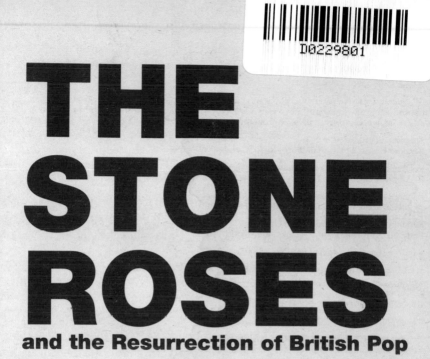

THE STONE ROSES

and the Resurrection of British Pop

John Robb

EBURY
PRESS

First published in Great Britain in 1997

10 9 8 7 6

This edition published in 2001
Random House, 20 Vauxhall Bridge Road, London SW1V 2SA

Random House Australia Pty Limited
20 Alfred Street, Milsons Point, Sydney, New South Wales 2061, Australia

Random House New Zealand Limited
18 Poland Road, Glenfield, Auckland 10, New Zealand

Random House South Africa (Pty) Limited
Endulini, 5A Jubilee Road, Parktown 2193, South Africa

Random House UK Limited Reg. No. 954009

A CIP catalogue record for this book is available from the British Library

ISBN 0 09 187887 X

Cover and plate design by PUSH, London

Cover photograph Kevin Cummins/Retna

Typeset by SX Composing DTP, Rayleigh, Essex
Printed and bound in Great Britain by Bookmarque Ltd, Croydon, Surrey

Papers used by Ebury Press are natural, recyclable products made from wood grown in sustainable forests.

Acknowledgements

Andy McQueen . . . the true believer, Jake Lingwood, Maria Cosgrove, The Gold Blade Gambinos, Peter Garner, Andy Couzens, Hall Or Nothing, Dave Simpson, Will Odell, The Roses Nation.

Roses fansite . . . I Am Without Shoes
      . . . http://odell.connect-2.co.uk

Roses fansite . . . Hobbits stone roses heaven
      . . . http://www.ianbrown.freeserve.co.uk

John Robb
      . . . http://www.johnrobb.co.uk

Introduction

The Stone Roses were *the* most legendary band of the late 1980s. They changed British pop by putting a cool street band back into the mainstream; they made pop and guitars cool again. They tried to operate outside the pop system and got themselves bogged down in a morass of court cases, bad career moves and chemical lifestyles.

And then they grew up and realised that they weren't really friends any more.

Just like real life really.

They were part of their times, but they were also a catalyst for the future. They took trad guitar music and breathed new life into it, and when they put out 'Fool's Gold' they virtually invented the perfect 1990s pop record.

This was a book that had to be written. It's a book about the band, the lifestyle. It's written from the streets of Manchester, and shares the same rehearsal rooms and venues, even the claustrophobic tour bus during their slow and grubby rise to the top; it staggers around E'd out of its head at their climax, and it sits around waiting for something to happen in their five-year stretch of doing nothing very much. It tracks the last stand and the downfall; and it enjoys their solo years, basically it's there at every stage, tracking the myth of The Stone Roses, feeling the force of a people's band pushed into the mainstream and beyond.

It grows up with the band from punk, through mod and the teenage gang wasteland, through the dreary 1980s, and explosion of good time that was acid house, and on into the 1990s.

It was a bastard difficult book to write, as looking at the past through a cloud of righteous skunk had warped many minds. But in this updated and revised edition I've elicited loads more new information, got the Roses to do some reminiscing and the result is the most complete and detailed history of this seminal band. It's a good job that I was there and sharp as fuck, or this tale of pop perfection would have been lost in the mists of time.

John Robb

The Big Day Out

THE BIG DAY OUT, BLACKPOOL 1989

And then suddenly the 1980s were over; the dreariest pop decade on record was finally getting the big heave-ho. The signs were all around: acid house had scorched the minds of a new generation, the iron curtain was crumbling, Ecstasy was all over the place – opening the doors to a drug binge that dwarfed that of the 1960s. Meanwhile, Manchester's The Stone Roses (along with fellow home-town pop hooligans, The Happy Mondays) ignored for so long, were getting ready to gatecrash the pop party.

And it was here in the flash Empress Ballroom in Blackpool on 12 August 1989 that the first rumblings that something was stirring in rock'n'roll and about to headbutt its way into the mainstream were being felt. The ornate Victoriana was filled with mad fuckers, indie heads, stoners and house fiends looking for some rock'n'roll crossover.

Suddenly The Smiths seemed to be a long time ago. In pop a few months can seem like a lifetime. Here were new gods for old, bowl cuts for quiffs, baggy cuts replacing indie styles. This was the dawning of a new pop era.

Manchester had been backing the Roses for several years but now it was time to go overground, to go beyond the cult underground status that had trapped any cool band from the last ten years.

The thousands of fans milling around the Blackpool streets knew that they were at an historic event. The Stone Roses had seized the times and there was an air of pop revolt where things were changing fast and you were either on the bus or off it.

Bob Stanley from *Melody Maker* was already head over heels in love with the Roses, he described them as 'Four blokes from the Stretford end and four teenage Jesus Christs. Pop perfection.' *NME* called them 'the future, the resurrection'.

A new generation was coming through with new styles – a clumsy appropriation of the flare and the baggy, loose-fitting clobber dictated by the sweat and freedom of the rave cultures, flares that appalled the punk warriors who had fought a mean style-war years before against the extra width. The Roses' fans had taken the look and completed it with Reni's beanie hat. It had been a long time since an audience had dressed like the band, a long time since a band had been a lifestyle; and Ian Brown, the totem of the new look, was playing today.

The swagger, the clothes and the anthems – in the summer of 1989 the Roses had the lot.

It was a sea change in popular culture and here they were, the bedraggled fans along the Blackpool Prom – a new youth army in way too much denim and attitude, new soul warriors fired by the Roses' bravura and great tunes.

For the first time in years there was a genuine rock'n'roll phenomenon coming off the streets. The Roses walked it like they talked it; and had the fanatical football-style following and it was here tonight that the whole thing was going to go overground.

It was a night when new reputations would get forged, a night that years later still seems legendary.

This was the perfect place for a pop coming-of-age. It was an audience who were ready for some kicks, a day out to the seaside with the greatest band of the coming pop generation at the helm.

For the Roses it was a million miles away from the perceived sneery hipness of London, most bands play their breakthrough gig in the capital. Typically the Stone Roses went for the ultimate working class playground – Blackpool.

Blackpool had its own magic and its own allure – for those from Manchester it was the number one holiday town, an extension of the brute northernness, a tatty seaside town. It meant long beery weekends, a quick shag in a seedy hotel, a ride on the donkeys in weedy youth days to throwing up after ten pints of weak booze in later teens. It was a rites of passage, windswept, full-frontal attack of pure undiluted bawdy British fun.

From the illuminations on acid, amusements in the blustery rain and skid-row hedonism, it was a glorious, gaudy, tacky place. A full-blown belch in the face of good taste, and it meant good times. It was a place of cheap glamour, even cheaper thrills and long drunken weekends; as a place for mad behaviour it was untouchable for Mancs.

And as a location for new pop kings to strut it was untouchable. Blackpool was a swift train ride, a bacchanalian break, and on top of that The Stone Roses, a band who had served a long and foul apprenticeship in the toilets and dungeons of the UK live circuit, were throwing a coming-out party. A band who had slowly smouldered were now ready to ignite in full pop pomposity.

Blackpool was awash with new pop pilgrims. Roses' shirts were everywhere as the new generation, already soaked with the Roses' anthems, cruised the town getting hammered and preparing for the summer's high-point.

All through the long warm months since the Roses' eponymous début album had been released that March there was real feeling that something was happening. The rave generation now had bands of its own to listen to while chilling out after a long night in the city's clubs.

Beatles tapes were getting supplemented by the Roses and the Mondays – two bands that walked and talked the new jive, and who seemed to have soaked up some of the surrounding culture. Two bands that, even if they didn't play the so-called 'indie dance' music, seemed to have got the flavour, the atmosphere and the vibe of the time infused in their tunes.

The Roses had the credibility – they may have had their roots in punk and post-punk glam, they may have steered a course through the fallout of The Jesus And Mary Chain and Creation Records – they may have been almost rock, but they had been affected by the times – they were the new breed. They had soaked up some of the new sounds, way ahead of the pack and although their début album was hardly acid house it had the infectious optimistic spirit of the times infused in its tracks.

It just felt right.

And throughout the summer they had been the soundtrack blasting out of bedsit windows, bouncing out of tape recorders in the clothes stores of Affleck's Palace, booming across the cracked concrete cancer of Hulme, the leafy bedsit bohemia of south Manchester to the red brick of north Manchester and into the surrounding knackered towns of the north – out on to the streets, everywhere – the soundtrack to the optimistic new Manchester determined to deflect its so-called moody image with a multicoloured tidal wave of optimistic partying.

This was a definite turn in pop fortunes, the band that months before had been a big deal in the north and totally ignored in the south was ready to flex its prowess in the centre stage.

This gig was for the nation.

Because in the 1980s, before Oasis made playing to 100,000 seem like a warm-up gig, even to dare to play to a hall holding 4,000 people this early in a career was considered madness. This was way out of order, too cocky, too arrogant; but the Roses had their fingers on the pulse and were armed with a stiff shot of self-belief.

This pop generation demanded big gestures, large communal gestures, waving-the-flag gestures. It wanted its bands big, bolshy and yet from the street, it wanted big spaces to celebrate, large-scale parties and big-time fun. The new rock bands that were going to survive had learned a few tricks from acid house, rock as community was back, and the Roses were here to provide the catalyst. 'The crowd is the star,' as singer Ian Brown had mumbled down a phone weeks before.

The band left Manchester early that day in high spirits. Their album had been selling consistently since its release in the spring and there was a clutch of singles gnawing at the back end of the charts. They weren't in the top ten yet but they were about to go silver. This was an unstoppable force – a band that was quite definitely on the up. They had caught the mainstream music business napping and were riding the rollercoaster.

Top photographer Ian Tilton, who documented the band from the start and then on through the pages of the defiantly on-the-case *Sounds,* hitched a ride on the band bus as it crawled into, ironically, his home town.

'For the Blackpool gig I travelled with the band. I wasn't commissioned by anybody but I knew that there was something legendary going on, so I decided to do pictures of them. We went over on the coach together with them and a few mates. There was Alan [Smith] with the gap in his teeth, Cressa who at the time was really big buddies with Ian – I got great shots of them back-stage, heads together, heads touching – looking at a yo-yo, playing around back-stage. It was cool the way they inter-acted together, they had an incredible intimacy doing exercises together; they were really close at the time.'

Even rookie Mani was already tight with the band after a year or so in the line-up.

'The atmosphere on the coach was great. That was a time when they had really got it together – even if Mani was a relatively new member of their tight-knit gang – they made him feel accepted. He was treated like a mate rather than as a musician. It was important for everyone to get along, he was like learning at the time. I did the first front-cover photo session the week he joined,' says Tilton.

If there were any nerves that such an audacious move as headlining a show the size of Blackpool may just be a touch over-ambitious, no one was showing it.

Tilton points out, 'They had this ultra confidence. They were getting a really big following in Manchester. It's this family thing again, this roots thing that all the great Manchester bands have. They made people want to watch them. It was all down to word of mouth. Nobody outside Manchester knew this was happening even a few months previously. I phoned the live editor of *Sounds* about covering them and he thought it was too early to do anything and even at the Hacienda show six months before he was still uncertain. I said they'll pack out the Hacienda. None of the editors in London knew the phenomenon; outside Manchester people hadn't really heard of them.'

But the tide was definitely turning, and only the week before Tilton had shot the band for a *Sounds* front cover.

'I'd just done a front cover for *Sounds,* four individual head shots on a colour background. Reni had his hat pulled down over his eyes, it made his chin look enormous – ha! ha! I left my camera at the back of the bus and went to talk to Steve Adge at the front. The band pinched my camera, and took pics of each other sticking chins out, taking the piss out of Reni, pushing out their jaws like Jimmy Hill. I don't think Reni was too happy about that shot.'

The audience building up at the Empress was a mixed bag: scene veterans, people who had followed the band from their roots in

Manchester, coachloads from all over the north, pop virgins, freaks, dealers, weirdos and fresh-faced pop teens. This was the day when the band finally got the crossover crowd, from the council estates to the rock press readers. It was everything that had been carefully worked on from the start – from manager Gareth Evans giving away tickets and T-shirts to kids who wouldn't normally be seen dead at shows for bands like these, and the disaffected former Smiths crowd looking for new heroes – and it was all coming together.

1989 was early days of ecstasy, when the drug symbolised good times, breaking down the barriers and the chilling out of football thuggery instead of the tabloid whipped-up death sentence it now carries.

In the late 1980s there was a new innocence, a new pop dawn, and a Victorian hall packed to the seams with pop kids ready to ignite was a big deal. It was a day of big gestures and grand partying, it was drugs, booze, chemicals, cheap weed and headache-strewn hangovers in cheap Blackpool boarding rooms and hotels. It was an unstoppable surge of flappy flares and greasy hair towards the Winter Gardens and into the Empress Ballroom, also where the vile Tory scum held their annual hooray-Henry, blue-rinse lunatic conference.

It was a celebration of youth and the rush of great pop music instead of the grim and forced showing off of the Tory faithful; it was a day to be bold and prepare for the grand excitement. The hall was all polished wood and chandeliers, a four-tier heap of balconies with posh stamped all over it; an unlikely place for a pop concert and a perfect place for the BIG gesture.

Pre-gig the band showed none of the tension you would expect for the big one, as Ian Tilton says. 'I remember Ian and John getting on really well, larking around. There was a film crew there, they had a pneumatic four-wheel trolley for a cameraman; Ian and John commandeered this and were pushing each other round the ballroom, they were really laid back – quite happy to sign autographs for people. Outside the Winter Gardens there were loads of people waiting in the afternoon. The band were not at all rock starish and they seemed to be really happy. They also seemed to hold back just a bit, keep something in reserve, make sure there was something enigmatic about themselves.'

It was the big day out for all the new faithful, the late teens who had finally got something new and tangible in pop culture to call their own, besides the faithful who had been following the Roses from the start. Tim Vigon was one of the new fans. He had picked up on them recently and was so star-struck and fired by the band's huge positive vibe that he had printed up copies of his own fanzine *Made Of Paper*.

'I had printed up fifty copies of my fanzine to sell in Piccadilly Records in Manchester, and to sell them, I made up all these flyers to hand out to queues outside. And as I was giving them out in the queue I remember promoter Simon Moran grabbing them off me and telling me off; I was only sixteen at the time so it all seemed like a big deal,' says Vigon.

There were hundreds outside, many without a ticket and, seizing the night, someone from the Roses' crew booted in the side doors of the venue and a joyous tide of humanity surged into the hall. The atmosphere was due for celebration.

'We wanted to give people a big day to finish their summer,' Ian Brown claimed later.

The tension in the hall was cranked high, the way-over-capacity crowd surged forward as the opening ghostly bass ran through 'I Wanna Be Adored' and rumbled through the building. Cool as fuck and into the gloom of the Empress the Roses stalked on-stage, Ian Brown limbering, bouncing like Mohammed Ali, overflowing with the cool arrogance that was his trademark, high-fiving the stage, lolloping on with the now legendary electric yo-yo, pimp rolling. He mumbled, 'Manchester in the area. International. Continental.'

Brown rode on the blast of adoration from the crowd, and the rest of the band threw ice-pops into the seriously over-heated audience.

'Manchester, Manchester,' the crowd roared, many of them from anywhere but; Brown stared and replied, 'Manchester, yeah yeah, I love you, 'cos I'm from Glasgow.'

The familiar chug of the bass sent shivers through the teeming mass, the deep throb being the opening hallmark to the Roses' live experience – the perfect opening. John Squire stood motionless, his guitar in an *Apocalypse Now* fog of feedback and squelching sounds before the delicious lick of the key-point melody curled in.

Once Reni kicked in, the Empress was bopping; from the third floor it was an impressive sight, a celebration of youth, vigour and rock'n'roll. It was like watching the Stones in their classic pomp of the mid 1960s. A great British rock'n'roll band prepared to go the whole way, a massive enveloping wall of sound curiously without that macho swagger that propels 90 per cent of rock. Almost gentle and yet packing its own power, the lazy narcissism of the song uncurled as Brown stalked the vocal with his northernness stamped all over the words. 'You adore me,' he sang, half to himself and half to the crowd, who quite obviously did. The stark atmospheric feel of the song, half gloomy and ice-cold, and half celebratory, caught the mood of the moment; it was an exhilarating rush of pop.

Ian Brown stiffly skulked the stage, all at once at home and oddly uncomfortable – an off-kilter balance that makes him such a compelling non-performer, the break with extrovert rock-god tradition that has already inspired the young Liam Gallagher.

Someone throws a pint of beer at Brown and he opens his mouth like a goldfish and pretends to catch it. Cool. A whole new generation is looking for the new dole messiah and Brown is there, prowling and hungry.

The guitar is back, ready to hang out with the DJ, and the singer stands there with his curious Paul Smith white shirt with the £ signs round the collar, maybe signifying that the days of indie paranoia over money-making are over. Brown walks on the spot, his head lolloping from side to side, an imitation of the gormless E-head spazz dance; everyone recognises the immaculate stoned moves.

Squire's almost skanking guitar intros 'Elephant Stone', the wah cranked up bigger and more powerfully than usual. The guitarist is re-inventing the under-used pedal. The wah, which would be the guitar sound of the next few years, had been dissed by punk after reaching its prime status with Hendrix, Sly and the early 1970s psychedelic soul kings. Its echoes were buried deep in some of the greatest music ever made; when the black cats went weird they stayed funky, Parliament, Clinton, Funkadelic, *Psychedelic Shack* by The Temptations, Hendrix, Miles Davis, Curtis Mayfield, Isaac Hayes – all the young kings. Squire is trying to dig into something more powerful than just whacking the axe, and it's something primal, something funky, something sexy.

Squire is getting close. His rock roots still hold him back but he is reinventing, tapping into a tradition that would inspire a whole generation of guitar players with a sound that would become synonymous with the new baggy fallout.

Mani is holding the bass down, his contributions tight, hard and always melodic – holding tight with Reni's drums, a shit-tight rhythm section . . .

By the time they cut loose with 'Waterfall' the Roses are coasting. 'Who's from Blackpool . . . anybody?' Brown is warming up to the MC thing with his off-the-cuff patter. 'Waterfall' is a gas, likewise 'Sugar Spun Sister', rock-solid classics that years later would still be staples of indie discos nationwide.

'International, continental,' murmurs Brown, obviously liking this line, as the band crashes into the anthemic 'Made Of Stone', the sliver of greatness that was their first total classic, a pure pop rush – it never felt better than when it was delivered at Blackpool.

To understand 1989 and the Roses in Blackpool, you had to understand E and the fumbling drug taking of a new generation of chemical adherents where there was hunger for a new way. Acid house had blitzkrieged through pop, opening up a new generation gap. But everyone still loved guitars, and the bands that were hammering the pill were the ones who could relate best to the new rock consensus. The Roses and the Mondays were at the forefront, and they knew about their home-town Manchester's new kinda kick.

'I Am The Resurrection' has now moved a few more gears, strung out, drawn out, cataclysmic, it's the Roses' grand finale, a huge song. Biblical and hypnotic, it's a moment of true arrogance, a song of great guitar playing, every lick carrying a tune.

During the long instrumental section Brown picks up the bongos and again does the shamanic stoned rock messiah thing; whether the bongos actually add much to the sound was irrelevant as it's a cool-looking manoeuvre.

After the show Vigon was one of a clutch of fans at the front of the stage desperate to get back-stage and hang with the band. As usual the meat-head security weren't into making things easy and were pushing the sweaty fans around. But the Roses were made of different stuff and were determined to be a people's band, as Vigon explains: 'Gareth (Roses manager) kept promising an interview with the band, but on the night he said that I couldn't talk to them as they were too stoned after the gig. I just wanted to get back-stage, I wanted them to approve of the fanzine. Security was saying that we couldn't go back-stage while Steve Adge was arguing with promoters, "Let these people back," and he literally dragged us over barriers in defiance of the promoters.'

Vigon made his way to the large room behind the stage, a curiously soulless space that was hardly the ornate experience of the hall. The band were chilling out after the show, keeping cool. John Squire sat quietly in a corner and Ian Brown was jiving around, the convivial host, the street hero coolly letting people into the Roses myth.

'At the party Ian was bouncing around. I've got a picture of him shaking hands with this big guy – I didn't know who he was at the time but later it turned out to be Martin Merchant from Audioweb who as it turns out I used to do press for.' says Vigon.

For the Roses and the Manchester scene it was the day when everything went off big time. Suddenly everyone had to agree that there was a new phenomenon on the doorstep. There was a new hunger in the air and there were new mainstream heroes to deal with, or as Vigon remembers, 'It was the first day when everybody wore Reni hats, it was the first time people wore baggy tops and the Manchester scene started. I remember going into Piccadilly record shop a couple of days later with the fifty fanzines I had printed up. They went through the roof at me; I hadn't even mentioned to them that I was putting out a zine and that their shop was mentioned on the flyer, and they said that already nearly 500 people had been in asking about the magazine. As it turned out I sold 3,000 of that first issue.'

The Beginnings
1962–80

IAN BROWN: EARLY YEARS

'I was born in Warrington and lived in Foster Street until I was about six . . .'

Ian Brown was born on the outside.

Warrington. Neither Liverpool nor Manchester. Bang in the middle. Right in between. Offering a tantalising glimpse of the big city on either side. Neither manc nor scouse – its lack of strong regional identity has provided some strange quirks.

British Telecom built a massive call centre in Warrington because it was found that the Warrington accent was the overall favourite accent in the UK.

Warrington itself lies just over the Lancashire border in Cheshire and is not typical of the smaller counties towns. A big working-class town in the Cheshire plains, the richest belt of Britain, real Posh Spice country.

A nether world of mixed affiliations. Warrington is one of the largest towns in the urban sprawl between Manchester and Liverpool. The Rugby League belt of St Helens, Widnes, Runcorn and Warrington joined together by industrial estates and Barratts homes, a never-ending sprawl between the two big cities.

Each town has its own fierce pride, its own accent, its own rules, its own fierce stubborn independence as if defying the inevitable swallowing up by the North West big city megapolis. Held together by the local rivalry of Rugby League (Brown was once spotted at Wembley with his father cheering Warrington on in the Rugby League challenge cup final).

Ian George Brown was born on 20 February 1963 to George, a local joiner, and Jean, a telephone receptionist at that massive call centre. The eldest in the family, he has a younger brother David and a sister Sharon.

He remembers his childhood as being relatively trouble-free, at least at home. His anti-establishment streak he attributes to his socialist and republican family. His father, according to Ian, was a 'sweet and shy' man and his mother an 'outspoken woman'.

He talked about his family to the now defunct *Uncut* magazine. 'We were poor, down to earth. My father was a joiner. He looks like me, yeah. I've got a younger brother and sister. I grew up in Warrington, which was grim but fun.

At school he was already building up a reputation as a loudmouth, a troublemaker.

Belligerent, unruly, already headstrong, the young Brown was already locked into a path of stubborn self-determination.

In 1969 the Brown family left Warrington and moved to the big city. 'We moved to Manchester and that's where I spent most of my life, but I've still got loads of aunties and uncles in Warrington.' Not that Brown has ever abandoned Warrington, he still has a house in the area. 'I came back here because I was sick of living in Manchester. I was getting burgled far too often and I just wanted the quiet life back in Warrington. I found a nice little house to settle down, and I'm usually there about once a week.'

In 1969 the Browns moved to Timperley, a few miles from the Manchester city centre. Timperley, also 'famous' for Frank Sidebottom, is caught between the never-ending sprawl of Europe's biggest housing estate Wythenshawe and the leafier suburbs of Altrincham – two very different worlds pulling in opposite directions. The very Manchester working class of Wythenshawe with its displaced population, moved out of the city centre after the late sixties demolition of Hulme, and the leafier suburbs of Timperley and Sylvan Avenue where Brown now found himself.

As a place to grow up this offered a collision of cultural references. Living on the edge of the city looking in, the streetwise pop culture of the council estates and the dreamy leafy suburbs – a scenario that pretty well captures the Roses' eventual audience.

The move to Manchester was a fortuitous one. It's difficult to imagine Brown bumping into like-minded souls in Warrington, let alone John Squire in a sand pit as the legend has it.

Manchester in 1969 was a very different city than the Euro wine bar, glitzy, neon, metropolis of the early 21st century. Back in 1969 it was a city that was just starting to emerge from its dank, dark, Lowryesque cloth-cap cliché, with its new air of sixties flash.

Manchester was beginning its long period of reinvention. It had its own mini Mersey beat scene, a post-Liverpool rush of northern bands of its own like the melodic guitar jangle The Hollies (occasionally quoted as an influence by the Roses), the ridiculous Freddy and The Dreamers who by now had been dispatched back to the cabaret circuit and Herman's Hermits, who had been the biggest band in the world in 1965, bigger, even, than The Beatles!

In football terms the city was booming. It was the city of flash. Manchester United were not only the kings of Europe but they did it with swagger and style. Since the 1958 Munich air disaster when the 'Busby babes', potentially the greatest British football team of them all were wiped out in an air crash, United had been building a legend and a footballing dynasty from the ruins. By 1969 Manchester United were on the ascendant, they had won the European Cup the year before and were the superstars of British football.

George Best was the flash king of European football, stick insect thin with his El Beatle haircut, mesmerising skill and pop star swagger. Impossible to miss for the young United fan, like Brown.

Fuck, in 1969, even City were winning the League!

Add on to this the fact that the world's biggest pop group The Beatles came from thirty miles down the road and you've got a couple of traditions getting a firm footing in northern folklore. Pop and football dominate the north-west psyche and the next thirty years were going to see plenty of reasons for these to get reinforced over and over.

SO YOUNG: IAN BROWN GROWS UP IN MANCHESTER . . .

Settling into Timperley Brown was the loudmouth kid, the ringleader. On his new street he occasionally bumped into John, the shy, quiet, kid but they were not great friends. It would be a few more years before his friendship with John Squire would tighten up.

It was in Timperley that music started to have an effect on Brown. He started ploughing through records that were left lying around. 'My auntie gave me a pile of seven inches. "It's Not Unusual", Tom Jones; "Help!", "I Feel Fine" by The Beatles; "Satisfaction", "Under My Thumb", "Get Off My Cloud", by the Stones; "The Happening" and "Love Child" by The Supremes. I would have been seven or eight and I had a little Dansette. They were the first discs I had. I've still got them.'

The seven inch single is still the classic pop salvo. Nowadays when the single has been reduced to a marketing tool, a boy band smirk or something to promote the album – the single was king. It's difficult to remember the powerful, all encompassing power of the seven inch classic . . .

The Beatles/Stones/Kinks/Motown – the glorious Sixties pop single practitioners were banging out endless singles a year, each one a statement, each one capturing a slice of time for ever, each one a mini symphony.

The first record that Ian Brown bought was 'Metal Guru', T Rex's classic 1972 Number 1 – and if that isn't a song that kicks all the right pop nerve ends then nothing is. Marc Bolan, the inventor of glam and one of the greatest ever British pop stars, was strutting in his prime when he put that one out.

Another key flavour was Northern Soul. Wigan Casino was the epicentre of the hippest scene in the north-west, a scene that was infusing the way everyone dressed whether they were aware of it or not. Flared trousers, star jumpers and even feather cuts/suedeheads were arguably popularised by the soul scene. All the hip kids in the schools were practising their back flips to the casino scene beat.

Phil Thornton, Runcorn's finest social commentator succinctly and cynically sums up Northern Soul and the way it infused a patchwork of pop cultures of the north-west in the early Seventies. A mish mash of competing styles that built the foundations for the post punk northern pop scene.

'Northern Soul was a direct antecedent of today's hedonistic clubbing scene but the majority of those on the periphery of the scene were never real soul disciples, merely followers of fashion. By 1976 Northern Soul was mainstream with Wigan's Chosen Few appearing on *Top Of The Pops* and reissues of tired old stompers diluting the passion for a crowd more interested in athletic showboating than a genuine appreciation of music. The youth clubs of the north-west were a melting pot of competing tribes in the late Seventies – soulies, punks, mods, skins, Bowie freaks, even heavy rockers – each armed with their own supply of cherished 7 inches and LP tracks for the DJ to play. It was hard not to take in all these influences and construct your own eclectic canon of influences – this is how Madchester was made; not in the aloof arty playgrounds of the city's bohemian elite, but out there on the council estates youth centre dancefloors.'

Its roots go back to the early Sixties club scene of Manchester. In 1963 the Twisted Wheel opened its doors for the first time with Roger Eagle (who ended up owning the International 1) as the house DJ. In the early Sixties it was a popular blues/R&B venue.

In 1966 when it moved to its new home in Whitworth Street where its legend started to grow, for many it became the home of soul in the UK.

It was probably due to this club's carrying the torch and its legend, that some Mods in the Sixties evolved into Soulsters. Turning away from the Sixties fashion thing, evolving away from the psychedelic take on the late Sixties and into a fashion all of their own, the backdrop was stomping soul records, crisp raw sounds and a vicious stomping backbeat.

The key singers were from the States who were frequent visitors to the Twisted Wheel. Such names as Ben E. King, J. J. Jackson, Oscar Toney Jr, The Vibrations, Jnr Walker, all helped to form the Legend of Northern Soul that was soon spreading quickly over the north-west.

Northern Soul was born out of this. In backwater towns and cities across the north of England, in places like Wigan, Stoke, Stafford and Blackpool, obscure post Motown soul releases were revered, the obscurer the better. The mods' love of oneupmanship, of the small label, of the hottest sounds was in its element here.

The Wigan Casino Soul Scene had come directly from a Sixties uptempo soul basis and stuck to this sound quite rigidly for a long time. Blackpool Mecca (or more accurately the Highland Rooms) considered itself a soul club before a Northern Soul club and stuck to the black soul sound of the Sixties while Wigan allowed the sound to broaden. Eventually, the Mecca started to play recent or newly released uptempo soul records, sometimes unknowingly and later deliberately. Over a couple of years the musical policy there shifted to the new sounds and then fragmented, allowing pure disco and funk.

Small independent labels in America pumping out attempts to emulate the success of Motown on a cheaper budget were ruling the roost. That their records were rawer, less polished and cranked full of energy was a huge plus mark for them. They may have sold jack shit in the States but to the youth of the north of England, wired on cheap speed, their records made a perfect backdrop to extrovert dancing.

Usually, the records sounded like Motown, Chicago soul or New York soul. Great wired performances by unknown or under-appreciated performers. The scene was soon dubbed Northern Soul because of the clubs' geographical location. Northern Soul continued to gain popularity until the mid-Seventies, when punk and disco stole its thunder. However, it never really faded away. Some clubs remained open and there was still a collectors' market for the singles, and many rare singles are going for astonishingly high prices, a price range that dominated the club culture.

A whole subculture was born, a subculture that in the early Seventies dominated school playgrounds as kids learned the dance steps and wore the clothes that were coming out of the clubs. By the mid Seventies, the mods had turned into suedeheads, then into skinheads and then the trousers got flared. It was a secret society, a fashion world of its own and far removed from the lumbering prog rock of the very lost guitar band scene.

Northern Soul provided the backdrop of cool in the early to mid Seventies. It was about clothes, clubs like secret societies, outsider culture with its own code, like the early acid house scene, the underground nature of rave culture, a big whispering cult held together by its own dress code (just check those flares!). Lines can be drawn with the Roses cult escape and the whole Manc baggy thing years later. Its very northernness and its own strict street cool, it was a whole new way of living 24 hours a day pop lifestyles.

Whilst the young Brown was navigating his way through the pop battlefield of the early Seventies he was also choosing idols from other mass media. 'When I was a kid, there was no one bigger hero for me than Mohammed Ali. I can see that '74 Foreman fight as clear as a bell, and I got all the books. My walls were covered in Ali pictures, and later it would have been the Pistols.'

Ali was the man. His indomitable fighting spirit, his fierce intelligence, his utterly astonishing boxing skill and his powerful political presence made him a crucial and inspirational figure. Not only was he knocking them down in the ring, he was knocking them dead outside the ring. He stood for the downtrodden and his black power Muslim leanings made him a controversial figure in the straightlaced world. He refused to fight in Vietnam and stood up against racism. He had a free and radical political agenda and a bucketload of charm to explain it to middle England. Ali is perhaps the greatest folk hero of them all.

His insolence and witty wordplay in the full glare of the world media, his radical agenda, his uncrushable spirit and self-made determination all struck home with Brown like it did with millions of kids worldwide.

Brown picked up on Ali's never-ending self-confidence and his righteous arrogance. It also turned him on to boxing and then on to martial arts – two disciplines that he still has a strong interest in to this day.

In 1973 Ali was joined by a new hero. Bruce Lee burst on to the scene and brought with him a revolution of interest in the martial arts. A revolution that would turn Brown's head. At school the myths would constantly circulate about Bruce Lee (Brown's favourite Lee film is *Big Boss*, also known as *Chinese Connection*). When the Bruce Lee double bill of *Fists of Fury* and *Enter the Dragon* were shown in Sale, Brown was there.

Already entranced by Ali, it didn't take much of a leap to get into Lee, martial arts' first-ever popular culture superstar.

The acting in the films like the stories was, of course, crap, but the fight scenes were something else and here was a fighting form that not only seemed ruthlessly effective but was graceful and had its own poetry and its own beauty. Brutality and beauty rolled into one, no wonder the young Brown was hooked.

Bruce Lee was on a fast track to becoming a superstar. Fact and fiction became entwined in his mystical legend. Most people didn't even know that he was already dead by 1973 . . . Lee popularised martial arts, his incredible physique and fighting skills became the unattainable dream of many geeky young teens in the early Seventies. Brown was bitten by the Lee bug as well and was involved in karate from the age of 11 to 18 when teenage kicks of a different type began to take over his life. He was well on the way to black belt status but his rebellious streak was getting stoked.

'There was this kid, the cleverest kid in the class, he was awesome, but he had his own mind. He wouldn't take his O levels and he wouldn't do his karate the way they told him. I sort of fell into that way of thinking as well. I guess it was a bit of a punk thing. The kid never got beyond his white belt. I think I took some of that attitude off him. Which is why I eventually left the club. I regret it now. It was a stupid thing to do.'

For seven years, though, karate was a single-minded obsession for Brown, an obsession that took a steely discipline and resolve a million miles away from the rebellious image he liked to portray. He would cycle four miles to the Dojo after a day at his new school, Altrincham Grammar.

The training, the physical and mental demands of the sport say a lot about Brown. When he packed it in when he was 18 it was because punk rock filled that space and he just got fed up with the relentless demand of the sport.

He had planned to go all the way, go to Japan to make the highest grades. And despite his rebellious streak he certainly has the discipline to pull it off. This steely discipline is something that lurks in Brown, that gritty patience and resolve that typified the Roses and their endless rehearsals, whittling their tunes down to a black belt perfection.

Brown quickly moved through several styles of karate till he found the one that suited him. In the local Dojos Brown first learned Wado-Ryu, a relatively modern form of Japanese martial arts founded by Hironori Ohtsuka Sesei in 1934. Developed from the Samurai martial art of Ju-jitsu and Shotokan it was a softer more natural means of self protection, even the very name Wado-Ryu means 'way of peace'. From this he specialised in Bujinkai, a modern form put together in the early Seventies which mixed Wado-Ryu with the Shoalin preying mantis form.

It's a far tougher discipline and takes some application. Ian says: 'I did Bujinkai, which is a mixture of Wado-ryu and phonebox boxing. I would start it again, but it would take me at least three years to get back up to the standard I was.'

Lee and Ali. These were role models and idols and part of the mid Seventies cultural backdrop. Superstars in the suburbs. And, like pop stars, unattainable idols. In the real world of mid Seventies Britain, things were very different. It was a world of shortages, bleak winters and confusion. A world where Britain seemed to be falling apart at the seams and the cities were slowly turning into mini Beiruts.

By 1975/76 the UK was at a cultural low point, the Sixties rock stars had run out of songs. They looked awful – straggly long hair and bloated middle-aged faces. They would spend years in the studio fucking about instead of making records, they were out of touch and lost. They needed a kick, a one-inch punch to the taste zone.

The talk was that pop had done everything it could. There was nowhere left to go.

For the teens growing up in the mid Seventies to be constantly told that they had missed the party, that the Sixties was the greatest time ever wasn't just grating. It was getting really fucking annoying.

Every generation needs its own defining point. Its own soundtrack. Its own standard bearers.

And just round the corner something was coming. Oh yes! There was some big time trouble-making to be visited on the lazy *Old Grey Whistle Test* world of pop, a smug dull world of singer-songwriters with manky stubble and knitted hats on their smug heads or earnest plodding prog outfits and stifling, laughably dull *Top Of The Pops*, full of chicken-in-the-basket losers pretending to be pop stars.

'Right now.'

Every time you hear it, it still sends a shiver down the spine.

'Ha! ha! ha!'

Followed by that cackle, that hideous cackle over the top of the fattest guitar imaginable descending into a beautiful maelstrom of sound.

Fucking hell. This was more than a pop single it was a music war . . .
It was 'Anarchy In the UK' by The Sex Pistols.
It was a generational calling card.
After this. Nothing. Would. Ever. Be. The. Same. Again!

YEAR ZERO: . . . PUNK HITS THE SUBURBS

Punk was just waiting to happen.

To understand just how exciting punk was you have to understand how
boring the mid Seventies really were. If the early Seventies had provided
some sort of action with the fab pop shakes of glam rock, the mid Seventies
was one of those periods of cultural hiatus. Pop music had got fat and lazy.
It was quite possible to be a cabaret act and hog the charts; the album charts
were full of long-haired buffoons in shabby denim with their dull anthems.

For the 14-year-old Ian Brown it was a call to arms as he remembered to
Record Collector.

'Punk changed everything. The band I most got into was The Sex Pistols.
My mate had "Anarchy In The UK". He got it in Woolies for 29p 'cos after
that *Bill Grundy Show*, they put the record in the bargain bin! I loved "I
Wanna Be Me" on the other side – that lyric about "cover me in margarine"
was great. Then I got "God Save The Queen" the day it came out. I was
fourteen. I remember thinking, "Oh wow, that Pistols record is gonna
change the world. And it did, in a way.'

Even in 1985 Brown was telling journalist Paul Greenwood, 'If I could
write a song as good as "Anarchy" I would be happy.'

The Sex Pistols' impact on the pop scene of 1977 can never be too
exaggerated. Those that fell in love with the band then are still out there to
this day, their whole mindset still fixed by the sheer power and pop
brilliance of the band. Not only did they affect people with their killer songs
and Steve Jones's awesome guitar sound, they threw up a whole mass of
ideas that are still settling now in the pop hinterland.

From situationism to anarchy, from the clothes that you wear to the way
you cut your hair, from telling the monarchy to fuck off, to questioning
everything about Britain. They were sex, style and subversion rolled into
one. Many of the questions they asked still remain unanswered. And for
many teenagers at the time, like Ian Brown, they were a U-turn in their lives.

The acerbic individuality and stark-staring anger of Johnny Rotten is very
much part of the Ian Brown psyche; the royalty-hating, rock-star-debunking,
myth-destroying psyche is still there in his schtick. The Pistols set Brown on
the way to becoming his own starman; they were a whole new template for
what a rock star could be. They called for bands to form in their wake but not
for copycat bands . . . like the Roses themselves would do ten years later.

But punk wasn't like any form of rock'n'roll before. It had one foot in the star system but another on the street. The energy of the Pistols was a supreme catalyst that bounced around the whole country. They played Manchester twice in '76 and inspired a whole local rock'n'roll infrastructure. The whole Manchester myth from The Smiths to the Hacienda onwards roots itself back to those Pistols shows.

The Pistols may have been the spark but the inspiration to get involved came from local Wythenshawe punk rock outfit Slaughter And The Dogs.

Local bootboy glamsters Slaughter And The Dogs transformed themselves into being a punk rock band. A form that suited them far more.

Suddenly punk didn't seem a million miles away. It was right on the doorstep in Wythenshawe! A wild riot going on, tantalising, just within reach. The message was 'anyone can do this, have a go'. It's perhaps one of the most powerful messages that pop music can give out. And here was a band having a go round the corner and getting some sort of national recognition for it!

The tales of Slaughter And The Dogs' wild gigs were hitting the teenage grapevine at Altrincham Grammar.

Your very own Pistols on your doorstep. Now that's something!

Brown's first gig was Joy Division in their earlier more punkier days playing some youth club near Sale, but it was Slaughter that gave him that adrenaline rush.

Slaughter And The Dogs are a band that Brown still mentions to this day as one of his favourites and at various points during his career, a key influence. 'Yeah, I got into them through that single, "Cranked Up Really High". My next door neighbour was a friend of Rossi, the guitarist. I saw them at Wythenshawe forum and the Belle Vue a few times.'

Slaughter had their first album produced by Mick Ronson, Bowie's guitarist and song arranger and an unheralded genius of British rock'n'roll. They also had a Northern Soul flavour and energy melded to their fat glam riffs with the stomping dancehall oomf of the casino dance floor belters.

They released a series of well-received singles which have since become collectors' treasures, including the early punk anthem, 'Where Have All the Boot Boys Gone'.

They also had a single 'Cranked Up Really High', one of the first records produced by a young upcoming producer called Martin Hannett. This would be a vital connection in the years to come.

'Cranked Up Really High' is an anthem to the cheap twin punk kicks of speed and booze, a celebration of the wild-eyed lifestyle even then getting sourced by Brown.

Slaughter were just another cog in an already burgeoning Manchester punk scene. Classic bands like The Buzzcocks, whose ultra melodic buzzsaw pop anthems neatly bridged the gap between perfect pop and punk speed freak thrills, were regulars on their home-town circuit.

'I saw The Buzzcocks a few times – at the Mayflower in Belle Vue and at a signing at Virgin Records. I saw The Clash in '77.'

In the couple of years that followed punk, Brown would pick up on some of the rawer edges of the national musical fallout. Groups like the tough psychobilly outfit The Meteors whose cartoon image and tough guy stance camouflaged an amazing guitar player and, initially, a great band. There were bands on the edges of the 'oi' scene like The Cockney Rejects and his personal favourites, the under-rated socialist skinhead band from the north-east, The Angelic Upstarts.

Ian told *Record Collector*, 'I used to go watch the Angelic Upstarts! Mensi – top kid! I roadied for them a few times. I've seen them fifteen/twenty times. Top band.'

The Angelic Upstarts were a South Shields based punk/skinhead band who released a fantastic run of singles that were charged with a righteous street anger. Their vocalist Mensi brought a street politic and anti-Nazi flavour to the band's lyrics.

Punk may have been a rigidly defined musical code to some but it also threw open loads of possibilities to others. Even groups like the Upstarts who could be considered a quintessential British punk band were bringing in music from their youth into the mix, all over the place there were hints of The Who, the Stones, even The Beatles, Northern Soul/ska/mod. The Year Zero of punk was fading as the new rock'n'roll generation starting looking at the roots of the new wave and rediscovering a whole canyon of like-minded crazed musics.

Into this new void people were evaluating late Sixties garage psychedelia, from Arthur Lee's Love to Iggy to The Doors to Hendrix to the Velvets – anyone who ever had any fire in their soul was reconsidered and honoured in a thousand teenage bedsits and bedrooms. Funk and a whole forgotten pile of great soul and R&B records were thrown back into the equation. It was a great melting pot of sound.

With punk and its influences swimming around his head Brown was on the lookout for like-minded souls to share his new passion with. He didn't have to look far.

That shy kid hiding behind his fringe four doors down had recently been turned on to the three-minute revolution by Brown. Their friendship was now firmly bonded by punk.

'John lived up the same road. We started hanging out together about thirteen or fourteen. He was into The Beach Boys and The Beatles but he didn't have any proper LPs, just compilations – that one with the surfer on the front and The Beatles' *Live At Hollywood Bowl*. I took around the first Clash LP and an Adverts single and turned him on to punk rock.'

BONDING OVER THE ADVERTS: SQUIRE AND BROWN BECOME PUNK ROCK BUDDIES . . .

In fact Brown and Squire had met years before.

There is the oft quoted sandpit story. Says Ian, 'There was a sandpit in the fields near our house. He remembers me being naked, but I don't know if that's right.'

The legendary meeting with Brown is part and parcel of British nineties pop mythology. The sandpit stand off in 1968, a story that has marked similarities with a certain Mick and Keef meeting in a sandpit when they were toddlers only to meet again years later as teenagers. Coincidence or rock'n'roll mythology, or just a good story?

Squire remembers his first brush with the Brown man. 'I've vague memories of meeting him at his friend's house,' Squire remembers. 'It was like an arranged marriage! A parental thing. The school catchment area had a line that went down the street. He was on one side, I was on the other, but eventually we went to the same secondary school. I didn't really get to know him until punk. He was somebody locally who was into the same music. We'd swap records and things. At the time it felt like an illicit underworld.'

Brown had taken his punk records to Squire's house. It was just another casual bonding through the new music. Another link forged in the molten heat of the post punk fallout. All over the nation lifelong acquaintances were being put together, bonding over precious punk rock vinyl, bonding over where to get non-flared trousers from. For those who dared to make the major jump from the mid Seventies mush to the brave new world of punk it was all about new relationships, new patterns of existence.

Says Ian, 'We became friendly at 13 or 14, when we were put in the same class at secondary school. I started chatting to him, and I took "God Save The Queen", the first Clash LP, and "One Chord Wonders" by The Adverts round to his house. I played him these punk records, and then a week later he'd bought The Clash and "God Save". He went mad about The Clash after that, following them all over.'

Brown also turned Squire on to Slaughter And The Dogs. Years later he still really rates the 'Cranked Up Really High' single. '"Cranked Up Really High" by Slaughter And The Dogs conjures up images of flailing fists and feet on Saturday night dancefloors in Manchester. It's a blistering track with the ultimate unintelligible vocal,' remembers John.

Brown and Squire were chalk and cheese. 'We were total opposites,' Ian recalled, 'I was very outgoing, the kid that would stand on the table in front of the class doing impressions of the teachers. I was the class joker and he was the loner. He got out of sports so he could do art. I think he was the first kid in the school to play truant, and he did that by himself. But at 13, 14, we'd walk the streets together and sit in each other's bedrooms playing records. He got his guitar when he was 15. The first thing he learned to play was "Three Blind Mice". Then he'd play his guitar for me when I went round. He's a funny kid. I know he's really, really quiet and doesn't speak to no one, but when he was with me he'd never shut up. Everybody knows him as a man of few words, but in them days he was garrulous with me, definitely. I did spend a lot of my life and a lot of the Roses' life talking for the kid. I knew him so well that I'd finish his sentences off. And then in the end . . . that didn't happen.'

'It was definitely a case of opposites attract," pointed out Squire. 'He was more popular, yeah. I was happy to be a loner. I prefer it. We hung about for a short period, then when we started the band it became more permanent.'

The late Seventies, for the two fourteen-year-olds hunched over the record player, was a whole new world of possibilities opening up. For Brown it was the exuberant nihilism of The Sex Pistols that fired his extrovert rebellious streak. The more arty Squire was besotted with The Clash.

He painted a mural of the band on his bedroom wall, wore the creepers repopularised by the band, tousled his hair like their guitar player Mick Jones. Another new friend, another local kid fired by punk who was starting to hang around with the Sylvan Avenue boys, Pete Garner, remembers just how much John loved The Clash.

'John would play The Clash's first album every day. I remember one day he turned up with a guitar string instead of a shoelace in his brothel creeper. It turned out there was a picture of Joe Strummer in the music press with the same thing that week. But that's what it's like when you're really young, that's the sort of thing you do, isn't it?'

The music may have been the common bond but as people they couldn't be more different. They were filling the gaps in each others' personalities. Where John was quieter, more introspective, Brown was already more outgoing, rowdier. Chalk and Cheese, Brown and Squire . . .

So who was this shy quiet kid, the polar opposite who lived two doors down from Ian Brown?

JOHN SQUIRE: EARLY DAYS

John Thomas Squire was born on 28 November 1962 in Broadheath, Lancashire. He was brought up in Timperley, going to a different primary school than Ian Brown despite living four doors down from him.

Even at an early age he excelled at art. He was the quiet kid with the shy half stare from behind his floppy fringe, daydreaming his way through school. Contemporaries describe him as being withdrawn and 'in his own world' and being especially gifted at art.

When Squire was a kid he got an autograph from *Blue Peter*'s Biddy Baxter. 'I sent her a picture of me guinea pig having a bath in a kitchen bowl,' he says. 'I got a *Blue Peter* badge and a signed letter from Biddy Baxter, 'cos it went up on the pictures-of-your-pets board.'

Like Brown when he was growing up he was surrounded by music. His parents listened to The Beatles, Elvis and Peggy Lee. A pop soundtrack that he soaked up. Especially The Beatles whose magical aura had been created just up the East Lancs Road in Liverpool.

Remembers John, 'I always consider them almost other worldly, The Beatles. The fact that they grew up in a northern working-class environment and still made it. That showed that you didn't have to come from London, or you didn't have to come from America to make it.'

PUNK

But it was punk that put all John's musical and art obsessions into focus. His curiosity in punk had been ignited by his new mate across the street and John Squire dived headlong into the exploding scene. It was a total inspiration.

'I think London punk bands had more of an effect on my motivation, than where I was from. The whole ethos of The Clash, Pistols, all that era, and the fact that they promoted themselves on the platform of "anyone can do it". I don't know if that was true, but it certainly made me think that maybe I could.'

And according to Squire, it was Strummer's impassioned example that was an inspiration. A chance quote from The Clash vocalist on TV had fired him up.

'This wasn't personal advice, it was TV advice. Joe Strummer from The Clash turning to the camera in a very stoic move. He was asked if he had any advice for the kids out there and he said, "Believe in yourself, you can do anything you want." That one went in and stayed.'

John Squire loved The Clash; he 'liked their painted trousers', he once explained, referring to one of The Clash's earliest looks when they splashed paint Pollock-like over their stage gear, an art school reference that can only have come from The Clash's artful bassist, Paul Simonon.

It also can't have escaped the fifteen-year-old John Squire hunched over his guitar that The Clash's engine room was the best guitar player from the punk rock generation. Mick Jones.

Armed with a Les Paul (the punk rock guitar, Steve Jones from the Pistols had a 1959 Les Paul – the classic guitar a hand-me-down from The New York Dolls Sylvain Sylvain and it was no coincidence that Squire ended up with a '59 Les Paul at the tail end of the Roses) and a sneer, the supa cool Jones was the link between punk present and a rock'n'roll past, looking like a starving Keef Richards.

And although Jones's super melodic energised guitar playing was a key influence, there were other guitar players who were also inspiring him. The Pistols' Steve Jones and The New York Dolls' Johnny Thunders were firing him.

'They were the only guys who were playing any sort of fast runs; everyone else just played chords,' says John. The Pistols' killer guitarist Steve Jones, whose fat Les Paul-driven power chords were putting a serious oomph into the band and firing them far further up the charts than any of Malcolm McLaren's hype, practically reinvented the rock guitar sound.

'I was 14,' he intones. 'There's a low note on "God Save The Queen", probably an A-string, just before the beginning of the second verse. *Dowwww!* Really fat and thick. One note . . . raw sex. I heard that . . . had to go and do it myself.'

Johnny Thunders was an incredible talent who burned out in a haze of hard drugs that eventually contributed to his untimely death.

Both guitar players were firing a young punk rock mind up in the suburbs of Manchester.

Squire worked hard at his guitar and even took a couple of lessons. 'I probably spent too long practising guitar on my own,' he muses. 'We didn't live in a musical street, and it wasn't until just before the first Roses album that I met another proper guitarist. This guy I used to work with used to go to a blues and folk guitar teacher in Rusholme; I went with him a couple of times and he taught me a lot. Apart from that, it all comes from books and cassettes. Plus I had the record player . . .' he explained to *Total Guitar* magazine.

Squire's industrious father wired up a train set transformer to the said record player, allowing, with a tilt of the dial, variable voltage. So not only could 45s be played at 33⅓, when the guitar parts got a bit tricky 33⅓s could be played at, ooh, 12⅕. 'It was so good when I got into Page, Hendrix and Clapton because I could slow everything down and pick out guitar lines. *Very* helpful.'

From here, Squire absorbed a smidgen of chord theory – 'I don't carry it up around here, though (*taps head*)' – and cherry-picked the best licks he could from a book called *Lead Guitar* by Harvey Vincent. 'It came with a flexi-disk and was all blues-based,' he remembers. 'That stuff just came easy to me. Dunno why . . . I just liked the sound. Still do.'

Squire's first guitars were the sort of cheapies everyone kicks off with. He swiftly moved on to a Höfner 335-style semi. A guitar that he still owns years later. 'I've still got it,' he grins. 'But I've, erm, painted it with a splash of household gloss.'

The Gretsch Country Gentleman pictured on the inside of The Stone Roses' lemon album was a live favourite, but John Leckie vetoed its use for the album's recording. 'He said it was too woolly, and he was right. For a lot of the first album I hired in a pink '60s Stratocaster which I ended up buying because it sounded so good. The Gretsch went missing . . .'

Looking for a fatter sound on *Second Coming* Squire's main guitar was a Sunburst '59 Les Paul Standard which was previously owned by Cheap Trick's Rick Nielson. 'The neck looked unplayable at first,' recalls John. 'It was so chipped – like a map of the Swedish coast. But it sounded really nice. I don't know too much about guitars so I could easily be sold a fake – but I know when one sounds special.' When the Roses' business affairs were liquidated, the '59 Sunburst was sold as, strictly speaking, it was band property.

Quietly building up his guitar prowess, sat in his bedroom spending hours with his guitar and his painting, Squire was perfecting the twin skills that would dominate his life.

In the meantime he was in the final year of Altrincham Grammar and there were new horizons to look forward to.

During the last couple of years at Altrincham Grammar, Brown and Squire bonded tight over punk rock. Walking back home to Sylvan Avenue they would talk their way through the usual burning topics of teen culture, from football to television to pop music.

Squire was still living in his dream world. Spending his downtime at home, day dreaming, creating an artistic Never-Never land. Meanwhile Brown was already mooching around the city centre, hanging with the city centre hooligans, the mid teen on the fringe of the late teen bovva boot world. The parallels and cherry reds of the football hooligan, the adrenalin rush of terrace culture transferred to the city street. Brown was on the fringes, getting kicks, hanging with the rough boys.

The soundtrack was Northern Soul, the adrenalised exciting music that had clung on in the north-west. Beyond national fashion, dance halls booming to the stomping beat, speed-driven all-night dance marathons still being belted out in unlikely hot spots like Wigan Casino or Blackpool Highland Rooms.

The skins, the suedeheads, the hooligans in town that the young Brown ran with were on the fringes of this kind of scene. It was part of Brown's pop psyche – one side would dive headlong into punk, the other would always retain the razor-sharp skin/mod mentality.

It wasn't safe. Manchester has always been a rough city, then and now. These were Brown's roots. Real roots, the glam of T Rex, the stomping bonding of Northern Soul, the hanging with the gangs in the city centre, the karate schools, Ali's sharp lyricism and boxing prowess and neat arrogance in the meanest of all sports . . . this was some melting pot of ideas. It was a melting pot of sources that would mark the kid's mind and would be transferred via The Stone Roses on to the next generation.

These excursions up to the city centre were the first mini travels by Brown; the foothills of his wanderings and he would relate these tales to John Squire, the sat at home artsy boy from four doors down who was quite content to sit in his bedroom, drawing, painting and day dreaming.

The two friends followed the punk fallout through their last couple of years at Altrincham Grammar School. They grabbed a bunch of O-levels and in the autumn of 1979 they started at South Trafford College, a large tech college on the south of the city with a real crossover of kids from all the surrounding suburbs and a whole new bunch of faces to mix with . . .

COLLEGE DAYS: FROM ALTRINCHAM GRAMMAR TO SOUTH TRAFFORD COLLEGE

It was the autumn of 1979 and, depressingly, Thatcher was about to beat Labour in the elections. The country was going through one of its bouts of turmoil where nothing worked and the whole system seemed to be collapsing. Punk was said to be dead.

In fact punk was splintering into a mish-mash of youth cultures. There were gang wars between rockabillies, mods, punks and metalheads. Some people swore allegiance wholly to one scene while others cherry picked from all the different tribes. South Trafford College typified this fallout. A minority of kids were immersed totally 24/7 in youth culture, while the rest ignored it completely.

Pacing the corridors between lessons – the corridors packed as two thousand students sluggishly moved from one classroom to another – the new intake would size each other up. Most of the kids were into nothing in particular so it didn't take long for the twenty or so punk-fired kids to spot each other. New boys Andy Couzens and Ian Brown noticed each other but it wasn't all bonding and record swapping.

In fact there was an element of tension. Says Andy, 'I'd seen them lot in there but I never really spoke to them, we just walked past each other in the corridors giving each other the eye . . . me and Ian. You know . . . "who the fuck are you!!"'

Couzens picks up on the fractured scene at the college. 'Everyone had that horrible crossover look between Joy Division and punk. There was a bit of mod starting to creep in here and there . . . There was a bunch of us into it . . . about two thousand students went there and there was ten or fifteen into punk/new wave . . . Ian Brown was getting into that mod thing proper with tonic suits and short hair with a sort of side parting . . . John Squire looked like Mick Jones – creepers, short leather bomber jacket, wrist band with studs . . . he called himself Johnny . . . Pete [Garner] wasn't at college there . . . I met Pete later . . .'

Pete Garner was starting to hang around with his elders. The punk thing was connecting people together. 'I didn't go to college. I was at Burnage High School and they were at South Trafford College. I had a lot of work to do to keep in the gang. You just don't speak to people in the year below and from a totally different school. We bonded over the punk thing.'

Pete had bumped into Ian and John in the fields just in between where they all lived. There was a river and small nondescript bridge that became the focal point. 'I met them at the bridge and all that . . . I'd seen 'em a couple of times before. I started chatting. There was a bit of piss taking going on! John was quiet, he didn't say much. John was really into The Clash whilst Ian was more Pistols and The Jam. John, for some reason, was never having The Jam . . . for me The Clash was always my number one, I love the Pistols too . . . but me and Ian really liked The Jam . . .'

THE BRIDGE

In between Sale and Altrincham there's this bridge and for generations kids have hung out there. Every teen lout across small-town England knows of the sort of place, a landmark, a meeting point, a place to get stoned and pissed, a place to fuck and fight – a focal point and a beacon for all sorts of crazed activity.

'The Bridge was like the meeting point, when everyone was ten or eleven they would hang out there and when they got to about fourteen – I guess they found something better to do and moved on,' remembers Garner.

Garner was hanging around there when he was an early teen. Just a casual young kid, mischief-making sort of stuff. He thought he was the coolest person there. He was certainly the biggest and most of the other kids thought that he was the toughest. It was something to play on in the jostling for power that dominates those long empty evenings of adolescence.

Sometimes a clutch of kids would come over from Altrincham or Timperley, bored and looking for some lightweight trouble and some laughs. Ian Brown and John Squire were just two of many that drifted around and hung out.

It was pretty fucking boring in south Manchester in those far off days. 'We thought that we were the king punks of the area. When Ian and John turned up we would give each other shit. I guess at some point there must have been some sort of mutual respect,' laughs Garner.

They started getting friendly when talk turned to what gigs they had been to. They exaggerated into the evening, inventing classic punk shows they had attended up in Manchester. It was mostly bullshit and braggadocio.

At the time, Garner was going to Burnage High School. It was there that by a bizarre coincidence he would also meet Aziz Ibrahim, the future Roses guitar player from the last stand at Reading Festival years later. 'He was a good lad, he would always have a guitar with him. He played it all the time whilst everyone watched him.'

Aziz himself remembers being in the same class as Pete. 'Burnage High School . . . top days! great days . . . best times. It was an all boys school, I was into sport there. Did really well at basketball . . . Pete was the school goth! He was artistic, really into his artwork . . . We were mates because I played basketball and his mates were on the same team . . .'

While they were bonding at the Bridge there were the first stirrings of some musical action. John who had become immersed in the whole Clash myth was taking his Mick Jones fascination one stop further and earnestly copping the licks off The Clash records. By grafting away he had become a comparatively useful if rudimentary punk rock guitar player.

But The Clash lover missed out on the greatest blag of the year and one of the best stories that surrounds the pre-Roses . . . the day they hung out with The Clash!

Brown and Pete Garner gatecrashed The Clash recording 'Bankrobber' in Manchester's Pluto studios, the long-defunct studio owned by the guitarist from Herman's Hermits on Granby Row, Manchester. The pair had heard that The Clash were in town recording somewhere and decided to see if they could find them. 'We got a train into town. Didn't know where they were going to be. Ian said a studio round here somewhere. It was pissing with rain. We thought this was ridiculous and this car pulled up and The Clash got out.'

Remembers Ian, 'We were in town in Granby Row, where Pluto Studios was. We heard these drums and it turned out it was The Clash doing "Bankrobber". So we knocked on the door, they let us in and we hung around for a day. They were nice, sound. Topper was just regular. Strummer was a bit of a weirdo. He sat under this grandfather clock, clicking his fingers in time with it. I thought, what a dick!'

'The one thing about Strummer I remember was that he was clicking his fingers to the clock,' says Pete. 'I thought he was a bit fucking nuts till I went in a studio to record and realised about studio time!'

On The Clash's Greatest Hits compilation there is a reference to these kids in Manchester hanging out in the studio.

The Clash were also a reference point for another local mate, a sharply bequiffed young drummer who lived a couple of blocks away.

Si Wolstencroft was in the same year at South Trafford College and from the same streets in south Manchester. He had cut his musical teeth on the bass guitar but had switched to drums. He had already played in Johnny Marr's pre-Smiths outfit Freaky Party with Andy Rourke and had jammed round the rehearsal rooms in town with various outfits.

Compared to Brown and Squire he was an experienced musician. He'd already been there and done it. He knew the pair through school and punk rock. It seemed inevitable somehow that the three of them would get together and start playing. They talked about doing something, getting something together.

It was at this point, sometime in early 1980, that the whole long adventure of The Stone Roses kicked off. In Si's parents' house where he had his drum kit set up, Squire came down with his guitar and Brown with his bass. They fucked about, jammed, got some rough tunes together, mainly built around John's half-inched Clash rifts. It was as good a place as any to start.

Si Wolstencroft was a pretty handy drummer. He had already been in proper rehearsal rooms like TJ Davidsons and had played with the big boys, people in their twenties! Oddly enough, some say, he had even played in a band with future Stone Roses' manager Howard Jones apparently holding down the beat for Jones's band, the Playthings . . .

He had his kit set up at home and the South Trafford team started to rehearse there. It made sense. An extension of the gang. Everyone who was touched by the hand of punk seemed to have some sort of band going now. Every bedroom, garage and youth club was rattling to sloppy riffs and spikey teen energy. And this crew were no different.

Ian had picked up the bass. It was the easiest instrument to start on and the ultimate punk rock instrument. The coolest person in every punk band was the bass player so why not? From The Clash's Paul Simonon to The Stranglers' J-J. Burnel – the bass had been elevated to the coolest instrument. No longer the thick sod standing by the amp, it was suddenly the poseurs instrument and Brown perhaps had some sort of empathy with the karate black belt, outsider rebel thug J-J. Burnel.

While his two band mates started to grab at the music power of The Clash Ian clattered along on his bass.

Now all they needed was a singer.

THE FIGHT CLUB!: ANDY COUZENS'S UNUSUAL AUDITION

Of course nowadays the singer is some sort of sensitive cove who builds a band up around his mercurial talents. Or something. But in the punk era the rules were a bit messier.

The Brown/Squire/Wolstencroft bedroom band knew they needed a singer. But where could they find one?

It couldn't be anyone. After all, there were already strong personalities at play here.

Punk rock bands required nutters to front them, not singers. Even Ian's hero Johnny Rotten, who was a contradictory sod at the best of times, covered up for an obviously shy side with a sneering tirade of hilarious and downright nasty put downs. They needed someone to front their Clash aggro, someone with a bit of craziness about them.

Mooching around the canteen in late '79, Ian Brown and Si Wolstencroft spotted a bit of a commotion. Never ones to avoid a bit of bovva they moved closer. The short-haired hooligan they had seen around the college was pounding some other kid into the floor. The other kid was in tears. It was a nasty, brutal exchange and they were impressed.

Andy says, 'I had a fight in the canteen. Some fucking lad the night before had given my little brother a bit of a going over . . . so I laid him out. He was crying by the time I had finished. It was the first fight I'd had for ages . . . It was at lunchtime with a load of people watching. There was a bit of a stunned silence. You just didn't do that at college. It was supposed to be further education and beyond all that!'

The silence was deafening. The laid back world of further education had just witnessed an unlikely burst of aggro.

So Couzens is standing there pumped full of adrenaline. He's just pummelled this kid. The refectory has gone silent. He wanders off. Gets a meal and sits down. He can feel the shocked looks of the rest of the college on his back. The confused silence that most people give off when they have been that close to some action fills the room.

He also notices two figures walking towards him.

It's that guy whose been giving him the eye since he came here and his sharp-looking mate. The one with The Clash style tight quiff and 'London's Calling' era Clash gangster punk chic.

'I spoke to Ian first . . . Simon Wolstencroft was there as well,' Andy recalled. 'He was into the later Clash look, creepers, crombies, quiff . . . kneckerchiefs and all that "London Calling"-look . . . I did this lad in and then I got myself a brew and some lunch and they asked me if I could sing! I always wanted to be in a band and I wasn't aware they had a band. I was always going to see punk bands but I couldn't play anything. They came over and said "Can you sing" and I said I'll have a go yeah! . . .'

Not that this is the way that Si Wolstencroft remembered how Andy joined the band. When interviewed by Fall Fanzine *Biggest Library Yet* his take on Andy joining was very different.

'The Patrol was my first band formed with John Squire and Ian Brown in the last year at Altrincham Grammar School. Andy Couzens was asked to sing to start with because his wealthy parents bought him an MG sports car when he went to South Trafford College (which we all attended for a while). This was a big novelty at the time.'

The band now had a singer. He had agreed to come over and rehearse in the next few weeks. And Andy Couzens, after years of drifting round schools and being the outsider, now had a gang of like-minded people to hang with. At last he had somewhere he could really call home. And that home was now calling itself The Patrol.

ANDY COUZENS

Andy Couzens was born in Stockport in 1962. It's not a town that he retains a lot of affection for. Stockport's like a village . . . it's weird. I couldn't wait to get out . . . I finished school and went as far away as I could which was . . . Altrincham!' he laughs.

He had moved constantly through his youth. 'My parents moved every two years. Always within the Stockport area and then out to Macclesfield . . . I was always moving school which didn't make life easy."

Having young parents had one hidden bonus. It meant that he was surrounded by pop music. Pop music that was not that far removed from his own generation. It was a great pop education.

'My parents were into the Stones and hated The Beatles. They liked loads of soul stuff like Wilson Pickett. My mum was 16 when she had me . . . almost like an elder sister.'

As the Sixties turned into the Seventies the parental soundtrack remained hip. 'My old fella got into Zep and Floyd and when you're a kid you pick up on what's around.'

It must have been frustrating – hip parents! But in the early Seventies there was the first real generational shift in pop. As the Sixties generation grew up into prog rock, the teenagers were busily finding their own sounds. While his father was going heavy Andy was getting into glam.

Glam rock has been snootily dismissed by 'musical experts' and 'pundits' for generation after generation but it was one of the classic British moments, homemade stars with a machine gun run of great seven inch singles. Couzens loved Slade and the rest of them but the band that he really fell for at the tender age of 11 was Bryan Ferry's Roxy Music.

'The first record I bought was "Pyjamarama" by Roxy Music. I still love it now, it drags me straight back. It reminds me of kids hanging out doing fuck all . . . '73/'74 . . . I really liked Roxy, yeah, I love glam, I loved Slade – ace band. Marc Bolan was great. "Metal Guru" is still one of my all-time favourites . . .'

T Rex are one of the greatest British pop bands that ever existed. Bolan was the inventor of glam and put out a fantastic series of pop singles and albums that have influenced a whole cross section of popstars ever since. Ian Brown, unbeknown to Andy, was also a huge fan at the same time.

'He was a big Bolan fan . . . T Rex was a great band, yeah! It's weird. I never got the sexuality side of it at all . . . I was too young really to note if stuff was sexual or not . . . Alice Cooper as well . . . That period had some great records, great singles . . .'

At school, being in constantly new face hell, Andy was the obvious target for bullying. The outsider just arriving in each school surrounded by kids who already knew each other inside out. It toughened him up. Fast. Kill or be killed. Andy had to fight back.

'When I was a lot younger I was quieter because I was moving often, so I was always the new face at school and you know what lads are like – wanna see how hard you are . . . so I learned to keep myself to myself . . .'

Already toughened up by his school experience and armed with a vicious temper and a keenness to fight, Couzens was drifting towards the ultimate male bonding world of football violence.

In the early Seventies, football hooliganism was massive. Like a reaction to the Sixties it seemed to define street culture in the Seventies. Peace and love didn't mean much in Stockport.

The skinheads were a reaction to the hippy shit and were transmuting into bovva boys and terrace thugs. Their hair was growing out into feather cuts. They retained the cherry red Doc Martens and parallel pants (often bottle green), hitched up to show off their neatly polished killa boots. Every match went off big style. It was common to see hundreds of kids chasing each other all over the place on match day.

The appalling condition of most of the soccer stadiums and the way that fans were herded round like sheep only added to the boiling pot of malevolence.

For Couzens it was escapism and male bonding and community all rolled into one. At last he felt like he belonged somewhere. 'When I got into my early mid teens I got badly into football violence. I'd go and see Stockport County every Friday without fail. There was always a battle on every Friday night. Always arranged at the tunnels at Stockport station.'

He dressed in regulation thug gear. 'Doc boots, cherry reds, parallels . . . sheepskin donkey jacket . . . the feather cut started disappearing, getting shorter and shorter like along with becoming a suedehead. Then I went to the bigger games in Manchester . . . United was always too clean cut and regulated so I went to Maine Road instead and that was serious nasty stuff . . . We were with a group of lads who went into Moss Side and met up with a bunch of guys called the Cool Cats, a bunch of black guy hooligans . . . and a few white guys . . .'

Andy Couzens was no shrinking violet when it went off. 'I've got a really bad temper, a really short fuse . . . The best thing about Maine Road was the Kippax, the police stand between the two massive high fences . . . and you could spit and throw things at them throughout the game. I got a right kick out of it. A bunch of us would go out on Friday night to Stockport and Saturday to City. The football was incidental, an excuse. I went to a lot of away games as well. It was good for a laugh on those Seventies football specials. They didn't have a seat in them, the windows were plastic and we had a riot!

This sort of life couldn't go on for ever and Couzens was no Neanderthal. He realised the violence was going to have to be tempered. He needed another outlet for his frustration and energy and one night in the summer of '77 when he was at home he flicked across the stations on the radio and was captivated by this fast snarling tune.

It was the first great pop record he had heard for years. Nothing had moved him since the glam heyday of three years before. The singer had a whining bratty voice but sounded sharp and intelligent as hell.

He was hooked. The group was The Adverts, one of the seemingly endless parade of punk rock groups that seemed to be spiralling out, filling the vacuum after The Sex Pistols had exploded.

He suddenly started to notice that there was this whole new sub culture going on. A new world, a new code, a new language and he was hooked. Greedily he started to soak up these new influences.

'I heard the tunes . . . I didn't read about it, I just heard the tunes . . . there had been a bit of a lull in music. I remember even buying an Abba album, ha! ha! ha! I remember buying a Wings album which I never liked. *Wings At The Speed Of Sound*. It was awful.'

At last there was a musical culture that felt like it belonged to you. 'No more Elvis, Beatles or The Rolling Stones,' crowed The Clash on '1977'. Fed up with being told that the pop party was over in the mid to late Seventies, teens were having their own party.

'I heard the music and you could tell there was something, the thing for me was that it sounded so angry. I related to that straight away. It was great . . . and then it opened my eyes. It changed everything for me. I started going to gigs. It was such a different world than my upbringing in Stockport. I was shocked, black people mixing with white people. Women on their own. A real eye opener. It changed the way I thought about everything. It buried my violence. Coming from where I come from all you aspire to is getting pissed on a Friday or Saturday, putting a suit on so you can get into pubs and being married by the time you're 21 with kids. Most of the people I went to school with did that. I meet them now and they look 50 years old!'

Manchester was great for punk rock. Outside London it was the second punk rock city. Every major band played there at the Electric Circus, and it even had its own scene, its own bands and Andy couldn't get enough of these groups.

'I saw The Clash at Electric Circus. I saw The Clash so many times, I always loved The Buzzcocks. It was all the sexual contradictions that always tickled me! The Pistols and The Clash were fantastic. The Adverts I liked but they let you down a bit, they didn't quite move you in the same way as the Pistols and The Clash and then the next thing that really hit me was Joy Division.'

By 1979 punk was becoming a straitjacket and although he still (like all the Roses) loved the simplistic rush of the three minute punk rock buzz for years to come, Andy was now fired by the new soundscape that groups like Manchester outfit Warsaw were carving from the punk template.

'I saw them when they were called Warsaw, playing in some fucking awful place at the arse end of Manchester, near the laughably called Northern Quarter. I'd follow them around a bit. Bands like that you could go and see and they actually meant it, which sounds so corny now. When they've really got some self belief and when you got an idea of their personalities from what they are doing, it's totally gripping . . .'

When Warsaw turned into Joy Division they really captured the post punk paranoia, the bleakness of the times.

'All the best music does, doesn't it? I met Diggle and Shelley loads of times. I met The Clash a few times. They were everything you thought they were going to be.'

Couzens was now settling into some sort of school routine. 'I was still at school now in the fifth year. Bramhall High School which was a nice safe little environment. It was a little bubble. Mike Pickering went to my school and Gordon King who ended up in the World of Twist went there as well. We were pretty good friends at school. He was always a bit more arty, with a bit more artistic flair, shall we say. He'd wear an Afghan coat and smoke draw and I was like more of a hooligan!'

Couzens surprised himself by sailing through his exams. 'I got O levels . . . about eight of the fucking things. The stupid thing is all that build-up to them. I never picked up the certificates. It was just a joke.'

He drifted into higher education. 'I went to South Trafford College. I did A level maths, physics and electronics . . . It was a technical college and had an arts side to it as well, which is where John Squire was.'

And it was at college that he was to make some friendships that were to change his rock'n'roll life. As he entered South Trafford College in the autumn of 1979 he quickly noticed a handful of other punk rock nutters but they were from another part of town and remained aloof. Couzens tried to keep his head down. Get some A levels and fuck off.

But that one slip. That one relapse to violence. That one moment of fury in the canteen had put him into an unlikely musical situation.

1980–81

THE PATROL

Early 1980 John and Simon hit the road for the first time for a tour that would dominate their musical thinking for the next few years. During January and February of 1980 they hitchhiked round the country to see The Clash at their peak on the legendary '16 Tons' tour.

Si recalls, 'The music we were starting to do with The Patrol was loosely based on The Clash. Squire and myself were massive fans at the time. I left college to follow them around the country on the 16 Tons tour in 1980.'

They were just two more fresh young faces in a sea of kids. The pair of them joining the ever-increasing pack of young waifs and strays who would hitchhike up and down the country checking out the greatest punk band of them all.

A whole generation of British rockers cut their teeth following The Clash from gig to gig, some of them crewing with the band, some blagging guest list places and some just turning up at soundchecks and getting looked after by the band. It was a big deal with The Clash to have this bond with their fans, even to the point of letting them sleep on the floor of the hotel rooms after the shows. Ian Brown remembers the pair of them hitting the road with The Clash.

'The Clash . . . yeah. John and Si were right into them. They'd go all over to see them. I preferred the Pistols, me. And later The Upstarts.'

Perhaps, more than following bands around, the most powerful message from punk was *do it yourself*. The whole notion, the whole inspirational idea was that anyone could have a go. All over the punk nation it seemed that every one was at it, blagging, buying guitars, forcing mates into being drummers, getting hold of youth clubs and putting gigs on. Rock stars were removed from the first-class lifestyle of mid Atlantic flights and were now strutting round estates, mooching around the suburbs.

Every ragbag collection of mates were now forming themselves into rock'n'roll bands. And the Timperley boys were no exception. John Squire had been glued to his guitar, listening to those incendiary Clash records, copping those Mick Jones licks. Listening and learning. The Clash's artful and adrenalised take on punk rock appealing to his nature . . .

And Funky Si, like John, was besotted with The Clash and learning his drums by copping rhythms from The Clash's remarkable drummer Topper Headon. The three mates were getting tunes together. Struggling to make music. The thudding fumbling that slowly turns into songs that was going on in garages all over the country.

The three of them had been rehearsing for a few weeks now. They had needed a focal point, their own Mensi, their own Strummer, a right nutter – and now they had one.

Perfect. And he had a car!

Says Andy, 'I arranged to meet Ian just outside Timperley train station. I was driving by then. They rehearsed in the back bedroom at Si's house in Hale Barns (starting a long band tradition of rehearsing in bedrooms). The first time I ever met John was at that rehearsal. I had seen him around at college. I thought there's that fucking Clash clone ha! ha!'

Andy plugged his mic into John's guitar amp and shouted his way over the songs, finding his way over the three chord workouts. 'Si had a good kit and he could play. John was pretty good but it was all Clash copy stuff. He played a bit of lead as well. He'd had proper guitar lessons. Ian was on bass and couldn't really play. He was a proper punk bass player. All fast strumming.'

There were also some tunes to work on. 'They had a couple of bits of music. They had had a few jams before I got there. John was the one who got it all together initially. They all went to Altrincham Grammar together. Had gone through discovering punk, all that sort of thing, so it grew from that really. No songs. Just jammed bits of music. John had brought some lyrics with him that he thought I might want to sing. It was a real Clash reggae type of thing called "Gaol Of The Assassins". Pete has a tape of that. Years later we'd always joke that Pete was the Bill Wyman of the gang, hoarding all the stuff! Reni tried to keep stuff as well but could never concentrate enough. In Sweden Reni kept a really detailed diary, came home and lost it . . .'

The rehearsals at Si Wolstencroft's mum and dad's place near Ian and John's in Timperley were going well. They had scratched together some Clash-style punk rock tunes. Squire was good enough on guitar to make the whole thing convincing and Si's drumming, already bolstered by more than a couple of years' playing in other ad hoc line-ups, gave them a good enough backbone.

The band's personalities were already at the fore in the tight confines of the hot bedroom. The muffled racket through the cheap amps and Andy's coarse vocals were further muffled by the fact that his cheapo mic was jacked up through John's amp which added to the distorted punk mêlée. As he shouted down the mic and attempted to put some punk rock life to John's lyrics, Andy had a good look at his new mates.

'Ian was cocky. Si was always quiet. John was dead serious, a lot of presence about him. Ian was cocky as fuck right from the word go – trying to vibe me out. I wasn't having any of it, I remember saying to him "so you are a fucking mod, are you? what's all that about!" The thing I remember about John the most was that he was very typically artistically natured. Quiet and shy. He always has a fringe to hide behind. I remember thinking he was quite interesting, you know . . .'

It was a wild punk rock baptism. Typical of the times you go from flared trouser nonentity to punked up iconoclast within a fortnight. From brawling madman in college to lead singer in 24 hours. Things were moving fast in pop culture and the message of the times was of being involved, of doing something!

The band rehearsed hard. The work ethic was already ingrained. Recalls Andy, 'We started rehearsing a few times every week. That was one thing we always did. We rehearsed every night. We never really had a night off. We would do it all the time, live and breathe it. It's the only way to get things done. I remember the songs were all real Clash-type things. "25 Rifles", "Too Many Tons" named after The Clash's "16 Tons" tour. It was all real Clash stuff. I did a few lyrics but they were mainly John's. It was all punk rock nonsense really. There was also one called "H Block".'

The Clash legend looms large over the Roses and their early incarnations so you can imagine how cool it was when the feeling was reciprocated. Years later Pete caught The Clash on TV being interviewed.

'I saw Strummer getting interviewed on snub TV just after I left the Roses. They asked him if he liked any bands and he said the Roses. I choked on my brew. I wanted to speak to John and say "Jesus!" Strummer had picked up on the Roses just when the album came out and we were still really underground. I'd love to meet him and tell him me and Ian had met him one time.'

Quickly the songs came together. Listening to a rehearsal tape from March 1980 you can hear a pretty competent band honing down its Clash chops.

The songs charge past, raw vocals over the slashing riffs, 'London Night Out', '25 Rifles', 'Human Disease', 'Stepping Stone', which sounds more like a cover of the Pistols' cover of The Monkees' song than the original, a rudimentary run through 'Johny B Goode' and, changing the tempo, the attempt at Clash reggae of 'Gaol Of The Assassins' which was named after a slogan on a classic Joe Strummer hand-stencilled T shirt. Also there was 'Stars And Stripes' which was 'our version of "I'm So Bored Of The USA",' remembers Pete, referencing The Clash's anti-Americana tirade.

Garner was sitting in with the band, hanging out at their rehearsals, part of the gang, pretending to be their roadie. They were surprisingly adept for a teenage punk band. Pete remembers how together they were.

'Si was into Topper. He was aspiring to that sort of level really. Ian's bass playing was pretty rudimentary – classic punk style, the guitar really Clash. One number was their sort of "Police And Thieves", a bit "Guns Of Brixton", not proper reggae by any stretch of the imagination, that was "Gaol Of The Assassins . . .", there was also "Up On The Roof".'

The Patrol were bonding over their musical tastes. This was a crew that knew their music. Says Andy, 'We were into the same stuff. Generation X's first album was a big one with all of us. We listened to everything from glam, to skin, to punk. We all delved into Johnny Thunders and the New York Dolls separately from each other. It was a real meeting of minds. We all had a core of stuff we really liked. We branched off into our own stuff as well. I was into Joy Division and the others weren't. I remember turning John on to some of the early Joy Division stuff. I had two copies of the first EP. I gave John one. He was bang into it.'

And always hanging around in the rehearsal room was their mate from the Bridge, Pete Garner, not playing anything just mooching about. The gang was still tantamount. Important. It was more than who was in the band, you can hear the banter on the rehearsal tapes, the debates about music, opinions getting formed, in jokes flying around and then songs crashing in and out.

Pete was right in there. After all, even a non-playing mate like him was not far behind some of the band members when it came to musicianship. Pete later recalled, 'That was what was so important. We knew so much about music. We talked about it all the time. We knew everything. It was an obsession . . .'

Even then, right from the start, the band were incredibly earnest about what they were doing. They rehearsed hard. There was no pottering about. As a result they swiftly tightened up. You can hear it on the rehearsal tapes, songs coming together quickly. Now they were ready to play some gigs.

On Friday, 28 March 1980 they played their first gig. The Patrol had managed to get on to a punk rock bill at the Sale Annexe Youth Club. It was a typical youth club affair. The felt-tipped and photocopied poster tells the whole story: for 30p you could see The Patrol supported by Stretford punks Suburban Chaos at the Youth Club 'behind Sale Town Hall!' screamed the missive which also has the curious slogan 'roadies don't wear jips' scrawled along the bottom. Even now a bashful Pete Garner won't explain what this means!

Andy Couzens recalls this first gig, 'Our first gig was at Sale Annexe, in some youth club in the middle of Sale, a really grotty youth club. A couple of other bands played. A punk band from Stretford played as well: I can't remember their name [Corrosive Youth!] a proper noisy punk band like Discharge. We went down pretty good, we were shocked! We had been rehearsing so much it was as good as that stuff was going to get. Ian doing his thing, sucking in youth culture, that's what he's really good at. We were all looking more Clash like. Me and Ian had short hair. I was jumping around. John used to move around as well in a Mick Jones style.'

The Patrol watched Suburban Chaos's set and were impressed by the band's fierce sound. Suburban Chaos were far closer to the full on leather, bristles, studs and acne assault of Stoke's fast and furious Discharge, a band who took the three minute protest of classic punk and crushed it into splenetic rushes of dark and viscous sound.

They accompanied this with a fiercer look, leaning more towards the bleached spike hair and leather jackets stuffed full of studs. It was the start of the punk look that had become accepted by the media as the nom de plume for the movement and Discharge's influence can be felt to this day in US hardcore and speed metal.

Suburban Chaos were a much fiercer punk rock proposition than The Patrol. They too had The Clash stamped all over their creativity but they had moved further into the ferocious spell of Stoke's Discharge and were knocking the finesse off the original punk style with a thrashier more adrenalised assault.

'When we arrived at the gig I thought "Hang on, I know these guys,"' says Pete 'and it turned out that a year before I was at some disco dancing to some punk records and these punks had piled in and kicked me in the face. I got up trying to sort them out and they just looked at me. There was loads of them so I left it at that! And it turns out that they had become Suburban Chaos!'

Despite this rather raw initial meeting with The Patrol's roadie, the bands got on well and planned some more gigs in the south Manchester hinterland.

Headliners The Patrol, in comparison, were almost lightweight, melodic. Their Clash-inspired workouts may have seemed tame in comparison but the sheer brutal edge of their frontman and their bass player's berating of the crowd helped them through. Their skinny guitarist, with his dishevelled mop and too tight leather jacket, played the Mick Jones thing to the hilt. They played a handful of songs and surfed on the adrenaline of being on stage for the first time. The small crowd were into it, after all it was punk and the buzzsaw attack was enough to pass the cred test. The bass player stared maniacally at the crowd and frantically assaulted his instrument and the drummer, hiding behind a tight quiff, held down the rat-a-tat punk rock beat.

The Patrol were now in the business of playing more gigs. Remembers Andy, 'We played a village hall out in Lymm and a youth club in Stretford to a bunch of punks. They ended up following us around, glueheads and punks – probably 15 to 30 people there but it felt full! We had about eight songs by then.'

On 15 May they played their second gig at the unlikely named Vortex in Lymm out in Cheshire towards Warrington. Again Suburban Chaos were supporting. Says Pete, 'Suburban Chaos had a song called "Anarchy In The

Suburbs" that was their anthem. They were alright. I mean everyone was sixteen at the time. We all became mates. They were Stretford lads, we were Sale lads. A bit like West Side Story!'

The next day The Patrol were on home turf with a show at South Trafford College. 'On the day after we played at South Trafford College. There was a couple of college metal bands supporting. Firecloud and someone else.'

The band bolstered by their run of gigs and with a set of their own tunes then decided to take the next step. That summer they were confident enough to cut their first demo, recorded on a 4 track.

'Yeah, we did a demo that was limited to a hundred copies but I don't have it any more. All my stuff got nicked years later so I don't even have a copy myself! We did a song called "Gaol Of The Assassins" and another called "25 Rifles",' says Ian.

It was their one and only demo. 'We did some demos as The Patrol,' recalls Andy. 'They were recorded in a Rusholme studio just off Great Western Street where Mick Hucknall did a lot of stuff with his punk band the Frantic Elevators. The only reason I know this was because we met him in there. There were three songs, "Too Many Tons", "Gaol Of The Assassins" and "25 Rifles".'

The demos show a band surprisingly adept. Far from being a youth club bunch of chancers, there is a touch of musicality about the band. John Squire's guitar is already the stand out, on 'Gaol Of The Assassins' his choppy rhythm playing hints at a future dexterity. The guitar, of course, has The Clash stamped all over it, the same sort of snarl, the sub reggae copped grinding chops that defined The Clash. It gives the songs their edge, their distinct flavour.

Si's drums are solid proof of a couple of years playing under his belt. They show touches of that youth club punk rush, that lust for putting the energy back into rock'n'roll. Says Pete, 'Si was a massive Clash fan as well and was modelling his drumming on The Clash's Topper Headon, which is not a bad place to start to learn how to play drums!'

Headon was, perhaps, the best drummer to come out of punk. He had spent years pre-Clash playing with soul bands and had even done a stint with The Temptations. Adding this knowledge, this arsenal of soul-infused drum rolls to his rock solid rhythms, he gave The Clash a dynamic, powerful, backbeat. As young Si drummed along to Topper, he was unwittingly picking up a whole history of pop music drumming from the skinny Clash sticksman. It was also a door to the many other musics that lay just beyond punk, a hint at the power of soul or the freedom of funk and would be a profound influence on his future drumming direction.

His partner in rhythm was Ian Brown whose bass playing was punk rock rudimentary. All Brown had to do was hold down the songs' riffs which he did with a bit more pizzaz than the one-note thrashing he's been accused of.

Not that there are any flash-like runs going on, this is strictly four note stuff, just holding it down.

Couzens's vocals are hoarse and shouted but they suit the punkiness of the tunes.

After recording the demo there was another clutch of local gigs. Ian Brown remembers, 'We played about five youth clubs with Corrosive Youth, a punk group from Stretford – we played in Lostock.'

The Lostock show was on 11 July. Ian forgot to mention that Suburban Chaos were also on the bill, the three bands now making up their own package of south Manchester suburban punk rock racket!

The Patrol's act was beginning to take shape over these shows. Inspired by the confrontational abrasiveness of punk, the band's more extrovert members were cranking up their punk schtick. Says Andy, 'Ian always had to have a microphone so he could shout at people. It was funny. It was good for a laugh. We played at the college and played the Portland bars in town as well . . .'

Andy remembers them supporting Seventeen who eventually became The Alarm at the Portland bars, although Pete denies this. 'Me and Ian had been to see them in a few places before,' says Andy. 'We just bothered the guy putting the gigs on there. He said he had Seventeen coming up and we grabbed it.'

Pete Garner can't remember The Patrol playing with Seventeen. 'I could swear they never played with Seventeen. We were aware of them but I'm sure we headlined at the Portland Bars with Corrosive Youth supporting.'

Andy later recalled, 'It was our first proper gig with a PA. It was total shock. I could hear myself . . . Seventeen were good guys. I liked the band but by 1981 they had turned into The Alarm. I was disgusted with them. One minute they were good and going in a certain direction, then they were all spikey hair and leather belts.'

Whether the gig was with Seventeen or not, it was their début in the city centre and was another big step forward for the band. Out of the youth clubs and on to proper stages. Things were starting to happen!

They also nearly replaced Adam And The Ants at another city centre show. A gig that Garner set up. 'That was the gig I booked for them playing when The Ants should have played the Osbourne. I rang up to see what time they were playing and they didn't make it. I said I know a band that could play, I'll get them down. Ian and Andy said brilliant but we couldn't find John anywhere. It turns out that he was sat in a field being artistic! It would have been a bad idea anyway, they were too young, a bunch of 16 year olds playing to an early Ants crowd. Big Mohican crazies . . . can't see it working!'

In between their intermittent shows in the middle of 1980 they would be in town checking out gigs, even getting out on the road watching bands. Ian was roadying for the Angelic Upstarts, the fiercely Socialist skin band who were in the middle of a fine run of hit singles of their own.

'Ian went to loads of their gigs,' says Pete. 'He knew Mensi . . . we always knew Mensi's politics were cool, he was a great guy.'

On 8 August The Patrol were back in action at Dunham Massey village hall, again with Suburban Chaos and Corrosive Youth.

A couple of months later on 14 November The Patrol played their last show, again returning to South Trafford College with Scorched Earth and Strange Behaviour. It was a whole 50p to get in. After the gig there was no set decision to stop. The Patrol returned to the rehearsal room. There was a feeling that it was time to move on. Branch out a bit. Get the music to do something more than just follow The Clash route. Explore what else could be done. Andy Couzens explains.

'We decided we were going to change it all. We were still rehearsing after the last gig. We were all trying to push it forward. We weren't going to push it any further forward with what it was . . .'

As already hinted at the gig, the line up was about to shuffle. The music they now wanted to make required more than a shouty singer who got the job because he beat the shit out of some kid in the canteen and the bass player was itching to step up to the mic. At the end of the set when Ian Brown started to sing 'Blockbuster' (a song that Squire was still listing in his top ten favourite records years later – '"Blockbuster" was an abiding memory from first watching *Top Of The Pops*, strange bricklaying transvestites who seemed to be on every week') on stage at Lymm, it was Ian Brown's first taste of being the frontman.

Pete Garner remembers well his elevation from mate/roadie to getting on stage for the first time. 'I had never played bass before they showed me the riff to "Blockbuster" and I just got up and hammed my way through it! It was the last time I played bass for years!'

Without knowing it The Patrol's centre of gravity had shifted during that exuberant cover of The Sweet classic. In a rush of excitement Brown handed his bass to their long haired mate Pete Garner and as Garner picked out the simple duh duh bass line, Ian Brown leapt around with the mic. It was pop history, Squire on guitar and Brown on near lead vocal, it was the first time that the eventual classic combination would be seen in public.

'Does anyone know the way! There's got to be a way to Blockbuster!' Not only was Ian Brown grabbing the lead vocal mic for the first time but the callow-faced youth with the long black hair on bass was on stage with his buddies for the first time.

For Pete Garner chugging away on Ian's bass guitar, it was his first time on stage and an appearance that completed the circle of the eventual Roses part one line-up.

South Trafford College was never intended to be the band's last-ever gig.

Within days they were back in the rehearsal room, working on tunes, looking for that change in direction.

THE END OF THE PATROL

They went back to the rehearsal room, keen to explore this new line-up's potential. Andy picked up the guitar.

'So Ian went on vocals. I learned a few chords from John and Pete came in on bass . . . just for a few rehearsals and then that fell to pieces again. By now we had a bit of a PA, turn it up and it feeds back. Everyone shouting at guitar players "too loud" . . .'

They even felt confident enough to look outside their tightly knit community to pull in another musician. Says Andy, 'First of all we got another guitar player in. I can't remember his name. I had to sack him because John and Ian wouldn't dare. This guy was on rhythm guitar. I think this was before we got Ian to be the singer. I've a feeling he was called Neil, I'm not sure. He was a bit of a beer monster. One of those types. I said to John, I can play the guitar instead, I can't sing! I never could, I never professed to so I moved to guitar.'

It was the moment Andy had been waiting for. There were limitations in shouting over a punk racket. He preferred the guitar. It was more him. The Patrol were trying to change. The new influences were adding to their natural musical curiosity.

'We had done a few gigs. Towards the end the music had started to change slightly. It went away from The Clash thing, more rock'n'roll for want of a better phrase. We were getting into Johnny Thunders, really drifting that way. John was pushing it that way. It's funny how bands work, you feed off each other. Playing off each other's stuff, arguing, and something gets spat out. You might have a riff, but the other person can't play it, or someone starts singing along with it . . .'

In the weeks that followed the South Trafford College gig they carried on rehearsing, messing about with the formula. But it was getting less and less enthusiastic. Says Andy, 'We used to call round for John and he'd be in his pathetic slipper phase and his brother Matt would come out instead. Matt is just like John but a . . . laugh! John would be in his bedroom making models . . . You'd go round, he was one of those guys who would melt plastic cars so they would look like they had a crash. You think how's he done that! They were all painted up afterwards . . . Fucking brilliant . . .'

Even as the band fell apart they remained friends. 'We were still mates. Because we continued to go out with each other and hang out one, two, or three of us . . . one night rehearsing, the next night not. I do remember Ian got a job working at the DHSS in Sale. Pete was working anyway in Paperchase in town. John was for a long time sat at home making models.

Si had a job in a fish shop in Wilmslow, and he started doing stuff with Andy Rourke and Johnny Marr. He did those demos with them.'

And The Patrol?

It wasn't happening. There were not enough kicks involved in being in a band for Brown. He was looking at the road. Looking for some adventure and the pull of the mod scene towards the scooter clubs was proving too strong.

A few weeks later Ian Brown sold his bass and bought a scooter.

The rest of them would go out, go round the south Manchester suburban sprawl, talk about life, punk rock, rock'n'roll, clothes and girls, the usual stuff. 'We even used to go in pubs and none of us drank, just a couple of orange juices and a coke. We would go to house parties in Sale. It was full of women, young girls, great . . .', Andy remembers.

Si took his drums to the pre-Smiths band put together by the then John Maher (eventually Jonny Marr), the Wythenshawe based Keef lookalike, who had put together the loosely titled Freaky Party alongside bassist Andy Rourke after their previous combo White Dice had dissolved.

They had already recorded a demo, 'Crack Therapy', at Decibel studios in Ancoats and were looking for a drummer who could push their funk-influenced band a bit further.

Through the grapevine a school friend Dave Columbo said he knew of someone from Altrincham, a drummer known as 'Funky Si'.

Si went round for a jam at Andy Rourke's house, checked the demo and joined. The funkier chops employed by The Freaky Party made a change from The Clash riffola of his previous outing, it was a new challenge. He remained in The Freaky Party for a year. They never gigged, preferring to hone down their sound with endless rehearsals. Their sound was the tuff, clipped, curiously northern take on funk, the sort of dark-hearted wah wah attack employed by the likes of A Certain Ratio. Si was now listening to Grandmaster Flash, broadening his musical horizons, getting funkier . . . Funky Si.

For the whole of '81 they rehearsed hard. But they could not find a damn singer, someone to front the outfit. They had some guy called Wade who could only do the John Lydon whine and was ejected only to become a male model. And the band got funkier, jamming hard, inspired by Marr's pile of disco singles.

Into 1982 The Freaky Party were rehearsing three nights a week in the city centre Decibel studios but the lack of someone to front the outfit and Johnny Marr's gradual loss of interest in the funk direction stymied the project. Si and Andy Rourke carried on jamming, writing and looking for singers.

Si wasn't the only one to start shifting away from his punk/Clash roots in that summer of 1981. Things were changing. Even a bunch of Clash diehards were starting to feel the post punk landscape shifting.

The mod thing was flavouring and cross-cutting the punk hinterland with new messages and ideas. If anything it finally eradicated the Year Zero theory of punk, the theory that there was nothing of any value in pop music and culture from before 1977. A direct line was established to the Sixties and gradually a whole new bag of influences would start to seep into a nation's rehearsal rooms.

The mod thing was affecting Ian Brown. Though he still loved punk, the skin/mod influences were now starting to cross pollinate his tastes. 'Ian was getting into all that mod stuff like . . . Secret Affair. He was bang into Madness, he loved Madness . . . ska, 2 tone was his big thing – Sham 69, Cockney Rejects, The Upstarts, which I must admit I loved as well . . . He was hanging out with Mensi, roadying. I went as well. I got right into the skinhead end of mod as well. Sta Press, Ben Shermans . . . I remember seeing Jimmy Somerville with the skinhead look, Harrington Levis and Doc shoes. Killed it. Every skin in the country burning his clothes! Ruined it over night! . . .'

Ian was the first to lose interest in The Patrol. He was bored with being in a band. There were now new ways of getting on the road. New ways of getting out and about. A bit of adventure. A bit of bother. And they didn't involve hanging around and rehearsing. Ian Brown was about to enter a new phase of his life and a phase that would influence him and his friends for the next few years and beyond. Ian told *Record Collector*, 'It wasn't serious. I never really wanted to be in a group so I sold my bass and got a scooter with the money – £100.'

1982

SCOOTER SCENE

To understand the late Seventies is to understand the proliferation of youth cults at the time. After punk there was total confusion. While punk itself had claimed that this was year zero and that to listen to any other music was a crime, there were hints from the top that this just wasn't so. John Lydon had mixed it up on a my-favourite-records-style playlist, name-checking dub, Can and Captain Beefheart in an eclectic run of records. The Clash were playing a whole host of styles, the sheer brutal energy unleashed by punk was finding new homes for itself, all the strands that had combined to make punk were unravelling fast.

There was a mod revival, a Ska revival (c/o 2 Tone), even a heavy-metal revival. For the post-punk street teens like the Roses and their gang of mates there was plenty of action to choose from.

Whereas the media portrayed all the youth cults fighting each other, there was plenty of crossover, especially when common interests like girls, travel and getting out of heads was concerned. The itinerant Brown was bored with being in a band. He wanted to get on the road now; at heart a cross between a skin and a mod, he hooked up with the scooter clubs, a melting pot of restless spirits.

The scooter clubs were just one of the many strands of culture that the wreckage of the punk rock generation clung on to after the fallout. Mods had been around since the late Fifties. Hip, cool, sharp and angular at the time, they gradually metamorphosed into skinheads or hippies depending on class, taste in drugs and the amount of violence in their souls. Somehow the culture had staggered along, clinging to the scooter clubs who had been shocked enough in the first place to be joined by all these barmy kids looking for some seaside action.

The scooter clubs were nominally clubs for scooter owners to take their machines out on runs. The mods hi-jacked the runs in the Sixties and had hung on by the Eighties to become an underground scene in their own right. For a lot of kids they were another gang, another excuse to get out of town and a great way to network up a huge bunch of contacts all over the country.

Ian sold his bass and bought a pink chopper scooter from Braithwaites in Stockport. 'My first scooter was a Lambretta J125 from '66. All over the north in the late '70s/early '80s, there were still loads of Northern Soul and scooter boys. East Manchester was heavy metal, but north of Manchester, it's Northern Soul. There were still loads of clubs to go to. We used to go to the Beehive in Eccles and the scooter boys used to fight with the lads from that area – where the Mondays were from, Swinton. So yeah, we used to fight them every week. Years later, we laughed about it.'

Andy remembers them all going out and buying their first scooters. 'I had a Lambretta . . . Ian had the first scooter . . . I went with Ian to buy a Lambretta. He's one of those people who breaks everything! Ian can't wear a watch, or anything mechanical. He breaks anything when he goes near it. He bought this Lambretta and it never worked for him at all. It never went! He was completely incapable with it! The thing with Lambrettas is that they don't fucking work. It's like owning an old motorbike. You have to take it apart and clean it. I could do that but he couldn't do it at all . . . So he went out and bought a Vespa. John bought a Lambretta. He didn't ride it that much, but spent a lot of time pulling it apart, painting it, getting everything copper plated. You could say each bike was a reflection of the owner's personality.'

Brown's next Lambretta has become legendary. A cross between Easy Rider and a Lambretta and painted pink. It was built to attract attention. Says Ian, 'Yeah, that was a Lambretta GP200 – extended forks, banana seat, leg shields off. Sweet and Innocent, it was called. And I had a Vespa Rally 200 with "Angels With Dirty Faces" painted on the side. I had five or six over time. We went to all the rallies – Brighton, the Isle of Wight, Scotland, Great Yarmouth. Two years later, I got John into it. He had a GP200 that he made up himself.'

Brown's scooter was long and thin with a wicked long wheel arch almost like an Easy Rider scooter. On the front 'Cranked Up Really High' was painted over the petrol tank – it was asking for trouble and he got stopped by the cops wherever he went. People can remember Brown lifting the scooter up the stairs of his Hulme Crescent flat at the time, leaving it down on the streets would have been asking for it to get swiped. He had moved to Hulme in 1980 and was to live there till '83.

John also picked up a scooter and had 'Too Chicken To Even Try It' – a line from The Clash's incendiary 'White Riot' painted over his petrol tank.

Squire remembers his scooter days with affection as he explained to Dave Simpson for an interview with *ID*: 'A Lambretta is a very desirable object. Ian wanted one. I got one. Did it up, painted it. I wanted to show it off to other people who had scooters.'

And that's what they did, meeting up at the scooter club's pub in Stockport. They would all stand around looking at each other's bikes.

The pair of them hooked up with the Stockport scooter crowd, but were never in the club, too maverick to really be members. They had the bikes and dug the music and went out on runs, hooking up with a whole host of unlikely people like Steve Harrison, who went on to manage The Charlatans, or Clint Mansell, the lead singer from Pop Will Eat Itself. It was a new network, a new chain of like-minded souls from the whole of the north of England, pop culture crazed nutters with a pocket full of speed and hi-octane adventure on their minds. It was an excuse to get trashed, get out of town and hit the road. It was running with a gang, a gang mentality that would eventually resurface in the Roses.

They would go away on bank holidays to Brighton and seaside resorts all over Britain. They were full on scooter boys – a road version of the mods, their helmets resplendent with the rabbit's tail that hung from the back.

'The biggest run we ever went on was to Scarborough,' recounts A.J. Wilkinson, who by now was a scooter boy as well. 'There were thousands of us, it was all the different scooter clubs like Wigan etc. all joining together. I remember there was some bother when we got there as well. This was about 1980 – it was well into the peak of the scooter club scene by then.'

The scooter clubs had been around for years. Starting off in the late Fifties, middle-class suburban weekend rebels were more fascinated in the nuts and bolts of their bikes than any sort of tearaway action. By the late Seventies it was a very different scene. It had been taken over by raw young recruits from the punk fallout and had become a home for punks, skins and hooligans as well as mods and scooter boys.

Mark Sergeant of *Scootering* magazine sighs as he picks up one snapshot of the time. 'There's a picture here of the Burnley . . . They had long hair, massive sideburns and flares and they were calling themselves mods.' It's fair to say that the scooter scene had wandered a long way from its roots.

Quadrophenia was to prove a massive turning point for the scene, putting it back into the centre of youth consciousness, and making mod and scooter culture fashionable again.

Mod is the youth culture that is at the roots of most of the malarkey in UK pop culture. The Pistols and The Clash and especially The Jam had quite definite mod roots. The coolest British bands have always been clothes and hair and drug obsessives, not being able to separate this from the music. In fact it's one of the things that the Americans always sneer at us for calling our bands 'haircut bands'. Style is all for the killer pop band and the gang that's at its core. Mod was the starting point and the backbone to many cool bands and it was going through some sort of renaissance. The massive success of The Jam in the punk era had definitely had some sort of knock on effect. Less extreme than punk, it was far easier to become a mod and many took this option.

As mentioned *Quadrophenia* had turned a whole generation on to something else after punk and coupled with 2 tone it had proved to be a special brew for the wild assed teens.

Overnight it was Ben Shermans, Sta Press and suede shoes replacing battered Docs, as Garner remembers. 'I was still the punk in the crowd and I was still hanging out with them but we would go to parties and they would be mod parties. People wouldn't let me in because of my punk clothes, it got to be a real drag.' Looking the spit of Mick Jones, Pete felt like the last punk in town.

Not that their social lives were totally modernised. People still remember Ian Brown turning up at Meteors gigs in town and going down to the Chicken Shack at Devilles, a rockabilly punk night as well as other clubs playing the same sort of music like Legends on a Thursday. While John Squire would go down to Pips and its legendary Bowie Roxy nights, the multi-roomed layout of Pips meant that there were about five clubs in one, some playing Northern Soul and oldies. Youth cults may have been fairly tribal on paper but for most teenagers if music was fast, exciting and fucked up, then they were having a slice of it, criss crossing scenes to get their kicks.

'The scooter boys were not mods,' Brown pointed out to the *Melody Maker* in 1990. 'We were a mixture of punks, skins, anyone who had a scooter. I used to see Clinton from Pop Will Eat Itself on scooter runs; we used to get attacked by bikers in Stourbridge till we followed Clinton down an alternative safe route. The police would pull mine up wherever I went. I was once fined £20 for having condensation on my speedometer.'

Ian Brown was travelling around for his musical fix. 'I used to go to Northern Soul all-nighters in Rhyl, Rotherham and Doncaster, very into it I was. All through the night till late in the morning,' he told *Q* magazine.

They started to drift apart – Garner getting deeper into the roots of punk – digging the Dolls/Stooges/MC5 axis while Ian got into Motown and Northern Soul.

Pete didn't see John Squire for months, believing that they didn't really have that much in common any more. One afternoon he bumped into him in Sale and with fuck all to do they checked out records in a local record shop. They picked up the first Dexy's album, because they liked the sleeve and the whole intense gang aura around the outfit. The band as gang thing was scoured deep into their consciousness. Nervously they took the record home. At the time there were so many false hopes and new beacons that nothing ever seemed to match the power of The Clash.

The fucking Dexy's did though, and to this day it remains another favourite in the canon. The combination of vocalist Kevin Rowland's soul scouring vocal and the band's bittersweet horn section, plus their wild-hearted outsider gang stance, struck a chord with thousands of post-punk wanderers. They were a key inspirational beacon for many and one of the greatest under-rated British bands of all time.

STUCK FOR A NAME: THE ANGRY YOUNG TEDDY BEARS (AND OTHER NAMES NEVER USED!)

After The Patrol fell apart the others took little interest in playing music for a long time, apart from John Squire who was continually playing guitar. He sat there getting better and better, putting in the hours that would make him one of the best guitar players of his generation a few years later.

By now he was more than adept.

Ian washed dishes in Friday's hotel in Northenden – financing his bohemian roving lifestyle. Meanwhile in 1980 John started at Cosgrove Hall where he was putting his art talents to good use.

Cosgrove Hall was a cartoon-making workshop in Chorlton that had made many an award-winning TV series. It was here that Squire made the models for *Wind In The Willows* and for *Dangermouse*. One of the stars of Cosgrove, there was even a story that because he was so brilliant he got to design the Bertie Basset sweetie man; the figure familiar to all the fat fucks who chomp on over-sweetened licorice.

Squire spent his days making the models for animation, getting spare time at weekends to pursue his own projects if he felt like it. It was at about this time that he bumped into future bass player and old mucker from the bridge days Pete Garner who was working in the city-centre Paperchase shop.

Manchester in the early Eighties was hardly the bustling youth culture capital that it is now. Now there are heaps of shops dealing in hip fashion, cool records and all the driftwood of pop culture. But back in the fallout days of post-punk there were plenty of bands, few venues and very few places to buy all the associated pop paraphernalia. That's what made Paperchase such an oddity – upstairs they sold greeting cards and every magazine and newspaper you could think of, while downstairs they dealt in the weirdest collection of cool records and total rubbish that was available in town.

Upstairs the lank-haired Garner worked behind the counter, ever the amiable host talking to punters, even buying in small fanzines to sell over the counter.

One afternoon, Squire walked into Paperchase and hooked up with his buddy from the Bridge and school days. They talked about making an animated film in Squire's down-time at the Cosgrove Hall. They wrote the first chapter for the story for which John would animate the models. They fucked around with the film for a few weeks and then shelved the idea, but no matter – contact was established and fate was moving its clammy hand.

John hadn't seen Ian for a while – Brown was off travelling or messing around with the scooter guys – but he had met Andy Couzens now and then and the pair of them had discussed starting the band off again.

ANDY AND JOHN GET THEIR GUITARS OUT AGAIN

So everyone had gone scooter crazy. Ian was hooked on the travel, seeking adventure on the road. The rush of the gang, the irresponsibility of the road.

It was a major buzz. Better than being stuck in a rehearsal room. John was happy painting his scooter. Pete couldn't give a fuck, I mean the fuckin' Dolls and Iggy had never hopped on to scooters! This was nothing to do with the rock'n'roll he was digging – bloody hairdryers! Pete was a rocker not a mod.

It looked like the band phase was over. Like thousands of teenage punk bands that had flourished in the tail end of the punk explosion, this was another youth club gang now looking for different kicks. The guitars were shoved back in cupboards, the dreams were put on hold. Some drifted off to jobs, some to drugs and some to new youth cults.

Some, like Andy, were missing the creative buzz of being in a band and a few months after The Patrol had fizzled out he decided to go round and see John Squire and see if he could get something going again. 'We didn't see each other for what seemed like ages but it was probably six weeks. I remember going out with John one night. Went to a pub in Sale which was weird 'cos no one drank. We decided then to get something else going on.'

There was also another reason for getting something going. By now Andy had left college, or rather he had been asked to leave college. Again his temper had got the better of him. 'I left college . . . I got thrown out of college. I took a swing at a teacher and told the principal to go and fuck himself. The rest of the band had all finished college and they had all passed.'

So at the tail end of 1980 Andy asked John if he was still up for a bit of playing and a loose project sort of got off the ground. 'It must have been later in the year. John and I started another band up with a guy from Hale, a drummer – a good drummer who popped up in a few bands later on. His name was Guy I think. Factoryish type of stuff. Good looking guy. Me and John playing guitar. I went round and said, let's do something 'cos I love it, the band thing. The Patrol was gone and I wanted to do something. Ian was off on his scooters.'

This loose outfit never had a name and, if anything, it served as a vehicle for the two guitarists, a way of learning those chops providing the groundwork for some future action, as well as keeping the flame of playing alive. Not that they treated it lightly. More than a bedroom jam, the band were keen, they even rehearsed about thirty miles away driving backwards and forwards to get their tunes together.

Says Andy, 'The core was me and John rehearsing in Warrington. I haven't a clue why we went there. It's really vague this period. We rehearsed above the YMCA opposite the town hall gates. There was that lad from Hale on drums sometimes. There was also another guy later on called Walt from Lymm in there as well. He was useless. A proper punk drummer. And we were trying to do something a bit more together musically. We got into The Beach Boys, although there was a lot of stuff like Generation X still getting listened to. I lent John my Beach Boys *Greatest Hits*, you know the one with the blue cover with the surfer on it? We liked the songs – they were a bit more musical than punk. We were just trying to get music going, nothing else. No one was singing.'

Built around the two guitar players, they knew they had something to offer and they worked well together. It was an ad hoc collection of any musicians they could get their hands on. Eventually, though, that drive to Warrington was going to break things up. It's bad enough having to set your gear up every time you rehearse but a one-hour drive before you get there . . .

There was also someone else floating around. A cheeky floppy-haired scamp who was coming down now and then and playing a bit of bass, an upbeat scally from north Manc who was going to play a large part in the future of this tale. Says Andy, 'Mani was just the same then as he is now . . . exactly the same guy. The one thing about being in a band is that you never have to grow up. If you make enough money you never have to do anything. You can be seventeen or eighteen for the rest of your life. This band was a funny period. This thing didn't have a name. It was a long drive as well to Warrington. Mani had his bass then. He had played with Clint Boon.'

And while the band eventually fell apart because 'going to Warrington was a pain in the arse', the foundations were set for the future. A few months later after they had knocked this project on the head they would reconvene as the unlikely monickered Fireside Chaps. Their part-time jamming bass player would also come with them.

Gary Mountfield who had spent the post-punk years floating around various north Manc outfits was now moving into that tightly knit gang of south Manc suburb punks.

MANI

Gary 'Mani' Mountfield was born on 16 November 1962, which makes him the oldest member of The Stone Roses by about two weeks.

Perhaps the most affable of the Roses, their eventual lynchpin bassist and current gunslinging pivotal bass player in Primal Scream, Mani was born in Moston in north Manchester, the other half of the city and a very different world from the south Manc suburbs. More Lancashire grit than Cheshire market town the north of the city is more working-class and less student-orientated than the south of the city.

Mani had lived all over north Manchester as he pointed out to *Reds* magazine. 'I'm a north Manchester boy, originally from Moston but I moved to Failsworth and Newton Heath in my early teens and I still go up there for a beer because that's where all my mates are.'

Football made a big impression on him from a very early age. 'I'm proud to be Manc, proud to be a Red. My dad was a mad United fan. Nobby Stiles is part of my family – my auntie's cousin or something like that and I was born to be a Red. I would have had my ears boxed in if I'd dared to be a blue. As for school, I went to Xaverian and after there I tried my hardest not to get a job and sat in my bedroom learning to play a guitar. My childhood hero was Georgie Best. My mam and dad were mates of him. I can remember waking up in the morning and him being downstairs in my house having a late drink when he shouldn't have been. I really had a thing for Gordon Hill too. Those were the days for me: Admiral shirts, Stepney, Nicol, Houston, Buchan, Albiston, Daly, Macari, Coppell, Pearson and the Greenhoffs. Good days going to United. I'm all for terracing coming back.'

Teenage Mani went through punk and then on to the scally/perry boy scene that was emerging out of the north Manc suburbs. Following United he was on the fringes of bother. 'Going abroad with the scals, doing a bit of this and that, getting nice trainers and that. I very nearly caught the ferry to Holland which kicked off with West Ham in 1986 but ended up catching a later ferry which was full of Everton. I had to keep my trap shut but I still made it to the Dam along with about a hundred others. I used to go to away games all the time with a lot of those heads from Salford. I can remember going to Luton when we were on that ten-game winning streak in '85. We met up at Salford Crescent, got in a van and went down to terrorise St Albans for the day. It's only in the past few years that I've had to cut down on going home and away . . .'

Mani had been going to matches for as long as he could remember. 'When I was a kid, I used to get the number seven bus from Failsworth which used to drop you by the swing bridge. It cost 50p to go in the Stretford End and I used to take our Greg, sit him at the front on a barrier, give him his Wagon Wheels and crisps and then watch the match. When we were old enough we used to get the specials through the '70s and '80s. I didn't miss many matches.'

Mani told *Reds* magazine about his most embarrassing match moment. 'I got caught spitting on the TV by my mam at a United v Leeds game. She was disgusted and said, "There's nothing big or clever about spitting young Gary."'

Like nearly every kid in Britain, Mani dreamt of football as an escape route from the drudgery of real life. That Peter Pan world of soccer showbiz was quickly negated when he realised that he just wasn't good enough to be strutting around Old Trafford, leaving one well-trodden alternative. 'I knew from the age of eight that I wanted to be in a band. I was never good enough to be a footballer and I'm lucky that I make a living out of music.'

Again inspired by the punk explosion, Mani realigned his dreams with rock'n'roll. Punk's message that anyone can do it, anyone can make their own dream, was hitting home yet again. He drifted through a whole bunch of north Manc punk outfits learning his bass. 'I'd been in a few bands previously including a punk band from Failsworth called Urban Paranoia who used to play at the youth club.'

He also hooked up with the South Trafford college crew after a run in with a local skinhead. As Ian Brown told *Record Collector*:

'Yeah, I'd known Mani from when he was sixteen. He was from north Manchester, we were from Chorlton. We'd heard about this kid with a swastika on his head, some bonehead who lived near Mani's who was bullying kids. So we got a crew up to sort him out. Twenty of us went to meet Mani's crew in this council house. I remember seeing Mani sat down. I'm thinking, he ain't no fighter. So, one or two of these kids dealt with the bonehead, put him to rest – and that's how we met.'

The Timperley mob quickly became mates with Mani. Getting picked up by Andy Couzens for that ridiculous long drive to rehearsal the loose jams were his introduction to the tightly knit musical world of the Timperley gang. Once in, he was gradually to become a permanent feature of their ad hoc line-ups and nights out in the city centre.

Hanging out, going out drinking and getting messed up in town with the boys, he was certainly part of their crew. Mani is famous for being easy-going, no one has a bad word for him. He's the most approachable of all the Roses. Tuesday night in town you'll probably see him doing something mad outside a pub or checking out a gig. Easy-going. Enjoying the good times, rolling with the band.

He went to school at Xaverian college, the Catholic Grammar school, with schoolmates like Vince Hunt who went on to form John Peel's faves A Witness and who remembers him as a garrulous, likeable, cheeky, popular classmate. 'I remember him having short spikey hair and being into The Fall and The Stranglers, The Clash and Elvis Costello, stuff like that.'

He moved on from punk rock and was digging Northern Soul (perhaps the ultimate music to learn bass to, just check Paul Ryder's work in The Happy Mondays). Drifting into the same twilight zone of scooters, mods and skins as Brown and Squire.

From there, he pioneered the classic scally look, a wedge haircut and a 'psychedelic shirt and dapper jeans' according to The Inspiral Carpet's Clint Boon.

Scallies were the precursor to the baggy scene, linking youth culture between the late Seventies punk explosion and the late Eighties, with a wedge haircut swiped off Bryan Ferry and fused with The Beatles, an obsession with training shoes and foreign sports clobber. It was the roots of designer label culture. With football overtones and a penchant for occasional violence, it was rough and ready.

It was this Perry boy/Scally look that he claims to have brought eventually to the nascent Roses, the final style ingredient that connected them with the mainstream, oh and his bass playing. Bass playing that by 1982 was being utilised again as Squire/Couzens were making yet another attempt at forming a band.

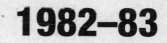
1982–83

THE WATERFRONT

Down in the cellar. What a crew! A couple of Perry boys, a couple of artsy south Mancs and whoever was up for drumming! Yet again Couzens and Squire were attempting to resurrect some sort of band. A creative spark should never be wasted, so the Warrington jamming band was put back together on a more serious footing. But this time no more mucking about in rehearsal rooms miles away. Even if it meant leaving a proper rehearsal room and returning to the cellars and garages of Manchester.

Andy Couzens's parents' cellar in Macclesfield to be more exact. It made it easier to piece together a group. A little less driving for Couzens. Less hassle all round.

They built the band around a combination of their south Manc cronies and the new blood from north Manchester they had been drinking in town with in the last few months. New bonds forged in the scooter scene.

Mani himself had been the obvious choice for bass. He brought down his good vibes, rudimentary bass playing and superbly sculptured Perry boy fringe. Mani also came down with a fellow Failsworth scooter boy they knew from the runs. Kaiser.

They had met Kaiser on their nights out in Manchester in the dimly lit clubs that were still playing all the great musics of the post-punk period. Kaiser remembers being approached by the shy John Squire of all people. 'I was hanging around in punk clubs like Berlin and the punk room in Pips. There was me and Mani and some of the other lads from the scooter runs. It was John Squire that came over and started chatting. He said he was starting a band up and asked me if I wanted to be the singer.'

The mates bonded over music. 'At the time we all still liked the old punk stuff. Ian Brown who was around but not in the band was into Madness, he loved them. John Squire was much more arty, none of us had ever heard of the stuff he was into, very strange! He was a very special type of person, John, very artistic and he really put his mind to what he was doing whether it was playing guitar or painting. He was working at Cosgrove Hall at the time. He took us down there a couple of times. He was making models there and he'd made a couple of adverts. He was very articulate. The people in the band were very varied from each other. John had a really different outlook on things than the rest of us.'

Andy Couzens remembers Kaiser. 'We had Kaiser, a mate of Mani's. He was a Perry boy, a pretty heavy guy, very sharp – he was serious about his wedge and the way he looked.'

In the mish mash of youth cults a new one was starting to emerge. One that would dominate the street looks of the city for decades to come. The

Scally/casual look or Perry boys as they were known in Manchester. Kaiser was one of the first people in the city to adopt the look. The first Perry boys were coming in from the mod/skin scene.

'Perry boys were coming out, just local lads really not trying to be anything . . . dead easy.'

The Perry boys were Manchester's pre-Scally scallies, Fred Perry tops and a neatly combed one eye wedge were the keys to the look. In the early Eighties they were listening to music on the fringe of the punk scene so it wouldn't be so unusual to see a few Perry boys in clubs like Berlin and Pips.

After meeting Squire and before The Waterfront coalesced, Kaiser hung out with the pre-Roses in the scooter clubs. He looks back on the scooter club days with great affection.

'The scooter clubs were great. They were like family. I knew Ian Brown from a long time back in the scooter days,' he remembers. Laughing, he adds, 'Ian Brown was a nutter then. Getting up to all sorts.'

It was Kaiser's scooter connection that stood him in good stead with his new bandmates. Says Andy, 'We sort of knew Kaiser 'cos we had been going out in town. He was part of our little drinking clique and a scooter boy as well. He had a scooter, a knackered old blue scooter with "I piss on Anderton's army" painted on the side panels in white paint. I had A.C.A.B. on my helmet and we'd get such shit from the police! They would stop us all the time.'

The Waterfront put together this mixture of north Mancs ruffians and south Mancs dreamers: John Squire, Andy Couzens, Mani and Kaiser . . . all they needed now was a drummer.

And, as ever, getting a drummer was a problem. Their old drummer, Si was branching out in town, making good connections, getting some good work together. He was busy taking his kit round various bands. Si was still jamming away with Andy Rourke, looking at getting that funk thing together. It was going well. They were sounding good.

Johnny Marr had asked him back into his latest band, an outfit built around a lanky bequiffed singer that he was putting together. During the summer of 1981 they went into Decibel studios and recorded two songs with their new singer, a right proper character with a quiff called Morrissey who had a way with words.

They recorded two tunes 'Suffer Little Children' and 'The Hand That Rocks The Cradle'. With the demo in the bag the group, now calling themselves The Smiths, had their first gig booked, supporting Blue Rondo A La Turk at a fashion show at Manchester Ritz on 4 October. Marr asked Wolstencroft if he wanted to join the band permanently and play the show.

But Si was still jamming away with Andy Rourke at their Britfunk style project and they had finally found their own singer. Si told Marr that he would help him out but that was as far as he could go.

The Smiths' new manager Joe Moss wasn't happy with this temporary situation and Si was out and Johnny Marr went in search of a proper full-time drummer.

All this didn't really help the new Squire/Couzens band. They needed a drummer quickly. Getting a drummer is always so damn tough in a band. No one wants to play drums. All that lugging around of gear and then disappearing to the back of the stage. All the work and no glory!

And again, it was Mani who bailed them out. He had another mate in Failsworth, Chris Goodwin, who was a drummer and was up for it.

So deep in the Macclesfield cellar another attempt was being made to coalesce their post-punk energy. Says Andy, 'We used to rehearse at my parents' house in Macclesfield. I used to go and pick up John in Chorlton and then go up to Failsworth to pick Mani and the rest of them up. Musicians are fucking lazy, aren't they! I was always picking people up. I was the organiser. Drive around, pick everyone up, then rehearse.'

The band perfectly captured the patchwork of post-punk looks. John Squire was still in his post-punk Clash look, Andy with his nutter short hair and denims and the three north Mancs had a look of their own. Remembers Andy, 'Mani's all into that flick look, Perry boys, Echo and The Bunnymen were big in Failsworth . . .'

It was typical of the times. A hotch potch of street looks and cultures all standing in one room.

Christened by Squire, The Fireside Chaps was an odd name for a band. Its ironic weediness, almost fey moniker, may well have appealed as an ironic in-joke, a loose dumb tag to snicker at while they were jamming around in yet another attempt to get a band going.

It was obviously not serious and not something 'That we could ever contemplate putting up on a poster,' laughs Couzens, who is also quick to pass the buck for who came up with the name. 'John Squire can be cringeworthy when it comes to names!' laughs Couzens, adding, 'I guess that the band was a continuation from the Warrington thing. That band might have stopped for a few weeks and then the new band started.'

And where was Ian Brown at this time? 'We didn't see much of Ian at the time. He was always away on scooter runs.'

They would jam, rehearse and fool about. Watch films like road movies such as *Two Lane Black Top* and *Vanishing Point*, a film that Primal Scream would be obsessed with enough to name their fantastic 1997 album after (the first one with Mani on bass). They would piss themselves laughing at Mani's Woody Allen take-offs. The ad hoc collection of south Mancs post-punk scooter boys and north Manc hooligans were having a good time. Too much of a good time in a very different south Manc suburb world, as Kaiser points out.

'Andy came up to my house to pick me up n his BMW! You never got posh cars like that round our way. We practised in Andy's house in a big cellar. It was in a big house in Adlington. A big mansion. An unbelievable place with a swimming pool. It was a real big shock to me and Mani. We had a great time just going in the swimming pool and hanging out with Andy and his brother who's a good lad.'

Things were going alright. Already songs were coalescing – and then they hit their first hurdle: Chris Goodwin split. Three rehearsals was enough for him and he quit the cellar jams, leaving his drum kit moulding away in the corner.

Again they were without drums but they elected to carry on without drums, just writing songs, trying to get it together.

As ever they rehearsed many times a week, long and hard. And at weekends they still socialised in town.

'The rest of us were going out into town a lot. I seem to remember going to the Cypress Tavern, places like that. We went down the Hacienda as soon as it opened. You know what it's like, fuck there is somewhere to go! When you're the only club in Manchester it's easy to get members! It was the only place to go. When it opened we ran down there to join really early on . . . in 1982.'

By now, a few months in, they decided to get a proper name. The band was sounding good and it was time to get serious. They had booked a studio to record a couple of songs for a demo and the thought of recording them as The Fireside Chaps was just too ridiculous for the band. Says Andy, 'One night, after rehearsing we sat down and watched the Marlon Brando *On The Waterfront* film. We all thought Fireside Chaps was a funny name but when it came to the point of doing the demos we thought, fuck, can't put that on a demo tape on the tape box. So thanks to Marlon we took The Waterfront for our name and went in and did the demos.'

The two track demo was recorded at the tale end of 1982 in some long-forgotten East Manchester studio. 'The demo was recorded somewhere in the back end of Denton. Somewhere round Mani's way. In a little studio someone had set up,' adds Andy.

The two songs they laid down were surprisingly competent. Even poppy. A lot less like the early incarnation of the Roses, the punkier Roses than the more jangly melodic '88 plus Roses. You can hear shades of Orange Juice. Any lingering traces of three chord Patrol punkarama have long since been shed, although the movement's energy and toughness can't help seeping in over the jangly guitars.

Mani's bass drives the song and puts paid to any lingering myth making about him only learning his trade when he joined the Roses full time. The bass work is really strong and the guitar is classic Squire with riffs, licks and melodic work cutting in and out with Andy Couzens really effectively.

Those guitars definitely hint at the sound of Young Scotland, and Orange Juice who took the brittle jangly guitars and made them into a template for a whole host of post-punk bands to use. The band, even though camping it up in a tongue-in-cheek manner, had been adopted by a surprisingly large quotient of ex punks and scallies who got off on their energised guitar pop. At the same time The Waterfront were digging Edwyn Collins's idiosyncratic outfit and so were Little Hulton's ramshackle gang of Dickensian hooligans, the Happy Mondays.

The outfits on the Postcard label have been somewhat written out of history over the years but both of them have inspired an unlikely rabble of outfits from the Happy Mondays right through to a whole gamut of outfits that have gone on to bigger things.

Even Kaiser's vocals are a surprise. His singing is pretty well spot on for a first demo and the expected gruffness is not apparent.

Kaiser explains his lyrics for 'Normandy', 'John wrote most of the songs and I wrote some of the lyrics . . . "Normandy" was about a trip that me and Mani made. We blagged our way to France jumping on trains, and we ended up in Normandy and we ended up walking down the beaches in Normandy. We were just Moston lads and we were gobsmacked, walking down there and I wrote the song about that and how thousands had died on those same beaches on D Day.'

The other tune on the demo, 'When The Wind Blows', is a faster affair dominated by a catchy if flat whistled section and some later period Clash-styled rhythm guitar chops from John Squire. Again it has the '88 period Roses feel to it albeit a tad less subtle, but the melody is there and the interplay between the guitars and the bass. There are definitely hints of something greater here, of some sort of potential.

The band were pretty surprised with the demos – they sounded really good! Fuck they almost sounded like a proper band. And Ian Brown? Well, he wasn't oblivious to what his mates were up to, as he explained to *Record Collector*, 'The Waterfront were great. They were like Orange Juice. They had a song called "On The Beach In Normandy". The Patrol was a racket so I got into scooters but John's still doing his band. He played me a tape and it sounded really good. I was impressed. I knew somebody who could play with that quality. Since '78/'79 John hadn't done much except play his guitar.'

Brown was now living in Charles Barry Crescent in Hulme. He was still in touch with The Waterfront, hanging out at the odd rehearsal, the two recorded tunes had knocked him out. Then John asked him if he wanted to join up as a singer. Ian was keen. He had been inspired to get back into rock'n'roll after a meeting. A meeting that has become one of the great stories that surrounds the Roses myth.

One night when he was having a party at his flat for Mitch his girlfriend's 21st birthday, a guest arrived that no one was expecting . . .

GENO! GENO! GENO! GENO!

In '82/'83 Ian Brown was living in Hulme, in one of the four huge flat complexes in the heart of the then run-down bohemian zone just south of Manchester city centre. Charles Barry was where most of the musicians lived in 1983 – people like Big Flame, Inca Babies, Ruthless Rap Assassins. It was all cracked concrete cancer and crazy graffiti – full of rat infested roach-ridden flats, junkies, squalor and filth. It was also, for the young tearaway with rock'n'roll on their mind – a great place to live.

Endless parties, easily available dealers, like-minded freaks as neighbours and a quarter of an hour walk from the city centre. It was a tight community. Hulme was probably the biggest boho drop-out zone in the UK, and in the early Eighties it was at its post-punk twenty-four-hour-party-people peak.

One night Ian Brown had a party in his flat and stumbling through the door came the unlikely figure of Geno Washington, one of the kings of soul, the don, the man with the sweetest soul voice, the man who Dexy's (one of the Roses' favourite bands) had honoured with 'Geno' their biggest hit. Walking up to Brown, Washington engaged the wired skin mod in conversation.

'You should be a star,' was his startling prediction.

Brown just smirked – he knew it would happen one day.

For a Northern Soul fan and a scooter boy, having Geno Washington knock on your door was one thing but to have him giving you some sterling advice must be another. Even if you weren't that sure who Geno Washington was!

Geno Washington was a legend on the Northern Soul scene. His Ram Jam Band had been the soundtrack to some serious dance floor action and he was still out on the circuit. He was already on a rejuvenated roll after Dexy's Midnight Runners had taken 'Geno' to Number One, a song that extolled the brilliance of the singer and the whole of the scene that he was a key player in.

On the night of the party Brown's flat was already experiencing some mad behaviour, after putting up the bass player who was in wild local punk outfit The Worst, as Ian told *Record Collector*. 'I knew their bass player, Woody! He slept at my house one night. He'd ripped me curtains down 'cos he was cold but when I go in in the morning, he's leaned up against the wall and the bed has burnt right round his body like a silhouette where he fell asleep with a cigarette, and the mattress has melted and it's smouldering. And he was fine! That's the same night I met Geno Washington, when he told me I should be a singer. That was '83.'

The party was in full swing when Washington arrived, fresh from a gig at the nearby Manchester University. He was looking for the now demolished Reno club in nearby Moss Side and was asking for directions. But on hooking up with the young Brown, he smoked some spliff and hung out. Says Ian, 'I'm at my party in Hulme . . . my mate's roadying at Salford University, and he brings Geno Washington down to this party. An' he's a superstar kind of guy, big personality, all over the room. He comes up to me and he says, "You're a star. You're an actor. Be a singer." I remember him on the street smoking a big spliff and this copper comes round sayin', "What are you doing?" And he's blowing his spliff in the copper's face, this is '83. And he's goin', "I'm Geno, man. *Geno Geno!*", singing the Dexy's song, really cool. And the copper didn't do nothing, he just walked away. A few weeks later, I'm thinking about what this guy's said. What does he mean I'm a star, an actor? Anyway, I thought we'd give it a go so we kicked Kaiser out and started the real thing, The Stone Roses, in March '84.'

In fact Kaiser wasn't kicked out. John phoned and the newly inspired Ian came down for the last few Waterfront rehearsals where they shared vocals. But Geno's spark, his comments were inspiration enough for Brown.

'He told me that I was a star and that I should be in a band. A few days after John rang up and asked me if I could sing and I thought, I'll go with that. I've got to, I just have to . . .'

So Brown was in The Waterfront.

I mean, what better recommendation than Geno's!

Ian was back down in the cellar. Sharing vocals with Kaiser. Hanging out with his old mates. Dreaming the star dream and getting off on the banter.

1984

FROM THE WATERFRONT TO THE ROSE GARDEN – HANGING AROUND!

The beginning of 1984 saw the various nutters and would-be musicians who floated around the varying line-ups, further away from realising any kind of musical dream than at any time since they were first fired by the punk explosion.

Ian Brown was working in the dole office or cleaning dishes at TFI Fridays in Didsbury. John Squire was working on 'Chorlton And The Wheelies' in Chorlton's Cosgrove Hall. Pete Garner had been selling magazines in Paperchase in the city centre right back to the days when he was The Patrol's roadie. He was the lank, long-haired, friendly dude behind the counter who always took your fanzines off you, a friendly easy-going soul who quickly got to know all sorts of people who drifted through the shop.

'I remember Morrissey coming in with the James Dean book asking if you could buy the lyrics for the New York Dolls albums. I thought he must live in a dream world if he thought such a thing existed for such a small group . . .'

The band that Si hadn't joined, The Smiths, was fast tracking its way to indie dominance and then to the grown-up charts beyond. And in Manchester itself New Order were critics' raves and hitting the charts regularly and The Chameleons were the biggest home town draw.

The Boardwalk was yet to open and the Hacienda was either a cold half full warehouse for touring bands battling muffled acoustics, or a student disco playing safe indie hits for cheap lager hunters.

For anyone bitten by the bug of rock'n'roll, gaps like this are dull and frustrating.

For a desperado like Andy Couzens it was a desperate time. Andy remembers this hiatus with not much affection. 'There is a gap between the bands because John started at Cosgrove Hall. He was always going home making models. I remember taking John down in a car with a bunch of models to Cosgrove Hall, he just wanted to do that. He always wanted to make an animated cartoon with models . . . he went off doing that.'

Musically Couzens was still broadening his tastes and like the rest of his occasional bandmates he was digging deeper into psychedelia, getting rootsier, moving further and further away from what the anti-rock dullard tastemakers were dictating. 'I remember starting getting into The Misunderstood and stuff like that. It goes back to the picture on that single sleeve they gave me when I joined The Patrol, that kind of look. I started getting into all that. There never seemed to be much on and the

International opened and loads of those bands came over. I remember it started having bands like Jason And The Scorchers, loads of stuff from The States. I went and they were crap – all rubbish. I hate all that yank shit anyway.'

Couzens even started digging some of the post-punk pre-goth outfits emerging out of London who were trying to forge something that was rock'n'roll but different.

'Brigandage showed a bit of promise but fell apart on their faces. It was a really horrible period, nothing seemed to be happening. Manchester was really horrible then. It was shite . . . I still lived in Macclesfield at my parents' house.'

Apart from that it was drifting around town at night getting into trouble. Andy was still seeing his old Waterfront cronies in late '83/early '84. 'We were still hanging out after The Waterfront. I still saw Kaiser, Chris Goodwin, Mani. In fact I last saw Kaiser a year ago on the way to the United match.'

The crew would inevitably run into fights in the city centre. 'I remember us having fights in Piccadilly Gardens. Fights with beer monsters waiting for buses. I do remember John getting his nose broken a lot, ha! ha! ha! One night we were coming out of Club Tropicana on Oxford Road, you know the one with the palm trees inside? I remember coming out of there one night and we got a right hiding. We used to go to Berlin a lot. Our first demo as the Roses got played in there one night just after we finished it, which was a shock . . .'

And it was this subterranean world of dimly lit clubs playing post-punk, goth and rock that was far closer to the Roses' roots than the shiny new world of the Hacienda. Clubs like Berlin have, of course, been written out of the history of the Manchester music scene. It was hardly a media haunt. You wouldn't find all the local journos hanging out there and it wasn't run by any local industry big wigs. It was a bit like Rockworld or The Ritzy are these days, busy packed clubs which won't fit into the story, the Manchester myth, the 'way things are'. Berlin was the first club to play the Roses' demos and records and they even put on some classical gigs there. I remember once seeing the Spacemen 3 supported by Inspiral Carpets down there.

As they hung around town and slowly drifted into the world of piss-ups and violence, the mind-numbing existence of weekend lads, it was almost inevitable that someone would gather the clan again for one last go at it.

It was into this aimless drifting existence that the Roses were finally born. Coming back from town Andy would quite often cut along Stretford Road and into nearby Hulme. He would then go up to the Crescents that dominated the middle of the estate and round to Ian Brown's place in the now demolished Charles Barry Crescent, the wildest and most partied out of the four Crescents that lay at the heart of Hulme in the mid Eighties.

At the time Hulme was a sprawl of squats, cheap council tenancies, students, artists, junkies, doleheads and families . . . a unique fucked-up sprawl of inner city living and bohemian squalor.

Couzens struck out from the city centre. He walked through the grim concrete council blocks that made up the notorious area. Past the squats. The bohemian sprawl. The nerve centre of the new Manchester underground. He walked to the middle of Hulme where the four huge imposing blocks that dominated the area sat still in the stoic murky Manc weather.

It was here that Ian Brown was still living. Recalls Andy, 'I'd go round to Ian's quite a lot anyway. He was living with Mitch, the mother of his children, she was at college with us in South Trafford and she was working on *Brookside* . . . All I remember was his wok! He loved his wok! He fancied himself as a bit of a cook.'

Couzens still wanted to make some rock'n'roll and he was determined to talk Ian into it. Usually he just went round to hang out and have a laugh. But today he was determined to talk his old band-mate into doing something. As he cut through the concrete sprawl of Hulme and up the piss-stained walkways he was pretty well set on getting yet another band together.

I WANNA BE ADORED: THE ROSES FINALLY GET THEIR SHIT TOGETHER

Andy wanted to play music. And he knew who he wanted to play music with. It was just a matter of doing some persuading.

The spark came yet again from Andy's fists. 'In 1983 the Roses started to get together again. I had all that shit from fighting again. I have one of those temperaments, some people have a short fuse, I don't have a fuse at all, bang and I'm gone. I just kept getting in trouble like that. I needed something. I had a court case coming up for fighting. I went to see Ian. I was hoping that he wanted to make some music again. I was keeping my fingers crossed. I said let's get something going, 'cos if I don't I am going to go down, I was staring at a jail sentence. They told me I was going to get six months.'

He had decided that he needed to get something to focus his life on other than drifting around town fighting, something to use his hands, something, anything, to get his temper under control.

Ian Brown wasn't so sure. 'I'd given up rock'n'roll in one sense,' he claims.

But Andy was very persuasive and there was fuck all to do in town. It was better than hanging around in Piccadilly Gardens fighting! Andy was giving it his best shot. 'So there I was with Ian in Hulme. I was saying right let's get something going again. We talked about it a bit, what the line up should be. I wanted Si Wolstencroft in and I know we were thinking of bass players, but who could we get?'

Obviously it should have been Mani but he was getting his own things together in north Manchester.

Pete was part of the gang and he went back a long way. Maybe they were just keeping things south Manchester. Back to their Patrol roots! Andy ponders the Mani question.

'He was someone you went out and had a laugh with. He was in that Failsworth gang. And we liked Pete. I always thought there was something about Pete. He's just a great bloke, Pete. Someone who is great to have around. Whether he could play or not was irrelevant. The fact was he was great to have around, which added to the thing. John came in in the end. It just felt right. We just ended up getting Patrol back together – the big reformation.'

Pete looked back at the band's formation. 'At the time just before we started I didn't see a lot of Ian and Andy. They were all into scooters.'

Pete remembers John mentioning that there was going to be another attempt at getting a band together. 'John said he's spoken to Ian and he had said he wanted to get something together again and did I want to play bass.'

Ian was keen but he knew that they needed John even if Andy was worried about how committed Squire would ever be to any project. Says Ian, 'There wasn't much else happening. Manchester was so dull at that point and it didn't take long for me and Andy to start getting excited again. A lot depended on how John would react. He was the only one who really knew what he was doing musically. And when we asked him it was so obvious that he was looking to do something musical that he agreed immediately.'

Phone calls were made. Everyone was up for it.

Si was back in. His band with Andy Rourke was now finally over as Rourke had left to play bass with The Smiths full time. A full line up! Pete Garner on bass; John and Andy on guitars, and finally Ian on vocals.

After four years The Patrol were back together.

Back in Andy's parents' cellar in Macclesfield they picked up yet again from where they kept leaving off. John brought down a song and quickly they put together 'Nowhere Fast'. It was a very productive first rehearsal.

Within a week they had added 'All Stitched Up' and 'I Can't Take It Anymore'. Not bad going when you consider the bass player couldn't actually play a note! Says Pete, 'You've got to remember that the only bass line I knew was "Blockbuster" from that Patrol gig years ago. I couldn't play the bass at all! I had only played once at that gig! At our first rehearsal everyone strapped on guitars and I was stood there saying "What the fuck do I do!"'

That first rehearsal must have been some scene. Plenty of chat. Plenty of fooling. Andy and John's guitars working together, Si kicking in on drums. And then John launching into the chords for 'Nowhere Fast' and Ian picking out some sort of space for his vocal melody. The buzz in the room. Good mates making music together. The gang back together. Top buzz!

Recalls Andy, 'The first rehearsal was at my parents' house. We actually wrote a song that first night. It was "Nowhere Fast". It had another title at the time. I can't remember what the name was now. John had a bit of a riff. He had the opening riff and the chorus and I had a couple of parts. Si started drumming and it came together. Not a bad start. We just worked on new stuff, no Patrol or Waterfront stuff. It was just a total clean break.'

All the gang members were there and it clicked. It clicked fast. John's guitar playing was already quite a few notches above just another run-of-the-mill garage band and they had Ian back on vocals, his self-belief and obvious charisma well up for the task and even if his singing could sometimes be a bit flat, well they weren't that bothered. This was a gang and anyhow the singer had decided to get himself some singing lessons.

Ian had decided to go and see this Mrs Rhodes near Victoria Station. Now getting singing lessons is considered to be just about the least rock'n'roll thing in the world. Guitar lessons? . . . yeah why not. Pick up some drum tricks? . . . why not! But learning to sing is a weird one. And it's something that can be very nerve wracking. Even for cocky upstarts like Ian Brown. But Johnny Rotten had had singing lessons and he was *the* anarchist!

As Ian told *Record Collector*, 'Yeah, we started a few rehearsals and I'm singing and everyone's like, fuck, we can't put up with that! You'll have to have singing lessons. So I went to this old woman over Victoria Station, Mrs Rhodes. She'd get me there at six o'clock, open the window, with everyone coming home from work. She'd have me wailing "After The Goldrush" or "Strawberry Fields" out the window. The crowds looking up and she's saying, if you can't do it, go home. So I thought, fuck it, I'll stick it out. So I did three weeks with her. She had an 80-year-old dear on the piano!"

It is one of the myths that has always hung around the Roses. The one that Brown can't sing. Sometimes his voice can sound rough but when he's on it, he has his own voice. It sounds like Ian Brown, surely the prerequisite of any singer is to sound like yourself. The early punkier Roses material he holds together with a brattish whine and eventually as the band become more melodic he even sounds, linking in with Reni, angelic on the records. In many ways Brown's vocal gives the band their distinctive edge, his stark northern accent instantly placing them.

A month in and it was coming together. They had a set worked out and the songs were moving on in leaps and bounds. They even had a name this time. A proper name, a name that didn't sound stupid and one that pretty well captured them as a band. John came up with The Stone Roses and out of all the suggestions it was the one that stuck. It captured their hard and soft edges, the lovelorn melodicism and punk rock edge, the angelic melodies and the tough street stance, soft songs with dark hearts, it was perfect, a double-edged sword.

Says Andy, 'We had no name at first but quite quickly we were called The Stone Roses. John came up with it. There was a whole list of names written down. Fucked if I can remember them! We had all written loads of stuff down . . . it's off a book I think, a book cover . . . the hard and soft thing was an explanation that was added later on . . .'

They never called themselves English Rose. It was The Stone Roses pure and simple.

Adds Ian, 'No, I don't know where that English Rose story came from. John thought up the name "Stone Roses" – something with a contrast, two words that went against each other.'

Back in the cellar the songs were coming on. Nothing was carried over from The Waterfront. This time it was going to be serious.

This time they were going to try and break that new ground that they had attempted after The Patrol, soak up all those new influences that they had been chewing on from the post-punk sounds of Postcard and some of the pre-punk neo-psychedelia that they had been listening to, mix it in with the punk rock they were still fired up on. They were really up for it.

And out there the music scene was changing. There was a mini revolution going on. A feedback drenched psychedelic rock'n'roll riot was goin' on in London. With guitars!

That year The Jesus And Mary Chain were setting the indie scene on fire with their feedback drenched pure pop, their sweet songs and riots. Hard and soft, like a stone and a rose, they were to have a profound influence on many upcoming bands on the scene and John Squire was listening.

'I loved the sonic action approach to the guitar overdubs and the endless permutations the brothers found for those three chords. It changed the way I thought about writing songs.'

After the Mary Chain there was Creation Records and Primal Scream, leather trousers and bowl cuts, sweet tunes and tuff street shapes. There was Alan McGee and his pop vision. It was a pop vision that kinda matched the Roses' vision.

Years later Alan McGee told me, 'Stone Roses were a beautiful amalgamation of Mancunian Pop and Psychedelia. Borrowing from the Three O'Clock and Primal Scream they made great Manc Pop. Ian Brown is, was and always will be, a superstar to me and a million others. The first LP is a classic. I love them loads and probably always will do . . .'

So there was plenty of ideas. Plenty of influences.

Even if they didn't have a proper rehearsal room . . .

WHAT A BUMMER . . . WE'VE LOST A DRUMMER!

Typically they were earnestly rehearsing hard. Down in the cellar several nights a week. No plans for any gigs, just getting the songs honed down. The work ethic again to the fore. This was never a bunch of musicians that would quickly get it together and then play. Nope! This was a meticulously planned and worked on set of songs played by a studious, hard-working bunch of players.

In the cramped cellar of the Couzens' in Macclesfield they started to work up tunes. They knew each other inside out so it was easy work. Musicians who have played together for some time have an inbuilt advantage. They've grown up together, got pissed together, all the same shit, the same in-jokes, the same musical tastes, the same horse trading of ideas and new bands to get into. It makes songwriting fast.

Says Andy, 'It just felt good again you know. It felt right. We just kept writing. All that very early stuff like "Mission Impossible". There was also stuff that didn't make it from that period of songs.'

Six months in, though, and they were dealt a bombshell. Si was leaving. He had been drumming for years and through his various contacts he was a known face about town. After all he had turned The Smiths down! He was the most successful and known musician among them. Getting back into the cellar after being on the verge of joining the band that was now dominating the guitar pop scene with a string of hits, was certainly something.

They kinda knew that trying to keep hold of Si was going to be difficult. He had been auditioning for bigger bands for the past six months and he finally got the job in Terry Hall's ex Specials new outfit The Colourfield. Adds Si, 'I was in The Colourfield with Terry Hall for a while, along with Craig Gannon on guitar. (I also got Craig the job with The Smiths.) I appeared on *The Tube* with him performing three songs, including Kim Fowley's "The Trip".'

Si got the Colourfield job and then drifted round the local scene playing drums with the Manchester hairdresser to the stars Andrew Berry (he used to cut everyone's hair in the basement of the Hacienda) Berry's band was The Weeds who had a couple of releases on In Tape. The Weeds supported The Fall on tour in 1986 and Berry was asked to join Mark Smith's outfit.

He was still mates with the Roses and in fact turned up at the Alexandra Palace show where I bumped into him during the soundcheck where he was buzzing on his former band mates' mega success.

In 2000 he rejoined Ian Brown where he now remains drumming, programming and doing the odd bit of songwriting. Another Patrol reunion! Another circle rejoined!

Si's departure from the cellar was a pretty big blow for the band. In fact it was a disaster. Getting a drummer is so damn difficult.

By now, they were a driven unit. That inbuilt inner confidence was being bolstered by some great tunes. 'Misery Dictionary' was written in the weeks following Si's departure.

But they needed a sodding drummer.

They put a phone call to the north Manchester posse and pulled their ex-Waterfront buddy Chris Goodwin back out from his never-ending stints in various north Manc bands like T'Challa Grid and Asia Fields.

Goodwin came down, but it was obvious that he didn't have any intention of sticking around too long. Says Andy, 'We were still at my parents' place. We got Chris Goodwin in. He came down for one rehearsal and left his kit. It was like he was just looking for somewhere to store it . . . in the cellar . . .'

Stuck again they continued to jam away drummerless while writing songs. 'We rehearsed for ages with no drums at all which is ridiculous when you think about it. These days you'd get a drum machine. But we were still writing. Either me or John would come up with a riff. Couple of songs didn't make it. We wrote stuff like "Mission Impossible" when I went to John's one night. John lived on Zetland Road in Chorlton. He had the top floor flat.'

Now two drummers down, they had run out of options from their immediate bunch of mates. So they also decided to advertise around town for a drummer. Cast the net a little wider than the South Trafford college crew and Mani's mates. See who else was out there. 'We started auditioning drummers. We put an advert up in A1 in town. The first person to answer was the ex-drummer from The Skeletal Family. He came down in his ginger Beetle. You only remember the funny ones, don't you,' laughs Andy.

Howard Daniels had been in The Skeletal Family for about a year, joining them in 1983 and leaving early in '84. The Yorkshire-based goth band were the poppier end of the goth scene. And the classic goth style of drums was a tumbling rumble of post-tribal toms. It may have fitted perfectly into The Skeletal Family but for the Roses music it jarred. Badly.

Daniels walked into the rehearsal room. Within seconds, with his fringed jacket and goth-tinged look both parties knew that this was not a happening situation, but in the etiquette of auditions they had to persevere anyway.

Daniels parked himself behind Chris Goodwin's dusty kit and they kicked off with 'Tragic Roundabout' and 'Mission Impossible'. Daniels's arms were pounding out incessant goth style tribal beats on the kit, powerful pounding drums. Fine if you're The Skeletal Family but not what the Roses were looking for. At the end of the song there was an uncomfortable silence.

The rumbling drums and tom tom stuff were the signifier to gothdom. At the end of the songs, Howard looked up, 'I'm not into this stuff. It's got no tunes.'

Couzens was among the smirking Roses as the drummer walked out.

'This guy walked in dressed in leather, a total goth. He was playing all this tribal stuff – it wasn't right. He kept saying, "I can't hear a tune." He didn't seem to be enjoying himself, so he didn't get the job.'

I guess the feeling was mutual!

Still drummerless they persevered and they started to pile up the songs. Andy says, 'I remember mainly the ones we ended up with: "Mission Impossible", "Nowhere Fast" – "Tragic Roundabout" was possibly from round that period as well.'

Their musical taste as ever was the ragbag of punk and post-punk. 'We were listening to old punk stuff. Also I remember Johnny Thunders being a big thing but also Orange Juice and stuff like that. All that stuff coming out of Scotland on the Postcard label, but also stuff like Empire (the remnants of Generation X after Tony James and Billy Idol quit who formed their own glam punk band). We all loved that album as well.'

But they were still drummerless.

As they faithfully put the ads back up round town they waited for the next bunch of freaks and weirdos to start ringing. What they actually got a couple of days later was a call from some extrovert sounding kid with a funny name.

RENI ARRIVES!

In 1984 one of the best places for a musician to find a band was looking at the notice board in A1 Music (now the Academy of Sound). It was in here that one afternoon while the band were drummerless, hammering away at their clutch of new songs in Macclesfield, a cocky young guy bounded into A1 and took one look at the advert.

The advert asked for a drummer into Gen X, The Clash and Empire – pointers to the way the Roses were thinking at the time. They were looking for the glam/punk crossover.

Not that this meant much to Reni. He was into metal. Van Halen's 'Jump' being his all-time favourite tune! He knew he could bag the job and pulled the ad off the wall to stop anyone else getting it.

As he left A1 that mid May '84 afternoon, 20-year-old Alan Wren knew he was good enough to be in any band in Manchester but there was something about this ad that intrigued him.

He went back home to Gorton, picked up the phone and booked himself an audition with the gruff voice at the other end.

The band themselves had pooled their money and booked the city centre Decibel Rehearsal Studios for the audition. No more fannying around in the cellar. This had to be done properly. They had never rehearsed in the city centre before but this was important.

'We moved out of the Macclesfield cellar to Decibel,' remembers Andy.

'We put an advert in A1 and listed a load of influences that Reni read and obviously knew none of them! He rang up. We were called the Angry Young Teddy Bears or some load of bollocks that week. Something someone had made up to wind people up with. English Rose? That was the tail end of The Patrol thing, never a serious name . . .'

Reni's call was to Ian Brown and dutifully the band arranged to meet the sticksman. On 31 May they had the rehearsal room booked. This time they were going to do it properly. They didn't want to make the mistake of losing the next one. What if he was really good? He might not want to join a tinpot outfit, they had to look more pro!

Decibel Studios was in Manchester city centre. Nowadays it's better known as Beehive Mill, a club come rehearsal room complex just to the north of the city centre. It may look rough outside the complex now but then it looked like hell. Inside it was a threadbare old warehouse with a whole bunch of bands rehearsing in there. These days they talk of turning the area into the 'Italian 1/4'.

Back then it was a deadzone. A rubble strewn forgotten area. The rooms were full of bands. Ian hopped into Andy's car and they drove round to Reni's house in Gorton. When Reni answered the door they were in for a shock.

According to Andy, the drummer answered the door dressed in a pair of furry moonboots and too tight jeans. 'Reni rang up, he denies it now but he called himself Renée on the phone. Me and Ian went to pick him up. We knocked on this door in Gorton. He came to the door. I seem to remember he looked mad. Big long coat on with these big furry moonboots. A pair of them awful stretch denim jeans. His dress sense was fucking terrible!'

He may well be exaggerating as when your author bumped into Reni a couple of months later he wasn't dressed too crazily. They put his kit in the car (Andy's big fuck off car again!) and set off to Decibel. 'We loaded his gear into the car and went to the rehearsal room. We took the gear up three flights of stairs, it was such a pain in the arse! . . .'

Reni walked in and set his kit up. You can hear the crackle of expectation on the cassette from that very first rehearsal. The explosive excitement as he connects with the band straight away. They run through 'Nowhere Fast'. It's the simplest one to play. It's Reni's first-ever song with the band and there is a palpable buzz of excitement. Suddenly they sound like The Stone Roses, those drums are so distinctive, so Reni.

Says Pete, '"Nowhere Fast", "All Stitched Up", "I Can't Take It Anymore", "Mission Impossible" were the songs Reni first rehearsed. We never discussed it, we knew he was in! He was fucking amazing! What a drummer . . .'

Fuck, you can hear it on the rehearsal tape. Reni explodes into the song. Even its complex structure is learned in about five minutes. This is a find.

What a player. You can feel the band buzzing. I mean Si was good. Really good. But this was special! Recalls Andy, 'When he started playing he was mad as a hatter. He played like Keith Moon. All those little things that he can do! Double hits! Unbelievable stuff, so fluent, no effort. He can actually do all that. Amazing . . . We wanted him in straight away, he was that fucking good. We weren't sure if he was going to have it! We weren't that good at all . . . Pretty rough in fact . . .'

Why did he join? A drummer that good could have joined a bigger band after all. 'He told me a while later that the thing that really struck him was how much we believed in ourselves. The sense of belief that he got from us all . . . He had been in [semi-successful local metal outfit] Tora Tora and if he hadn't joined us he would have ended up as a jobbing musician.'

On the tape Reni is not sure about the songs. He thought they may not be strong enough. That's until they launch into 'Tragic Roundabout'. Now he gets it. Now he knows what they are capable of. He can hear this one. Remember Reni comes from the rock world, indie music means little to him. Where's the tune? Where's the song? This is a whole new discipline for the band and a good one.

'I'll bounce ideas off you,' says Reni. There is laughter and the band crash into 'Roundabout'.

Pete's stub-toed bass intro rumbles in yet again and again something magical happens. Reni's drums have the stamp of the Roses all over them, the loose Keith Moon rolls, the tricks, the gleeful unrestrained joy of playing, the unrestrained extrovert energy so rare in British musicians. It sounded like magic dust has been sprinkled all over the songs.

Here we are in May 1984 and the Roses' sound ready formed: the stop start of the song, its clever structure, its overflow of melody and the twin guitar work of Andy and John's guitars cranked to max treble. You can hear the flavour of the Postcard bands in the guitars, the brittle treble, the tunefulness and yet there is still something darker and more sinister in the song.

'Keep going, please keep going,' yelps Reni as the song stops. There is a lot of laughter as they try to explain to the new drummer where the song goes, like he really needs to know, his confidence is outrageous . . .

Reni knocks around with the Max Wall snare drum rat-a-tat. The band laugh and then goes into yet another version of the tune. After what seems like a million attempts, the band finally get to a version that includes Squire's melting solo.

It's a nightmare song to audition anyone with, its endless parts, its continually evolving structure, its hardly 1-2-3-4 and then one beat, but Reni's on it.

'We can do this, I know we can,' says Ian.

They have a break and Reni asks what's going on with the band.

'We got loads of chances of gigs, got to get on with it. We know GBH and we know Peter And The Test Tube Babies . . . and that's about it.' A voice, possibly Andy's, comes out of the gloom, name checking two unlikely punk outfits. 'We like all kinds of music . . .' They explain to their drummer. It is some sort of truism, because even though they are still wearing their punk roots firmly on their sleeve their music is a long long way from the far more hardcore nature of where the punk underground has gone. This is back to the roots of punk, the garage psychedelic licks, the twin guitar melodicism that roots back to the core of classic six string pop. At the same time the FX laden guitar unintentionally nods towards The Chameleons. Even from that first rehearsal with Reni you can hear all the hallmarks of the Roses sound that would captivate the upcoming generation five years later . . .

After that uplifting pep talk, they crash into a few bars of 'Coming Of Age'. 'I can't remember the tune,' laughs Ian as the song falls apart after a few bars.

'We're coming of age and you can't take it away,' intones Brown over a Who style workout.

And then they dive back into 'Tragic Roundabout', the band's relief at actually being able to play along with a drummer again after all these months is readily apparent. These songs have been waiting to be pushed by the drums. They are pretty well finished. Arranged. Ready to go. Getting anyone to drum on them must have been a buzz. But getting a drummer like this must have been quite a moment.

The songs are stuffed full of licks and the guitars peel off for mini solos and tuneful riffing. The song ends.

'That sounds really good, know what I mean . . .' enthuses Reni as 'Tragic Roundabout' clatters to a close, the tune being the only one that he actually really liked at that first rehearsal!

At the end of the rehearsal they huddle together. They want Reni in. He thought about it and said 'Yes.' It wasn't so much for the music, he later claimed, which was a bit slipshod, but the band's confidence, their total belief.

The allure of this fierce tightly knit crew appealed to him.

The Roses were ecstatic. They will always readily admit that the real turning point for them was when Reni joined the band. Now they had a foundation to build on. Says Ian, 'Finding Reni was crucial. John was a punk guitarist when we met Reni, but Reni could play anything. He'd been brought up in pubs, so he'd practised and practised on his kit and played with proper pub entertainers. He had a musical talent that none of us had. We all had to graft and work, but he was born with it. Pete Townsend saw our first gig (Moonlight, 1984) and said he was the best drummer he'd seen since Keith Moon.'

Reni's metal angle was just another obtuse influence to add to the band's stockpile of sounds. Says Ian, 'We liked The New York Dolls, still do John, Andy and Pete were very into Johnny Thunders, Reni was into Van Halen. He'd never heard reggae when we met him. He'd been brought up in east Manchester, which was more heavy metal. He was into Thin Lizzy and AC/DC. He was a proper rocker, used to go to Donington. We used to rip the piss out of him. But we were very enthusiastic. We just wanted to make a noise.'

So just who was this manic drummer, this wiseguy from east Manchester who would 'play every song completely differently every time'?

JUMP! RENI

Alan 'Reni' Wren was born on 10 April 1964. He was a streetwise kid from the Ardwick/Gorton part of the ring of rough estates that surround the Manchester city centre before panning out to the cosseted suburbs.

Already famous in his area for being a cocky, confident character, he was also known as the kid with the drums. Even at a very young age he was thrashing around on drum kits set up in his parents' pub where a kit was permanently set up for pub bands to play on.

The local kids thought Reni was a freak because he was such an amazing drummer, a total natural. Reni didn't care. He was already jamming along to anything and anybody. Stepping in with bands in the pub playing along with whoever was around or just by himself. Says Pete, 'Reni's mum and dad ran a pub and they had a drum kit set up for bands in the pub. After school he would come home and play on the kit . . . when he joined us he was already in two other bands. He was checking out who was the best bet – I'm not definite about this . . . He thought we looked interesting. We had something!'

Graduating from the pub he was playing in mates' bands, just going nowhere sort of stuff round Gorton. It was somewhere to sharpen up his act – get those drums tighter and meaner – but it wasn't enough for someone who knew how good they were.

By the early Eighties it was time to break out and try his hand at something more serious, maybe the spur was his close drumming mate getting a dream break. It had only been a few months before that one of his best mates, Simon Wright, had answered an ad ('drummer wanted must hit hard and heavy' was the blunt message with a PO box number) to join AC/DC.

It had been a long shot but Wright had got in. Some scruff from the estate and now he was in one of the biggest rock bands in the world at the peak of their powers. It was like a dream come true. Simon Wright sat there thrilled in his Man United shirt – a total star, a yob from the street playing the world's stadiums.

Adds Pete, 'Reni had played in loads of bands before. There was some kid round his way in AC/DC. He had a Man United shirt on TV playing with AC/DC. Simon Wright was older than Reni – showed him some stuff . . . Tora Tora, I think? He was in them at some point I think . . . I'm sure he was in them.'

Seeing his mate in the stadiums must have been a spur to Reni. It must have sharpened his resolve to get hooked up in a band. Some say that he stepped into Wright's shoes in Tora Tora, a local Manchester rock band that his mate had drummed in before moving on to the awesome Aussie rock giants but no one will confirm it.

Reni then began to scour the ads around town . . . and now he was in the Roses.

THE THREE RS . . . WRITE, REHEARSE AND RECORD – SUMMER OF '84

During the summer of 1984 they rehearsed for a couple of months at Decibel but the studios' scummy environs and some missing equipment made them less than happy with that situation. So they moved a few blocks further into town and to Spirit Studios in Tariff Street and it was here that the whole myth and legend of The Stone Roses really started to er, flower!

And it was here now, bang smack in the middle of the Manchester music business, that they started to make the right sort of contacts that would link them into the city's infrastructure instead of flogging away forgotten out in suburban cellars. They would swagger around the tight corridors. Reni would turn up on an old battered scooter looking like a little kid but was always a full on talker, cocky as fuck. The kid seemed to have nerves of steel. Other bands in the rooms included my band, The Membranes and Carmel.

Says Andy, 'We stayed in town. We rehearsed in Decibel for a good while and then we went to Out Of The Blue fleetingly and then on to Spirit which became our base for a long time.'

Now with a permanent home and a steady line-up coalescing, the band's songwriting began to hit top gear. 'When someone joins and you get a new rehearsal room then loads of material seems to get written. If you dry up then go to a new room and start again! The songs will come! In Decibel the songs we put together were "Mission Impossible" and "Nowhere Fast". In Spirit the songs we started getting together were "Tragic Roundabout" and "So Young", "Tell Me", "Fall".'

They worked hard in Spirit and continued to pile up the songs. 'In Spirit we wrote a lot of the Hannett stuff, nearly all of "Getting Plenty".'

They also rehearsed in Spirit's other rehearsal rooms out in Chorlton, flitting backwards and forwards from the city centre to the suburbs with fellow Spirit outfits like Carmel and The Membranes. The Chorlton studios were a two-room affair carpeted with a good vocal PA. They were spacious affairs and it made you feel like a proper band going down there.

As The Membranes rehearsed in one room we would wonder who the tough-looking bunch of short hairs were in the neighbouring room. The music pounding through the rehearsal room walls sounded good. Anthemic powerful rock music, it had the spirit of The Clash but had gone somewhere else with affected guitars and powerful drums. You could clearly hear Ian Brown giving it his all over the top.

One day I had to go next door and borrow some guitar strings off the band. It looked like it could be a bit heavy but I knew Pete from hanging out in Paperchase and Reni and I had met a few times. The Roses were affable, they seemed easy-going. In fact they helped us get our gear back to our west Didsbury bolthole, loading it into Andy's big white van.

And it was in Chorlton that the band entered the second phase of their songwriting. 'Then we went out to Chorlton writing "I Wanna Be Adored". By this time Pete used to sit out a bit and I'd play the bass while we jammed basic things out then give the bass back and show him what I had been playing. Likewise John would do the same. We also wrote "Here It Comes" there as well.'

While the Roses were toiling away in the rehearsal room, fellow Mancs The Smiths were well on their way.

The Smiths were in their ascendancy. Much has been made of the Roses' dislike of The Smiths, but this isn't totally true. Ian told *Record Collector*, 'I liked the fact that The Smiths came from our home town and I knew Andy Rourke when I was a kid, so I was happy for them. I liked "What Difference Does It Make?" but after that, no, not really.'

Andy will admit, when pushed, to some respect for The Smiths. 'We had this song, "Boy On A Pedestal", it was very Smithsy, the title and the lyric. We sort of hated them but had a secret adoration as well for them . . .'

The Smiths were not an influence for the Roses. They may have both had a jangling guitar framework and idiosyncratic charismatic lead singers and the Roses would eventually take a huge chunk of The Smiths' crowd as Morrissey and Marr's outfit collapsed just before they broke through, but the Roses always liked to keep their distance from them. Despite this there were the odd musical parallels between the bands: the very English atmosphere that surrounded both bands' musics and some of the Roses' early songwriting reflects not a wholesale take-off from The Smiths, but a definite flavour of the outfit.

Spirit was not only a place where the Roses first really got their band together and wrote nearly all of their early material. It was also the place where they began to infiltrate the Manchester music scene, coming in from the cellars and the suburbs into the city network.

The first important contact they made was with Steve Adge.

Steve 'the Adge' Atherton who was helping to run the rabbit warren of rooms. Adge was a tough-looking ex-rockabilly who was a fistful of years older than the band, but with a similar musical background. He hit it off with them immediately. Recalls Andy, 'Spirit was where we met Steve Adge – another nutter. We always seem to attract them! He's from Hyde and they are a bit strange out there! He was a lot older than us. We were in our early twenties. He was like in his thirties.'

Says Pete, 'He was playing in a band called Third Law with Mark Adge, his younger brother. Third Law rehearsed down there. I bought my bass amp off Steve.'

Ruffians with a love for rock'n'roll, it was obvious that Steve Adge and the Roses would bond.

The Roses, also, after a few months of intense rehearsal wanted to get some songs down to tape. Because at the tail end of August they had felt ready enough to cut their first demo.

THE NO-ONES MAKE THE FIRST STEP TO BEING SOMEONES: THE FIRST DEMO

On 26 August the Roses took advantage of the studio downstairs in the Spirit rehearsal studios. Shunting their gear down the narrow stairs they decided that they were ready to cut their first demo. Twelve weeks after Reni had joined, they booked two ten-hour sessions and recorded four songs, 'Tragic Roundabout', 'Misery Dictionary', 'Mission Impossible' and 'Nowhere Fast'.

Says Pete, 'It sounds better than the Hannett album we recorded later on! A lot more raw. You can hear Reni's drums. I never thought that Hannett suited the band. Listen to our earlier stuff! This is what we really sounded like!'

Down in Spirit there is an 8-track round the back. Generations of Manchester engineers have learned their trade in there. For this session the Roses worked with Tim Oliver. They handed him a tape of their glam punk heroes Slaughter And The Dogs. 'We told him that's the sound that we were looking for,' laughs Andy Couzens. For the south Manchester lads, heads filled with glam and punk, this Wythenshawe-based punk band with their 'Where Have All The Bootboys Gone' anthem was the closest that they had to role models in the search for the perfect pop sound.

They commenced with the first of the two ten-hour sessions, recording 'Tragic Roundabout' and 'Misery Dictionary'. It was at this point that they decided to change the name of 'Misery Dictionary' to 'So Young' because it sounded 'too Smithsy' and if there was one thing that this crew didn't want, it was to get confused with fast-rising new superstars of the Manchester scene.

In the next session they recorded 'Mission Impossible' and 'Nowhere Fast'.

Anyone who has heard these demos will tell you that they are a lot more representative of what the band was about. You can still hear flashes of the poppier end of punk on the Buzzcocks rush of 'Nowhere Fast' (or 'Just A Little Bit' as it would become), the first of their anthems on 'The Misery Dictionary' (note the added 'the', trainspotters!), 'Mission Impossible', and the bass driven 'Tragic Roundabout', the first Roses song that Reni really liked and the one that convinced him that not only was this an attractive gang to hang out with, but one that had the potential to write some top tunes.

Ian Brown singing vocals in the studio for the first time since that Patrol demo sounds so young. His double-tracked voice cutting clearly through the twin guitar attack that would dominate if it were not for that explosive drummer.

'Reni never played the same thing twice,' laughs Pete admiringly, 'which was pretty mental when it came to recording!'

They copied up the demo on to a 100 cassettes and John did his first piece of Roses artwork, photocopying the band's hand-drawn logo stuck on to a paisley shirt.

Armed with a demo and a proper set, it was time to get playing. 'We'd buy *Sounds* every week and Ian noticed an advert for a benefit gig in London with an address to send a demo to and Ian, being the main hustler in the band, phones up and sends a tape to this woman called Caroline Reed who was promoting the show at the Moonlight. We didn't really expect to get a reply, but Ian told her that we were massive in Manchester. I guess that must have swung it,' remembers Garner.

Ian remembers sending off the demo. 'The first Roses gig was at the Moonlight in Hampstead, an anti-heroin benefit that Pete Townsend put on. I'd seen an advert in the paper saying they were looking for bands. I lived in Hulme, where everyone was on skag except me. So I wrote a letter saying I'm surrounded by skagheads, I wanna smash 'em. Can you give us a show? And they did. The other groups were Mercenary Skank and High Noon, who all wore cowboy hats like Gary Cooper!'

This was the demo that was going to do good business for the band in the next six months. Straight away Ian started scouring the music press looking for places to send the tape.

It must have worked. They had a gig in London in eight weeks. A début show. The demo was already doing its work. The first of many positives it scored.

That September they piled into Andy's van and went to London to meet Caroline Reed, talk about the gig and other bits of stuff. Nothing official, like. And when a music biz contact of Steve's called Howard Jones asked the Adge if he knew of any cool bands rehearsing in town and to keep a good look out for anything out there, then Steve was only too happy to oblige.

Late October 1984 Adge rang up Jones and said, 'Yeah there's something here you may well be interested in looking at. They're called The Stone Roses.'

Howard Jones, who had just left the Hacienda, was a man with a mission. He wanted to prove to the Factory mob that he could cut it on his own. He was looking for a band with whom to spark a different empire off and the Adge was raving.

Jones, the ginger-haired maverick music nut, made a few calls and prepared himself to check this band out . . .

But first The Stone Roses had already booked themselves a début London show and, unbeknown to Jones, already had some sort of London management and a gig.

23 OCTOBER 1984: THE ROSES' DEBUT GIG

Ian Brown was once asked if he rehearsed his stage moves in front of a mirror.

'Well, when you do karate, you train in front of mirrors – so I'd always looked in mirrors. A few Ali moves but I never stood there with a tennis racquet,' he answered. Stagecraft. Now, there's something the Roses crushed out of the generation that followed. But in the earlier days the speed-driven band were riding on a surfeit of energy and Brown was a bug-eyed wildman diving around the stage. In the rehearsals up to their début gig this was uppermost on their minds. Their high-energy rock'n'roll demanded some sort of confrontational stage chops and Brown was getting ready to develop them.

They had rehearsed hard over that summer. The addition of Reni on that last day of May had made the massive difference. Suddenly this felt like a proper band. Far ahead of anything any of them had tried before.

And now finally they had a gig. Not just a local circuit gig. But a show with fucking Pete Townsend! Of all the Sixties bands The Who were the closest to the Roses – a wild drummer, an introverted artistic guitar player, a dynamic (at the time) frontman and a rock solid bass player. You've got the same love/hate dynamic that made The Who spark.

An anti-heroin gig at the Moonlight Club, London. What a start! Garner still has the poster to this day, a photocopied A3 with the Roses' name scrawled on in felt-tip alongside secret headliner Pete Townsend and the other support, Mercenary Skank.

It was a cause close to Brown's heart. His junkie neighbours in the Hulme high rises had got him down. The sheer waste of time and life because of the heroin monster were something he disliked. Brown was always very anti hard drugs. These were reflections of his martial arts background and The Sex Pistols confused anti-drugs stance that venerated speed, didn't mention marijuana and was betrayed by heroin!

The demo and Brown's gab on the phone had certainly done their job. The recipients were buzzing. The recipients of the demo were the aforementioned Caroline Reed, the then manager of Mercenary Skank, and Andrew Tunnicliffe, the guitarist of the band. They were blown away with the demo.

Reed rang back not only with the go ahead for the show, she also asked if they wanted her to manage them.

Nothing to lose, the band piled into Andy's white Chevy van and went down to London to sort out some sort of management deal.

Mercenary Skank, at the time, were an up-coming punkier version of The Alarm from the same town, Rhyl, as the Welsh band and also former roadies of Seventeen (the band that spawned The Alarm).

Andrew Tunnicliffe, now lives in Exeter where he restores antiques. When called upon to restore antique memories of the Roses he is keen to talk the band up.

Tunnicliffe remembers the Roses' demo. 'They did the anti-heroin benefit with us at the Moonlight Club in West Hampstead. The first impression of them was when they sent our management company a demo tape. We thought it was fantastic. We played it all the time. Being management we'd get the odd tape. The management was part of the band as well. At the time there was no one we really liked. The Stone Roses sounded like they had the same kind of bloodline, like The Clash and the Pistols and stuff like that. It was a really good tape. I remember "Misery Dictionary" being really good.'

Andrew and Caroline Reed were buzzing on the tape. They decided not only to put the band on at the anti-heroin benefit but also to manage the group. Before the gig the band met up with Andrew and Reed. During that September and October, the Roses made a few visits to London.

Recalls Andrew, 'So Caroline contacted them and they came to meet us in Hammersmith. It was way before the gig. They all came down. They had a surly, shitty attitude which we liked. They seemed to like to do things en masse. Just taking the piss all the time, anti everything like young bands should be.'

'So we went down to London before the Moonlight gig,' says Pete. 'Always the whole band, everyone, went to everything. Loads of people said we seemed aggressive at the time. I didn't see it as aggression as I was in the bubble. People said that they were intimidated by us, they assumed everyone in the band was a wanker because we were pretty arrogant about it.'

This surliness didn't put Andrew Reed off the band. 'We said that we liked them so much that we would like to help them. Caroline wanted to sign them to her company – Before the Storm Management. She asked them to do gigs with us. They seemed pretty keen to get involved.'

This unexpected London angle suited the band, because the Roses had a plan. It wasn't a foolproof plan. But it was a plan. The band that had come together in the suburbs outside the city's hip inner circle had a complete contempt for the Manchester music scene. This was the band that had already written the anti-Hacienda Factory song 'Fall', had no time for The Chameleons and were not big fans of The Smiths. In short the Roses were no flag wavers for their home city.

In the years since the big Manc boom a myth has been spun. The 'myth' of Madchester. It runs from punk to Joy Division to The Smiths to the Hacienda and then the Roses and the Mondays. All the pundits will always keep hammering away at this myth, like there was some sort of connection between all this activity, all the bands hanging around the Hacienda while the Hacienda were busily inventing acid house.

Of course in real life it wasn't quite like that. Bands like the Roses were on the outside of the Factory/Hacienda axis. In fact they violently hated it, the way it had become the unelected spokesman for the city's pop culture, the way that label had become the so-called conduit for the city's cool.

Being punk/mod/scooterists, the Roses had their own definition of cool, a cool that was a long way from Factory's anti-rockist art school version of events. While Factory were celebrating the whole morass of post Joy Division outfits, the Roses were still sticking up for bands like Slaughter And The Dogs and were banging on about Northern Soul.

They felt like outsiders in Manchester, the city's scene had developed a long way away from where they were going. They were on the outside looking in before they had even started.

So, fuck Manchester!

Let's go and play in London first.

Manchester can wait.

We are the Roses.

Says Andy, 'We didn't want anything to do with Manchester at all. We opposed all the raincoat-wearing Manchester Factory bands. All that cliquey elitism.'

And now things were up and running at the other end of the country. Their first gig was to be outside Manchester. It was the first time any of them had played outside the city. And there was talk of some sort of London management. This was doing things differently and it appealed to them. They were going to do this from the outside. Fuck all that local band shit.

The upcoming anti-heroin gig was on 23 October 1984 and they were secretly buzzing at the Pete Townsend connection. I mean, The Who! You've got to respect Townsend, the eloquent king of the mods himself!

Townsend was fresh off a stadium American tour with his day job superstar band. He had had his problems with hard drugs and was a good person to be playing a show like this. Pass that experience on to the next generation, try and turn them off smack, the least rock'n'roll drug in the world!

The band hopped into Andy's white Chevy van (again!) with Kaiser at the wheel. 'When the Roses started I used to help them out. I would drive the van and help set the gear up.'

They hit the motorway to London. No one had been on stage since 1980. Four full years of rehearsing or hanging out, scootering or working and at last they were about to get the adrenaline rush of being on stage again. And this time they were armed with an amazing drummer, a drummer who had his own explosive way of playing. Pete Garner is still buzzing over Reni's playing.

'Reni never played the same thing twice. You'd do a song and then five minutes later when you played it again he played it completely differently. He was amazing. It was like having ten Keith Moons playing all at once.'

The band dutifully turned up for their soundcheck and blasted through a cover of The Nazz's 'Open Your Eyes'.

'The Moonlight was interesting as we played the only full cover that we ever did,' recalls Pete Garner. 'We did a version of The Nazz's "Open My Eyes". Me and John were mad on The Nazz. It was one of our favourite groups at the time. Pete Townsend told us we remind him of the early Who so we had hard-ons all the way home!'

The Nazz were built around Todd Rundgren (who also produced The New York Dolls!). Rundgren had formed the band in 1967 in the USA and the four piece's dedication to the British invasion saw them decked out in Beatle mop tops and a deep love of Roy Wood's The Move. 'Open Your Eyes' was their first single but they fell apart by 1969 after a disastrous attempt to move them into the teen market.

The Nazz's sharp looks and clever songs made them a hit with John Squire and to a lesser extent Pete Garner and 'Open My Eyes' was the only fully played serious cover the Roses ever did. The Nazz have since slipped out of the pages of rock history. But somehow in Manchester they had two youthful fans dedicated to their cause.

The Roses exploded through the song: they just completely went for it, wired on adrenaline and buzzing from getting out of the van after the long dark journey down to London.

Now normally in sound checks the rest of the bands stand around looking as bored as the group going through one. For most bands the soundcheck is a chore.

But the Roses were going ape and the rest of the bands stood there open-mouthed. After they finished the tune the assorted musicians clapped.

It was a supreme accolade and a pointer to just how good the Roses actually were after all those months of endless rehearsing. And The Nazz song was perfect for their warm up.

Says Andy, 'That first gig at the Moonlight. In the soundcheck the song that we did was "Open Your Eyes" by The Nazz. The version we did was really tough. It's a great song live, really good and people were going fucking hell. People were coming up and saying, where are you from. We had had that much whiz by this point, that everything was very intense.'

Cowboy hat wearing indie rockers High Noon played first and then the Roses hit the stage for their set.

There were no nerves. Nothing. Just confidence. A speed-fried confidence. There was a supremely arrogant frontman giving the crowd his combative staring eyes attack, a lank, long-haired bass player rocking with his bass, letting his lank black hair hang over his face. Also there was a guitar player moving backwards and forwards while shyly looking out from under his fringe, the other guitar player was a tough-looking version of the singer with a tight quiff. They looked like a street gang, a right bunch of moochers.

The set was just about all the songs that they had managed to finish writing in the past five months since Reni had joined: 'Mission Impossible' opened the show, and was followed by "Nowhere Fast", "All Stripped Down", "Tragic Roundabout" and the set ended with "Heart of Staves". This was a band that was making no apologies for its presence.

There were other factors playing their hand that night. Couzens laughs as he looks back on that awesome début show. 'We were doing loads of speed that night. In those days we were massively into speed – that was the main thing for us. We hardly ever drank and we never smoked dope. Speed was the drug for us. We took it religiously. The only person who never did any speed was Reni but he was such a natural speed head he didn't need any.'

Says Kaiser, 'That time they played the first gig, the anti-drugs gig, they were all out of their heads speeding!' But then the Roses, like most of the punk generation, didn't look on speed as a drug. Smack or dope were drugs. Hippy shit. Speed made you think fierce. Made you more aware. Crazier. It was sharp and dangerous. It didn't mong you out. Well, not for a few years anyway!

Another of the reasons that the Roses really flew that night was that they had worked their asses off for the show.

'We rehearsed like mad for that gig – we put everything into it,' recalls Andy. And not just musically: 'We worked out all our moves and what we were going to wear, everything. We knew that we were special, we knew that we were very good.'

The Roses had spent their whole post-punk lives living for this moment – this gig was everything that they had been dreaming about, waiting for. For a northern band to début in London was always an experience of mixed fortunes. It was the big moment because the whole music business was for some reason based in the capital and every little band in the country had to come down sarf and show themselves to the lazy A & R departments of the early Eighties.

Pete Townsend was blown away. He couldn't wait to get the loose-limbed kid up there for his encores. Remembers Ian, 'Reni did "Pictures Of Lily", "Substitute" with Pete Townsend. He was made up – his first-ever gig and there he was with Pete Townsend! We come off stage and Townsend was like, you look really good up there and your drummer's great. Then he said, as an end-of-the-night thing, I wanna play a couple of tunes. Do you want to do it? Reni's like, yeah! We'd do soundchecks and Reni had people with their mouths open!'

Andrew Tunnicliffe from the Skank recalls that moment as the young cocky drummer held his own against the superstar musician jam (well, half superstar jam – Mercenary Skank played the guitars) and the Roses as well. 'They were great onstage. Pete Townsend was particularly impressed with Reni and asked him to get up for "Substitute" and "Won't Get Fooled Again".'

Couzens, like the rest of the band, acted as surly as possible: 'We just said to him "Who the fuck are you?" That was our attitude at the time,' remembers Andy, adding, 'He had asked if he could borrow our drummer and we just pointed to this heap on the floor and said if you want him he's over there, just go and ask him.'

Recalls Andy Couzens, 'Everyone had a colossal ego in the band. I remember at the end of the set at those times Reni would collapse on to the floor. It was hard to tell whether he was putting it on or not, although he put so much into it, it could have conceivably been true.' When Townsend played 'Substitute', Reni who was a fan of sorts, but not a massive one, turned to Pete and shouted 'How the fuck does it go?'

Says Pete, 'As if he was bothered, know what I mean, he could just drum to anything, he was a total natural.'

They followed it up with a last run through of 'Won't Get Fooled Again'. The rest of the band just stood there laughing. What a night.

The gig was a major success for the young band. They had impressed some of the most respected old boy musicians, they had blown everyone away with their sheer raw power, they had drawn an instant offer of management by a London manager and to cap it all the music press was down at the gig in the form of Gary Johnston from the ever perceptive and sadly defunct *Sounds* and he seemed to like it. He was going to review their first-ever gig and arrangements were made for an interview in *Sounds* in the next few weeks.

What most bands achieve in a year The Stone Roses seemed to have achieved at their first-ever gig.

Pete Townsend was impressed. 'It's great to see five arrogant kids on stage,' he smiled, perhaps sensing that the great baton of street bands was being handed, yet again, from one generation to another.

Buzzing they climbed back into the white Chevy for the long haul back to Manchester. They had come down to London and blown everyone away. They knew that they were good. Maybe that inner confidence wasn't just bullshit, maybe they were a band that was going to tear it up and tear it up quickly.

The gig also got them their first review of sorts. Well nearly! In the crowd was the lugubrious Mick Mercer – writer of the goth manuals, some-time editor of *ZigZag* and all-round eccentric. Then writing for *Melody Maker*, his review appeared on November 10. The band, press junkies at the time, scanned the review. They were mentioned in the list of bands at the top of the piece but Mick had neglected to mention them in the review itself.

'We came back to Manchester after that gig thinking that we were The Beatles and went to buy the paper and there was no mention at all,' laughs Garner.

Stop! start! stop! start! – that's band life for you!

So it was back in Spirit and with a renewed vigour they attacked their songs, wondering what to do next. Caroline Reed had offered them another couple of shows playing with Mercenary Skank at the end of November. There was somewhere in Exeter and another show in London at the Ad Lib club, a mini tour! Two dates on the road.

And Howard Jones wanted to meet them. He was talking about band management and record deals – were they interested?

Yeah, they were but they had two gigs to play with Mercenary Skank on 21 and 22 November. They arranged to meet Howard the week after.

They had already agreed to let Caroline Reed manage them, but what the hell! More managers means more gigs. Let's see who can do the most, eh!

THE ROSES GET THE JONES

Howard was buzzing. He could trust 'The Adge'. The tip-off had got him thinking. Apparently there was a hot band in town right under his nose. First, though, he had to get everything into place. What's the best way to show the Factory up about record labels! I'll form my own!

And who better to do it with than another ex-mate of Factory, legendary producer and wildman Martin Hannett.

Before going to see the Roses, Jones rang up Martin Hannett, the maverick Manchester producer who had made his name with his imaginative work with Joy Division and a whole run of Factory acts.

The two met up. Hannett was was looking for a new band to work with. He loosely decided to come in with Jones and get a new label together. On 12 November the pair of them met up with Tim Chambers and formed Thin Line records.

Now he was ready to meet the band.

On 29 November Jones went to Spirit to meet the Roses. He was full of attitude as he entered Tariff Street. He had something to prove. 'It had become a bit of a thing for me to find a good band in Manchester. I went down to Spirit to check out the Roses and . . .'

Picks up Andy, 'Howard Jones came down. He had just lost his job as General Manager of the Hacienda. He said he was setting something up with Martin Hannett.'

He went down the stairs into the tight warren of corridors and up to the rehearsal rooms. The dull thud of other bands rehearsing away, the confusing mush of sound that makes up the eternal din of rehearsal rooms worldwide greeted him. He then pushed the door open and apprehensively entered the room. The Roses were in there, looking young, tough and mean, but were also deceptively polite. The band started to play and at first Jones was very confused.

'They were absolutely fucking diabolical. It was a racket, but one of those kinds of rackets that are so exciting. They had songs there. I couldn't believe some of the actual lyrical content. It was brilliant. I'm into lyrics as well – I love Dylan – and Ian Brown's lyrics were great. I was thinking does Ian Brown realise how evocative his words were? They work on so many different levels. Does he understand how powerful these words are? I eventually got to know Ian and got to realise how deep a thinker he really is. There isn't a thing he doesn't think about. I thought this guy is a great songwriter.'

In the murk of the room and in the endless racket Jones started to notice more than the songs.

He was instantly struck by the way the band hung together. There was no slacking here. This was a band that knew how to be a band. Says Howard, 'They looked great. Like a gang. Each one was different. Like a tall one, a thin one, a hard one, a soft-looking one, and John looked like if you said boo he would jump. Reni looked so young, I didn't realise he was so young. I couldn't believe it [he was 20 and they were 22–23].'

Despite the 'racket', despite everything, Jones had to think on his feet. There were decisions to be made. 'Everything is about instinct. I'd heard a lot of bands that were better than them and more ready musically, but I thought this band has got legs, this will go. I was full of it anyway. I was the big time Hacienda head honcho, Mr Manchester who didn't pay to get in anywhere!'

The rehearsal had made an impact, although they had been loose and ragged and very, very loud. Howard knew instinctively that here was a band that he could kick start his campaign off with. Get this crew in the studio and some of those songs that are buried in the noise will leap out. Martin Hannett would make sure of that. There was potential there . . .

The next day he went back to another rehearsal and they talked it out. Quickly Howard found that there was some sort of rapport between him and the band. They definitely knew what they didn't like. 'They hated the way Hacienda and Factory dominated the Manc scene . . . They saw me as an insider except when I gave them my spiel about how I was nothing to do with Factory any more. Steve Adge had warned me about this – about how they hated all that scene. I told them that I'm resigning from Factory and starting my own company. By this time I had spent a lot of time recording with Martin Hannett who was also pissed off with Factory. I told them that we're going to start a label and the first band I'll sign will be recorded by Martin. If you go with me now you will have product out within months.'

They agreed that Howard was now their manager. Says Ian, 'That was Howard Jones, the original manager of the Hacienda, who became our manager in 1984. He formed the label so we could release the single, rather than go for a deal.'

The band now had a proper manager. It was an odd feeling. 'Howard was like having your dad round. All of a sudden it stopped being a racket. It was a bit more serious. He said the same thing: we made this racket, couldn't make out the songs because it was so loud and distorted, but there was something in the self belief and conviction that we had that made him think yeah these are great . . .' remembers Andy.

Jones told the band that he wanted to sign them to this new label. He said it would rival Factory and they would be the first band on it. They would also be able to get loads of free studio time in Strawberry Studios, the main north-west studio based in Stockport because Hannett had some down time owed to him there. They may all be night sessions but what the fuck, they were free! They could record an album for next to nothing with one of the hippest producers in the country . . . This was the man who had produced Joy Division and masterminded the whole Factory sound.

Big deal, thought the sullen band. That means nothing to them. But they remembered that Hannett was also the man responsible for Slaughter And

The Dogs' crisp neat and powerful production on 'Cranked Up Really High' and this impressed them so much more, when they eventually went to the studio. This was the record they took, trying to get their melodic anthems crossed with the sheer visceral thrill of Slaughter And The Dogs' amphetamine rushes.

So the Roses had found themselves a manager, a manic sharp-looking geezer who seemed to appear from nowhere.

He came down, and liked what he saw but there was something rankling him.

'Your bass player's great but he needs a haircut,' was his summation of the situation.

'I thought, you cunt,' guffaws Garner. 'I told him to fuck off. I wasn't happy at all.'

But Jones still became the group's sole manager. Or so he thought.

What they had neglected to tell Howard was that they already had a manager of sorts, having hustled themselves a loose arrangement with Caroline Reed.

Recalls Howard, 'I didn't know anything about Caroline Reed. What happened was that she thought she was managing them and they never spoke to me about it! She was ringing Andy and he never told me. The first time I met her was four years later when I was going to Berlin with The Buzzcocks. I didn't know anything about Caroline.'

Meanwhile their other manager was getting busy. Caroline Reed (who also videoed the first gig and has the only copy ever made of the video of it – the only ever copy, rock memorabilia buffs) had got them some press. She had pulled in a mate of hers from the rock press, *Sounds* writer Gary Johnson, who had seen them at their début gig.

'That November Gary Johnson had rang up because Ian had sent him one of the August demos as well. We all read *Sounds* and Ian knew that Gary Johnson was the one writer who could be into us. He rang us up and came up to Manchester to interview us on 30 November,' remembers Pete.

Johnson had been writing for the paper since his mate Gary Bushell had got him on, covering that mish mash of post-punk rock that fringed on 'oi' and also the mod bands that had exploded a couple of years previously. Being a long-lost Clash fan he got off on the bands fired-up rock'n'roll. In short he loved the band and dragged down A&R, like Steve Tannebum, to check them out but to no avail.

The band set out on the road again for two more shows set up by Reed. The first of which was supporting her other charges, Mercenary Skank, on 21 November at Exeter Labour Club. The Skank's Andrew Tunnicliffe remembers the show.

'I'm sure the only other gig we played with them was Exeter Labour Club. I can't remember the London show at all! They were great, even better the second time. They had a different guitarist then. They were a bit like The Clash. The guitars were full on! They went on stage and made a racket. I particularly liked them. They really reminded me of early Clash. For some reason I remember John Squire having some sort of flares on. He always had his distortion pedal full on! I tried to tell him he didn't have to do that. Andy and Ian Brown would career about the stage. They also had a very glam, long haired gothy type in the band as well. Whoever turned up at the gigs really liked them as well. They might have had an attitude but they were really nice people as well, polite even! Their attitude reminded me of what we were like when we started in the punk days . . .'

Now Exeter is one motherfucker of a drive from Manchester and it takes hours to get there. But the Roses were buzzing after the success of The Moonlight the month before.

In their naivéte the Roses set out on the long drive, believing that this gig would be the same sort of thing as the Moonlight, the same story as London – an astounded crowd surfing on their sheer talent. This is how they saw it and it made the seven-hour drive rush past far quicker. Naturally it was a damp squib, a dead crowd of about 40 people who stared back at them totally disinterested.

Welcome to the real world of the road.

Fuck, they were going to have to work a damned sight harder than they had figured.

But that work didn't mean the usual thing of slogging around in Manchester like other bands, as Couzens points out.

'Manchester was a pit. There was nowhere to play. We just thought we may as well concentrate on London. Me and Ian would go down to London and do some hustling as well as the stuff that Caroline Reed sorted for us.'

The day after Exeter they were back in London, playing with Mercenary Skank again at Kensington's Ad Lib club. This, according to witnesses at the time, was their best gig yet.

The Ad Lib gig was billed as the Christmas punk extravaganza in an attempt to get some heads in the place. A curious venue tucked away in some posh looking Victorian blocks, the Ad Lib was a regular gigging venue in the mid Eighties with people like Johnny Thunders playing there what seemed like all the time.

The Ad Lib gig was reviewed in *Sounds*, their first ever proper piece of national music press before the *NME* and *Melody Maker*, and printed on 5 January 1985. The journalist was Robin Gibson, a firebrand Scot who loved his Stonesy glam punk as much as any of the band and knew what he was talking about and never minced his words.

Gibson hated the Roses and slated the gig. Years later his hatred is just as strong. 'They were crap, man. I never understood the whole thing. I just don't understand why they were so popular, I remember when they started taking off, years later, and Hall or Nothing (their press people) gave me ten singles to hand out around the office and everyone went on about how crap they were. Weeks later there was a clamouring to write about them. I still didn't get it.'

Gibson stuck the boot in in the review, claiming the Roses were like Mercenary Skank before they got any good and that they were hindered by their singer. He did admit that they had the power but not the songs. Gibson wasn't having it at all.

An interesting footnote to the Ad Lib gig is the small shot on the inside of the *Garage Flower* album showing the band on stage at the venue. Ian and Andy look remarkably similar, in white kecks and short hair, while John and Pete hold up the glam end of the band. Already, though, they look like a band, a gang.

Their 'London manager' Caroline Reed was still enthralled by the band's young drummer. Says Andrew, 'Musically Reni was the main strength at the time and she was in total adulation of him. She tried to nick him from us. She wanted him to drum for Mercenary Skank and if she could have got him she would have.'

But Pete maintains that this could never have happened. 'By this point there was never any question of him joining anyone. We were locked in by then. It was the five musketeers and all that. Even if AC/DC had asked him he would have turned them down. You only get one chance with people your own age and you're all mates and we all knew it was our one chance to do it.'

The Ad Lib hadn't been the same sort of buzz as the gig last month at The Moonlight, but they still went down well and still got the right people talking.

They returned back north buzzing over their raids on London and ready to get a début northern show under their belts.

They had a big crew of mates, c/o the scooter scene and Steve Adge's ready-made crew of muckers from Hyde as well as the Failsworth connection and their own south Manc boys . . . mates who were starting to buzz on their tales of gigs in London, starting to buzz on the demo that was floating about. Everyone wanted to see the band play up north. They returned to their rehearsal room and carried on rehearsing till the end of the year. There was talk of gigs in January and February and that *Sounds* feature was to run just after Christmas.

Meanwhile Jones was getting organised. He blagged Hannett and some downtime at Strawberry for their first proper sessions in mid January.

The Roses were ready to record their début single and début album.

1984 was a good year. What would 1985 hold?

1985

JANUARY: FIRST FEATURE

Traditionally the first music paper of the year has the journos' tips for the upcoming year. Half the fun is just how spectacularly wrong these can be. Flicking through *Sounds*, the band were astonished to see that they were tipped. Gary Johnson was now well on their case.

Over the years there have been several claimants to being the first journalist to get on The Stone Roses' case. Not even in Manchester had anyone picked up on them. They didn't hang out on the local media scene. They were outsiders. No one has ever mentioned Johnson who went on a one-man campaign for the band, dragging A&R down to their gigs, dropping their name off to all and sundry, really pumping them up.

He predicted great things for the Roses when he had to choose his predictions for 1985. Printed on 29 December in *Sounds* Gary Johnson's predictions stated that 'The Stone Roses will have a hit indie single and album in the next year . . .' Not much, but some positive press at last.

Note that he was one hundred per cent right. He also tipped the Immaculate Fools at the same time!

And the feature was to be running in the next couple of weeks. A chance to go national!

Getting a feature in the music press is a big deal for a new band. It's the first big break, serving the notice of something happening. The Stone Roses were taken completely by surprise by their début feature. After all they were three gigs old, unknown in their home town, unknown anywhere really.

They knew that they were on to something good but they didn't expect it to come together this fast. Usually a press agent hustles some press or there is a record out; there is a reason for the article, apart from a writer's hunch or intuition. Johnson was well on the ball here even if it would be a few years till he was proved correct.

This was the mid-Eighties and this was *Sounds*. *Sounds* was always hot for new bands. Certain writers could just walk in and put bands into the paper that they were quite literally raving and frothing about.

And *Sounds'* Gary Johnson would quite often rave and froth about a group.

Things were moving fast.

Johnson, who was brought on to the paper by Gary Bushell, was a gum chewing 'Oi' poet who had progressed to live reviews and was now on to features. Digging out new bands is the lifeblood of a new gunslinger writer. It makes or breaks a reputation.

On 4 January 1985 they played their first headline show at the Fulham

Greyhound by default. It was intended to be another support with Mercenary Skank but the Skank pulled out of the gig because their front man, Scratch had laryngitis.

The Roses were supported by Doncaster's long forgotten, Last Party (raved about in *ZigZag* by Mick Mercer and an amiable outfit). The Roses played hard, driven by Reni's sweat-soaked Keith Moonisms. Gary Johnson was, yet again, on their case, dragging down A&R from Rough Trade.

At Fulham they decided to close with 'Getting Plenty', a brand new song. Up till now they had closed with 'Tell Me' because its extended instrumental sections gave Ian Brown the chance to wander into the crowd for his confrontation with the audience bit.

The only problem was that 'Getting Plenty' was too new and, typical of a new song getting its first gig, it fell apart. Not the climatic exit to the set that they were hoping for.

The following week they were back in London again. The ubiquitous Gary Johnson had managed to blag them tickets to one of those showbiz parties where freebies were rained upon the celebs and the guest list was stuffed full of wannabies, ne'er do wells, chancers and attendant scum.

It was the day before the *Sounds* feature went in and Johnson also took them around a few record companies with their demo. The band's London excursions seem to have been conducted without the knowledge of their other manager, Howard, who was still setting up his label in Manchester!

They first checked out CBS and then went down to Arista.

Sat around in the air-conditioned vacuum of Arista they were stunned to spot David Cassidy pacing around the offices. No one had heard of him for years and here he was on the verge of a not very spectacular comeback. They sat there staring at him, the young bucks versus the desperate old guard – that's the showbiz way. They pitied him still slogging away and chasing the magic dust after all this time.

None of the labels was interested in the Roses, what the fuck! what do they know anyway!

The party was a spectacular rooftop garden do. Everyone, apart from the Roses, was famous, the place was crawling with mid Eighties celebs, the Rolling Stones, Slade, Bananarama, Captain Sensible, The Cult and again David Cassidy. That was cheesy enough but these were the coolest people there, because lurking in the corners were Chris Quinten, fallen semi-star of *Coronation Street* and Tik and Tok (two utterly banal New Romantic mime artists) and it slipped further downwards from there to hungry 'B'-list celebs, the sort of no-marks that scarred the decade with their big egos and tiny talent. It was a guest list from hell and made the front covers of all the next day's national press. Pumped with an endless supply of free food and beer, the Roses wandered around swigging free champagne out of bottles and lobbing the half empty bottles over the balcony.

The Roses must have felt totally out of place. All those months in the rehearsal room and now here they were in New Romantic London!

'We felt like imposters,' spits Pete Garner, adding, 'we met Captain Sensible and we were excited. We loved The Damned. We told him that "Idiot Box" [obscure Damned track from their critically slaughtered second album that was one of the sole Sensible contributions to their canon and a way cool tune to boot] he couldn't believe it.'

'We also met Who bass player John Entwhistle. It was all the people you read about.'

Towards the end of the party, Garner, wasted on the free champagne, made a beeline for the bogs. Staggering in, he kicked open the door of one of the cubicles. Inside was Limahl, the lead vocalist of Kajagoogoo, perhaps the nadir of Eighties naffness.

'He's sat there having a crap, and he literally shits himself ha! ha! ha! ha! He's cowering in the cubicle and I'm standing there totally bemused – it's a strange scene.'

'It made the gossip columns of the following week's *Sounds*, how I'd beaten Limahl up at the party, while the party itself was noted by the dailies as being party of the year.'

The Roses themselves capped the evening by having their picture taken with Bruce Foxton of their beloved Jam, all except for Clash fan John Squire, who apparently, hated the Woking trio.

THE FIRST FEATURE

Gary Johnson had scored a feature on the Roses in November and had travelled up to Manchester to interview them in the greasy caff on Piccadilly just by the bus station and underneath the massive slab of concrete skyscraper that dominates and insults the city centre.

When the feature went into *Sounds* in mid January, Johnson had even managed to blag the Roses' name on to the front cover of the paper.

Under the headline 'Flower Power' (the first of years of crap puns on the name) the picture of the group with the piece had them staring meanly at the camera. Ian and Andy's hair was slicked back, Pete had a Stooges/MC5 style black bob and Reni looked like a 14-year-old kid, while John was in glam punk mode. It was a variation of that shot that crops up every now and then when someone wants to call them goths, and, if they do look a bit of a hotch potch mob, they were quite definitely not goths. Gary Johnson raved: 'The Stone Roses have an indie smash single and album inside them.'

Couzens is still bemused by this early burst of press activity. 'We were staggered. From then on we thought that Johnson was a really good contact and we thought, right, let's dig deep into this guy and see what he has got for us. We stayed at his house, me and Ian – a couple of head cases on speed – he was like a like-minded soul, he was a speed freak and he always wanted to be in a band – that was his whole thing, he'd put on The Small Faces' "Lazy Sunday Afternoon" and sing along to it.'

Johnson wanted to be in the gang, it's an attractive proposition.

In the piece, The Stone Roses also fibbed to Johnson. Claiming that they had coachloads of fans that followed them everywhere. A self-fulfilling prophecy – as months later when the Roses played Preston the coachloads turned up – they were one of the first new generation bands to get that huge street following. Years later the tradition would continue as the fans would cram buses and coaches and travelled across Europe on a booze and drugs-fuelled binge to check out their heroes in another bout of incredible street decadence. A tradition that roots right back to the scooter gang background of the Roses.

RECORD THE FIRST SINGLE

On 13 March the band decamped to Stockport's Strawberry Studios to record 'So Young' and 'Tell Me' with Martin Hannett. They informed Hannett that working with Joy Division was all well and good but it was that Slaughter And The Dogs sound they were really after. Fine sentiments but as a band they didn't really sound much like Slaughter. There was none of that incendiary speed-driven Wayne Rossi guitar going on here. Even on these two more up tempo songs the Roses were dealing in FX laden guitars and fluctuating dynamics.

Hannett set about recording the band in his usual painstaking manner, adding effects all over the place, carving the sound into whatever landscapes he wanted. For this he was ably assisted by engineer Chris Nagle.

It was Hannett's status as a living legend that was useful for giving the label credibility – more usefully they also managed to get the band four free days in Strawberry Studios and this was where they recorded their début single.

Between 13 and 17 March the band trooped down to Strawberry Studios in Stockport to grab some of Hannett's downtime, to cut their début single, 'So Young'/'Tell Me'.

Strawberry had been set up by 10CC in the mid-Seventies. At one time it was the best 'state of the art' studio outside London. By the mid-Eighties it was still the premier studio in Manchester, with Hannett working on most of his classic cuts there.

Hannett had invented his own sound over the years, in the studio. He was behind the monumental sound of Joy Division's two crucial albums as well as ACR, John Cooper Clarke, and a whole host of Mancunian tracks.

His harsh, cold sound perfectly suited the groups. He was a total legend as much for his excessive lifestyle as for his production techniques.

Couzens vividly remembers the experience of working with Martin Hannett. It was a key educational moment for the band.

'I loved it, even though he was a total mess. He was bad on smack at that point. He kept going on about trying to destroy his ego. But whatever he did, he did it instinctively. The record was engineered by Chris Nagle, and Ian Brown just didn't get on with him. He kept saying that he couldn't get any response from him, so you've got that, and Martin asleep on the couch. It was a weird way to record a record.'

Working with Hannett was always an interesting experience. Making up his own techniques along the way, linking together chains of effects to create strange new sounds and textures. To some he was a genius and to others a drink and drug-addled, crazed wildman.

Sometimes in the studio he would be inspired and brilliant and sometimes he would fall asleep under the desk, leaving engineer Chris Nagle to mop up, do the work.

The unassuming Nagle, who was as talented as Hannett, went on to produce the début number one albums for The Charlatans and The Inspiral Carpets. A lack of ego has made sure that he has never really got the credit that he deserves for helping to create several groups' sounds.

Howard Jones, after working in the jaw of the beast, was obsessed by Factory and fascinated by its corporate image and artwork. You can see it in the press releases he put out for the band at the time. They are blatant total rip-offs of the in-house Factory style – all stark visuals and sharp lines. This didn't make the band too happy – they were hardly massive fans of the Factory machine.

The plan for 'So Young' was for it to come in three entirely different mixes – each with its own separate catalogue number like Factory mixes. Mix number one was the song proper, mix two was to be a DJ-only mix and mix three was, crazily enough for a small label on a tight budget, to be finished off in Nashville (yup, that's right, the country-and-western town – someone had a bit of a pipe dream obviously) with all the connotations that that entails. The fact that none of these mixes ever happened shouldn't surprise anyone.

'Imagine trying to get Hannett in and out of the country,' laughs a well known Manchester scenester, 'what a field day the Customs would have had with him!'

Both tracks released later that year showcase the Roses' early sound. All powerful rock bluster and mid-Eighties Chameleons style phlanged guitars, but even at this early stage you can hear Brown's English, almost folk melodies, rising above guitars. It was a younger, more aggressive, speed-driven Roses that sits in the vinyl here. Both tracks are in-your-face, no-nonsense rock and both songs are not Roses classics as even Ian Brown admitted.

'I wouldn't give 20p for that single,' sniffed the lead singer a few years later.

HOWARD JONES GETS THINGS MOVING

Now in the management hotseat, it was time for Howard to prove that he could pull a few things off. He began by shaking down a few local contacts. City Life was already sorted. How about some radio?

Tony the Greek (Tony Michaelides) was the DJ on the main local indie radio show on Piccadilly Radio and he was slipped one of the 100 demos. Liking what he heard he put it straight on his show and on 3 and 10 February he played a couple of tracks from the tape.

Unusually the songs caused an instant reaction with the listeners. There were phone calls. It seemed that the Roses tunes had something. Tony the Greek booked them in for a session. Says Pete, 'People were ringing up. It was very rare that people rang up. Then we were booked for a session on the radio on Sunday, 24 March. At this point we hadn't even played in Manchester.'

Adds Howard, 'It was the first live radio session on Piccadilly radio for ten years. At first we were going to do it acoustic with just John and Ian but eventually we decided to do it with the whole band.'

This is not quite the way the band remembers it. Pete laughs, 'I've never heard of that. The only person who would have thought of that is Howard. It was never mentioned to us. I mean, why would you do it? It would be a total non-representation of the band and acoustic versions of songs that no one has heard anyway. Pointless!'

The session booked, Howard printed up a flyer in a neo-Factory artwork style to flood the city with publicising the session and a couple of upcoming shows. The buzz was building.

Radio Piccadilly had been asked to put together a showcase of local bands at Dingwalls in London. The bill had already been fixed but Tony managed to get the Roses added on last minute. So on 8 February they set off yet again in Andy's van for a London gig.

Dingwalls has been the scene of many Manc triumphs over the years. Only the year or so before I had seen The Smiths' début headline London show there to a half-filled room and a huge heap of gladioli left on the floor as the curious looked on, and only a couple of years later the Manc baggy scene would be introduced to London via the venue as both the Mondays and the Roses played classic shows there.

That February 1985 the other Manc bands making the furtive run down to the city included Glee Company, Communal Drop, Fictitious Names and Laugh who eventually transmuted into Intastella. The hosts were Bob

Dillinger, a local singer-songwriter come comedian, and Mark Radcliffe, who was working at Piccadilly at the time. All very pre-Rave Manc.

Laugh were one of the first bands to play so-called indie/dance music when they released 'Sensation Number 1'. They were melodic power pop and good at it. They were great players with cool songs but always seemed to be fated to fall between the cracks somewhere and never get the success that they deserved.

The idea of a Manchester showcase, pre-1989, was fairly meaningless. Since punk, the city had been banging out influential and important groups but there was no scene as such, there was nothing connecting these groups. It was assumed that Manchester would soon run out of groups. It seemed like the punk first generation had given up all its sons and daughters and the next generation had nothing to offer.

Michaelides, though, was a mad enthusiast. He was filling his show with whatever new bands there were out there. He was also the first person to play the Roses on the radio, hammering their demo tape, week-in, week-out, especially the track 'Misery Dictionary'. The reaction had sparked talk of a live session.

There was even talk of recording as a live gig for the radio. The Gallery had been booked under a secret name, The Stoned Bozos, and word was out. But the plan was shelved and the gig put back a few weeks.

Of course being the Roses when they finally trouped up to Piccadilly to record the session they did things their way. Says Pete, 'There was some throwing of chairs in the studio – a pretty reckless thing to do! But it gave it an edge!'

For the session they recorded a newly written thing called 'I Wanna Be Adored', giving the now legendary song its first public hearing, and they played a harder, slightly faster version of 'Heart On The Staves' and the anthemic 'Tell Me'.

The session has gone on to become one of the most sought-after early Roses bootlegs. But what the fans don't realise is that they may not be getting the actual session itself. Recalls Pete, 'The radio session we did live and it went pretty well. Then as we were about to take everything down and go home, the recording engineer came in and said I forgot to press record! He'd put it out live but he hadn't recorded it. We had to do three songs again and it wasn't half as good. They repeated it quite a few times after that, playing these not so good versions and these are the ones on bootlegs. All the versions I've heard are the shit ones. We'd done our work! Trying to be for real the second time just doesn't work.'

About the same time *City Life* did a bigger write-up on the band, again the journalist was Bob Dickinson. Says Pete, 'He called us "deviant Mersey beat" and wrote "Can you like a band that does the finer points of the debate without the psychedelic drugs and the social vision?"'

More local press and the radio session were increasing the band's standing in Manchester. A band was starting to emerge that couldn't be shoe horned into the shiny new Manchester music scene. All their mates and their gang buddies were screaming for a hometown gig. Fuck! they'd even travel and when plans for a gig in nearby Preston were announced then an ideal opportunity presented itself for a show of strength from the Roses' fan posse.

WHITE RIOT, I WANNA RIOT: THE FIRST NORTHERN SHOW

After recording the single, The Stone Roses went back to the rehearsal room and carried on tightening up the band. Back in the Chorlton Spirit recording studios, the band were working hard.

You'd see them going in and out of there all the time. They would rehearse the same song over and over, honing it down, note perfect (curiously the early Oasis would be like this when they rehearsed next door at The Boardwalk, countless versions of 'I Am The Walrus', as Noel disciplined the band to perfection).

The Chorlton rooms were not your usual dank, mouldy, sweat-soaked semen-stained shit-holes – these were carpeted spaces with good PAs inside.

There was some more excitement in the camp when a phone number Ian Brown had picked up on a jaunt in Europe during the summer of '84 turned out to be a good contact. Brown had met a Swedish gig promoter called Andreas Linkaard and blagged the geezer with tales of how big the Roses were. Linkaard told the singer that he would sort out a tour of Sweden for the band.

Ian shoved the number in his back pocket and forgot all about it till one day in early '85 he decided to give it to Jones. 'Ring him up and sort out a Swedish tour,' he gruffly asked his manager.

And indeed Jones had been on the blower and the dates were sorted out. There was talk of a mini tour coming up in March. The band were raring to go, rock'n'fucking roll! A European tour, total gonzoid fun to be had! Jones wasn't so sure.

'I thought it wasn't the best time to go away. We were just building things in Britain and then we would be away for three weeks. I was worried by that.'

But before they went to Sweden there was another British date to play.

The band were booked for their first northern show. It might not have been Manchester but it was close enough. Down at Spirit they told us they were playing Preston which was always a great town for playing gigs in. Our band The Membranes had played there a few months previously and there had been a riot. The bouncers had got on stage and it had really gone off. We had to leave fast. We warned the Roses that it may be a bit lairy.

On 29 March, the Roses were booked into Preston Clouds. This was the outfit's first northern concert and the band's first chance to play to their hometown crowd who were already buzzed up on the reviews and rumours about the Roses' gigs in London.

Everyone was going up to the show. Manchester was buzzing. There was quite a crew going up to Preston.

At the time Clouds was a big disco, the sort of place, where, during the week the straights would groin exchange to the thump clod of bad disco. On Fridays it was alternative, the biggest indie night outside the main cities in the north-west – a gathering of the clans from the Pernod-and-black soaked crowd of indie goth rock to mad fuckers chicken-dancing on the dance floor – looking for sex or kicks, coy kids, mad kids, bored kids and a lot of very drunk kids.

It was a pot boil of good times and staffed by mean bouncers. The bouncers hated the freaks – they always have done – it's a British thing, everywhere you go there are bouncers employed to stop trouble.

Being the first Northern gig it meant that the Roses were going to be taking a huge crew of Mancs up there with them. The last few months had seen the band's legend spread in their hometown. All those London shows and all the press that had come their way had helped. Combined with the fact that they hadn't played a hometown gig intrigued their mates and the hometown pop kids. And the Roses had mates, hundreds of them – they had networked the whole city in their scooter post-punk days.

'I had mates all over the town, not just from where I was from, I was hanging out with kids everywhere,' remembers Brown.

Says Andy Couzens, 'Steve Adge was the leader of the gang and there were all these punks, goths and skins from Manchester there. Steve loved a rumble and that night with all the tension there was plenty of opportunity for that.'

There was going to be some big handy crews going up there, Chris Griffiths and Phil Smith who would eventually be the core of the band's crew went up there with them as well. They ended up pinning the drummer from another Manchester-based band to the wall after spotting him lobbing bottles at the band. Even before they hit the stage it was tense.

During the set just to add to the tension the Roses' gear decided to pack in, typically at a big show – the one where you get to show your mates the power and precision of your band – teething problems crept in.

Andy Couzens turned around aghast, after a lot of crackling, his lead packs in – he can't get anything out of his guitar. It's the ultimate nightmare for anybody in a band; total silence. Howard Jones leaped on to the stage and attempted to repair the lead – only to feel the power of Couzens's shoe leather booting him off again.

'That's why we always called him "the rhino", we would always give him shit and he would always come back for more.'

It takes ten minutes of fumbling around to find another lead. A complete nightmare. When you've taken the stage you want to take it seriously, you want to own that stage – run the building, you want to make it your home turf. A one-minute gap can feel like a lifetime but a ten-minute gap lasts for ever. It's ten minutes of silence and tension, it's ten minutes of a fidgety crowd tanked up on watered-down booze and snide drugs, it was a loose match to the powder keg that has been building up all night.

In the lull in proceedings, in the dreadful silence that all bands fear more than even getting electrocuted on stage, Squire decides to kick into one of their rare covers that they had been knocking out in rehearsal. To the shock of the few sober members of the audience and the amusement of the band he crashed into the space-age Eddie Cochran chug of Sigue Sigue Sputnik's classic 'Love Missile X1-11'.

The London-based glam shock outfit had burned a bright and fast trail in the sky rather like the love missile itself in the video of the song. Sputnik were a brilliant group, a way-over-the-top dress sense – like a skyscraper New York Dolls on angel dust and a pulsating rock'n'roll disco rush of songs had grabbed them a massive deal and a fistful of hype. They had burned bright and they burned fast and then disappeared but their back catalogue is well worth checking.

Their glam riffing was an instant hit with the glam-punk-digging Squire. Halfway through the song they gave up. They had decided to play the song for a laugh after they saw the video for the track on TV when a simultaneous appreciation of the band occurred. It was an unlikely flame in The Stone Roses canon.

Finally a lead is found and the band kicks back into action. The atmosphere is hot and some of the negative energy gets turned into the white heat of adrenaline excitement, but then more problems occur halfway through the set. Pete Garner's bass string snaps. It's the E – the thick one – the one that never breaks – the one that some bass players have on their bass for years, especially if they dig the dead sound. Another yawning gap occurs as the band stand around aghast. It's a total disaster.

Garner fixes on another E string – he's as aware as anyone that the tension is building. His hands shake with adrenalin but the damned string is now on, only now the tuner is bust and he can't get the damn thing into tune. Fuck when will this nightmare end? This is a total fuck up, he tunes by ear and the band kicks off again.

It's stop – start – stop – start.

'Trust A Fox' goes out of time as the band, normally so tight, is knocked clean off its tracks by all the mishaps. They soldier on to 'Tell Me' and then Reni, sensing the frustration and fucked off with all the disasters, kicks his kit over and Andy smashes his guitar up. A pop-art statement that's no big deal when you're getting bank rolled by the fat and rich but a pretty good measure of the desperation of someone on the dole with one guitar.

It's absolute chaos, bottles and fists are flying – the atmosphere is ugly.

'The thing about Ian being a kick boxer is that he can look after himself in those situations. He didn't feel frightened and neither did Andy because Andy is quite rough and tumble but John and Pete in particular are not fighters and they were terrified . . .' recalled Howard.

The Preston riot was the first big myth in the Roses canon. The moment when they realised the power of rock'n'roll, the way it could release some loose energy into a building. It hadn't been pretty but it was a buzz and everyone was talking about it. It also meant that the regional stringers who were reviewing the show for the national music press were left distinctly unhappy with what they had seen.

Says Pete, 'Ro Newton from the *NME* came back-stage and said, "Do you condone any of that violence that has gone on?" She was trying to get Ian to do the "Oh yeah it's a terrible thing", but he wouldn't do it . . . so she went totally against us at that point. I was glad I wasn't in the audience. It was a really lairy load of Mancs who came down . . . fighting with people from Preston. All I remember was that when we were playing there was tension in the air beforehand from a load of people, from another city. We went on and it erupted into a Wild West salon thing . . . It was pretty naughty!'

One piece of Roses history had been made though. Scruffy and falling apart and marred by bad sound and a band just about holding it together – 'I Wanna Be Adored' makes its live début. It's the first notice that from the raucous rock that the Roses were currently dealing with that they were about to write classics that will still be loved years later.

It was a sign that the band were starting to get to grips with dynamics, pacing and great songwriting and it's a sign that they are getting confident enough to create deceptively simple songs.

Two days after the Preston riot, Piccadilly repeated their session and a week later they packed their bags for Sweden. In between on 5 April there was to have been a gig at Oldham Oddies, but the plug was pulled on that. 'It was a good job as well,' someone notes. 'That was ripe for a riot, that was a rough old venue and the Roses were now getting a bit of a reputation.'

Maybe it was a good time to go to Scandinavia.

'WE WERE LIKE ANIMALS': SWEDEN

Sweden was the Roses' Hamburg, that pre-fame stint in Europe that moulded The Beatles, that jaunt away from home in harsh conditions with a string of gigs that tightened the band musically and as a unit. Says Andy, 'It was our first big proper break. It was where we went serious. We made John give up his day job. We got him on the phone in Sweden and made him do it. Ian was signing on and stopped.'

Sweden moulded the Roses. Continues Andy, 'I don't think we played anywhere in Manchester till after we had been to Sweden. Even John Squire reckons that was the best time for the band. That was where the band first became a proper band and gelled. It was our Hamburg really. We were there for a month, but it seemed like forever! In Sweden the gigs varied. It's not difficult to make it big in Stockholm. It's only a small music scene, especially if you're going out every night causing the mayhem we did. We were all over the papers, women chasing after us . . . We didn't know how long we were going for when we went.'

When during his Euro jaunt Ian Brown bragged to Andreas Linkaard, a stranger on a train in Germany about his band, he wasn't really expecting a tour. After all there was no proof that his band even existed let alone that they were massive in the north of England. If massive meant one fucked up gig in Preston and a handful of supports in London then maybe he was telling the truth, but that was the mark of the man, he could be utterly convincing if he needed to be.

Remembers Ian, 'I was in Berlin and met this kid whose friend was a promoter so I told him we were a big group from Manchester. He set up about eight or nine shows. We were living in his flat in Stockholm for about a month. It was great. We got in the daily papers . . .'

But then north Europe back in the mid-Eighties wasn't really like Britain. It was far richer and had far fewer bands – plenty of bored kids who love music and loads of disposable cash. Add to that a traditional interest in just what those rowdy Brits have new in pop.

Whatever Brown said, it had been enough to bend the ear of the Swede who arranged the gigs with the help of his father (who was a concert promoter). After Howard Jones's follow-up call he promised the band a couple of shows that March. It may not have been a whole European tour, in fact it wasn't even enough gigs to justify a trip, but no one was thinking about the details. This was the Roses, right! and this was a band that was going to the top. Music press, London gigs and now a European tour (of sorts).

Smart.

Sod planning, let's rock'n'roll. Recalls Andy, 'We literally threw the gear in the back of my big white Chevy truck. We knew nothing about customs and carnets. We just drove there and got off the boat and drove up to Stockholm . . .'

Here was a chance to go on holiday – bum around Sweden and get the band super tight – this was going to be a great experience.

Two weeks after Preston they set off in Andy's van. Says Howard, 'Me, the band and the roadie, Gluepot Glen, went on the trip. As usual Andy wouldn't let anybody drive his white Chevy – so he drove all the way there! We were all crammed in the back with the gear, thank God they only had small amps! John and Andy had small Roland amps and we all sat on those.'

Like any party of rock'n'roll droogs on their first tour, the band partied hard. It was a triumphant vibe. It always is when you're on the car ferry. The dullest of environments, a floating motorway service station on a ten-hour ride can be turned into a superb jaunt . . . adrenaline, high jinks and a rare drinking spree for the band combined to make this a memorable trip.

Arriving in Sweden the next morning the band were a little worse for wear. Even with spring on the horizon Sweden is a fucking cold place and a desperate place for a vanload of pissed-up musicians with no petrol and a very vague plan of action. It slowly began to occur to them that the tour organisation was a tad suspect. Howard laughs, 'We didn't know what gigs there were, where we were staying, or how much money we were getting. We were due to meet Andreas at 8 o'clock on 9 April at Stockholm Railway Station, that was the only plan that we had! I often wondered what would have happened if he hadn't been there. We would have been fucked! We didn't have his phone number or anything!'

Even getting to Stockholm seemed fraught with danger. 'We arrived in Sweden with no money at all. We needed some Swedish cash to get petrol. We had got off the ferry in Sweden. We couldn't get petrol. We suddenly realised that there's only twenty quid in the kitty! We were stuck in this blizzard with no petrol and the engine turned off and no heat in the van. We could have frozen to death! We sat there in the cold getting colder, hungover from alcohol. And then in the blizzard a car pulls up, it was the first one in an hour. I jumped out and banged on the car window. The Swedish guy inside opens the window. I said, "Look I've got no money, help!" He just pulled his wallet out and just gave it to me. It had about 150 quid in Swedish money in it and he just drove off. I must have looked like some sort of lunatic mugger appearing out of the snow. With a van load of lunatics behind me in the van.'

Eventually they arrived in Stockholm and hooked up with Linkaard. After 24 hours on the road they gratefully dossed down in his flat.

'We drove solid for 24 hours. We got in his flat at 6 o'clock and Andy didn't wake up till 5 o'clock on Tuesday afternoon . . .'

Two days later on 10 April they played their first gig at the Big Bang Club in Linkopping, a Swedish logging town. Ian's mate, Andreas Linkaard, the man on the train, not only booked the shows but had previewed the band in the local papers and eventually reviewed the shows as well – a one-man music biz machine – it was all part of the service Swedish style.

Ian Brown, though, wasn't about to reciprocate this charity – remembering old John Lydon's combative band/audience stance he opened the début show with 'You're all Swedish twats', a phrase that he had managed to pick up in Swedish. That's the Brits abroad for you – taking a massive interest in local customs and languages and learning key phrases to share with the locals. After that scene-setting salvo, the band crashed into 'Mission Impossible'.

Despite Brown's obvious disdain for the audience, the Roses went down well and their resistance to doing encores finally crumbled. When the baying crowd hauled them back to play another song from the set, they, like all young bands, simply didn't have enough material. They had to dip into the set and replay tunes.

The review of the gig, melted down from Swedish and back into English, describes a band buzzing with full confrontational powers. 'Singer Ian runs around like he has rabies,' it also points out that 'he rolls around on the floor'. He also likes The Stone Roses music, 'because it is violent and has a close connection to punk, and then indeed describes the music as psychedelic punk.

Getting hot with the encores, the Roses banged through two the following night at The Olympia in Norrkopping. Spring was in the air, it had been a few months since that début gig and now they were touring abroad and struggling along with life on the road and all that entails.

The band had never encountered anything like this before. Having no idea of tour finances – after all they had stumbled into their tour van with a handful of money cashed from their giros. Now they were in Sweden they were flabbergasted by the high cost of living in Sweden, reeling at having to pay £4.50 for a pint of lager – they were totally skint already. There were plenty of long and frustrating gaps in the touring schedule, time for broke band members to starve and where inter-band tension could thrive.

Fortunately the drummer of the local tour support band, Toxic Toy, was the manager of a local supermarket and stole food for them – even then they fought like dogs over the scraps. It was the real rock bottom tough life – the sort of backs-to-the-wall situation that shapes up a band.

Andy Couzens recounts the struggle. 'On the road it was horrible. We were so broke we became like animals, we fought over food and we fought over money, we took it all out on Howard – he became the band punch-bag.'

The manager had to put up with all kinds of pranks – some of them fairly amusing in a typically dumb, bored, on the road sort of way. Unless you were Howard Jones, who bore the brunt of all the jokes. Says Andy, 'One place where we stayed we took all the slats out of his bed and it collapsed when he went to bed in it . . . I guess it's funny the first night but we did it every night,' laughs Couzens, who also remembers Reni putting slabs of bacon in Jones's bed and the band's desperate thieving for food.

At one point relations between the band and their manager slumped to an all-time low point, with Jones being kicked out of the van in the freezing late-night foul storm of Sweden and left on the roadside.

'It was about minus 20 outside,' says Couzens, 'there was a row as usual over someone sitting on the bench in the van. I opened the door and kicked him out and left him in the middle of nowhere. He had to walk for an hour and a half before he got back to where we were staying.'

The Roses were tasting rock'n'roll stardom in Stockholm. It may have been low-level stardom but they were flouncing round the Stockholm bars, living it up.

The rest of April they swaggered around Stockholm, partying like kings and living like pigs. They also managed to cram a few more gigs travelling out of town to Boras (where they didn't bother to play – 'the venue was a shed,' laughs Pete, 'so we didn't play and then we found out that people travelled for miles to see bands there and it was one of the main venues in Sweden!') and Vastertores and then back to Stockholm on 23 and 25 April for two unlikely shows, one supporting the Go Betweens and one headlining at the Studion.

At one Swedish gig it kicked off and there was a riot – the police came down and arrested the whole crowd. This sounds like ace fun – any rock'n'roll band worth its salt enjoys a good riot and the cops raiding a venue is an adrenalin rush worth a million.

On 30 April they played the last of two shows at Lidingo and then got back on the ferry to the UK. It had been just over three weeks since they came to Sweden. They had done their rock'n'roll rite of passage. Now they were ready to take on the toughest gig of their career so far.

The home town show in Manchester. But where could they play? – after all they were no mere *local band*.

The Swedish experience tightened the band up. It also taught them the rules of the road, the mean and tough existence of living with no money in a strange land. They generally played to few people, they had a run-in with the cops, they fought with each other, they returned to Manchester in late April, worn out but with valuable lessons learned.

FIRST NIGHT IN MANCHESTER!

Before they had gone to Sweden Howard had booked them a gig at Manchester International 1's 800 capacity hall. Not a bad size of venue for a band who had only played a handful of gigs.

The Roses' début hometown gig and they are booked into Manchester International, the venue run by Gareth Evans and the biggest venue a local band is going to get for a showcase event.

A good crowd turned out, pretty guaranteed now, the Preston riot proved that there were quite literally plenty of kicks to be had at a Stone Roses show although the International passed off peacefully. International manager Gareth Evans had been pumping up the attendance, helping out the band that he would eventually end up managing by handing free tickets out around town. One of these tickets ended up in the hands of a young Noel Gallagher who mooched down to the International for his first sighting of The Stone Roses as he related to Jade Gorden.

'It was the Lord Mayor's parade – we have mayors in Manchester, 'cos it's out in the sticks and that – and this fellow walked up to us in the street and gave us a big bunch of tickets. The Stone Roses were playing at International 1 and he said, "Have these and bring all your mates." So we were like, "What the f***'s all that about?" It subsequently turns out that the fellow that handed us the tickets was Gareth Evans, who used to do this quite regularly in town – he used to go round all the people who looked like scallies and he'd give them all tickets.

'So it was a Saturday night and we were round our way with nothing to do, so we all bolted down there. But it was full of students, so we all congregated at the bar. The Roses were in mid-Goth, early scally period then. Ian had a harlequin shirt on and a walking stick and slicked back hair, like Dracula.'

The band were in fine swagger. Their intro tape is the hilarious Tom Jones full on sex anthem, part ironic and part of their background, 'It's Not Unusual'. Brown hit the stage oozing arrogance.

'Hey, why don't you over there come here,' he yells at the crowd. 'You might learn something.' The voice is deadpan, arrogant. Spat out like John Lydon. The band play 'Mission Impossible', 'Adored' purrs in over a chundering Joy Division very Manc slice of gloom, Garner's bass the backbone. 'I Wanna Be Adored' sounds virtually the same as it would do when it becomes the anthem of the baggy generation, a blissed out rolling tune that captures a future summer lost in an ecstatic daze. Back in '85 the context is very different, but the song already sticks out from the rest of the set.

The two guitars are phlanged, heavy effects dominate. The band are in full rock mode. The sound has the punk aggression and anger. It's got an Eighties psychedelic tinge added with the cheapo effects that were flooding the market at the time for guitars. The songs already have the twisting and turning structures that dominate the classic Roses work, drop downs, stop and starts, long build-ups and explosive choruses, hook laden guitar licks and frantic Keith Moon drumming, false endings and a hint of Eighties stadium big soundscapes dominate the sound. There is even the coldness of the sort of soundscape that dominate the parallel goth scene, not that the Roses are even a goth band by any measure.

Brown's vocals have an anger and arrogance. There is that deadpan northern vowel flatness all over them and, typically Manc, no effort or concession is made to singing 'nicely' or 'properly', It's like a celebration of all that is brilliantly unmusical in the northern voice, a 'like it or lump it' attitude that dominate the areas' vocalists from The Fall's Mark Smith through to New Order's Barney. Even the rising star of Morrissey has one of those voices, albeit a lot nicer . . .

The band are tight. That month in Sweden had done them a power of good. Even if they are getting a good reaction Brown is still skulking on the stage. 'Stop talking fucker,' shouts Brown, sounding angry. The anger sparks the song into life and Brown sings the song furiously.

They end with 'Tell Me', Brown spitting: 'This is your last chance to dance, anyone who is anyone already knows it . . .' he takes his long mic lead for a walk into the crowd as the song ends: 'I am the garage flower,' he spits over the 'Thanks for everyone who came, a pitiful display . . .' And he throws his mic on the floor.

Years later Liam Gallagher's sneering ad-libs will have Ian Brown stamped all over them, the manic speed driven Roses singer is already the rough model for all those Nineties Brit vocalists . . .

POST SWEDEN COMEDOWN

After the excitement of The International the band had a few low-key gigs to play. There was the show at Manchester Gallery where on 24 May under the assumed name of the Stone Bozos they had been booked by Howard ostensibly to play a live show for Radio Piccadilly, an idea that never came off in the end. The gig was meant to be secret but, as Pete remembers, it didn't really turn out that way.

'The Gallery put on their flyers the idea that we were going to blow it out but we couldn't in the end and did it anyway. Everyone knew we were doing it. All those people who see us knew each other. Word got out fast amongst friends of mine and Reni's and John's and the scooter lot, the hardcore mob. And Ian knew them all! You get to know fifty guys pretty well if you're into shit like that.'

After a couple of months' break they returned to London on 4 July supporting Dr And The Medics of all people at the unlikely Croydon Underground. It was another weird show, more treading water while waiting for the single to get pressed up.

Says Pete, 'I remembered the girls in Dr And The Medics putting their wigs on in the dressing room and thinking it was pretty funny. It looks like a weird gig now but it was a gig . . . at the time we would play anywhere but not in a pub.'

Just when it seemed the band were wandering around with nowhere to go, Steve Adge came up with another masterstroke, a masterstroke that would truly define the way they operated as a band.

One afternoon in Spirit he asked them if they were up for playing a warehouse party that he was arranging.

THE FIRST WAREHOUSE PARTY

They needed something to give them that mystique, that edge. Something to take them beyond the local band support treadmill. They had a few fans and the thuggish-mate following, they had the numbers, they were worth more than a few mediocre supports.

It was Steve Adge that came up with the idea.

The warehouse parties were a stroke of genius. In 1985, years before the acid house scene made them the norm, the thought of grabbing a warehouse and putting on a party was pretty novel. Inspired by his trip to London The Adge was working out the logistics of an all-nighter in Manchester.

The whole idea was to have a powerful effect on The Stone Roses and the way they operated in the future. It sparked the belief that they could be a powerful pop force and play outside the established music business network. The way that they promoted their own shows at Spike Island and the tent gigs – even the way they took five years out of their lives to make their second album and the low key launch of that record. It could even be said that this staunch outsider policy was their eventual downfall. But when they were burning brightly, their very independence and unpredictability was one of their most powerful strengths.

Every classic band has mythological moments and the Roses have certainly had plenty of these built into their career. Like The Clash and the whole lineage of 'great British bands' they were certainly very astute at peppering their career with defining moments.

Already they had played the classic début gig in London, done their 'Hamburg' in Sweden, had their very own personal 'white riot' in Preston and recorded the first live radio session for years for the local radio station that was getting plenty of street talk in the town. They were working with one of the hippest producers in the UK, a man who had almost single-handedly built up the Factory sound.

Not a bad start and not a bad myth.

The Roses thought special.

And a special band doesn't bother itself with chugging round the local circuit. There are always a mountain of other local bands to clamber over, all mini versions of whatever's going on in the big time. It's a rat race. And a band like the Roses who by now had been playing music for five years in various guises was above all that sort of 'three local bands for one quid' nights.

Nah! They wanted something to suit their new mythic status. They had done some local shows and it just wasn't worth it.

Steve Adge had been meaning to put on a warehouse party for ages. It wasn't going to be easy. A small city means the cops can sniff out some sort of party action pretty damn fast and in the mid Eighties the cops were busting to get involved. After all these were the days of Anderton's barmy army. James Anderton, the iron-fisted, big-bearded God's cop who was already making his presence known in Manchester's club land with raids and strange biblical proclamations, would hardly be a big fan of a gig like this.

The Adge pressed ahead and scored a warehouse in Fairfield Street, one of the grim Victorian back streets peeling off from behind Piccadilly Station.

Being a master blagger Adge phoned British Rail and hired a railway arch on Fairfield Street just behind Piccadilly Station. He didn't exactly tell British Rail what he was hiring the arch for. He paid the money, hired in the PA and kept schtum.

Says Pete, 'He booked it and secretly photocopied directions of how to get there. People bought tickets without knowing how to find it. He'd been to London, buzzing about a warehouse party he'd been to. He'd sold all these tickets which told you to ring Spirit and find out where the gig was. He rented the arch knowing that if they found out about the gig they would pull it. "The only dress restrictions is no blue uniforms" was handwritten on it.'

Just like going to a rave three years later.

Armed with a handwritten scrawl and a hand-drawn map, the punter walked past Piccadilly Station and then the first road past the Star and Garter pub and then down a bleak and uninviting looking alley. It was all very well worked out, a military operation. Manchester's first ever warehouse party was under way.

The tickets screamed 'Blackmail records presents Manchester's first warehouse party', adding 'warehouse 1 the flower show with special guests The Stone Roses'.

The party was on 20 July. After the sound check the band went round to Ian Brown's flat on Charles Barry Crescent in Hulme to hang out and get through the long wait to stage time in a bit more comfort than in a freezing warehouse in the city centre. No one knew what to expect. It had been a cool plan, but would anyone show up?

One of the faces around at the flat was Steve Cressa. 'We met him down in the Berlin club. He was always like a young kid in there, running around being pretty sharp,' recalls Couzens, adding, 'I spoke to him and he sort of joined the gang. He was one of the few people that we let into the rehearsals and hang around. There was always loads of people that wanted to come down and watch us rehearse but we couldn't really allow it. It would have been really horrible.'

For Brown, Cressa was a soul mate and an inspiration as Couzens recalls.

'He was a real culture vulture, always taking things from people, Ian looked to Cressa as some sort of entertainments manager.'

Then wallowing in the rotten hulk of the Hulme flats, Brown and his inner coterie of mates and gang members were living the rock'n'roll dream, careless and carefree. These people knew that they were destined for big things, and tonight's show was just another peg up the ladder.

When they eventually hopped into the car and left for the gig, though, they were apprehensive: maybe no one would show up, maybe no one would find the place.

When they arrived at about eleven o'clock ready to play the show, they were shocked by the number of people wandering around. They sat in the car wondering what the fuck all these people were doing hanging around Fairfield Street – till they realised that they were down for the show.

Inside the pop kids were buying raffle tickets for their beer – another Adge wheeze, who figured that if the police raided the joint then they couldn't get done for selling beer. It was a wheeze that the house generation would pull off at countless warehouse parties themselves three years later. The band sat around ready to play, but unlike a normal gig there was no set time to hit the stage.

They had to wait around till about 1.30 am before they played. Another myth about the party was its 'pumping acid house soundtrack' as attempts have been made to put it up as some part of the eventual rave scene of the late Eighties.

'The music was nothing like that,' remembers Pete. 'It was nothing to do with dance music.'

Mike Joyce from The Smiths was there. 'I saw The Stone Roses at Fairfield Street. There was a danger aspect about going to see them at the time you know "come on let's have a big fight!" . . . The gig was a word of mouth thing.'

The gig starts off with loads of feedback . . . loads of 'woos woo' from Ian Brown . . . Again Reni's amazing drumming powers the set, it's very rock'n'roll sounding . . . not exactly acid house, is it? Ian Brown's vocals are shouty and angry, they sound strong, sound good . . .

The band filed onstage looking cut and mean. Decked out in black, they had hit on yet another image. This one really worked. It gave them a sinister edge, an almost Joy Division angular scowling presence, a dark-hearted street gang look. They looked like a unit. And it was all encapsulated by their frontman with his cropped hair and his pouting scowl.

Brown dead-eyed the audience, his stark staring eyes looking right through the packed throng, a throng buzzing on excitement on the band's post-Preston reputation and gossip, a throng made up of mates from the scooter club days, local music scene drifters and word of mouth junkies. Two girls at the front had home-made Stone Roses shirts on complete with a rose hand-drawn on the back, the band was already building a following – a following a long way from the portals of hip.

After all the electric gunk of guitars being picked up and the loose feedback of gear waiting for action, they crash into their set. The band go berserk. This is not the dosed-up-on-cool Roses of the future but a gang of young punks, full of testosterone and energy. Ian is in and out of the crowd, his long lead clutched in his fist, Andy Couzens zig zags the stage slashing the root chords on his guitar and Pete Garner swings his bass about, his raven black hair flapping in his face, looking studied rock'n'roll cool, copping shapes from Johnny Thunders, Mick Jones and the whole pantheon of post Keef dyed black hair punk rockers.

Reni is stripped down. Topless, his wiry kid frame in a pair of adidas tracksuit bottoms, he's just a blur of sweatshod energy. His drumming is remarkable. The bass drum is so damn constant that it makes a mockery of every other British drummer on the scene, his constant rhythm barrage driving the band on to a different plane.

The early Roses, the so-called 'goth' Roses, are a special band. The raw power and belligerent energy of this set makes you wonder what would have happened if they had ever recorded this tuff stuff properly, with a more sympathetic producer, one that understood the classic British rock'n'roll sound that they were honing down here, a sound that fits into the lineage of prime-time Who, The Clash, the Pistols, a very different line than the one they eventually chose to pursue (although flashes of this fearsome rock'n'roll power would flash up occasionally in the years to come, like their last ever Reni show at Glasgow Green).

This is no early version of a band fumbling around with the keys of greatness but a fully fledged, fully formed band complete with its kick ass sound

There was no real press there, although the City Life man on the spot described them as 'stunning and loud'.

It was this night that the legend of the Roses in Manchester was truly born. The band was talked about on the grapevine for weeks afterwards. They hit the stage and blew the place apart, Couzens remembers certain band members really going for it.

'Reni never took speed normally but that night he was really buzzing. Normally he's fast enough as it is but at this gig he was like a hyper version of Keith Moon.'

For Couzens the warehouse parties were the peak of his career with the band.

'They were the best two gigs that I ever played with them. There was nearly 400 at the second one, it really felt like a major event. It was brilliant,' he enthuses.

For The Stone Roses it was their first Manchester triumph; for Steve

Adge it was something to work on. He would be the warehouse party promoter. He went in to promote A Certain Ratio in similar circumstances soon after and the Roses again on 30 November. From then on he gradually moved into the band's tight inner circle ending up as their virtual manager in later years. That début warehouse party meant a lot to the band. It meant that The Stone Roses had finally arrived in their hometown and on their own terms, setting a precedent for future off-the-wall gigs.

A perfect frame of mind to go in and record their début album.

RECORDING THE DÉBUT ALBUM

During the summer of 1985 The Stone Roses began to record what would have been their début album. The tracks, which eventually came out as *Garage Flower* years later, captured the band at their hard rock peak. Their so-called eponymous début in 1989 was, in many ways, their second album.

Listening to the 1985 tracks years later sees the band's harder edged sounds mixed with Hannett's cold, hard electronic edge. It sounds like a very different band, but there are hints of what's to come, especially since two future classics, 'I Wanna Be Adored' and 'This Is The One', are on the record.

Fortunately it never got the release, leaving them time to put together what would be the eventual début album four years later. An album this early into their career would have seriously debilitated the myth.

Mid-1985 the band were on a high: the warehouse party had been a real buzz, a real indication that the band could take off. It wasn't just a case of bravado and coasting on Brown's inner strength. There was some serious business going down here. Even so, the decision to record the album that August was, in hindsight, a tad hasty.

Howard Jones was keen to get on with the album. The single was ready for release now and they needed something to follow it up with. They booked Strawberry Studios from 3 to 26 August, plenty of time to get their live set down on tape.

First there was another London show at the so-called legendary Marquee, and the Roses, like most bands with a bit of fire in their souls, had managed to get themselves banned. They were added to an ever-lengthening list of outfits blacklisted from the club after Ian ran foul of the management of the Marquee. He had taken his Lydonesque stage act thing a touch too far and shoved a mic stand through a monitor at the front of the stage. Ever confrontational, the wiry front man was rubbing people up the wrong way.

Back in the studio they recorded everything that they had. They put down the live set and a few extras: all the tunes that would eventually end up on the 1996 released *Garage Flower* album: 'Getting Plenty', 'Here It

Comes', 'Trust A Fox', 'Tragic Roundabout', 'All I Want', 'Heart On The Staves', 'I Wanna Be Adored', 'This Is The One', 'Fall', 'So Young', 'Tell Me', 'Just A Little Bit' (formally 'Nowhere Fast') and 'Mission Impossible' (Haddock' is a loose bit of feedback that was never a song and which was run backwards and put on to the *Garage Flower* album by compiler Andy Couzens in the Nineties).

They were getting studio time on the drip. The decision to record with Hannett at this time may well have been a financial one as well as a creative one, Hannett having plenty of down-time from his never-ending sessions in the studio.

Yet it couldn't be helped thinking that they were a band in the studio too early – a small following in London and Manchester under their belts hardly put them in a position to cut their début album. The three weeks they spent in there were three weeks that were quickly telling them the truth.

They weren't ready.

They were also changing as a band. Typically when a band hits the studio to record a set of songs they are already moving in a different direction. Even while they were spending long night hours in Strawberry working away at the tunes the Roses were instinctively moving away from their rockier roots.

Listen to *Garage Flower* now though and the songs sound a lot better than people will lead you to believe. Their anthemic quality, their inherent rousing rock'n'roll power and their inspirational anthemic ruin may never be the sort of music that is ever hip with music biz pundits but there are some great moments going down here.

For some this was the Roses' best period.

There were already flashes of the inspirational redemptive songwriting that would eventually make it the key band a few years down the road. 'I Wanna Be Adored' was recorded by Hannett in its slightly faster heavier version. But it was 'This Is The One', written after Martin Hannett locked the band into the studio and told them to write another tune, that saw the band make the first of several creative leaps forward into the next few years.

'This Is The One' itself was a triumph. Built around Garner's pumping bass line the song, which is still many people's favourite Roses tune, builds and builds till it hits that soaring climatic chorus. It really is the bridge between the two Roses, the anthemic punky version of early years with Ian's exhilarating almost shouted vocal, 'This Is The One' has the same sort of soaring shouting chorus that marks out 'So Young' and 'Tell Me'. It also, even in this earlier slightly faster rockier version, has some of the amazing guitar interplay that would become the hallmark of the classic Roses sound.

Perhaps one of the greatest songs of their career, 'This Is The One' is a surging, monumental anthem. It would be the high point of their set for years and one of the key point tracks of the eventual début album.

Couzens remembers the moment with pride. 'At the time we had two classics, "All I Want" and "I Wanna Be Adored".' Now we had three.'

The band was never happy with the final album. They felt that Martin Hannett had somehow suffocated them and it's true – Reni's drums sound subdued.

This didn't stop Scott Piering, the top indie record plugger in the country, at the time, who was having a lot of success with The Smiths, representing Rough Trade in London, from attempting to set up a deal to release the record. Rough Trade would be involved in negotiations with the band for years, attempting to put out the album until Silvertone came in and eventually snapped them up.

Couzens believes that the album's non-release was a blessing in disguise. 'It's probably a good job that it didn't come out at the time, because like most bands in the studio for the first time, we weren't quite sure of what we were doing. We were all really fucked up, the sessions would go on all night. It was a difficult record to record, but I think that it was worth bringing out years later as a document of what we were like in the early days. But despite the mayhem, Martin taught us one thing – he taught us how to write.'

Martin Hannett's soundscapes have made some bands, enhanced others and merely got in the way of some. Add on to this the fact that the Roses just weren't ready to record an album. The songs were good but the band had only played live about twenty times. They hadn't gelled as a live unit in that deep sort of way that really makes a band. The trip to Sweden may have bonded them as a live unit, it may have been their Hamburg, but The Beatles spent four years going backwards and forward to Hamburg.

Even while they were recording what was their live set they were already moving forward as songwriters. Towards the end of the session they came up with a couple of tunes that pretty well signposted the direction ahead and put the brakes on the album and its release.

While Martin Hannett was sleeping, burnt out by his crazed chemical surge through the rock'n'roll lifestyle, the band took him up on it, they decided to lock themselves into the studio until they came up with something.

According to Couzens, the Roses were about to go into creative overdrive. Whilst '"Here It Comes" came from a riff that John had "Sally Cinnamon" was a riff pinched from The Walker Brothers. We would jam stuff out for hours on end. Reni was crucial for us at this point. He was brilliant to jam with.'

For a gang of south Mancs yobs coming out of football violence, petty hooliganism and punk rock modernism, they were going through big changes. The Roses were now starting to listen to music a long way away from their punk roots, they were checking out stuff that had been pathetically classed as hippy music.

'I wish I had heard Jimi Hendrix earlier, I wish I had heard his records when I was twelve,' Ian Brown once told the press.

There was fear of the classics, like admitting to anything pre-punk was admitting to the total defeat of 1977; whole swathes of great music were ignored. The result of this was a desperation to be modern, resulting in the whole of the Eighties becoming an empty vacuum of naff chancers grabbing the money while most of the talented players were crippled by their fear of selling out and fear of letting the punk straightjacket slip.

'The Jesus And Mary Chain were a really important band in many respects,' Couzens recalls. 'They opened a lot of doors for people like us. Before them you weren't really allowed to listen to loads of groups but they turned people on to a lot of great bands. From that point we started listening to Stones, Beatles, Byrds, Misunderstood and Sixties garage bands. The flavour of our songwriting started to change.'

Crucial changes were afoot in the Roses camp. Pre Hannett they were dealing with rock with a punk edge, it was cruising along one dynamic, and had very little variation in its style. After Hannett, after the Mary Chain, they were dealing with a lot of new flavours, and it was at about this point that Squire's guitar would really start moving to the fore.

They would eventually enter the home strait that saw them create a 'rock classic', a template and a blueprint for a whole generation of bands to follow.

Hot from the studio they played Manchester's Hacienda that August, a gig recorded on 8 track by Martin Hannett who was also mixing the sound that night. The support band was Playne Jayne, a swap gig with the London based psychedelic outfit was played at the Marquee in London the week before.

In the murky acoustics of the Hacienda's muffled hall, Hannett did 'amazing things to the sound of John's guitar', Garner remembers. 'It was brilliant. Everyone was gob smacked.'

Some say that the Roses were in fact no big deal that night. That they were not the sort of band that should be playing that 'temple of cool', the Hacienda. For the band it must have been interesting to hit the stage of the venue that represented most things they didn't like about the Manchester music scene.

At the gig Brown was as wired as ever. At one point he jumped into the crowd for his walkabout. The packed Hacienda dance floor freezes with fear. No one wants to be that near a singer at a gig!

Garner reminisces, 'During the encore Ian jumped in the crowd and everyone went mad. We thought he was gone for, we thought that he was going to get killed!'

'MUCH TOO MUCH, MUCH TOO YOUNG': TELL ME ABOUT 'SO YOUNG'! – SEPTEMBER 1985 THE ROSES RELEASE THEIR FIRST SINGLE

At last after all those years of being in bands the Roses had some vinyl to shout about. The début double 'A' side single produced by Martin Hannett was a two-song salvo that perfectly captured the younger, rockier, speed-driven Roses, a Roses fronted by a manic, crop-haired, paisley-shirted madman who would dive into the crowd with his mic on a long lead trying to get a reaction, trying to get a confrontation.

You can hear it on these tunes. The songs tap into one of those Manchester sounds that is never really written about, the phlanged guitar, rock rhythm raw power that made and still makes The Chameleons one of the city's most popular bands. It's a sound that younger bands like Puressence would pick up on years later.

'So Young' (originally titled 'Misery Dictionary', the title changed to avoid confusion with The Smiths'-style titles and also to hook into the more upbeat rabble-rousing nature of the song) is Brown shouting 'c'mon get up!' from his Hulme balcony at the dope-stained bohemian community. Brown was appalled by the wasting away culture in Hulme. It grated against his work ethic (although, it must be said, it's a charge that could easily be levelled against the Roses themselves in years to come!).

Says Ian, 'Mainly the lyrics are about personal experiences, about my friends or about how I feel. The single "So Young" is about when I lived in Hulme, everyone who lived there seemed to think it was great to stay in bed until tea time. It's just a waste of life. I'm saying you've got to get out of bed today. They could be doing something more worthwhile with their time.'

It's unfair to say that Hulme was an area where people did nothing with their lives. Meshed in with the drug culture and the twenty-four-hour-party-people scene there was a lot of creativity, a lot of cutting-edge ideas, it was, and to a certain extent still is, the area that gives Manchester a rare bohemian flavour.

But the (mostly) anti-drug sentiments of the song are still something that Brown will go on about today, years later.

'Tell Me, is Brown adopting his Lydonesque drop-dead stare and co-opting the Pistols frontman's lyrical arrogance. With its 'you can't tell me anything' and 'I love only me' howls, it could be something off Lydon's first Public Image album, that same sort of stark cold belligerence that was so important for both Brown and Lydon to survive.

Thin Line now moved into hyper drive. With the band in the studio recording the album they whacked out the début single, 'So Young'/'Tell Me'.

On 9 September the single finally came out on 12 inch only. As a weird precursor to what would happen in the future, The Happy Mondays also released their début single, the 12 inch of 'Delightful' on the same day. At the time, though, both bands were bands out of their time. Eventually their careers would tie together for the two-pronged attack on the UK music scene.

It seemed a touch early to be putting out records. Perhaps Thin Line were hoping to consolidate the local following, it was certainly a tough call if they were aiming at the charts. The Roses were one of those bands that would fall between two stools, too polished and too rock for the indie sector and too raw for the mainstream. They were too northern and also too rock for the music press and there was very little potential radio play outside the playlist in the mid Eighties.

In effect they would have to rely on a strong live following to sell a single, and this they didn't have outside Manchester. It was too early, maybe Thin Line thought they could bludgeon the band through, maybe use the single to get the gigs to build up the live following.

The first review of the record was in local music paper *Muze* by Paula Greenwood. At the time Paula was a big fan of the Roses and would support them in local papers. She eventually moved on from journalism and set up Playtime Records, putting out the first records from The Inspiral Carpets and New Fast Automatic Daffodils. Armed with a keen pair of A&R ears, she was hot to the Roses' hustle, writing, 'Every gig is an event and this, the long awaited début single, is big, loud and beautiful. They have certainly matured since their demo and with the help of Martin Hannett they have become smooth and hard.'

They found themselves at number two in the Piccadilly charts. Piccadilly was the main indie guitar record shop in town. Always a key player in building up local bands, Piccadilly's enthusiasm in pushing groups from the turf had been the key to many band's ascendancy.

The demo had been getting played hard in clubs so it was no surprise that the single did likewise. It certainly did well locally, being one of the top selling records in Piccadilly records.

Zigzag commented that the record 'had a good production that brings the best from a tested song', while *City Life* claimed that it was 'very unManchester'. The Roses, now, quite definitely had a strong local following in a city that traditionally supported its homegrown bands enthusiastically.

That was not the problem, the problem was getting known nationally, an idiosyncratic well-supported local scene like Manchester was great for creating new bands but a band could get stuck ending up like James, The Chameleons and a host of other groups, hometown superstars with little fan base south of the Mersey.

If the single meant nothing on a national scale, it sold strongly locally and consolidated their local mini fan base. Compared to The Smiths it was nothing, but the Roses were now off the mark.

A couple of weeks later Paula Greenwood interviewed the band in *Muze*. Ian was in full Ali-inspired flow – firing off quotes with an arrogance and self belief way beyond the band's current size. He claimed that the reason that the band had played comparatively few gigs in Manchester was that venues were 'too small-time' and, fired up by the warehouse shows, that they were into playing gigs that had 'no bouncers, no law – everyone can have a good time'.

He still felt no fear of the audiences, preferring to see 'rows of blank faces or jaws dropping when we go berserk'. He finished with 'we just want to do it and do it big and once it's done it's done.' Telling words for the future – especially underlined with the following quote: 'We'll either be massive or fizzle out, there is no in-between for this band.' Brown was obviously already working to his own itinerary.

The Mondays' 'Delightful' was confusing people even more and even with the backing of the much bigger Factory label, it was hardly flying out. The Mondays were currently too raw and too strange while the Roses had yet to fuse their rock with the molten melodies that would get them the lift off. The two bands, though, at the time were aware of each other. Cressa even went as far as bringing Mondays' bassman Paul Ryder to see a Roses show in Liverpool.

The Mondays were the real deal, they didn't give a toss about notions like credibility. They were out to get what they could. They looked rough as fuck, they didn't have any sort of conventional pop look. At the time they looked like a mad bunch of fucked-up thieves more than a band, but they played weird left-field rock with a fab funky bounce, mainly provided by Paul Ryder's Northern Soul fused bass lines. The surrealism was punched in by Shaun Ryder's brilliant stream-of-unconsciousness lyrics.

Paul Ryder definitely left an impression on Pete Garner.

'I knew he was a shit-hot bass player. Everyone in Manchester was raving about him being the best thing in the Mondays. We thought that we were going to be the band that broke out of Manchester and yet here was this other band that really looked like they were going to do it as well.' Garner looks up. 'After we heard the Mondays we knew that there we were not going to be alone.'

The band's demeanour, their whole pimp roll, easy-rolling natural vibe was to have a big effect on the Roses who were still trussed up in their leather-and-rock look.

Just two days after the single was released on 11 September, they were back down in London playing a launch party for Dennis Morris who was releasing a photo book of The Sex Pistols at the Embassy club in London supporting The Chiefs Of Relief. The Chiefs featured the former guitar player from Bow Wow Wow, the late Mathew Ashman, and, on drums, the legendary ex Pistol, Paul Cook, whom the Roses, being avowed Pistols fans, were pretty excited to meet. It was, according to Garner, a disappointment.

'He was like a dull brickie. He had no aura at all,' remembers Garner.

On 26 October the band took yet another trip down to London to play another show in the capital. This time they played their 23rd gig at a rock week at the Riverside studios.

The week of gigs featured headliners like Mighty Lemon Drops, The Membranes, The Shop Assistants. It was a smattering of the available 'underground' talent, bands whose confidence was already drained by the post punk scene. It would be a few years yet before anyone would make it really big again. In these times no. 41 in the charts was where hot new bands seemed to get jammed while the crappy Eighties jamboree raged all around them.

The Jesus And Mary Chain were about as big as you were going to get if you had some sort of attitude that spilled over into the music. A couple of bands like New Order and The Smiths had taken a more pure pop approach and had been awarded Top Ten hits, apart from that it was a scramble, it was a frustrating time.

At the Riverside the Roses supported That Petrol Emotion, the Irish band that was dealing some great pop coupled with sharp political comment, especially on the Irish question. First on were Banjo Fury. Apart from the Petrols the whole night was played out to a fairly bemused crowd at The Riverside.

They copped another review in the *Melody Maker*. It was getting pretty clear that, apart from Gary Johnson, no one was really going for the band in a big way. The *Melody Maker* sharpened its claws and went in, Ian Brown copping the brunt of the attack.

'What's this whirling torso, an undiplomatic spunky splash of energy . . .' It also talked about the 'wretched state of the dire dirges'.

Back home it was a different matter. Manchester University main hall holds about 800 and is the first serious port of call for any band that is attempting to break out. When the band rolled up in their van they were surprised to see grateful students help carry the gear into the venue for them. This was the first time this had happened, strangers carrying the gear, the most hated chore in rock'n'roll and some other schmucks were doing it. This was a pretty neat taste of the big time.

In Manchester, the word of mouth was out – here was a tight new rock band with this cool lead singer. It was time to cash in on this new support and on 22 November they played the main hall of Manchester University. Garner was surprised by the reaction.

'It was the first gig where we got out of the van and people carried our gear in for us. There were loads of students helping us to carry our stuff in. Slim was roadying for us with Gluepot Glen. It was an easy day for them.'

Slim was something of a legend on the Manchester scene. A big fuck off guy, Slim has been crewing for bands for years. Garner knew him back from his school days.

'Slim battered me at school when I was in the second year in the playground,' Garner recounts. 'You just didn't wander into the big kids' playground but we were playing football and our ball went in there. I went in and got it. Just when I put my foot on the ball this fat guy ran up to me and smacked me in the face and I went straight down. After that, years later, I saw him at loads of punk gigs,' he recalls, adding, 'He was a trouble-maker! He was always standing on the balcony gobbing on people!'

Support that night were The Brigade, ironically a Clash style band reminiscent of The Patrol. They seemed to be on the circuit for years before fizzling out.

Buzzing from the début single and the university show, they played another warehouse party on 30 November.

People at the show remember that the warehouse was massive and that it was really cold. This time the Roses told British Rail that they were filming a video.

'It was at a different place . . . fucking freezing . . . We hired a massive room. It was not as intimate as the first one, there was a dead high ceiling. I remember doing the soundcheck with gloves on. We played these songs all day every day. It wasn't a big deal that Ian didn't go to soundcheck. Andy sang in the soundcheck. I've got that on video, that's funny!' recalls Pete.

This time there were even more people at the show than the one before. It was obvious that as far as Manchester were concerned the Roses were getting to be a cool band to be into. The two warehouse parties had served the band well. They gave them an outlaw edge, an underground dangerous vibe, an added hipness that took them out beyond the ruck of local bands slogging around the circuit.

Kevin Cummings, the fast-rising local photographer who would eventually take some of the classic Roses shots, took pictures that night.

The set also featured a new song, the melodic jangling 'Boy On A Pedestal', a tune pointing the band in a different direction. Unfortunately the song had only been written the day before and predictably fell apart.

The gig was reviewed by local face and DJ, Auss, who has been a fringe member of the Manchester scene for years DJing and hanging out. He noted that the gig was the first time for a long time that people had been seen to be enjoying themselves. Garner remembers things a touch more earthily.

'There was some woman pissing in the street,' he recalls.

The set hung together well, despite the logistical difficulties in putting a show on in such awkward circumstances. It wasn't until 'Getting Plenty' that the generator which had been humming almost as loud as the band's set, blew up ending the gig. Karen Ablaze who put together the cool *Ablaze* fanzine and was one of the eventual key players in the inspirational Riot Grrrl scene, was there.

'I remember at the end of the show Reni leant back and smashed the window at the back of the warehouse. It was really freezing. The band were great that night, it was the first time that I saw them. They were much better in the early days. I really liked the sort of stuff that they were doing then, it was much more soulful, it was much more them.'

In November the *NME* finally reviewed the single. Mat Snow weighed in with 'the great lost Martin Hannett produced this and a right silk purse it is too, pure post-punk apocalypse, even that won't persuade me to play it again.'

Bob Dickinson followed this up with a 28 November review in *City Life*. 'The sound leaps violently out, The Stone Roses are truly teenage,' he raged, despite the fact most of the band were now in their very early twenties. He also noted that they were 'pretty self confident.'

In the home city their only true rivals on the non-Factory, more rock-based scene were The Chameleons, again a hard-rock-fused-with psyche-delic outfit with a fast building local following who would always have a problem consolidating it around the rest of the country. Recently The Chameleons had been picked up by Geffen Records and were looking further afield. Although they would never have the mass success of the Roses they would retain a huge and loyal local following year after their demise, even up to the present day.

There is even a weird story that still goes round that Geffen was sent over to Manchester to sign this new stadium rock band that's doing the rounds in the city. The A&R man on the track of the Roses stumbled across The Chameleons instead and signed them. If true, the deal would have been a disaster for the Roses. They just were not quite ready yet for the big time. Some changes were going to have to be made.

As 1985 drew to an end, and 1986 kicked off the Roses entered a period of inertia. The first eighteen months had been a buzz, they seem to be heading somewhere, but the album was just not right. Already they weren't happy with Howard's management. Something was going to have to give.

SMEARED! THE GRAFFITI CONTROVERSY

Record Collector: 'There's also the famous story about you spraying "Stone Roses" all around the city. What's the true story?'

Ian Brown: 'Me and Reni decided we'd been ignored for long enough. We'll cover the city with "Stone Roses". So we sprayed everywhere at about seven/eight o'clock at night. Reni was spraying the front of a library and there was a copper stood just around the corner – but the copper couldn't see him!'

In fact the band's next move was to mire them in a controversy that hung round their necks for years. The first time that the Roses came to most people's attention in Manchester was with the dubious 'controversial' and much copied graffiti campaign. It gave a stick to those that wanted to beat them and cemented their thuggish image with the scene hipsters.

All the way from Burton Road in Didsbury to the city centre and, especially on the walls of the circular library building, their name was sprayed. The band always claimed that it was an over-zealous fan while graffiti experts pointed out that the graffiti went all the way from their current bedsit HQ in West Didsbury and along the bus route into town.

Whatever and whoever, someone seemed to have graffitied the whole city.

Looking back years later, Couzens is hardly ashamed of the campaign. 'Ian and Reni did the graffiti. We used to go and watch Seventeen who were a great power pop mod band who eventually became The Alarm and wherever they went they sprayed their name. We thought that this was a really cool idea.'

This version of events is still disputed by others close to the band. 'It was a fucking fan that did it right, for fuck's sake, they were not that sort of band,' gruffly recalls an unnamed associate.

The campaign by the band or 'over-zealous fan' had a dual effect on the band's Manchester profile. It made them instantly notorious. It pissed off the bookish wing of the Manchester scene – like The Smiths-loving south siders.

The band were instantly ostracised by *City Life* and the *Manchester Evening News*; even the local Granada TV news felt obliged to jump on the self-righteous bandwagon. If anything it helped to make them feel more like romantic rebel outsiders and may have affected the way that they perceived the press and media for years to come.

Muze magazine was one of the first to lay into the band, screaming 'It's own up time, who's responsible for the graffiti? The band themselves deny involvement because "it's too tacky",' they screeched.

It seemed as if everyone on the city's music scene was outraged – a combination of sudden civic pride and an inevitable backlash on the spotty new brats on the block was biting deep. It's hardly like Manchester is the world's most beautiful city. The city trades off its pop heritage. The same self-righteous denouncers of the graffiti were the very ones living in the shadows of the bands that were using any means necessary to project themselves on to the public.

Couzens is still amused at the repercussions of the campaign. 'It finished us off in Manchester. We could get no gigs, no press. Tony Wilson was slagging us off and made moves to make sure that we couldn't do anything. We tried for a rehearsal room at the Boardwalk and they wouldn't let us in there as well. We were outsiders, we had total notoriety.'

The graffiti made the front pages of the *Manchester Evening News* and the letters pages were filled with annoyed missives. In one way the spray painting had worked – it had made the Roses notorious.

The Roses were the talking point of a city music scene suddenly overcome with self-righteousness. Graffiti and rock'n'roll are hardly new bedfellows. Most band's music is aural graffiti and all the better for it. Pop is not meant to be respectable. At the time Norman Tebbitt was handing out awards at pop ceremonies and the Eighties, post Live Aid, saw pop become horribly sanitised.

It was a burning controversy that took years to calm down. While everyone raged and got on their high horses Pete Garner took a trip to town with his mother. He passed some of the spray can work and cringed with embarrassment waiting for the inevitable dusting down, but was surprised at her reaction.

'Someone has sprayed your band's name on the wall over there,' she gushed in awe, adding, 'You must be getting famous.'

And even in the daft world of rock'n'roll Mum knows best.

1986

BOYS SEEKING A PEDESTAL: THE ROSES IN LIMBO

The inertia built up in 1984/85 seemed to have dissipated. Time for a change. A new broom. A new direction. The album was pissing them off, they felt that they had better songs, it had inspired them to retreat to the rehearsal room where they had come up with 'Sally Cinnamon', a big jump forward in their capabilities. Pure shining pop, 'Cinnamon' opened the door to a new Roses.

Says Ian, 'We wanted to move as far away from "So Young" as possible.'

Howard Jones was now out of the picture. Says Andy, 'We weren't sure what he was doing. He had brought in Tim Oliver to help out. We didn't even know who was managing us.'

Jones had got Rough Trade interested in releasing the album, which could have been a good break. Rough Trade certainly had the clout to make something of the record. The main problem was the record itself. The Roses had no interest in it any more. They knew they were going somewhere else musically. So all plans were shelved, plans that included the album and the two follow-up singles to 'So Young' – 'I Wanna Be Adored' (which had even gone as far as having a sleeve designed for it by John Squire, a sleeve that would eventually be used for the cover of *Garage Flower*) and the single after that, 'This Is The One'.

So it was all change. The first of many in a chaotic eighteen months. First Jones left the band. They had pulled the brakes on. Then the Roses scrapped the album. The band's swagger needed a proper soundtrack, a new soundtrack. They could do better than this.

They sat and listened to the tapes. There was something not quite right. They felt that they were in the studio recording an album far too early into their career. It could still have come out but they binned it. The début album, the Roses's eventual début album to all intents and purposes, is their second album. No wonder it sounded so accomplished! For a band stuck on the dole to scrap an album takes some discipline. Takes some guts. But they were perfectionists.

They had done something very rare in bands. They had put their foot down. They turned their back on the record deal, the album, the fucking schedule, the deadline, the whole sodding career inertia thing.

Not for the first time in their career The Stone Roses took matters into their own hands. Instead of letting the gradual groundswell of public and industry support push them into the mainstream they stopped in their tracks.

It was time for some proper songwriting. Time to let the music really talk. Instead of getting bogged down in gigs they retreated to the rehearsal room, disappeared from the scene and started writing songs. Proper songs.

They changed the way that they wrote – no more working up riffs and making them into songs. They started to relearn the whole creative process and learned how to write songs.

This also saw a slight shift in the band politic. Instead of John or Andy throwing riffs into the rehearsal room and Ian huddled in the corner putting his words to them, Ian and John worked together on the tunes round at John's flat.

Listening to a rehearsal tape from March 1986 you can hear a different band beginning to emerge from the 1985 one. The guitars are tuned down. They are janglier. More melodic. More thought out. There are dynamics getting applied. Quiet bits. Loud bits. Bits where Ian Brown can sing instead of shout. A bit of tension and then a chorus. Melody is the key. There is less thrashing and more finesse. Reni is still a power-house but the complex song structures are letting him toy with the rhythms even more.

In these tunes you can pretty well hear the classic Roses sound getting put together. Here is the rough template finally being moulded, the sound of '89 is getting stumbled on early in 1986 in Spirit recording studios in city centre, Manchester.

By the time they got back on the boards to play a gig on March 5 after a break of four months they were a different band. Back on stage at the King George's Hall in Blackburn they were faced with a rather bored crowd waiting for Paul Cook and Matthew Ashman (ex Bow Wow Wow)'s Chiefs Of Relief to come on stage. That night they débuted new songs 'Sally Cinnamon' and 'All Across The Sands' and an innocuous song with a typically dark lyric.

The 'crowd' though were in no mood for such double-edged songs and stood there bored and listless. The Preston Riot was in no danger of getting repeated here.

The band had had enough of the crowd and as a wind up the Roses dredged up their Sigue Sigue Sputnik cover from Preston Clouds the year before. This time they played 'Love Missile' four times in a row and left the stage snickering.

Sweet revenge.

It had been a long time since the Roses had done anything. It is a tough time for a band when the initial promise seems to fade. The surge of gigs, press and music biz attention sometimes comes to nothing – at this point many bands fold. They see the dream is an empty dream, that there is nothing worth pursuing and pack it all in, going back to their normal lives.

The Stone Roses were already dug in too deep to believe this. There was a massive emotional investment to the gang and they really did believe that they were going to get somewhere.

'So Young' had hardly set the world alight. Typically for a new Manchester band it had sold well in the hometown and done nothing anywhere else. Manchester was supporting its bands like football teams.

There was already a big Manchester scene early in 1986. It was starting to get its own look, its own idea of what it was about. The Hacienda, although nearly always empty, was looked on with pride. It was a hell of a prestigious club to have in a city of this size. There were Manchester bands like The Smiths and New Order who were big ground-breaking bands, the city was hip and there was a feeling in the grass roots of the city that there was something else going to break.

But the Mondays and the Roses? You have to be kidding mate! The Mondays were a bunch of hooligans that had puzzled everyone by blagging a deal with Factory. They sold no records at all and their prospects of a breakthrough looked very dim. And the Roses – even worse! They were just a rock band with a penchant for spraying buildings with graffiti. Just thugs who would dash off bad-tempered letters if journalists slagged them off. Journalists like Paul Lloyd who reviewed them for the Poly arts mag *Pulp* and received a hatful of hate mail from Ian Brown as a result of a rather negative piece.

The pundit's money at the time was on a whole host of no-mark outfits. Everyone was looking for the new Smiths. It would take acid house, ecstasy and the end of the student dominance of the city's music scene to mark the next key shift and that was a good few years off yet.

It had been eighteen months since their *Sounds* feature, but without a press agent they hadn't really followed this up. At the time bands had no idea of the press bustle that characterises the current scene. Bands in the modern era know the whole system and also go with the dictates of the system. At the time, though, bands would be shocked at getting in the papers and then would disappear for ages, bemused at their lucky break.

On 25 March they played their first Midlands gig at Warwick University supporting Love And Rockets, the remnants of ultimate goth band, Bauhaus, who were playing in a home town gig and would eventually go on to have a number two hit in the States.

Recalls Pete, 'I was a big Bauhaus fan but they were arseholes. Would not talk to any of us. They didn't want to associate with us. That was their third band in the spotlight. We must have been like little kids to them.'

By now, the Roses were always ending the set with 'This Is The One' instead of 'Tell Me'. This brilliant song was an effective and all defining full stop on a set that was slowly but surely moving away from the rock kernel of its roots and into something more flowery and more melodic. Slowly evolving, moving on up towards the sugar spun pop . . . All they needed now was some sort of human dynamo to point this new pop nous in the right direction.

Maybe this ad that someone had spotted in the paper from a local manager looking for a band could be the answer. It was from the bloke that ran the International 1. He must know some people.

ENTER GARETH EVANS

Sometimes a band's manager is a quiet figure, plotting and scheming away, someone like Oasis's Marcus Russell with his low-key approach, doing the deals and just getting on with the business. And sometimes the band's manager is a larger-than-life character who just can't help getting to be almost as famous as his charges.

Gareth Evans is such an ebullient character, and while the Roses were going through their initial growing pains he was making his own moves on the city's music scene.

In the mid 1980s, along with business partner Matthew Cummings, he bought up two venues on the south side of the city – the International 1, a former cabaret venue where the likes of The Glitter Band could be found flailing away, and the International 2, a huge barn of a venue which had been an Irish drinking bar for several years.

Swiftly the two clubs were turned into rock venues and a whole host of bands would pass through their doors. They were archetypical rock spaces: plastic glasses, beer-stained floors, shabby interiors and great nights of cool bands. The International 1 was the smaller of the two, aimed at bands that were coming through, while 2 was for more established stars chugging around the circuit.

At the International 1 Evans would often be on the door letting in local musicians for free and stopping journalists from getting in just for fun. It was here that one night he stopped Yasmin le Bon from getting in to see Duran Duran play a low-key secret gig. 'I don't care who you are, luv, get to the back of the queue,' he snapped at her. It was the measure of the man, no airs and graces, and no matter how loaded he became he would always travel second-class on the train, hating the whole concept of first-class.

Evans was a hustler, looking out for the main chance, but he also lived rock'n'roll, and when he finally hooked up with the Roses he totally believed in the band, using his money and the power of the Internationals to back them to the hilt.

It was a crucial coupling and one that really helped the band break through.

Evans's vision was one that didn't fit easily into the late 1980s. Here was a man who thought that anything was possible. He believed that a guitar pop band could take centre stage in Britain again, and that The Stone Roses could be as big as The Rolling Stones.

He saw no problems, no obstacles, and he managed the band the old-fashioned way. When they played their early shows at the International he gave away countless tickets to fill venues up, this starting to build up a mass street following in Manchester.

He stood in the garden of a local journalist while he typed out a feature on the group for *Sounds*, making sure that it would get done. He rang up the paper's editor promising him a holiday if he printed the article.

His belief was total.

He was old-school and he disregarded the polite rules of combat that infested the music scene. He thought that there was no reason for the same feature to be printed for the *NME* once it had been in *Sounds*. Evans needed guiding towards press agents, and was given the numbers of Hall Or Nothing and Jeff Barrett, the two best press agents in the UK. He ended up with the former.

There was no such word as 'can't' in the Evans canon. He bulldozed his way through, making street pop a spectacle again. Evans' belief coupled with the Roses' self-belief propelled the band and British pop into a new era. The whole Oasis schtick has its seeds here.

And how did the Roses hook up with the garrulous impresario?

It was as banal as a simple small ad.

'We saw an ad saying that they were looking for demos of new bands and the address was for the International. So we drove down there and burst into his office and demanded a meeting,' says Andy Couzens.

The Roses' impetuousness must have impressed Evans, a man who would have probably done the same thing in the same circumstances.

It may have been a measure of their desperation though, as they had lost interest in the Hannett album and relations with Howard Jones were getting strained. 'We didn't think that Howard was up to the job. We argued with his ideas. We never signed a contract with him; he never got his dollars out of it.'

The Roses felt that they weren't really getting anywhere and needed a new input, a new push. In a situation like this it's either change the band or change the manager.

For the time being they would settle for the latter.

The office at the back of the International was really a narrow corridor with a tiny room at the end. When the Roses entered it must have been quite a sight, the arch hustler and the young band crammed into a tight space, each party wary but doing the hard sell, as Garner remembers: 'We launched into a massive spiel at him. We were dead cocky. "You will be our manager," we told him.'

In some ways it was an odd decision, since they had never really met him before. They were impressed by Evans' quite large control of the Manchester music scene, as with two venues outside the Factory axis he was getting pretty well known by the bands.

Evans instantly clicked that this was a band that he could work with. He decided to show them some of his hard-sell skills. At the time he was selling novelty underpants.

'He told us that he could sell anything to anybody. He was just going through this spiel when he dropped his pants and showed us his underwear; he told us that he was selling those as well. He tried to sell us a pair of pants!' says Pete Garner.

Maybe they didn't buy his pants but they bought his spiel. 'It was at that moment that we knew that he was the right man for the job,' adds Garner.

The band also liked the fact that they could get into his club for free and get complimentary drinks at the bar all night. This was more like it, the rock'n'roll lifestyle on the dole.

Ever the flash man, Evans took the starving band out to a spaghetti house a week later and signed the management deal with them in front of Paula Greenwood, the still loyal journalist.

They screeched down Burton Road in West Didsbury in two flash cars, trying to get a local journalist to join them. It was all high spirits and hi-jinx at that point, and the meal ended up with them throwing spaghetti around the restaurant.

When Evans produced the contract that would later cause so much grief, he stated that he would sign them for ten years to which the band joked, 'Make it twenty, Gareth!'

Evans looked up, and without a trace of irony he stared back at them. 'Can I?' he answered.

RIOT PART 2! THE DUBLIN DISASTER AND THE SIMMERING TENSION BETWEEN GARETH AND ANDY

With Gareth at the helm The Roses now slowly entered a new phase. They moved rehearsal rooms from the cramped Spirit rooms to the stage at International 1. A proper full-on stage to get it together. Bliss! No wonder they started to sound like a big band! With a full PA to work their tunes through they further developed their subtleties in their daily rehearsal regime. Says Pete, 'We would rehearse every day. Well you would wouldn't you? Its your job.'

Ian and John were starting to bring proper songs in. The band were moving. Out of everyone's faces and in the rehearsal room. Lying low.

Behind the scenes Gareth was in hyper-drive. Constant phone calls to record labels and local media. This was a one man campaign. A promotional whirlwind.

The Roses demo tapes were getting mailed out everywhere. The follow-up phone calls were raining in, a blitz of enthusiasm and self-belief that would even take the band aback!

And yet there were still no takers. The Roses were still stuck in limboland. And the band's internal dynamic was also beginning to change. Gareth was meddling with the chemistry. He had his own idea of how this band worked. And to him it was the Squire/Brown axis.

Says Andy, 'Me and Gareth never got on. We had screaming rows. He would go on at me about loads of things. It was starting to get a bit frustrating.'

The tensions were beginning to show. Evans was concentrating on Squire and Brown.

And there were mutterings in rehearsals. The two wings of the band had always been Ian Brown and Andy Couzens on one side and Reni and John Squire on the other. Pete Garner, being the most amiable, was the mediator in the middle.

The first cracks had begun when Ian and John had started to draw together, becoming the band's inner-core. Andy instantly felt frozen out; he wasn't a no-hoper tagging along for the ride. He could write tunes and organise a band as well and he would later prove this when he formed The High who nearly made it themselves a few years later. Couzens was in the Brian Jones boat, the talented outsider.

As Brown and Squire gelled creatively the die was cast. All the great bands, the pair reasoned, had a song-writing duo at the core. Lennon and McCartney, Jagger and Richards, Strummer and Jones, it was all two-man songwriting teams playing off each other. That was at the core of all great pop, so Ian and John too were a team.

The Roses now had a songwriting machine and no space for outsiders. Up until now things had been cool; they would still split the money five ways. After all they were still mates and they still believed in equality and all that.

But the main two songwriters were beginning to see things differently – they felt they did all the work, they wrote all the material. They were in effect the band. It's the conundrum that has ripped apart many great bands. There are no easy answers and both methods of splitting the royalties have good arguments going for them.

The only way is to come clean and sort it out before the big money comes in, avoiding the day when the royalty cheques arrive, which is usually the day when most people find out that while they continue to sign on, the singer is moving down south to his fat-cat mansion.

Early that summer Brown and Squire decided that they would come clean and tell the rest of the band where they stood.

On the day Ian and John walked into the studio, the rest of the band could instantly tell that there was something going on. The pair of them made the announcement that as things were getting serious and that since they wrote all the songs they would not only take the credits on the record, they would take the money.

The rest of the band would earn mechanical royalties etc but the bulk of the band's money would be going to the main pair and that, as the songwriters realised, was the largest proposition of money that any band ever earns.

The rest of the group were agast, Andy Couzens and Reni left instantly. The Roses as a gang was torn apart. They had always been more than just about making money – they were a gang, a united front, they were there for each other or so they had thought. It was a salutary lesson, but the ever loyal Garner decided to stick it out with what was left of the group.

Couzens was livid, but Reni, though, realised that this was the best band he was ever likely to get in and returned. Says Andy, 'The argument at that point was about songwriting royalties. But at first it was more the aesthetic thing of having two names on the labels like Lennon/ McCartney etc. It looked good. But the reason I eventually left the band had nothing to do with money.'

The remaining outfit was relieved, as you could be the best songwriting duo in the world but without a drummer, and especially one of Reni's clout and class, you were never going to get above the soul destroying bog circuit. The fact that Reni was also starting to provide all of the harmonies on the band's songs and had the sweet voice of an angel had not gone unnoticed by his colleagues.

The band returned to some sort of normality but as an effective unit they were shattered. It could never be the same again.

They still had some gigs pencilled in, including a trip to Ireland for a gig that Gareth had booked within twenty four hours on May 31st.

It wasn't all doom and gloom as they boarded the ferry to Dublin. For Manchester bands, even ones without the mythologised Irish heritage (and the Roses were, on the whole, as English as you could get), there was always something exciting about playing Dublin.

The city had a vaguely exotic air of a hip and happening bohemian town – it was also rough as fuck with some of the meanest estates this side of

Europe, but that meant nothing after living in Manchester.

The place the Roses were to play was McOnagles, a subterranean city-centre dive with a roof that looked like it was spat-out papier mache. A small venue, it was also the spot that most biggish touring bands made their Irish début. Normally a prestigious gig, someone had ballsed up big-time when the Roses arrived.

In their early mythology this was always looked on as the most bizarre gig that they would ever play. They had been booked on a heavy rock night.

The soundcheck went swimmingly and they went for a walk around the summertime Dublin streets, which is always a great experience, full of life and good vibes often missing from the beat at home. When they returned to the venue they were appalled to find it packed with what they termed 'stinkers', rockers who at the best would be digging Thin Lizzy and at the worst would be dug deep into some retard Neanderthal sludge.

The band's stage-wear didn't help matters, either. Brown and Squire, along with Couzens, Garner and Reni, were decked out in matching Beach Boy shirts which John had made. They looked more like a bright and breezy clean-cut pop team than the rawhide leather and beer-swilling troupe that the urkos were braying for. There was an air of expectant trouble when they shuffled on to the stage, the sort of air that Ian Brown always thrived upon. Squire played it funny, making out that the band were a cabaret band.

The audience naturally didn't really get the joke and were braying and howling insults from 'Fuck off you English bastards', which was about as polite as it got, to threats of violence. The hordes weren't even barracking for fun; this was undiluted hatred. The promoter was either a prize buffoon who couldn't tell his demo tapes apart or someone with a mean sense of humour.

It was going to be a testing night.

Halfway through the sets Squire decided to liven things up a little, and between songs he started to hunker out the stub-toed riff that was the totem, the alpha riff for the grease boys, 'Smoke On The Water', and as it rang out across the creaking retard PA the place erupted. They thought the band was taking the piss!

This time the violence was going to be more than a few beer-stained insults – it was going to be blood and war. It was sacrilegious to even tamper with the holy heritage of dandruff, and Squire had just put a dainty hoof in there.

The band retreated to the dressing-room where they had to barricade themselves in as the venue exploded. The promoter burst in through a back door and was livid. 'I'm not paying you fuckers for that,' he screamed.

He was met by a typical Roses response. 'You either pay us or we go out there and the place gets trashed,' they stated as cold as ice, prepared to go all the way with either option.

They stayed where they were while the bad-tempered crowd slowly dispersed.

Years later Garner met a girl who was at the concert, who claimed that it was the most frightening night of her life and that she had to shelter from the smashing glasses that were flying around everywhere.

Straight after the gig the band got ready to return to Manchester, whilst they got in the van Andy Couzens went to the airport to catch a flight back to Manchester paid for by himself. It seemed a fairly innocuous move but it was one of the last straws.

'The gig was booked at short notice and I had arranged to see my girlfriend and I had to go to work the next day, so I was in a rush to get back.'

Andy's flight back from Dublin was just the sort of lever that Gareth was looking for.

As he sat on the plane over the Irish Sea, Andy was flying home from his last ever gig as a Stone Rose.

For Andy Couzens the following years have been filled with frustration.

Hooking up again with Howard Jones as manager, Couzens formed The High in 1989, whose classic guitar pop got the big launch the year after the baggy summer. They had the best press agent in London, Jeff Barrett, and with London records pushing them, they all but fell short of the top thirty. The songs were there but they were missing that crucial X factor – that element of danger and unpredictability that was Ian Brown's unwitting genius contribution to the Roses.

From five members to four, the Roses were about to kick-start a new era, but without the twin guitar attack, they would need Squire to up the ante.

And the quiet guitarist was definitely about to do that.

FROM FIVE TO FOUR

The first gig without Couzens could have been disastrous. The four-piece Roses had worked hard as at first there had been a gap. Andy had been a driving rhythm guitarist, his hard riffing had given them that rock edge that had grabbed all the attention so far. In pictures he very much looked like a member of the gang, sharing the same sort of slicked-back hair as Brown and the same sort of angular demeanour.

The band debated whether to replace him but it was obvious that Squire was more than adequate at taking over and playing the guitars.

He was fast becoming the best guitar player on the scene; his artiness, his depth of pop knowledge and all those hours of hard work were paying off. His guitar playing was becoming phenomenal and the band was finally moving in another direction, away from the amphetamine-driven rock and into the dope-smoke haze of the more psychedelic pop. The Roses were enjoying a surge of confidence that often comes after a band sheds a member, that tightening up, and like a football team with a player sent off who then raise their game, the band were starting to gear up to write the classics that would turn around their career. And how.

But still no one outside of Manchester was taking much notice. The band had gone through its first crisis and it was ages since the début single, but there was nothing on the horizon; only Gareth Evans' persistent buzzing and hustling, and the band's strong resolve kept things going through this frustrating period. In many ways that summer of 1986 was a real low point for the band. They played the Three Crowns pub in London and were poorly received. Brown sat on a stool in the middle of the set looking bored, and that night it must have seemed that it was going to be impossible to ever break out of their trap.

Back home, they played the Monday night gig at the Ritz (Mondays had been the goth/student night for years) with The Flesh Puppets supporting. It was their first home-town show without Andy Couzens, and they had to put up with countless people asking where he was. But the new four-piece Roses was looking and sounding good, Squire more than comfortable playing the equivalent of two guitars.

At the tail end of August they played the Mardi Gras in Liverpool supported by The Danny Boys. It was almost like they were starting from scratch again, playing low-key shows. The year was nearly over and they were getting nowhere, and the odd gigs combined with a massive gap between records, was leaving the band floundering. The local press was down on them after the graffiti campaign, and they were perceived as witless thugs while the literary pop stomp of The Smiths was in its ascendancy. At that point the Roses were seen as throwbacks, no-hopers, just one of those Manchester rock pop bands with an intensely loyal small local following, and that was all.

But at the heart and soul of the band things were very different. Phase two was kicking in, and with the air cleared, they were writing a phenomenal amount of songs. It was the greatest writing period of their career and at that otherwise unremarkable late August show at Liverpool's Mardi Gras they revamped their set. In came 'Sugar Spun Sister' and 'Sally Cinnamon', wonderful bitter-sweet pop. Catching the Roses that night would have been a glimpse into the future, with nearly half the set now of songs that would be classics to the just emerging new pop generation.

Things were moving on; the old songs seemed dated and they were getting fed up with playing them.

Fan Sharon Bampton was at the show: 'I hadn't really heard of them; there weren't that many people there. It's all a bit of a blur now. I remember that they weren't as "goth" as people were saying that they were in the end. There were moments when they seemed quite poppy. I remember Ian Brown really staring out at the crowd, he was quite fearsome in those days.'

'We hated doing "So Young",' recalls Garner. 'It was like our "White Riot", we were getting really sick of it.'

Slowly but surely a very different band was emerging. It was the keynote of 1986, the year when, on paper, they didn't do very much. Maybe in public there was little sign of any activity but this was the year when they started putting together the proper début album that would shake the British pop scene. Rehearsing away, learning their craft and fired by influences like The Jesus And Mary Chain and Primal Scream, they were coming up with real nuggets, drop-dead classics that would define a later pop generation.

They already had 'I Wanna Be Adored' and 'This Is The One' from the Hannett album, and now they had 'Elephant Stone'. New gear was also influencing the very sounds that they were dealing with.

'John had just bought his first wah-wah pedal and just written "Elephant Stone". It was a move forward. We thought that we were ahead of the pack again, when we heard The Happy Mondays' "Freaky Dancing" and realised that they were there as well,' says Pete Garner.

The two bands were moving symbiotically again.

The Mary Chain and Primal Scream were key influences on the Roses. Their 1960s-fused pop hinted at a myriad of new influences, bands that the Roses started to greedily chew on. They had the look, the rock'n'roll cool and the gang thing that also scored heavily with the style-obsessed south Manchester group.

It was at this point that the Roses started to dig out the paisley shirts and leather pants; they had bowl haircuts and roll-necked pullovers. It was a northern street take on the Creation leather look of the time. Creation Records, the label set up by Alan McGee, was the original home of The Jesus and Mary Chain and the current home of Primal Scream, and in the mid 1980s the whole label was decked out in a pimp leather crossed with a classic 1960s look.

John had the bowl cut and Brown was growing his out into a short rude shock of gelled spikes, Garner had the psychedelic pants and Reni, well, he had his own thing going. For many bands at the time, the Mary Chain were the alpha group.

The Jesus and Mary Chain were sullen biker leather and beautiful arrogance. Their gigs would collapse into sullen semi-riots, and their huge warm enveloping wall of pop sound seemed revolutionary – a mixture of 1960s girl groups, battered 'Nuggets' garage-track compilation LPs, garage rock and British psych freaks. They had simple but killer bruised melodies, they sang softly and sweetly of darkness, despair and love. They rang a chord with The Stone Roses. Their drummer, Bobby Gillespie, was so cool that he left to concentrate on Primal Scream, the band that he had started off before the Mary Chain, two key bands in one.

Kicking off as a metal percussion wind-up landing between Public Image Limited and Einsterzende Neubaten, Primal Scream soon incorporated Bobby's love of pristine pop. When he eventually got the band going good and proper they quickly became renowned for songs that seemed to last for seconds and were shots of pure melody. Again they were tough guys singing soft songs, love songs dripping in sentiment and sung with a stone-cold sneer. It was that classic clash of opposites that a band called Stone Roses could appreciate.

Music press photographer Ian Tilton remembers an early Primal Scream photo session that tells all about the band: 'I was out in the hills near Glasgow doing some pictures of them and they were all about this melodic pop music, almost sentimental in a way – when along flies a butterfly and lands on the guitarist's shoulder. One minute they are all looking at the camera and the next he claps his hands and splatters the butterfly all over the place . . . that summed them up really.'

The Primals had been lumped in with the ridiculous C86 (it was originally a cassette – the C part being given away free with NME in 1986, the 86 part) scene, a press-created scam – rounding up disparate underground acts in an attempt at making a movement, which smacked of cruel desperation. It was a scene that the likes of the Mondays and the Roses must have spat on.

The Primals as well, even though they were included on C86, thought bigger and wanted bigger. They believed that they were a top pop band. They had a song, a B-side called 'Velocity Girl', that was ninety seconds of killer pop and collapsing chord changes. It struck a bullseye in many hearts, especially with The Stone Roses who would make a rare trip into town and see the Primals, hearing echoes of their beloved Love.

In fact The Stone Roses loved 'Velocity Girl' so much that they half-inched the chord sequence for 'Made Of Stone', and took the Primal's song one step further and turned it into a bona fide classic. That's what pop is all about – influencing, changing and altering. If you like it, you have it; take the original and improve.

Bobby Gillespie knew this: 'Aye, people have mentioned that they took "Velocity Girl" over the years. But if they did, they made it better, much better – "Made Of Stone" is a classic.'

And Bobby, the astute professor of pop, is a man who knows.

That December 12 The Roses recorded their first demo as a four piece in the basement flat of a house in Chorlton, Manchester. During the session they recorded 'Sugar Spun Sister', 'Going Down', 'Sun Still Shines' and 'Elephant Stone'. 'Sun Still Shines' featured the odd mono mix of all the bass and drums on one side and the guitar and vocals on the other.

The disconcerting sound mix was provided by Garner who managed to get his hands on the controls. This demo was the first time that they had started to take an interest in what they sounded like as a band and not just their own parts. This demo is the point where the band started to take control of their sound, a control that leads directly to the début album. The tunes drip melody and a summery pop feel. They are so close to the 'Lemon' album sound and yet three years away from its release.

Creatively 1986 was ending on a high note!

1987

CAT AND MOUSE – EVANS PLAYS THE WAITING GAME

As 1987 kicked off the Gareth Evans machine was kicking in. Full On. Behind the scenes he was spending hours on the phone. Hustling. Hoping. His self-belief was outrageous. On paper the Roses were in a desperate position. Way out of sync with whatever crap fashion or dumb cool was knocking about, they were a couple of years down the line and still getting nowhere. Their original crew of fans had dwindled – confused by the new melodic direction the band had undertaken. Slowly their replacements were beginning to appear, new recruits and new faces previously not sure of the band's reputation who were getting hooked into this unsuspected pop gem.

On January 30 they played Manchester International 1, yet another crossover gig for the band. The new Roses audience was making up the majority of the crowd, the last two demos had floated around town and new faces were now checking them out. The pop kids were appearing, the word was out the Roses were not so much the hooligans of yore, they were actually, possibly the best song-writers in the city since The Smiths! They were writing pop tunes that were dripping classic guitar pop licks.

And where were these tunes going? There was still no sign of a record deal. Factory turned them down, everyone turned them down. Then one afternoon Gareth had some good news. Some record label in Wolverhampton, of all places, was interested.

GARETH SCORES A RECORD DEAL

More demos. More work. Gareth was mailing that demo everywhere. And there was very little reaction. The only record label that were even returning Gareth's calls were the Wolverhampton based Revolver FM. A curious label to be interested in the melodic guitar pop that The Roses were playing, but a label none-the-less.

Revolver FM had been releasing low cost glam metal/rock CD's and selling them into the lucrative Japanese market as well as releases from the UK Subs and The Vibrators. The label's boss was Paul Birch who ran the operation from his large country house just outside Wolverhampton or from a Mayfair hotel room, his partner was Dave Roberts who had played in Silverwing, a glam/metal outfit from Macclesfield. Roberts had gone on to freelance for *Sounds* before getting involved in running a record label and then pooling his resources with Birch.

As the calls began to intensify between Manchester and Wolverhampton Gareth was working on building the Roses profile up in Manchester.

Owning the two International venues left him well placed to do this. He would put the band on at the smaller International 1 and knock down the ticket price, give away tickets, anything to get the crowd in. In the past two years the band's audience had been changing, the word was getting out, the Roses were appealing to a whole new audience with their jangle pop thrills.

Gareth was merciless in this line of promotion pulling in local bookers like Sandy Gort to help him out. Sandy managed the Macc lads who had been signed to Revolver FM and had the dubious honour of being the label's first Japanese flop but the initial contact between Gareth and Revolver came from here. Also Revolver's number two Dave Roberts, would be at the International reviewing bands for *Sounds* and Gareth, as was his wont, would always look after journalists.

Realising that the band needed some sort of release Evans decided to go with Revolver FM. One night Gareth cornered Dave Roberts in the International and told him he would have a permanent place on the guest list if he could get his boss to finally release the Roses on his label.

A few days later Paul Birch relented and signed the band on a reverse deal (the band are the ones to provide something on signature not the company).

Gareth was looking for a one off deal to get The Roses into the indie charts, up their profile and hopefully score a proper big time deal. Revolver, in, for this one off, would set up a subsidiary label called Black Records. A meeting was arranged.

Jumping in Gareth's jeep they made the ninety-minute journey down to Wolverhampton.

It was two worlds colliding! Paul Birch with his long flowing hair and leopardskin pants was rock incarnate (hurray!), a million miles away from the Roses sullen Manc cool (and remember this is the Roses fresh out of leather and bandanas and they still found his appearance too much!).

Birch preferred the bands earlier rockier stuff, he could smell the glam influences that were in the band's music. The touch of The Clash, the hint of New York Dolls, the half inched bass lines from the MC5. Despite reports to the contrary, there was a link between the two parties; the Roses had always had a love of glam punk – after all there weren't many people in the country who had dug the post Generation X outfit Empire! but for the sake of northern cool these earlier influences were now getting swept under the carpet. The band was moving in a different direction, the new jangle pop was about cool, a studied cool and John Squire in his new army fatigues and Soviet Union badge, was hardly dressed like a glam metal freak.

But it was a marriage of convenience, the band desperately needed a release and Paul Birch was astute enough to hear the pop potential of 'Sally

Cinnamon' and one of the oddest deals in the history of the Manchester music scene was done. The Stone Roses had a one off single release on a midlands metal label.

On the way home, as if to excise the past, Gareth, a man of wild gestures, threw the last remaining boxes of 'So Young' in the road and reversed his Jeep over them. The band looked on smirking and surprised. 'That's the ghost of Howard Jones removed forever' their manager shouted, adding 'the new era starts now!'

A week later Gareth looked through the contract and signed it. There was no time to fuck about, there was also no leeway to manoeuvre. In hindsight the Roses, with their now legendary status, signing goofy deals seems crazy but you have to realise how tough it was at the time to get anyone interested.

For Revolver signing the band may have been a favour but it was one that gives the label an odd footnote in the history of rock'n'roll.

And now Gareth Evans decided to pull them off the crap supports that had been an occasional gig for them in the last couple of years. He concentrated them on the big shows in Manchester, utilising the International 1 and 2 to showcase them to A & R men, giving out free tickets to students and indie heads – filling the venues up – giving the impression that The Roses were far bigger than they actually were.

Now armed with tunes that were backing up their grandiose claims, The Roses would spend '87 frustratingly on the slow curve towards ascendancy. They were getting bigger and bigger in Manchester, this was the year that they became a proper big draw in the home town. Elsewhere they were still ignored. But they were still powered by that enormous belief. A belief now being translated into great songs.

Self-belief, though, doesn't pay the bills. They were so broke at the time that Reni was apparently working as a Kissogram. It was a measure of the poverty under which they were living.

But at least they had a home for their second single and that May they released 'Sally Cinnamon'.

SALLY CINNAMON

The Roses sound was now changing. Pulling back from the amphetamine assaults of their earlier years, they were discovering a more melodic side to their music, a less angry uptight sound. Its a difficult transition to make and one that plenty of bands should never make. But the new melody-soaked Roses seemed to suit the band. They retained some of the earlier flavours of the song-writing, the anthemic huge choruses and the inspirational rallying call songs, but this time they were more dynamic, more subtle. They were learning about song-writing and finding out that it really suited them. Ian

Brown explained the new Roses sound to *Record Collector* who asked about the oft quoted Byrds influence on their sound and the painstaking song-writing process the band now set out upon.

'The Byrds came later. John got into them around early '88 but I've never owned a Byrds record. No, the influence was a nice tune. We never deliberately tried to copy anyone. We ended up writing tunes that sounded like the Beatles. We'd have 'I Feel Fine' or 'Daytripper' but with different lyrics, accidental. So we'd drop them. Me and John went to Italy once just to write and we slept rough – we took an acoustic guitar and sleeping bags. We came back with three or four tunes. Wow, this is great. Well, no, they're like the Beatles!'

And evidence of this new Roses sound was stamped all over their upcoming 'Sally Cinnamon' single, even its title was telling a different story.

One night in the International 1 an excited Gareth Evans ushered me into the tiny corridor at the back of the club that served as his office. He handed over a twelve inch single. It was the Roses second single and the manager was positively exploding with excitement.

Released on May 28, 'Sally Cinnamon' flipped with 'Here It Comes' and 'All Across The Sands' is pure unadulterated pop. Bagged in its curious black and white sleeve photo (taken by John's brother Matt) of sweet dispensers outside a shop.

Recorded in Wolverhampton it's as about as far away from their rock as they could go. Says Pete, 'We produced "Sally Cinnamon" ourselves with Simon who was our soundman at the time. He did the Happy Mondays as well.'

It offended some of their old fans like Karen Ablaze who told Ian Brown of her worries. 'He wasn't happy about that. He got really angry. I didn't like the new direction that they were taking. I really liked the older stuff like "Heart On The Staves", it was also more soulful.'

Karen was now in a minority. The Roses were starting to attract a whole new host of fans, disaffected pop kids, indie fans bored of the charisma bypass indie shufflers, were all starting to buy into the band. So far these were hometown indie fans only, the rest of the UK still wasn't getting it.

'Sally Cinnamon' hints at all those dynamic chops and changes in tempo that would be the band's trademark along with the non-stop rush of melody, when they finally released their début album. The flipside 'Here It Comes' and 'All Across the Sand' followed suit; here was a band steeped in sweet tunes and a band in '87 totally out of sync with the times.

'Here It Comes' features one of Brown's first classic lines, 'I'd rather be no-one than someone with no-one' a typical piece of homespun Brown philosophy, an anti-celebrity sneer, a swaggering plea that directly bonds with the audience. When its sung in the song as a rousing piece of polemic it really hits home. 'Here It Comes' is yet another song that bridges the band between their punkier initial phase and already burgeoning new melodicism. Live in the early days it was an aggressive workout and had recently been dropped as the band's subtle change of direction had made the aggressive side of the band more and more redundant.

The single came out and didn't even get in the indie chart, meanwhile in Manchester it sold by the bucket load aided no doubt by non-stop radio play on Tony Michaelidies key 'Last Record Show'.

Andy McQueen, perhaps The Stone Roses' biggest and most eloquent fan, remembers going out to buy the record the day that it was released. 'I went into Virgin records to see if it was there and you couldn't buy it there. I met Ian Brown in Virgin and we were both disappointed that you couldn't buy it there.'

It seemed like the mainstream was a long way off. They sold out the 1,000-pressing of the single, it was enough to prove that somewhere someone loved them but it was hardly going to guarantee any chart action.

A couple of years later Revolver FM re-released the single and charted it, pissing the band off with a naff video that resulted in its offices getting the legendary repainting job. At the time the single got no national air play and no national press reviews. The local writers writing for the national press were now frothing at the mouth, pointing at The Roses' huge hometown following and the classic pop that they were by now effortlessly parading, but it was going to be some time before London got it. Live reviews editors on the national music press were just not having it.

'I rang up about covering the band,' remembers one journalist, 'and they told me that there was no way a band could be that popular in the north if no one in London liked them!'

If there was one thing that The Roses managed to achieve when they finally broke massive, it was that no one would get ignored again just because they didn't go drinking in Camden.

4 BECOMES 3

In June they were back out on the road. Around this time Pete Garner told them that he wanted to leave the band for good. It was a difficult decision but he felt that something had been lost in the band, the core bonding friendship had been broken since the money row the year before.

He'd carry on playing gigs for them until they found a new bass player. This was a pain in the arse for the tightly knit band. Getting someone to play bass, on paper, is far easier than finding a drummer. But finding someone who fitted in as well as the affable Garner was going to be difficult. It would have to be a mate, and it would have to be someone with the same sort of mentality and experiences.

Pete, though, loyally continued to fill in at the gigs that they had coming up on the small-town northern circuit where they were starting to build on their Manchester following with just-out-of-town shows.

On 26 June they played the International 1, a gig Gareth Evans invited the music business to, and really papered the house with free tickets. He shouldn't have worried though, as the band were by now pulling in a solid following.

They had been rehearsing in the International, and the advantage of playing on a large stage through a big PA was starting to tell on the group. They now sounded like a big-stage band. Instead of being crammed into some vile rehearsal room squashing their sound down they could experiment with space in their music, letting it grow, feel big.

The day after, on 27 June, by one of those weird quirks of fate, the Primals played the same venue.

In many ways Glasgow's Primals were the sister band to the Roses; both bands were from tough cities and both bands had a deep love for the underground pop classic tunes that they fused with their own brutal post-punk outlook, and created melody-strewn sensitive pop. The Primals would be one of the few bands that the Roses would check out when they played in town, although they always denied this.

In mid-July the Roses travelled over to Sheffield to play the Take Two club, and the set had now been radically shaken up: 'Elephant Stone', 'The Hardest Thing In The World', 'Sugar Spun Sister', 'Here It Comes', 'Sally Cinnamon', 'Where Angels Play', and 'Your Time Will Never Come' (the last being one that they never recorded and is still one of superfan Andy McQueen's favourites), 'She Bangs The Drums', 'Sun Still Shines', 'Mersey Paradise' and 'This Is The One'. The set was now taking shape.

Ever the political animal, Brown hated flags and all the heavyweight symbolism they carried with them. The support band's girlfriends were waving a Confederate flag at him, and this was a red rag to a steaming bull, as Andy McQueen remembers: 'Ian stopped the gig and went into a speech about the flag and how it represented slavery, white supremacy and racism.'

He didn't care that this sort of heavy-duty necessary stuff would make little impact on the rock pigs in the crowd.

Then it kicked off again. 'There were these rock-chick girls, friends of the band, who were heckling the Roses. Ian, during "Sugar Spun Sister", said something back and one of the girls threw a pint at him. He went back, had a swig of water and spat water at this rocker bloke. Then everyone jumped in and told him to calm down.'

The Roses also played Liverpool at Planet X to about fifteen people, where Ian Brown was, as ever, the young lion. The band's music was developing but Brown was still into his confrontational stage bit. Prowling around the venue with his long mic lead, shorn hair and a thousand-yard stare he would go right up to people at the bar and stare them in the eyes, demanding attention.

Journalist Paula Greenwood remembers the Roses' aura, 'Everyone says that they were a goth band but I never thought that. They didn't come on-stage dressed in black, singing miserable songs. Everything about them was positive. They were optimists and they had something that no other band had at the time. Ian had an arrogance on-stage. He demanded attention and got it. He controlled the audience. You could never get away with talking at a gig. Ian made sure of that, by getting off-stage and walking into the audience with his microphone in his hand and going right up to people.'

Brown just didn't care. After four sulk songs he went up to some hecklers at the bar and gave them the mic for 'Sally Cinnamon'. The speed-driven Ian Brown was looking for some sort of reaction, even if it was totally negative.

Between the gigs the band was now in creative overdrive. Ian Brown could be spotted walking down Burton Road in west Didsbury lugging a set of keyboards over to John's in Chorlton. 'They are better for writing melodies on,' he would smile. Never was their creative partnership as strong as in this period. At the time John said, 'The amount of songs me and Ian have to reject! We want perfect songs. We've got loads that aren't quite good enough. We want to be like The Beatles . . . they could change their style as much as they wanted, yet they were still undeniable as their songs were so good.'

On 11 August, the Roses played Larks In The Park, a mini festival that took place every year in Liverpool's Sefton Park, the large green space next to the crumble of Toxteth.

Days before, Brown had threatened to pull out of the gig if it was raining, remembering The Happy Mondays' recent balls-up in Manchester's Platt Fields where only thirty people turned up in the rain-sodden mid-summer afternoon.

Eventually he relented and the turnout was far better than expected. In 1987 Larks In The Park was the usual ragbag of local outfits but with a couple of pointers to the future. Liverpool's The La's, who had been working the bars and pubs of Liverpool and had built up quite a following with their skiffle pop, were in the same boat as the Roses, pure pop with no national audience. They were the main event along with the Roses themselves, and quite a few fans travelled from Manchester that hot August afternoon.

The Stone Roses played on the stage surrounded by the grassy slopes with loads of stoners sitting back and getting smashed in the summer sun. The band played next to an ornate pond which Ian Brown ended up jumping into, probably wrecking his leather trousers.

For many pundits it was The La's that seemed ready to lead the charge of northern pop bands that were waiting in the wings, but an idiosyncratic pace of work and an erratic recording schedule put paid to that. Lee Mavers's band had to virtually succeed on the coat-tails of their Mancunian neighbours before burning out far more efficiently than the Roses; The La's blew it in a way that the Roses could only dream about.

Another chapter was about to close for the Roses, as Larks In The Park was Pete Garner's last gig for the band.

He went on to manage a record shop and be one of the cool heads hanging around town, eminently likeable; it seems that everyone has a good word for him. He was never bitter about the band and would even carry on going down to rehearsals for a good stretch into the future. He remembers watching a rehearsal just after leaving and they played him 'I Am The Resurrection'. He was stunned. He knew that the band were moving forward fast.

He remained good friends with them and was recently spotted dusting down his bass guitar for a long-awaited return. An under-rated bass player, he was never the goth of legend, and his melodic bass runs contributed enormously to the band's burgeoning new sound. He left right on the edge of their success, the great lost member of The Stone Roses.

The line-up crisis had re-emerged after one year. Where do you find someone who could slot into the gang, the tight-knit unit that was the Roses? Ian and John were knocked for six. Sure they knew that Pete was leaving, but they hoped that it wouldn't actually happen. They would spend the next couple of months in the doldrums.

Afer all, just how do you get a new member for your gang?

THE RETURN OF MANI!

It wasn't easy for a band as close as this to get a new member who would fit into the ranks. They didn't really deal with outsiders that easily. So when Pete made his decision it was a very dejected-looking John Squire and Ian Brown who bumped into Clint Boon, who had now formed The Inspiral Carpets, down on the Boardwalk one night.

'They said that they were looking for a bass player and did I know anybody,' says Boon. 'At the time we had Scott Carey in The Inspiral Carpets. Scott went on to form The Paris Angels, but he was a massive Roses fan. I could have suggested him, but that would have broken the band up, so I told them that I would think about it and left it at that.'

While Clint is keen to point out that he doesn't want any credit for this vital last cog being put into place for The Stone Roses, he did bump into Mani's brother Greg in Manchester city centre the next day and told him what was happening. Whether Greg told Mani what was going on, and then he got in touch with the Roses, is lost in the mists of legend.

Even though the Roses and the Mondays would never openly acknowledge the Inspirals, relations between the bands were quite cordial as they started to break through in the next couple of years. There was a point when the Inspirals were actually looking like the best bet to break through.

'We would drive past each other on the motorway everywhere and say hello. When the Roses started to make it I realised that they were a lot cooler than we were. But in the end we toured the world five times, we got everywhere. We had a good pop career and I'm sure they must have wanted that at some point. We were completely in the shadow of them, everywhere we went people asked us about them, they were a one-off band,' Boon is honest enough to admit.

One weird twist in the tale of the bass player is that for one week there was another bassist in the Roses called Rob Hampson, who Pete Garner gallantly attempted to teach the bass lines. He even appeared in a photo session done by Ian Tilton, but when push came to shove he just didn't seem to be arsed enough about being in the band; he was last seen as a cloakroom attendant in the club South.

The same couldn't be said about Mani who, from the day he joined the band, was like a bolt of enthusiasm, and the garrulous wide-boy joy at being up there on the big stage was infectious. The man of the people who'd got the big break was the final piece in the jigsaw.

It was an enthusiasm that he would always bring to any situation. Mani was the rogue Rose.

Mani's début gig was at the International 1 on 13 November 1987. He fitted in instantly, and as he'd always been a fringe member of the gang he knew the moves. He walked the walk, he talked the talk, he was a Rose before he was even in the band.

The legendary line-up was now complete, and now it was time to go and collect.

The show at the International was a triumph and the set they played was: 'Sally Cinnamon', 'Elephant Stone', 'Here It Comes', 'I Wanna Be Adored', 'Mersey Paradise', 'Going Down', 'Your Time Has Come', 'The Hardest Thing In The World', 'Waterfall', 'She Bangs The Drums', and 'This Is The One'.

They were supported by The Waltones, another guitar-based pop band who at the time seemed omnipresent but just couldn't survive the great pop sea-change that was looming on the horizon.

1987 BURNS OUT . . .

'Sally Cinnamon' was massive in Manchester. Gareth's policy of handing out tapes of the song around Afflecks Palace, the city-centre clothing emporium, was beginning to pay off. The plan was to get the student/ music paper readers into the band but to break out to the people who lived beyond the campuses. The story still goes round of Gareth driving down Blackpool prom handing out Roses shirts to the coolest-looking people he could find, a bizarre old-school touching method of management. It was this belief in working from the grass roots up that would eventually hit pay dirt two years later.

The Smiths were at the tail end of their career and something new was needed, something similar but with a more street edge. The times were toughening up and more attitude was required. The Roses and the Mondays were getting really good at just the right time, and there was something in the air, something was going to blow.

In mid 1987 small clubs were playing house music and the word was on the street about E; the hip were out looking for this wonder drug, a new way to blow your mind.

Around Manchester raincoats and long faces were getting put into cupboards. A city long associated with glum serious pop was about to throw a massive party, and all were welcome.

It was to be a tantalising and fascinating turnaround in a city's pop culture and it was a turning point too in the fortunes of many people.

Evans was creating an air of mystery around the band, and A & R men would scuttle up to Manchester and see the band play huge local shows that were becoming more the norm and less reliant on free tickets.

The band were still in leather and psychedelics, with Squire's Pollocked artwork dripping off the guitars and the drum kit. They were now finally looking like the classic pop group. At the shows you could sense that something was happening, and that after all the toil they were becoming very much a contender.

Stephen Kingston wrote in *Sounds*, 'Ian Brown fancies himself as a bit of a star', but added that he liked the songs as 'somehow they suck you in'. Another *Sounds* writer raved about the 'Man-United-style terrace ovation that greets the band. The Roses are to the Stones what The Smiths are to The Beatles,' while Penny Kiley raved about their show in Sefton Park in *Melody Maker*. The northern journalists were convinced, they were on the shop floor, and they knew that despite of or because of Gareth's wheeling and dealing, combined with the Roses now total brilliance, that this was a band that was bursting through.

At the time though, even with the rush starting to happen, it seemed hard to believe that Britain could go for songs as melodic and sweet as these. It seemed that classic rock'n'roll bands would be permanently fated to fall outside the mainstream.

Just getting to the edge of success, the 1,000-capacity halls and the back-end of the top forty was about as far as it was feasible to go. It was going to have to take something really special to break out of the rut. The 1980s had all but killed classic pop music. The Roses were by now fighting a battle with a disinterested national media and a sceptical music industry, a battle that most bands that followed through their slipstream in the 1990s wouldn't have to contend with.

After The Stone Roses dramatically burst through, a totally different media and business machinery was in place. The national press, having ignored the Manchester breakthrough, have never since missed a band. The journalists have been on the case – chasing every lead up and down the country – powered by enthusiasm and excitement. The labels are there as well.

In the mid to late 1980s there was a massive scepticism about anything that rocked the boat; rock was of course 'dead', most pundits claimed, and nothing was ever going to change again.

They, of course, didn't count on acid house, the Manchester boom or Kurt Cobain, three totally differing sources of a new pop revolution that beautifully upset the apple cart and set up the 1990s, the best pop era of all time

1988

HERE IT COMES: THE DEAL, THE ALBUM, EVERYTHING!

Early in 1988 The Stone Roses played Dingwalls, returning to the venue where three years before they had played as part of a Manchester package. This time they were headlining to a sparse crowd of devotees, mainly made up of fans who had come all the way down from Manchester to see them. I caught the gig as well and it was obvious the band had moved on from the Liverpool gig of the summer.

Not that the band were the slightest bit phased in the cold venue. Ian Brown bounded into the venue like a champion, and when they played the show later on, they oozed their guitar pop. Ian had finally toned down his aggressive long lead forays into the room and the classic king monkey moves were in place, a new arrogance, a new fronting had replaced the speed-driven confrontational Brown of before. The new guise stood there challenging the audience to do something, to do anything. It was a pose that would be adopted by Liam Gallagher and a whole generation of British frontmen to varying degrees of success, a frozen drop dead cool that many of the frontmen didn't have and left them looking like a sack of potatoes left out on the stage.

For Brown it worked perfectly.

The band were now picking up on the street scally look, their new bass player with his Perry boy fringe, perhaps instrumental in the new look Roses, less rock'n'roll, more casual. Maybe Cressa's influence was coming to the fore, but for a band immersed in pop culture, dressing smart and dressing street was something that had been part of their schtick from punk to scooter boys and onwards. Also John Squire had applied his love of Jackson Pollock's paint dripping technique to his own paintings and then, drip drip drip, allowed the paint to decorate the drums, the guitars and even some of their clothes. It was a neat pop and art connection. The band were quickly evolving into their final stage. The songs were there, the look was there and they still had their own idiosyncratic twist and if the audience wasn't there, then hey! they will be there soon enough!

And for the Zomba/Jive posse that were present at the gig it was the music that did the talking. McKenna had been buzzing up Zomba (Silvertone as a label didn't exist yet) that this was a classic band that was really going to happen, even in the non-guitar dead zone of the late Eighties, where even the thought of a band trading on three-minute pop songs built around shimmering guitar shapes, seemed a pretty laughable notion.

But there was something about this band that really worked.

Not only were the Zomba/Jive people getting buzzed up on the band but Lyndsey Reade had brought down Geoff Travis from Rough Trade to the gig. Travis was also blown away with the band. He said he's sign them on the spot.

Despite Zomba/Jive looking like the favourites to sign the band, Gareth got Rough Trade to pick up the upcoming studio bill for the 'Elephant Stone' single. Rough Trade were looking for a one-off deal. That was not enough for Gareth who was looking for something a bit more long-term but that didn't stop him from letting Rough Trade pick up the upcoming studio bill.

What no one seemed to be thinking was would the band be happy with getting released on some southern version of Factory? Just another trendy indie label. Never their thing really!

But with Rough Trade's money they hired various northern studios where they started work on their intended third single, 'Elephant Stone', with New Order's Pete Hook. Roddy McKenna wasn't panicking, he knew he could buy back the tapes when he needed to.

BASS VIKING AT THE CONTROLS: STONE ROSES RECORD 'ELEPHANT STONE' WITH THE LEGENDARY HOOKY!

As 1988 kicked off, the Roses went into Strawberry and Yellow 2 studios in Stockport to begin work on their third single, 'Elephant Stone'. Says Ian, 'At that time we nearly signed to Rough Trade. In fact, Rough Trade signed us to do "Elephant Stone" with Peter Hook.'

For 'Elephant Stone' though they were already hooked (ha!) in with the esteemed New Order bassman. 'Hooky was a mate of Slims who was roadying for us – he used to roadie for New Order. Hooky's engineer, Michael Johnson, did most of it but Hooky played a part.

'I'd say it was Peter Hook *and* us that produced it. We wanted Reni out there. We wanted people to hear what he could do.'

Peter Hook points out that it was Gareth that got him involved with the single. 'Me and Barney (New Order) knew Gareth from the International. He was one weird character (laughs). He'd come up behind you with a bottle of Pernod and some cans of beer and then run off! In the end we got talking!'

Gareth told Hooky that the band had been working on 'Elephant Stone' and weren't happy with the sound of 'Sally Cinnamon' and this time they wanted to get it right. Could he help?

The single was recorded at Revolution Studios in south Manchester. Hook was amazed by the band's musicianship. 'They were great players. We tracked up loads of guitars and I bored the band with anecdotes! Gareth was always popping in like a wildman. One day he turned up dressed as Mani holding a bass! He always had loads of cash on him and would pay for anything the band needed. He really looked after them. If someone's hi-fi was broken he would go and buy another one!'

A two-inch tape of it sat in Suite 16 for years discarded, forgotten about, lying on a shelf with a mountain of local bands . . .

Shan Hira, the owner of the legendary, now closed studio in Rochdale, remembers his then business partner Hooky giving him a desperate ring during the sessions.

'He asked me if I could come down to the studios and sort something out. They had a problem, they needed some hi-hats over dubbing on to the track, and Reni had gone missing. They couldn't find him anywhere.'

Hooky asked Hira, who was once the drummer in the seminal Stockholm Monsters, the Factory-signed act who were the first gang of drugged-up funked-up yobs pre-Happy Mondays but were too crazy to make it. Hira was a great drummer and a potential life saver in the session.

'I wasn't happy about doing it at all. I sat there in the studio putting down the part when in walked Reni. His face was icy, it was a really bad situation. I felt really awful about it and got out of there as soon as possible.'

Hooky remembers this well. 'For some reason Reni wouldn't play this hi-hat part so I got Shan to do it. It was Christmas Eve and I thought no one was around and then in walked Reni!'

Hooky notes that the Roses' drummer was a powerhouse player. 'Singing drummers, eh! Reni wanted to do everything, he wanted to be the lead singer of the band, he was always coming up with vocal parts. I had to stop him!'

Peter Hook, himself no stranger to the pratfalls of rock'n'roll, muses over the Roses' eventual career. 'They could have been massive, couldn't they? They really had it. It reminds me of Joy Division really. We would have been massive in America like they would have been if we had just got there at the right time, but we lost a singer and the Roses wouldn't go because Gareth told the record label he wanted screaming girls at the airport like The Beatles or he wasn't going to go!'

The single's flipside 'Full Fathom Five' was the Roses' first venture into running their songs backwards. Flipping the two inch of 'Elephant Stone' over, the band got off on the trippy wash of backwards sounds. It was the beginning of a Roses tradition.

The sessions over and 'Elephant Stone' was in the can where it sat for most of that year, waiting for whichever label was going to release it to come forward and do the job. White labels were pressed up and were floating around Manchester that summer where again the hipsters dismissed the band for being out of date. But the fans were buzzing. It sounded like another step forward for the band and they had finally got themselves a deal.

There was talk of recording an album. Producers were considered. 'I was asked to do the album. But I had to go and record a New Order one instead, so I was out of the frame,' adds Hooky.

Rough Trade, acting like they were the record label, were making creative suggestions. Label boss Geoff Travis, an astute music head, came up with a blinder. He thought that for their next batch of recording the Roses should work with John Leckie.

Says Ian, 'As we were doing "Elephant Stone" Geoff Travis said try John Leckie, I think he'll be good for you. Zomba then bought "Elephant Stone" off Geoff. Zomba were offering us eight LPs and Rough Trade were only offering an LP or two. But we met John Leckie and we got on. We thought the Dukes Of Stratosphear LP had a good range of sounds – a clever mind that's made it. So, he obviously had some knowledge of equipment.'

Geoff Travis's suggestion of Leckie as producer had struck Roddy McKenna as a brilliant idea as well. Leckie's history, dating back through two decades of great music from being the tea boy on Pink Floyd and Beatles' records to producing some of the cutting-edge, post-punk bands and those authentic psychedelic Dukes of Stratosphear records, stood him in good stead to work with the Roses.

The stage was now set for some classic rock'n'roll action. The last remaining piece in the jigsaw was the record deal.

And that was pretty damn close.

SILVERTONE STEP IN!

Zomba were now closing in on the deal. In March there was a big pow wow in the Britannia Hotel between Gareth, his lawyer, Matthew, Lyndsey Reade and Mark Farmer from Zomba. Zomba had given Gareth a contract fully expecting Gareth to get it checked over by a music lawyer and were pretty surprised that he had got his own lawyer, a property lawyer, to run through it. This was hardly conventional!

Nope, not conventional business practice, but then Gareth wasn't a conventional manager. Gareth's policy was to get Zomba to rewrite the contract when the Roses hit the chart. This he got a handshake agreement on. Evans felt that the group, when they grabbed the rewards that they were so rightly assured of, would be able to renegotiate their deal.

In many ways the deal was a relief – they had finally found an outlet for their music.

After a bit more haggling they squeezed £27,500 advance from Zomba, more than the label was expecting to cough up but a lot less than the usual pay-out for a hot band. Then Silvertone sat back and waited for Gareth and his lawyer to work their way through the contract, deleting clauses, arguing over points, the usual stuff, the usual haggle.

They were pretty surprised when no argument was forthcoming and the contracts were quickly signed.

Who knows what Gareth was thinking? Maybe he figured the contract was perhaps not perfect but was banking on renegotiating within a year when the band broke massive as he knew they undoubtedly would. He also realised that contracts were hardly worth the paper they were written on. How many people reading this are in bands and have seen the best negotiated contracts thrown back in their faces when the money comes in? Plus Gareth was probably relieved to get the band a deal. This was the band that was considered dead meat outside Manchester, they may have been a great band that was getting better but the music business was hardly tripping over themselves to sign up bands like the Roses.

Gareth had done well. He had scored the band a deal. After three years of stop/starts, and setbacks he had got The Stone Roses a release at last and a chance finally to get that album recorded.

By the spring of 1988 the band was also so utterly ready with Mani gelled perfectly into the ranks and the songs in perfect condition that the Roses were not just going to record any old album. They were going to record one of the classic all-time British rock'n'roll records. Fuck, even Gareth with his wild eyes and crazed enthusiasm can't have seen this coming!

And Zomba, despite being buzzed up by Roddy McKenna's enthusiasm were about to play an unwitting part in a soon-to-become legend.

Their first move was to set up a label to accommodate their new rock signings Silvertone.

Silvertone, despite having one of those classic names that makes it seem like it has been around for ever, was in fact a brand-new label. The Stone Roses would be the first single the newly set up label released in October '88. Set up by Zomba, the huge South African publishing house that already had the Jive label, Silvertone was set up by the parent company on Roddy McKenna's insistence to be a label for renowned A&R man Andrew Lauder to sign bands to.

Andrew Lauder, Silvertone MD recalls, 'Silvertone certainly wasn't formed for The Stone Roses. I'd been talking with Zomba about bringing my rock experience to them somehow. It was obviously better to do this under the banner of a new label, so I came up with the name of Silvertone and, virtually on the day I signed the deal, 18 April 1988, they told me they'd just signed this band that might be ideal for the new label, so I took the demo tape home with me and really liked it.'

Lauder had a long and distinguished career in the music business. In 1967 he moved to London and started working for Liberty Records, doing promotion for new bands like The Bonzo Doo Dah Dog Band and Roy Wood's Idle Race.

He then became a label manager, bringing Credence Clearwater Revival over to the UK market, becoming head of A&R. He took underground acts like Groundhogs, Man and Hawkwind on to his more mainstream label, seeing off the look of panic on his bosses' faces when Hawkwind scored a Top Five smash with the classic 'Silver Machine'.

He then signed the great and gritty Dr Feelgood and masterminded their unlikely crossover success which included the first ever live album, *Stupidity*, to go in at Number One.

With this apprenticeship over he was ready for punk, signing The Buzzcocks and The Stranglers. Post-punk he launched Radar Records who released Elvis Costello for a short time and Brian James once of The Damned and then in the cool but totally overlooked Tanz Der Youth.

After this he moved on to F Beat which spawned Demon and Edsel – two excellent labels dealing in the maverick, both current and back catalogue. Bored with the re-issue scene, Lauder was looking for something more exciting – he was looking for a new act to break. So when Zomba got in touch and asked him to head a new company he was more than pleased to accept.

When Roddy McKenna came a knock knock knocking on his door with The Stone Roses stuff, he was ready, and despite a cautious record deal he must have instinctively known that there was something definitely exciting in this pile of demos and underfed photo shots.

'I like outlaw bands,' he told the *Observer*, adding, 'I tend to be interested in the band that record companies find difficult to deal with . . . that's what makes it interesting.'

He was just going to find out how difficult a band and a maverick manager really could be in the next few years.

THE FIRST OF THE BREAKTHROUGH SHOWS: ANTI-CLAUSE 28 GIG AT THE INTERNATIONAL 2

Record Collector: 'Didn't you also headline a double bill with James?'

Ian Brown: 'Yeah, we did an anti-Clause 28 benefit gig – remember that thing about homosexual literature in schools?'

'Clang, clang, clang, went the bell, clang, clang, clang,' Ian Brown crossed the stage clanking a huge tolling bell, ringing times up for the old Manchester and ready for the new.

This is the one.

The anti-Clause 28 benefit was special. Special because the Roses never did supports in Manchester, but fuck it was a good cause and a chance to remove the old guard from the stage. James had been around for years. They were a south Manchester band playing their home turf.

The gig was put on by local indie DJ, Dave Haslam, as a call to arms against the Tory party's oppressive new piece of policy, which, with typical hatred and bigotry, decided to put a clamp on the homosexual community as well as a host of others not considered in the mainstream of society.

In times to come Ian Brown would claim that this was 'a perfect Stone Roses gig'. He was at the height of his crowd confrontation phase and that night was pushing it as hard as he could.

In 1988 Ian Brown wasn't the immaculate frontman of later years – he was wired, angry, spiky. Probably fired more by speed than dope – this was some confrontational conflagration of a frontman, his hair was a crop of gelatined spikes, a tuff fringe crossed with a scally mop, while his shirts were Jackson Pollocked psychedelic slashes. This was an angry young punk with a burning intensity. But this old skool Brown was slowly being superseded by the stoner Brown, this gig was the bridge between the two.

The Manchester cognoscenti were still looking at them a little warily as if they were yobs gatecrashing the bookworm party. The media has never been comfortable with punk and raw rock related activity and, although the Roses at the time were still packing enough subtlety into their jive via Reni's awesome multi-flavoured drumming and John's delicate guitar work, they still had their so-called yobbish following mixed in with the new pop kids who were quickly picking up on them.

Eileen Mulligan, one of the Roses' original fans, remembers, 'Steve Adge was always really cool to us. He would always get us in, all the fans that followed them like Theresa, Collete, Shirley, Andy McQueen, the Hyde lot, Simmy . . . all them lot. The Roses always looked after their fans.'

It was a lesson learned from The Clash, the top bands, the street bands always looked after their fans, it was a special bond.

For promoter Dave Haslam this gig was a perfect opportunity to combine two upcoming local bands and a good political cause.

'The International 2 gig . . . Paul Cons at the Hacienda was quite active in AIDS awareness at that time. He didn't know any bands so he asked me if I could put on a couple of gigs to raise some money for anti-Clause 28. They wanted to set up an office in Manchester to co-ordinate the anti-Clause 28 campaign up here. The shows were the Roses with James at the International 2 and The Brilliant Corners at the Hacienda. I knew James would be up for a cause like that. And I thought maybe the Roses would be up for it. I had noticed a change in their attitude from aggressive to allowing a bit of femininity into their lives. I liked that mix of hardness and sensitivity in a band.'

When he got the go ahead the gig was swiftly put together. 'It was easy for me to set up. Gareth charged me twenty-five quid to hire the International 2.'

Over the years there has been a lot of talk about the Roses delaying their stage time to aggravate headliners James and take the whole crowd. Some claim this was their policy on the night and that the whole show was an attempt by the Roses to move up the musical ladder. This is not the way

Dave Haslam saw things.

'Around that gig there is a lot of myth making. Some say that there was an attempt to scupper James . . . that there were various power plays going on. I remember having to fit both bands in the bill. Both bands had pretty big followings in Manchester at that time. I needed both bands to get on before curfew. I wasn't aware that they were trying to hold back to piss off James. Everyone knew that both bands were capable of being headline bands that night. At the time James were more established so they got to headline the show. Afterwards it seemed the Roses were saying we did this and that . . .'

Gareth is on record detailing all the strokes the band pulled that night. The posters round town with their name as headliners, delaying their stage-time to play at the headline time and leaving the crowd to go home after they had played – powerplay that visibly pissed off James frontman Tim Booth . . . and to a certain extent it worked.

More importantly for Dave was the money that was raised for the cause. In light of later accusations of homophobia against Brown, the gig puts the Roses' realpolitik in a good light. Dave Haslam: 'It was great. They were so up for doing the gig. I realised they weren't being cynical about the show when I talked to Ian about it. He also went on the anti-Clause 28 march a couple of weeks later round Albert Square. Ian was in the crowd. He'd gone as a normal punter. He didn't use it as a place to be seen. He understood the clause. Ian Brown genuinely understood what was going on. I was quite impressed by that . . .'

At the International 2, the Roses seized their opportunity, a high-profile gig with a big hometown crowd. It was a gig that demanded a special attitude and Brown was taking no prisoners, as Andy McQueen pointed out. 'Ian Brown walked a tightrope at that gig.'

The benefit was a chance for the Roses to gather the clans, to break out from their fiercely passionate audience and into the student audience.

That afternoon they cruised in and sound checked with 'I Am The Resurrection', the song that only months before Pete Garner had been stunned to hear in the rehearsal and was fast becoming their anthem. Fleshing itself out, it transcended its influences and turned itself into its own sprawling monster that a year later when released would become one of the anthems of that long and strange summer of '89. The Stone Roses sounded good and sounded ready.

Due on at nine o'clock they didn't hit the stage till eleven. Building the tension up in the hall, making sure that when things started to happen they really would happen and also making sure that they got to play to the maximum crowd.

Gareth Evans will always maintain that the band deliberately went on late and the sight of the punters leaving before headliners James came on may have looked like a tip in the scale of the local band hierarchy. But all this competition between bands is pointless power playing and in the next couple of years both bands would mutually benefit from each other's successes.

For the first time ever they opened with 'I Wanna Be Adored'. It was a smart move, the perfect opening, building with the sonorous bass line that for years would be the spine-tingling call to arms, letting John coax himself in before kicking off big style.

Ian Brown stalked the stage, looking like trouble. Maybe he was aggrieved at the unfamiliar support role or maybe it was time to really ride the rush of adrenalin. There was a nasty edge to him that night and it worked the music hard.

A scuffle broke out at the front during 'I Wanna Be Adored' and he stared into the space. 'It's kicking off.' He sounded dispassionate and cold. When the crowd clapped with excitement he answered with a mock clap. He was giving nothing back except for attitude.

'I never set out to be a singer, I'm an exhibitionist and a lyricist,' as he told Paula Greenwood.

They ended with 'This Is The One', Brown sitting on the drum riser, staring out at the crowd – echoes of Lydon at San Francisco ten years earlier as the Pistols crumbled to defeat. That defiant not-playing-the-game frontman role – sulky and dangerous. It was pure pop art. Instead of putting a downer on things, it made the music seem more aggressive and dangerous, a pivotal display.

It was a non-performance performance that Oasis would make into an art form nearly ten years later, and it was this gig that fired the 16-year-old Liam Gallagher and made him want to sing in the first place. Liam was in the crowd that night and Brown's mesmeric anti-performance 'was doing my head in', adding 'That was my favourite gig of all time, killed me dead, changed me fucking life. If I hadn't gone that night, I'd probably be sitting in some pub in Levenshulme.' As inspired by Brown's stage presence as the band's music from that night, he vowed to front a band.

His brother, Noel was there too, celebrating his birthday, standing next to a certain local band member who was bootlegging the show. It was a real Manchester night out. The upstairs bar was packed with scene bands. Bands who were about to break as well the following year, like The Inspiral Carpets who at the time looked like the next band to break out. They had just released their début *Plane Crash* EP with 'Garage Full Of Flowers' one of the four tracks – the old Ian Brown lyric that they had turned into their tribute to the Roses.

At the time Ian Brown was asked by Andy McQueen for the now-defunct *M62* magazine if he prepared his mood before a gig. 'No I can't, because I don't know what the crowd is going to be like, because I never go out and have a look before we go on. I just like to walk on, you know, not knowing whether it's full or not. Just walk on and see what happens.'

You always seem so disappointed with your audience.

'No, that's not true.'

What about the gig at the International 2?

'That's just how you saw me. I wasn't upset. That's just how you decided I was. I was dissatisfied with the lack of movement on the balconies. I'd sooner look out at the crowd and get excited watching people get into it. Not people just stood there leaning on a balcony watching me, I just want people to watch us and participate. Why should we do all the work? Why should I do all the work? That's what I think.'

McQueen then pulled the decisive words out of the reticent Brown.

Did you actually enjoy the gig?

'I think the anti-Clause 28 gig was a perfect Stone Roses gig, because you had all the people down the front who were so obviously lost in it all. And then you had the people on the balcony who either couldn't understand it, or wanted to drag themselves away because they were guilty watching the group thinking, "Oh I shouldn't like this group", but they couldn't drag themselves away.'

Manchester's International 2 saw the band poised.

Finally the years of self-belief were paying off.

That night Roddy McKenna took Andrew Lauder up to see the Roses for the first time. Lauder was suitably impressed but was worried about the contract being too weighted in favour of the label. Things like that can cause problems.

And, in the crowd, was John Leckie checking out the band for the first time. He liked what he saw. And John Leckie had seen some bands in his life.

JOHN LECKIE

John Leckie has one hell of a track record. Post Roses he has become one of the top British producers, an award winning name to drop, the Roses' album finally pushing him into the mainstream of hip producers.

Leckie himself is an easy-going laid-back dude. Every year I bump into him at Glastonbury soaking up the sun and soaking up the vibes. And it's the Sixties vibe that is his roots.

Leckie started his career at Abbey Road in February 1967, joining straight from school. He had originally intended getting into the ACTT and then into the film industry. Straight into the deep end – he was the teaboy on Procol Harum's *Salty Dog* album; the next day he was working with George Martin and Ringo Starr on Ringo's *Sentimental Journey* album; it was like a tour of rock legends because the following day it was again making tea, this time for Pink Floyd working on their *Atom Heart Mother* album.

It was a hell of a first three days but then Abbey Road was the pop mecca of the world. It was where The Beatles had virtually recorded all of their hits, so you would expect better work than just knocking out local bands demos.

Within a couple of months he started making all the usual studio promotions. This time to tape op, his first job was with Phil Spector and George Harrison on *All Things Must Pass*. This was an incredible grounding and his reputation swiftly grew working with the Floyd or BeBop Deluxe.

A contemporary of Martin Rushent and Trevor Horn, Leckie was one of the producers who came out of the punk era before moving into the Eighties new angular pop scene. His production début was on XTC's *White Noise* before moving on to the likes of The Adverts and then XTC's perfect pastiche of psychedelia – *The Dukes of Stratosphear* – which typically of all band jokes backfired and outsold the master group. Noted for its brilliant guitar sounds, the album was held up by many guitar players as a definitive collection of vintage guitar sounds.

Always a music man Leckie told *International Musician*, 'Try playing The Beatles *Revolver* or some of Captain Beefheart's albums and they really stand up. Technically maybe they don't quite match the records made nowadays. But the melodies, the quality of singing and the overall construction of the songs are classic. You can't beat a good combination of a good tune, a good rhythm, a good sound and a good arrangement.'

Leckie pointed out that The Beatles and Jimi Hendrix were pretty much required listening in the Roses camp although Leckie was surprised by how they didn't like Pink Floyd.

Pink Floyd was still a no no for the scooter boys! It was only two years ago that they were asking Martin Hannett to recreate his Slaughter And The Dogs production!

When asked in 1990 what he thought of the band then, he replied, 'They were a bit of a shambles the first time I saw them. I got the impression that Reni was the star of the show and that a lot of people had just come to hear him drum. These days he's not trying to be Cozy Powell so much.'

In many ways John Leckie was to become a key figure in the band's story. Although they had toyed with getting Sly and Robbie in to do the album, Leckie passed the litmus test.

When they met him they, for some reason, asked him about Buddhism and he replied, 'Don't give away your possessions and never live on a commune.' Stark advice from a man who had been there and a reply that scored with the band.

Leckie had a good honest approach to production. 'I think that my job as a producer is to make a record which showcases the band. That's certainly true of the way I work with The Stone Roses. I think their record should sound like their best gig. And so I try to get them into that sort of mood and that sort of frame of mind when we're recording. It's the same with the mix – I think it's good to highlight everyone's little bit.'

Looking back at the Roses' début, Leckie recalls, 'As an album *The Stone Roses* was quite difficult to record because we set ourselves a very high standard and scrapped a lot of songs. I was specific that they should play as a unit. They didn't want to sound like they sounded live but at the same time they wanted to have a band sound. Which meant the drums and the bass had to be real. We pushed ourselves hard to make sure we got good live takes with no session players so they could reproduce them live.'

International Musician asked him what made the Roses' demos really stand out from the heaps of stuff that he was sent to listen to.

'Commitment, of course. What struck me most when I first heard The Stone Roses' demos was immediately how much more commitment they had than most bands you hear.

'Plus they have a crazy manager in Gareth Evans which is always a big help in my book. People take more notice of a crazy manager than a sane and sensible one. If he's crazy and bolshy, he'll get noticed more by the record company and the press.

'People really do respond to total belief. Gareth forces it upon you endlessly. Even now after two years he still phones me up and chews my ear about how great The Stone Roses are. My wife always says there is more to life than The Stone Roses, but you wouldn't believe it the way Gareth talks.'

More than a producer, Leckie had astutely put his finger on one of the reasons for the Roses' success and the sheer importance of Evans in creating the whole damn myth.

The great guitar sounds can't have escaped the ear of John Squire, a man who was always looking for some way to fuck around with his sound and make his pop symphonies sound even greater.

WHERE LEGENDS ARE MADE: RECORDING THE DEBUT ALBUM

The album was recorded in downtime in London's Battery Studios which were part of the Zomba group who also owned the Roses' label Silvertone, which was in the same building across the courtyard.

Walled by ten foot walls and behind automatic gates, Battery is almost like a mini version of Abbey Road, but with a scaled-down glamour. Hidden away from the dull surroundings of Willesden, Battery is an excellent place to grab a load of downtime to build up a powerful new pop record.

The ingredients were all there – a band with five years already on its clock and songs that had been worked on for a long time ready to cook, a producer with years of experience who could link them directly to the Sixties classics but also with a foot in the Eighties. This was a band at the peak of its powers. They had been around long enough to perfect their muse but not too long to get bored of it.

It was a mouth-watering prospect, and the Roses worked hard and meticulously slowly, piecing together the record. Their work ethic surprised Leckie who had seen some real rock'n'roll wasters in his long career.

Soaking up the current pop scene, the Roses certainly listened to a lot of house music and John Leckie remembers them playing it in the studio all the time. It made very little direct crossover into their actual sound but listen to it they certainly did, as Ian Brown noted, speaking to local DJ, Dave Haslam, the following year.

'We're always getting fans coming back stage and hearing tapes we're listening to and going "How can you like this?" and we'd tell them to listen again.

'It's never true that if you are a guitar group then all you listen to is guitar music. In this group we can't get enough music. The first music I listened to was The Beatles and the first record I bought was "Pretty Vacant". Music had a pretty lean period in the Eighties – that's why hip-hop and house have made such a huge impact.'

Leckie was impressed by the meticulous way the band worked. 'There was no discernible musical leader. Each member of the band was equally important. They hardly ever drank. Ian Brown didn't even drink any beer. That impressed me.'

At last they were getting 'I Wanna Be Adored' down on tape for proper release. It can't have taken Mani for ever to learn that bass line! But he now made it his own. There was a killer new song, 'Made Of Stone', with its amazing chorus and Mani's signature bass run and some awesome guitar from John Squire. There was the pure pop shakes of 'She Bangs The Drums' and the falling arpeggios of 'Waterfall'. No wonder the band were buzzing. No wonder the mood was good. Four drop dead rock'n'roll classics and this was just for starters.

For the second session the band moved across London to Konk studios, set up by The Kinks' mainman Ray Davies. Konk is another great sounding studio, mainly used for mixing but with a neat live room that potentially records a cracking drum sound. I have produced some stuff there and can vouch for the place – you even get to see Ray Davies.

Here they recorded 'Badman', 'Shoot You Down', 'Resurrection', and 'This Is The One', the anthems, the long extended jams, the amazing playing, less the straight three minute pop anthems, more the band showing just what they were capable of. Guitar, bass and drums as magical as it gets. And then they started to fuck with stuff, run things backwards.

Ian pointed out to *Record Collector*, '"Waterfall" may have sounded like a Simon and Garfunkel song, "April She Will Come". But we've never consciously stolen or copied anything.'

The track 'Don't Stop' was one of Ian's favourites.

'It was accidental. We got a tape of "Waterfall" on the portastudio, which plays both sides. It sounded great backwards. We could hear lyrics coming out, words suggesting themselves. We went back into the studio, turned the tape over, put the vocal down and then put a forward drum over it. That's my favourite thing on the first LP. There's twenty seconds at the end that's a killer, the little rhythm that comes in.'

And 'Resurrection'?

'"I Am The Resurrection" had a Motown kind of beat. It reminded me of "You're Ready Now" by Slaughter And The Dogs – (sings) "you're ready now, you're ready now".'

Reni recalls how they wrote 'Resurrection': '"I Am The Resurrection", started out as a reverse bass pisstake of Paul McCartney on "Taxman". Mani used to play that riff every day, I'd come in and John would doodle some Fender over the top and we'd do it for a laugh at soundchecks. Finally we said, "Let's do it properly – this joke song actually sounds really good!"'

John explained to Total Guitar, 'I also like the fortuitous ending of "I Am The Resurrection". We had some bits left over on tape which we just dropped in at exactly the right points – that little rhythm guitar bit at the end. Also the acoustic jangly stuff on the end section, too; I'd recorded it on this little Philips ghetto blaster and I got the engineer to drop it in. It's a bit out of time, because we were just pressing Play to try and get it in sync. I think we only tried it twice, so it's a bit out of time. I like it, though.

'The low point on the album? I'd have just done less overdubs, had stronger main guitar parts.'

The record itself was shaping up to be guitar pop perfection. Demo tapes that were leaked out set tongues wagging. There was some serious business going on in that studio.

Despite the fact that the album was sounding amazing, the band themselves have never been happy with the sound of the record. John Squire sums it up in one word: 'Twee.' Adding, 'I think it was mainly the production. We saw there being a huge gulf between the live sound of The Stone Roses and that first album. It was mostly recorded on an SSL desk, and it just didn't sound fat or hard enough. From a guitar point of view I see my approach as the main failing; I completely deconstructed what I played live and rewrote everything for the studio. That just seems a bit simple, and the switch from chordal to solo stuff just doesn't seem to work. The album just doesn't have the stamp of a real guitar player to me, apart from a couple of the solos. It sounds like a two guitar band, which we weren't.'

But there were creative high points that even the perfectionist Squire enjoyed. 'But I do like the guitar playing on "Bye Bye Badman". I worked through the guitar parts for that in this little breeze-blocked room at the back of the studio where all the air conditioning and mains switches were. I was just sat there with my little Portastudio sitting on top of its cardboard box; we were getting right down to the wire in terms of time, and when I went in to record I still didn't really know the part. I really enjoyed doing that.

'I like "Don't Stop" a lot too. It's the tape of "Waterfall" backwards, with the bass drum triggered, and the only real overdubs are the vocals and a bit of cowbell. I wrote the lyrics by listening to "Waterfall" backwards and writing down what was suggested, what the vocal might have been. It's good fun doing that, because you sort of remove your involvement from the song, you don't really know what's going to come next.'

Despite certain reservations, despite the band being worried about the record's 'monochrome' sound they knew that they were sat on a classic record. And when they moved over to Rockfield in Wales to finish it off and mix it down the vibe in the camp was positively upbeat.

Rockfield was a wheeze as well. Set in beautiful countryside, the band chilled out and finished off the record, they loved the place so much that it would virtually become their musical headquarters for the next few years.

'ELEPHANT STONE' GETS THE RELEASE

Finally released that October by Silvertone, 'Elephant Stone' was another move forward, another hint at the golden groove that the band were about to hit. The song was pumped full of tunes and had those chops and changes that would eventually become a total feature of their sound. Riding on Squire's choppy wah wah, it was a fast-paced rush through classic guitar pop. Ian Brown's sugar-sweet vocals were dripping an unlikely innocence: how could such a yob sound so angelic!

The 'B' side, 'Full Fathom Five', was the first of those backwards things that must have sounded great in the studio at four in the morning. Flipping the master tape of the 'A' side over they were intrigued by the weird rush of backwards sounds that flew out of the speakers and decided that this must be a flipside. Ian Brown's backwards vocals sound like some Byzantine monk singing in a spooky Far Eastern chapel as the crazed slurping rush of guitars scorched past him.

'The Hardest Thing In The World' was one of their older songs, but it was obviously picked because it was not one of the 'rock ones', it was a pure blast of melody. Listening to this makes nonsense of the claims that Brown couldn't sing. The solo is crystalline Squire; what a great pop solo player he was. A non-macho guitar hero, John could dash off the greatest licks that were just total pop. The song was a medium-paced, dark-hearted ballad showing the emerging introspection of a band that was daring to admit to more than full-on rock and in-your-face psychosis.

It was also the first single to feature Squire's Pollocked artwork. 'Elephant Stone' was Silvertone's début release for the band and only managed to scrape into the indie charts at number twenty-seven. What the fuck were they going to have to do to get this pure pop to the people?

Andy McQueen was disappointed. 'Ian Brown phoned and said that he had a copy of "Elephant Stone" for me. I cycled over, the record sounded very disappointing – slovenly, scrappy and "live" . . . John later told me that he couldn't bear to listen to that version. Ruined it.'

The press reviewed the record this time. *NME*'s Edwyn Pouncey said that readers should listen to The Velvet Underground's 'Sister Ray' instead – a bizarre suggestion. *Record Mirror* told them that there was more to life than 'Lollipops, psychedelia and flakey grey skin' (just wait till next year!) and the radio ignored it.

Still why should they care, they were sat on top of this amazing album, and they were thinking of pulling one of their newer songs, 'Made Of Stone' off it as a single for early 1989.

And what a single that would be!

1988 PLAYS ITSELF OUT

With the single recorded, I interviewed the band for *Sounds*. It was their first piece of major press since Gary Johnson had given them a page in the same paper three years before. It was my first major piece for the paper. Hopping into Gareth's Jeep, I made the short journey over to Reni's house in Ardwick.

The band were all sat together in their briefs in bed. The whole house seemed to have virtually nothing in it. The bedroom was stripped floorboards, a bed and a tape recorder.

In fact the house looked like someone had stripped it all down. There was nothing inside it, except for wooden beams. Every ten minutes or so Gareth Evans's head would pop around the door all excited, hoping for some sort of action. Evans himself was oozing enthusiasm – it was contagious. His beaming face was hilarious, his excitement thrilling.

The band talked about their love of The Hollies and pure guitar pop and talked about their big ambitions. They also played some rough mixes from the album. I took home a tape of 'Made Of Stone' and was in a rush of excitement at how brilliant that song was. It sent shivers up my spine, it felt weird that people I'd known for a long time could actually come up with such a classic song. I knew at that point that this was a band that was going to be more than just a big indie band but a special band.

They were all growing sideboards. 'It's a band thing,' they smirked.

The interview was finished off in a couple of days later around Ian Brown's flat in West Didsbury – a tight, crammed space with a poster from *If* on the wall.

It took several weeks for *Sounds* to print the piece. In the meantime Gareth Evans would stand in my garden and knock on the window, hassling for the publication of the piece. According to the then editor of the paper he offered a holiday in the Bahamas to him if the story ran. Because of this the editor deliberately stalled the story!

As ever the interview was littered with self-belief and made-up stories. Brown claimed that Reni used to be a biker and that he had once attempted to bully Brown at a fair 'for 10p'. Brown claimed that 'Martin Hannett taught us all about writing melodies' on the shelved album and that in Manchester 'we have grown up in public' when pressed on the band's gradual change in image and style over the years.

The band were affable, easy-going, there was none of that stonewalling the questions or blank stares that they were to become famous for. Ian Brown was quite adamant that he was concerned with 'the truth' and would answer any question straight.

Reni raved about Bootsy Collins and how he was listening to 'a lot of Parliament at the moment'.

Reni talked about his first rehearsal with the band. 'When I auditioned for them I thought they were a horrible racket but they were exciting and totally committed. I was struck by how different the whole band were. Long-haired scruffs and short-haired smoothies.'

Ian Brown claimed that they were going to call the album that they were about to start work on 'Bring me the head of James Anderton on a plate' referring to the stern, bearded, Victorian principled, Mancunian police chief of the time.

At the tail end of 1988 they continued to work the circuit. They had a single out to promote, so it was back in the clubs again. On 26 November they played the St Helens Citadel. Back in the days when bands played in St Helens, the Citadel was the circuit venue, a cool, well organised place, everyone went through there. It was the beginning of a long nine month haul by the Roses through the small clubs of the UK, playing mainly to empty houses even after the album came out until word of mouth caught them up in such a spectacular manner.

It was, typically, for an outside Manchester Roses show, pretty empty.

Andy McQueen was there, of course, and was asked by Ian Brown to make up the set list for the night. It's an honour for a fan to get this close to the machinations of the gig. With trepidation he lined up the following: 'Here It Comes'/'Elephant Stone'/'Mersey Paradise' ('I Wanna Be Adored' was tucked in mid set, McQueen obviously not noting its killer potential as the set opener), 'Waterfall'/'Sally Cinnamon'/'Made Of Stone'/'Sugar Spun Sister'/'Shoot You Down'/'She Bangs The Drums'/'I Am The Resurrection'.

'It wasn't that good a gig actually,' McQueen remembers, adding, 'Gareth drove me home in the really thick fog and asked me if I had ever had "some of this E". I said no and he asked, "Why not?" We stopped off at the International 1 and he gave me a copy of "Sally Cinnamon" and "So Young".'

Ecstasy was, by that autumn, a big craze. All that summer acid house parties had been kicking off all over the UK, all of a sudden bands and gigs seemed dated, very old-fashioned, like clumsy dinosaurs compared to an all-nighter in a field. Sometimes thousands of people would turn out for a night of rampant hedonism. This sure beat standing in a dank, mouldy venue with a few pints and a half-assed band as entertainment.

And the drugs! The rush of ecstasy was extraordinary, it was the greatest feeling and the music seemed to match perfectly. You couldn't stop moving, grooving on the music. Touching other people was a thrill, it was an incredibly tactile drug, it made the user feel warm and horny, the love vibe was high! Tied in with the big warm bass end-beats and hi-speed gallop of acid house it was a perfect combination.

The camaraderie and the outlaw nature of the raves pissed all over the respectable indie scene. Going to see an indie band was like going to the library, it was sensible, boring and dull. It was tied by convention and rules. You paid your money, came in, stood about checking the band and went home. Where was the wild looseness that you demanded from rock'n'roll? It was as staid and sensible as DIY, just not sexy.

The first rave you went to was a wild carnal experience. Off your head on drugs and lost in this new alien music, the clothes were loose and bright and the vibe was a massive rush of positive joy.

And no wonder the government was coming down hard on it, people can't have that much fun! They came down hard on ecstasy which, of course, fucks you up, but nowhere near as much as cigarettes and alcohol, two drugs that are not only legitimate but virtually forced upon you.

Equally appalled by this new scene was the rock establishment who, being as conservative as the government, made big noises about the raves. It was one of those sudden generation gaps that appears in pop. It was a call to arms. It was time to decide. Just which side are you on?

The coolest bands would be the one that took acid house on and let it influence their moves. Ian Brown, ever culture vulture, was checking things out, he and the Roses would almost instinctively use some of the trappings of the house culture and fuse it with what they were doing. It was mainly the approach they were interested in, and oh, the drugs as well.

Back in the indie world they took one of their occasional trips down to London to play what was a desultory affair, supporting The Chameleons' off-shoot Sun And The Moon in a tiny room at Central London Poly. It was a shoddy gig, watched by a tiny pocket of punters. It seemed like the band was going nowhere. But they still retained that steely resolve. They knew that they were going to break big. They had come a long way and there was no turning back now.

On Tuesday 29 November they played at Olives in Chester. Again they were supported by 'some crap metal band', the bane of a touring band when it takes its first steps out on the circuit. The promoters, unsure of what the band are about, will always couple them with the most unlikely supports.

Jo Taylor, who went to a lot of indie gigs in the late Eighties and first saw the Roses at Chester, was blown away. 'They were just about there when I saw them. Friends in Manchester had been going on about how good they were as a band so I went to check them out. They sounded like the band that broke through the year after. It seemed odd at the time that there wasn't more people but you knew then that it was only a matter of time before they broke through.'

On 11 December they played Edinburgh Venue. It was their first trip to Scotland. Andrew McDermid, who would go on to manage Stone Roses fanatics White Out (the band that Oasis would later support on their first national tour) remembers getting into the Roses at about this time. This was the first gig he saw them at. He was promoting bands over in Greenock, it always meant that he was hip to what was coming out.

'I had booked the Mondays from that Manchester agent, what's his name, aye, Brian Turner and he sent us "Elephant Stone". We were all Primal Scream fans so we were hooked immediately, deffo.'

McDermid went to The Venue and was blown away. He'd also, by now, booked them for his own club, Ricos, in Greenock. It was the first thing that he was genuinely excited about for ages.

'I was booking stuff like James Taylor, The Chills and The Weather Prophets – all that indie guitar stuff was not happening, that was the size of the groups I would put into Ricos. We had the Roses booked for Monday, 12 December, and then they cancelled. We were told Ian had tonsillitis. Imagine how gutted I was, already I was a massive fan.'

Glasgow and especially the cluster of towns to the west of the great Scottish city would become a stronghold for the band.

The Roses also recorded their first TV towards the tail end of the year appearing on Granada on one of Tony Wilson's arts and entertainment guides. They played 'Waterfall' and the session became part of their legend due to Ian Tilton's photos of the band which eventually became the pictures on the inner sleeve of the album.

Says Ian Brown, 'We did "Waterfall". Wilson did the Hacienda and our manager did the Internationals and they were rivals so Wilson never used to give us any space. The only reason we got on was because Paul Ryder told Tony Wilson we should be on his show.'

Those black and white pictures (check the photo section in the book) capture the band right on the cusp. Stark images of a sharp and angular group, dressed in clean-cut mod gear, a band on the verge of the baggy revolution.

1988 again was another slow year, another year of struggle and delay, but the necessary bedrock had been built. For the first time in their career they had a proper record label behind them and as the year closed they also had a brilliant début album under their belts. The Roses had their sensual new pop sound together.

All that long work in the studio was beginning to pay off.

If 1988 had promised, 1989 was finally going to deliver.

1989

AT LAST! THE 1980S COME ALIVE

Every now and then pop, culture and the times coincide with a ferocious force to create a whirlpool of excitement. Think 1956 and Elvis putting sex into the mainstream, think 1963 and The Beatles and the Stones copping the high-energy rush of optimism of the 1960s, think 1977 and the punk revolution, and think 1989 for the year that the crap 1980s music scene finally got trashed.

When 1989 began it didn't really feel that there was a revolution about to start. Rock, terrified of the rave culture, seemed even more conservative. As The Stone Roses took to the circuit they were playing to 'crowds' of ten people in backwater towns, and it was hard to believe that within eight months they would be at the Empress Ballroom in Blackpool.

But the 1980s were grinding to a halt. All over Eastern Europe, the Communist old guard and their vile, cranky leaders were being overthrown by the people. Years of repression were coming to an end. Maybe it was time for the repression in pop to be overthrown by a new generation of bands hip to what was really going on out on the streets.

Ecstasy was massive now, and every week you'd meet some ex-champion of guitar action looking all glazed and ranting on about house music. The clubs were packed. The Hacienda, the club started by Factory Records, had spent 1988 becoming party central, finally being a byword for the cutting edge in pop. Manchester was the fulcrum of the whole culture. Remarkably it had re-invented itself as the dance capital, and all thoughts of The Smiths had been banished. Ecstasy was one powerful drug.

The Stone Roses were looking looser and baggier. Ian Brown now wore those famous green cords that he got from Steve Cresser. The rest of the band wore parallels, they looked great – one step in and one step out of fashion – the way pop bands should look.

LET THE TOUR COMMENCE

During February they confronted shocked indie fans at Warrington Legends and Sheffield University, looking like aliens compared to the staid wardrobe of the punters, their loose cuts directly opposed to the rigidity of the indie scene.

On 23 February they played Middlesex Polytechnic. Sally Williams helped to promote the show: 'We put them on in the canteen. We had spent the whole term putting on really small bands, we had no money and we couldn't afford any bigger groups. But we thought that we should do well with this one. But only thirty people turned up – I couldn't believe it. I think it was the next night they were playing the Hacienda and they were going to get 3,000 quid. They had this really massive fan that followed them around everywhere called Little Julia. She had Jimi Hendrix Experience written down one arm of her jacket. She was mentioned in Bob Stanley's *Melody Maker* review. They both stayed over at my house that night . . . I think she ended up following Dr. Phibes around the country after the Roses. That night The Stone Roses were brilliant. The next time I saw them was at Dingwalls in May and there was a big queue outside and then after that it was at Ally Pally . . . all in the space of a few months. It was astonishing how quickly they took off.'

The set they played that night at Middlesex Poly was: 'I Wanna Be Adored', 'Standing Here', 'Made Of Stone', 'Waterfall', 'Sugar Spun Sister', 'Elephant Stone', 'Where Angels Play', 'Shoot You Down', 'She Bangs The Drums', 'Sally Cinnamon' and 'I Am The Resurrection'. It was pretty well the same set they played on this seminal tour.

This was the first time that Bob Stanley, the mastermind behind Saint Etienne and at the time a journalist for *Melody Maker*, had seen the band. He was the first London journalist to get it since Gary Johnson, and he reviewed the gig: 'They sound like someone has sneaked a tab into your Tizer, they sound like the best thing I've ever heard. The Stone Roses. Jesus Christ . . .' Bob was on a rush, and from then on he was campaigning strictly on behalf of the band, eventually hooking journalist Everett True into the group, and bringing *Melody Maker* on board.

It had been a long time coming but at last The Stone Roses were starting to get some press attention in London.

KISS ME WHERE THE SUN DON'T SHINE, THE PAST IS YOURS, THE FUTURE'S MINE

As it moved into March it was clear that the rest of the nation was still lagging behind Manchester in its support of the Roses. But not for long.

On 1 March they played Bradford's Club Rio, the next day Cardiff's Venue and then Dudley's JBs, circuit gigs that were ill attended but which kept the band's soul fire burning. The 1989 tour was a gradual roller-coaster and the word of mouth was beginning to spread that here was a band coming through fast that captured the spirit of the times, playing a pop so pure, that it seemed remarkable that they had been ignored for so long.

It was at Dudley's JBs that they were supported for the second time by The Charlatans (they had already done the Warrington show last month) still in their earlier Baz Ketley fronted phase. The two bands got on. They were both plying a colourful guitar pop. But as the Roses effortlessly hit first gear it became obvious to the support band that they would have to do something if they were ever actually going to catch up with their northern contemporaries. A line up shuffle and a slight overhaul in style and The Charlatans would be there and there about when the Roses had finally kicked the barn doors open.

The press were fine, and what the Roses needed now was the single to break through. 'Made Of Stone' was days away from release, and they had new radio pluggers, Beer Davies, on the case, who said that they were getting good reactions down at Radio One. The mainstream resistance was finally wearing down.

SINGLE NO. 4!: MADE OF STONE

For many people, seemingly out of nowhere, 'Made Of Stone' released by Silvertone in February hit the racks. This time the press were on the band's case; *Melody Maker* may have compared it unfavourably to 'Spear Of Destiny', but *Sounds* raved and *Record Mirror* was buzzing.

Richard Skinner, who was then hosting the early-evening slot on Radio One, picked up on the record and suddenly the word was out. Into a pop scene slowly being infused by ecstasy and confused by acid house, a brilliant traditional guitar pop song with echoes of Primal Scream and The Rolling Stones' 'Paint It Black' was released.

A brilliant record, 'Made Of Stone', had all the effortless cool of The Stone Roses at their peak. Introing with a shimmering guitar arpeggio before the bass enters, nailing down the minor-key melody, the song rips molten melody. The verse intoned by Brown is icy observation just waiting for the tug of the chugging guitars to lead up to the crescendo of the chorus. The chorus itself, when it comes in, seems to shift a gear. It's a beautiful and tragic piece of music, uplifting, dark and scary – pure pop but with a black soul.

On release its dark heart and shimmering psychedelic edge hinted at the oncoming summer. It was the 1960s, but with a definite late-1980s edge. 'Stone' was ice-cold and yet it melted the heart; it boasted one of the greatest uplifting choruses of any pop song ever released and it still sounds like a masterpiece today.

Their first total classic, 'Made Of Stone', remains to this day one of the Roses' five greatest songs and one of the best singles released in the 1980s. From the first demos right through to the final release it sent shivers up the spine.

The record captures Manchester's teaming rain and restlessness, while cold-hearted streets and casual nihilism infuse the chorus: 'Sometimes I fantasise, when the streets are cold and lonely, and the cars they burn below me. Are you alone? Is anyone at home?'

Ian Brown's vocals are perfect – the deadpan hushed crooning is at once menacing and celebratory – the arrangement is perfect and it boasts a soaring solo from John Squire.

Joining 'Going Down' the band's ode to oral sex, the single's 'B' side on the 12 inch, was 'Guernica', another chance for the Roses to stretch their sound out and another chance to run the A-side tapes backwards and put the vocals on forwards. Named after Picasso's awe-inspiring painting inspired by the savagery of Franco's army crushing the socialist-anarchist resistance in the Spanish civil war. Amazingly 'I Wanna Be Adored' was mooted for the 'B' side before being held back for the album.

The freak-out section was inspired, according to Ian Brown, by jets taking off at Manchester airport, the all-night café that overlooks the runway now being one of the band's favourite haunts.

Brown told *Melody Maker*'s Bob Stanley about 'Guernica': 'We go to Manchester airport and watch the planes land and take off. Your eardrums feel like they are shredding with the volume of the engines. And the fire coming out of the back – it's an awesome sight, being thirty feet from a plane. We want to get that sound on to the record.'

If there was a single moment when The Stone Roses broke out then this was it.

Simon Williams made it single of the week in *NME*, calling the Roses 'macabre Monkees, dreamers haunted by their own shadows'.

'Made Of Stone' was a marker of things to come, a signpost on the road to the big time. Surely it would only be a matter of months now until the big breakthrough. 'Are you all alone? Are you Made Of Stone?' was the exit line, and seemed to sum up the Roses' ice-cold cool in one line.

'Made Of Stone' began doing the business, and instead of having a battle to get the band known Silvertone were suddenly sat on a mini indie goldmine. The single crashed into the indie charts at number four, and made a brief excursion into the top 100 of the main charts. There was now a small but hungry national fan-base to start complementing the huge Manchester one.

The word was out as people were raving about this new band from Manchester, and their friends and their friends' friends were beginning to take notice. As April melted into May the venues the Roses played that had once been empty began to fill up; hey they were now nearly half full!

As the summer started to kick in and it seemed like everyone was blissed-out on E, this shaggy pop group from Manchester were walking the new walk and talking the new talk. Along with The Happy Mondays, they seemed to be the harbinger of a new working-class psychedelic (un)consciousness that contrasted so sharply with the far more middle-class 1960s phenomenon.

This time the hallucinogenics were in very different hands, and this time they would be in bloodstreams of new crews of crazed-drug outlaws, scallydelics and acid casuals as the press misnamed them at the time.

And it all seemed to be coming from Manchester. The city became synonymous with drugs and good times. It was going to be one hell of a summer. It seemed like a never-ending E-fuelled trip through some of the craziest pop scenes for years. Acid house had sparked a cultural revolution and now the guitar bands, after assimilating the new culture, were ready to reply . . . And what a reply! Hot on the heels of 'Made Of Stone' The Stone Roses released their début album.

On Monday 27 February, The Stone Roses broke into the media mainstream. They played the Hacienda; the club that Ian Brown had once hated so much was now the hippest space in England. It was a master stroke, coming in from the suburb clubs like the Internationals and into the city centre, they were a band about to break in a city that was by now seeking the twenty-four-hour party. They looked right, they felt right and they sold the place out.

Meanwhile publicists Hall Or Nothing organised the first big press for the band, and all the papers were there to review the show. It was make or break for the Roses and the triumphant gig was crucial to their eventual ascendancy.

The Roses' career had been going up in steps in Manchester, from the warehouse gigs to the Internationals, last year's bash with James at the International 2. It was time to move on up, raid the fashion palaces, get a foot into the door of the trendy. Filmed for *Snub* (a BBC2 pop programme), this was the gig that started the media rush.

The Hacienda was going through something of a renaissance. It had originally been a live venue, a big, cold, modern barn with a dripping ceiling and a dreaded sound system. It had struggled to make ends meet until acid house and the likes of Graeme Park and Mike Pickering had made it the hippest club in the UK. It was the nerve centre for acid house – reputations were forged on the dancefloor, hushed rumours went round that the first-ever Es in the city were sold by Bez in the dark corners of the club, the erstwhile Mondays' percussionist/dancer hot-rodding a cranky old van up and down the M6 supplying the new drug generation with their pills.

In the last eighteen months the club had become very hot indeed. It was the key place in the city and everything revolved round it.

But for a guitar band it was still looked on as a difficult gig as the Roses had found out when they last played there three years ago.

This was the perfect moment, this was the moment when acid house and rock were going to fucking get together and the Roses were one of the two bands, along with the Happy Mondays, who had the swagger and the nous and the understanding of street culture to pull it off.

Andy McQueen was buzzing. 'I got down to the Hacienda at quarter to six just before the soundcheck, and there was a real sense that an event was about to take place. Ubiquitous baldies and longhairs stalked about and the gigantic PA just boomed *The Vanishing Point* soundtrack and *The Spirit Dive* [Shirley Bassey]. It sounded crystal clear and very loud. The band arrived in dribs and drabs, all clearly excited, especially Mani, who was leaping about and slapping hands with everybody. I was very excited.'

The excitement was tangible all evening. Playing the Hacienda then was a very big deal, and was as big as you got, if you were cool, long before your GMex's, long before Britpop and the big aircraft hangers, this was it. There was nowhere else to go; if you could just get on that stage and play, you seemed like you were a massive band. Fuck the rubbish sound system and the barmy acoustics, this was the big time. Bands yearned for the chance to hit that stage.

The Roses felt that they were on to something here.

In the soundcheck they attempted to play a new song, 'Where Angels Play'. Andy McQueen was simply stunned. 'It was gorgeous, really catchy, just classic pop. I had that familiar feeling, the tune was so great I felt it was a cover, it sounded so perfect.'

Even Andy felt that no one could have the audacity to be writing such great guitar pop in the late 1980s. That was the crazy situation that the Squire found themselves in at the time. They had the whole thing nailed down perfectly: the tunes, the look, the arrogance, the buzz – but who would ever buy British groups making guitar pop again?

It was something that we were traditionally brilliant at and yet it was something that, at the time, almost sounded avant garde. The Stone Roses were neither indie or mainstream, instead they were heading for that dead zone, caught between two fanatical polar opposite worlds.

And that was the beauty of the Roses: they, more than anybody else, destroyed that barrier for once and for all and unleashed a tidal wave of pop that had been pent up for a decade back into the chart. For the first time since punk rock everyone felt included in the pop process. They got the council estate kids interested in being in bands again, but they didn't exclude the students. This, by accident or design, was their singular key contribution to UK pop culture.

McQueen hung around the soundcheck spellbound. 'Here they were mooching around in their outdoor coats making such beautiful music. It was what was so great about the band, it was like they made no attempt and yet they were effortlessly making brilliant music.'

The soundcheck, typically, took ages. There were lots of details to take in. A lot of texture to be honed. Ian sang all the versus of 'Resurrection' and they went on to play 'Where Angels Play' again, 'Shoot You Down', 'Sally Cinnamon' and repeated half of 'Resurrection', before diving into the drawn-out bluesy ending of 'Resurrection' separately. Ian lent down and played the tom-toms, detached.

Later that night the band took the stage and pop became a celebration instead of a chore. Guitars suddenly seemed modern again, effortless, the band were coasting, cool. The *NME* and *Sounds* raved, and suddenly the Roses were finally in favour. The press were thrilled; here was a band that could replace The Smiths. So were the fans and it was from The Smiths that the Roses got most of their audience.

The sound was spot-on, miraculously crystal clear; again 'Adored' kicked off the set and again Ian was taunting the crowd, mouth gaping, eyes staring, the king monkey moves apparent. Total attitude was required and delivered.

'Here It Comes', 'Waterfall', the new single, 'Made Of Stone', segued into 'Shoot You Down', 'Elephant Stone' – it was becoming a legendary roll call – 'Sally Cinnamon', 'Sugar Spun Sister', a rush of pure pop, and the full stop. No encore.

'These brightest of sparks actually do merit your adoration,' enthused Andrew Collins in the *NME*.

After five years The Stone Roses were the hottest new band in Britain.

MEANWHILE BACK IN THE REAL WORLD

The tour continued on 28 February, travelling all the way down south to Brighton. In total contrast to the Hacienda last month, in Brighton at the Escape Club fifty-two people paid £3 each to enter the upstairs room of a well-kept pub with a tight, small stage and a lop-sided bar. The Roses obviously didn't like it at all – they played four songs and left the stage, walking into the crowd and down the stairs as there was no exit on the stage itself. The last song of the set was 'Sally Cinnamon', and Ian Brown never even bothered to sing; he just sat there playing the bongos like a kid with a new toy, dispassionate, bored. He cold-shouldered the 'crowd'; 'Aren't you people polite clapping like that,' he sneered at the smattering of between-song applause.

It was in Brighton that they went to the Dolphinarium and checked out the dolphins. Ian Brown let his tough street pose drop in an interview. 'We went to see a dolphin in Brighton. It was really sad because it was in a tiny little pool. None of us said anything for about half an hour. We just stared at it. It kept going past and turning its head and smiling. There was a load of people standing around the pool and it only jumped up when it saw us.'

It was a sensitive side that would occasionally seep out in the band's music.

The Roses had never toured like this before. But from the first gig, a show in Ian's hometown of Warrington at the Legends club, on 17 February they were pretty well on the road for the rest of that year. Playing to sparse crowds the Roses were one step ahead of the pop audience, but this seminal tour, one of the classic pop tours, was taking a whole new pop culture to a new pop generation and when the kids got it, they got it en-masse.

THE STONE ROSES DÉBUT ALBUM RELEASED AT LAST: MAY 1989

That album, the soundtrack of the period and the kick start of a new rock'n'roll generation still sounds as fresh today as it did years ago. For ever ending up near top of lists of classic records it's easily survived the past decade. Even the doubters at the time who dismissed the band as 'hype' have had to swallow their words.

The Roses' début is up there with all the classic British rock'n'roll records and proved that a British band could easily throw off the yoke of The Beatles and the other heavyweight classics that mostly crush the spirit of any upcoming band. This record is as good if not better than most of those so-called classics.

Opening like their best gigs with 'I Wanna Be Adored', the album was thought out, planned. The track listing was perfect, all ebbs and flows. The bass chugs in, lulling the listener into a strange unease as the crystalline guitar announced itself with a series of sound FX before the chords slash in. There is no other way you could start this album, 'Adored', once planned to be the Roses' follow-up single to 'So Young', is now virtually the anthem to a new pop generation. The song, Brown's third person paean to sin and craving for adoration, neatly uncoils itself. The beauty of 'Adored' is the way it is so easily misunderstood – in the context of an arrogant singer intoning the lyrics in front of the adoring faithful it took on a meaning quite different from what Brown intended. *But* then that's the beauty of pop, misinterpretation, making the song mean whatever you want.

Riding in on that bassline, the song, written almost right back at the beginning of the Roses' career, finally finds its home, at the front of the album and, finally, at the beginning of their live set after spending four years floating around in the middle of the set list since its début in Sweden.

'I Wanna Be Adored' slowly uncoils, all menacing, ominous and yet riding on a total pop melody. It's a great opener to an album.

'She Bangs The Drums', the song that eventually gave the band their first Top Forty hit later that July, is a glorious, near Monkees, pop rush. Every twist and turn of the song seems to be crammed with another riff, another hook; hooks that sound at once so familiar and yet you can't quite place where you heard them before. The Roses having the imagination to twist pop into new shapes. Great lyrics as well from the songwriting duo with Ian's uplifting swagger bounding along on the edge of pure arrogance.

John weighs in with the lyrics to the chorus planting a seed of self-doubt in the song, but all that is lost in the music. The Roses literally swagger their uplifting pop out of the grooves of the record. Two songs in and we're already celebrating a classic record.

The other single pulled from the album, 'She Bangs The Drums' was pop as innocent as The Monkees, a saccharine blast of guitar pop that seemed to change tune with every twist of its fluctuating structure. It showed a band that were oozing a cool confidence. Most groups would have built a whole song around one of these tunes. The Roses would almost discard them instantly before moving on to the next one. They were the new young kings of total pop.

'Waterfall' rides in on that burning arpeggio. A spooked figure, it shimmers with that updated psychedelic that the band were now so adept at trading ... when the acoustic guitar drops in near the end it shifts another gear, you sit back and wait for one of those glorious churning endings that the Roses specialised in but it tantalisingly goes to a fade out.

'Waterfall' is further evidence of the sheer depth of Squire's guitar playing. It seems like every trick he's got up his sleeve is at play here from the trademark wah wah to spine-tingling acoustics, the non-macho guitar hero! There is a total sensitivity at play here.

The lyrics are, according to Ian, 'a song about a girl who sees all the bullshit, drops a trip and goes to Dover. She's tripping, she's about to get on this boat and she feels free.' Ian sings softly. It's a long way from 'So Young' and Reni's backing vocal perfectly complements the song. Oh, and deep, resonating dub bass is closing in on that Jah Wobble sound (amazing bass from John Lydon's post Pistols Public Image Limited. Wobble's bowel-rattling deep dub bass was PIL's signature. If you're a fan of Mani's bass sound, then check out Public Image's *Metal Box* album).

And now the going gets weird. As if to prove that pure pop is too pathetically easy, the Roses flip the two-inch for 'Waterfall' over for one of their backwards tracks 'Don't Stop' (they did four all together). By now this backwards thing is rapidly becoming one of their trademarks, every release must have one! In the Sixties The Beatles had run the odd guitar or cymbal backwards but the Roses were not stopping there! For some fans this track is the low point of the album, an annoying break from the rush of pop perfection, but it neatly slaps the listener across the face – a break from the melodic easy listening, a neat reminder of just what we are dealing with here.

Plus it fucking works. It's not a lazy filler. 'Waterfall' does sound great backwards – a real trip. The lyrics, some of which are the original words slurring backwards with new added ones written by John, are equally bizarre. John always claimed they were just what was suggested to him by the track running backwards. For some listeners they drip some sort of hidden meaning. For me it's just great to hear the word 'imbecile' in a 'pop' song!

'Bye Bye Badman' is all brisk, frothy and light on the surface and is a classic case of the Roses soft on the surface and tough on the message (underneath the sand the paving stones perhaps!). For many a love song – but it was actually about the '68 student riots in Paris, a time when pop radicalism nearly brought down a government, a time that must have been dear to Ian Brown's heart. A rock'n'roll romantic, Brown believed in the power of revolt.

'If you go home and listen to "Bye Bye Badman" and then imagine it's someone singing to a riot policeman on the barricades in Paris '68 you'll get a picture of what we're about. The song is a call to insurrection.'

The song's theme continued to the cover of the album. The cover painting by John Squire (his best sleeve for any Roses record), is called 'Bye Bye Badman', and the painting is littered with references to the song, from the daubed *tricoleur* down one side, to the lemons (Ian Brown had read that the students in 1968 used to squirt lemons in the air to negate the effects of the CS gas fired by the cops.

Says John, 'The lemons aren't a part of the picture, they're real lemons, nailed on because it was photographed on the wall – the photographer didn't have a rostrum camera. It ties in with the lyrics of "Bye Bye Badman", to do with the Paris student uprisings in May 1968. Me and Ian saw a documentary on it and liked the clothes: there was a guy, chucking stones, with a really nice jacket and desert boots. The students used to suck on lemons to nullify the effects of the tear gas. That's why the *tricoleur* is there. The green is inspired by the water at the Giant's Causeway in Ireland, where we went before a gig at Coleraine University.'

It was another neat twist in the Roses' mythology, another hint that there was something far deeper going on just underneath the surface.

There is something far more disturbing, something far more dangerous and political to the Roses that most people perceived.

'It's important to retain your aggression as you get older,' Brown told Simon Reynolds of the *Observer*. 'People like Tony Benn and Michael Foot do. The current Labour leadership can't compare with them. Labour's outdated and gone. It's been left behind, it's served its purpose. If you read the *Crossman Diaries* or books about Harold Wilson they tell you that when Labour does get in it can't actually change the country, that's just the way, it's set up.'

And it was this radicalism that is much less subtly stated on the next track. 'Elizabeth My Dear', with the melody half-inched from Scarborough Fair, was Ian Brown intoning an anti-Royal paean; the short track ends with a gunshot. These boys were not in the hunt for MBEs.

At the time the song, which quite specifically calls for the end of the monarchy, was put into sharper focus when Brown said he would be the man to suffocate the Queen Mother. This set off a bit of a shit storm in the tabloids.

Written in late 1986, 'Sugar Spun Sister' is one of the older songs on the album and one that they had already demoed. That original demo displayed a poppier touch than this final recorded version. It's hard to grasp just what the song is about. It could be about love, it could be about tripping, some say it's about a prostitute!

'Made Of Stone' released as a single the previous month, makes even more sense in the context of the album, just another atmospheric rush of great melody in a breathless surge of pop.

John Squire, talking to the *NME* cryptically, attempted to explain just what the rush of the song meant to him. 'It's about making a wish and watching it happen – like scoring the winning goal in a cup final, on a Harley, electroglide, dressed as Spiderman . . .' Well, that explains it then.

'Shoot You Down' sees the fingerprints of the guitar genius, Jimi Hendrix, all over the song. Jimi had been fast becoming a major influence in the Roses camp, obviously with John's guitar playing, there's no way you're going to go near a wah wah and not think about Jimi, but it goes deeper than that. The spiritual soulfulness of prime-time Jimi seems to have rubbed off on most of these tunes and the man's music – its loose limbed funkiness and melodic riffology – is also key in the Roses' creative canon. With only the ending of 'I Am The Resurrection' to be added on, this was virtually the last song to be recorded in the album sessions. Brown's sinister vocal is a great counterpoint to the song's almost mellow groove. Again there is something nasty, something dark, hovering just below the surface, the contradiction in the name Stone Roses is still being used as a creative yardstick by the band . . .

Next up was one of the Roses' (written in 1985) first anthems, 'This Is The One'. Built around a tight looping riff, the song builds up to a massive anthemic crescendo. The song seemed to capture the feeling of freedom and the youthful exuberance of that crazed and chaotic year (even if it had been written four years previously the intense rush of excitement that the Roses helped to unleash. Building slowly from the simple start, the outro of the song literally does soar. When the Roses hit these sort of grooves, they really were on a planet of their own.

When you finish an album you want that last track to be a bit special, something that really stretches the band, something that takes you somewhere else. And with 'I Am The Resurrection' the Roses perfectly fit that bill.

'I Am The Resurrection', one of the Roses' finest moments, was a song that ended their set for years, a rousing anthemic song that captured that euphoric rush of rock'n'roll adrenalin in a spiritual manner. The musicianship is incredible. All those hours in the rehearsal room were paying off big style! The stop/start and false ending, the tease of the song's climax . . . Awesome stuff. In 1989 it seemed to be on forever in every club that you went to in town. The anthem of a never-ending summer!

It sounded heavyweight and dark and yet was burning bright with the adrenalin of great R'n'R.

'We saw "I Am the Resurrection, I Am the light" on a church notice board,' John Squire said to the *NME* while Ian Brown told Simon Williams of the same paper, 'I believe in God. There must be some substance in Christ, because the myth has lasted so long. Like 2,000 years, but it's convenient because you don't have to make your mind up till you get to the gates.'

If the guitar gives the record its musical edge, Brown personalises the record, singing in his home-town accent, spitting out the vengeful lyrics with their shades of prime time Bob Dylan. This is a real put down of somebody, contrasting neatly with the euphoric rush of music that surrounds the voice, making it a valid voice for rock'n'roll. Apart from Manchester underground band, The Fall, Brown was the most northern voice you'd heard on a record at that point. It gave the Roses a particular identity, adding to the almost folky melodies. He gives the album its very British edge.

Lyrically the record hints at something far deeper and darker. Broadly speaking Brown's lyrics were the Old Testament biblical tracts and the revolutionary rhetoric while Squire's were the cynical cutting shots. Both lyricists were on burning form for the début, with a dark humour fusing the anti-establishment love songs at every corner.

The package was completed with a bunch of great black and white shots taken by Ian Tilton that captured the band at their coolest. John hunches over his guitar deep in concentration, his long slender fingers doing something complicated to the arpeggio on 'Waterfall'; Ian Brown looks angelic and surly, oozing a menace and a danger. Mani looks like the scally that got the big break, his Pollocked bass looks too big for him.

In the background, behind Squire's Fender amp, Cressa is caught between dancing and changing the guitar player's bank of effects.

Reni has got the drums and the super harmonies down. He too, oozes a malevolent innocence. It just all looks so effortless, a band naturally stalking its domain, months before the peak of their powers. The shots were taken in late 1988 at a Granada TV appearance and they captured a band that was totally in its stride. Pre flares, in parallels, the band look cool, like any rock'n'roll band at the moment when it all clicks.

Ian Tilton remembers the session. 'Gareth rang me at the last minute. They were on Tony Wilson's *Other Side Of Midnight* programme. I had the feeling that Wilson didn't really like them that much and booked them in as a last gasp replacement for someone else who had dropped out. Gareth got me really cheap for that session and it ended up on the massive selling album. Ha!'

Tilton had to be on his toes, dodging the fast-moving cameras as he captured The Stone Roses running through their first TV appearance. 'We had a bit of a day out. We sneaked on to the *Coronation Street* set.'

Years later John's brother, Matt, a really good photographer as well, would work at Granada taking stills for programmes.

In May *The Stone Roses* was released. It was obviously the most important album of the year but it didn't steamroller the press. Reviews were mixed, sitting on the fence of fashion.

It was, though, about to change everything about guitar pop in Britain.

It was the resurrection of British pop. And it started here!

THE TAKE OVER

On 4 May the Roses played Liverpool Polytechnic, and witnesses remember that there were definitely far more people there than there had been before. The Stone Roses, now, had their own small brand of fanatics in each town. In Liverpool, though, they had broken through.

Keith Curtis, now the bass player in Gold Blade, was there: 'I got in just as they started the first song and it was packed. You could tell that there was something going on. The crowd was really into it. There was a definite atmosphere.'

The 1989 tour is looked on by the hardcore fans as the band at its very best. Oozing the magic that would make them soar, they were a catalytic force, and all over the country amazed indie fans saw that there was a new way to be. Bands were springing up in their wake.

They were still only getting fifty to a hundred people at most shows, but the grapevine was well and truly buzzing.

One of the myths about The Stone Roses was that they were hyped by the press, but this isn't true. By spring 1989 the word was out and they were going to happen anyway. The press could only hitch along for the ride and report this whole new pop scene that seemed to explode from nowhere.

The day after Liverpool they played the Queens Hall in Widnes. This was a large Victorian hall in a chemical town bang smack between Manchester and Liverpool. If the Roses were going to really mean anything then this was the kind of place where they were going to have to cut it. In the surrounding towns, though, the story was out, people were hungry for the Roses, and the gig was yet another example of how far the story was starting to spread.

By now the band were in the middle of a press storm, grabbing plaudits by the handful after years of being treated as outsiders. The graffiti-spraying thugs, the goths, the rock band, the ignorant boors smashing The Smiths' party – it was all getting swiftly forgotten. They were suddenly being feted and, not surprisingly, they were a tad bitter, so when asked if this press was enough by *Uptown* magazine while standing on the steps outside Widnes's Queens Hall, they just stared back and dead-panned, 'It's never enough is it? We're disappointed that we haven't had more.'

What's it like to be big in Manchester?

'We're not massive in Manchester,' said John Squire, adding, 'There are a million and a half people in Manchester and we only get 2,000.'

Confounded, the journalist asked them why they were so arrogant with the press.

'We're not arrogant, we are real. What do you want? A bunch of fakes with prepared answers?'

They were then asked about the 1960s comparisons.

'People who say that have no knowledge of music,' said Ian Brown. 'I don't know of any record in the 1960s that sounds like ours.' He looked up and added, 'We don't have to sell ourselves. The music will sell itself.'

When the talk turned to their immediate rivals, Brown smirked, 'We had people coming in last night asking us to autograph over their Smiths T-shirts, so I think they are finished.'

With Widnes and Liverpool buzzing, the Roses were on a roll, and it was now time, on 6 May, to play their home-town again. This time they would move up another level.

The International 2 show was their biggest yet and for many ultra-fans, their best yet. A sold-out crowd was at fever pitch as they hit the stage. Chants of 'Manchester la la la' filled the hall, and there was a real pride about the scene, about the town – suddenly everyone felt that Manchester was beginning to mean something, that this 'grim' northern city had its own pop scene, a pop scene that meant something and could take London on its own terms.

The stage was bathed in stark ultra-violet light and a slide of a Pollocked Union Jack was ripped across the back. The atmosphere was electric. The album, not even out yet, was already making massive inroads into the listening of the city, and everyone seemed to know the words.

The Roses played it straight and aloof, no more leaping into the crowd with a long mic lead for Ian Brown, who was working on the pimp roll now. Swaying and swaggering in his own world, stoned instead of speeding, floating about two foot off the floor, he stared vacantly at the crowd. It was still the menace of the Lydon-influenced tearaway but put through a weird stoned grill.

He didn't speak to the crowd, there were no encores, they sloped off and left the hall rapturous. They didn't communicate a single bloody thing, except for total cool.

At the time it was what Manchester demanded and got.

The night was a celebration.

Manchester was now party central and clubs were opening up all over the city. Last year's Smiths' fans were dropping E, clothes were getting looser, accents were getting stronger and hair was getting longer. Uptight no longer seemed to exist, and there were mad parties in fucked-up flats all over the city. From Saturday nights in the Kitchen in Hulme, to the Hacienda's explosions of dance solidarity to rambling houses in Whalley Range, grubby cellars in Rusholme – everywhere was booming to the big bad bass drum of acid house. And everywhere there were the pills: in pubs in west Didsbury you could buy them over the counter, in dark corners of the sudden plethora of clubs playing acid house you could score a handful, 'In The Area' revellers yelled, nonsensical slang was becoming codified, and crazy handshakes with freaked weirdos in clandestine deals in the bogs of nightclubs was the norm. It was a drug heaven. Strung out, cabbaged, whacked and plain weird was the mental currency of a city gone completely off its axis.

Sometimes pop is so powerful that overnight everyone seems to have shifted a gear. There was money to be made – Afflecks Palace buzzed and Identity boomed as a T-shirt store – its 'On the 7th day God created Manchester' T-shirt became a design classic.

Eastern Bloc stopped being a stall that sold hardcore punk records and became a booming dealer in indie, especially dance. House music seeped from every pore of the city, the powerful boom of the bass drum was the keynote, guitar music was temporarily on a back burner, until everyone realised that chilling out post-rave, post-E, to the psychedelic 1960s pop of The Beatles and the Stones was a perfect comedown; the final compliment would be to have some contemporary bands to chill out to.

And Manchester was about to provide them.

The Roses themselves were missing a lot of this Manchester euphoria as they were still on the road. The tour was starting to turn into a triumphant victory celebration; on 7 May they were back at Sheffield University, and the day after they were in Leeds at the Warehouse, where scenes of unbridled enthusiasms were reported.

The tour was gaining momentum but in a way decidedly different from usual. Instead of having to drag locals to their shows outside Manchester, the Roses took their own crowd.

Dave Simpson from *Melody Maker* was at that Leeds show: 'The whole thing was just kicking off. I'd only just heard of them. I'd heard them on Richard Skinner of all places, he had played "Made Of Stone" and it just got me straight away. It was so brilliant. The Roses were coming up to play in Leeds and to tell you the truth the reason that I was going was to see The Hollowmen, who were like a local Leeds band that I was really into and were the support that night.'

Getting to the Warehouse, the main venue for up-and-coming bands in Leeds at the time, Simpson was struck by a curious thing. 'The place was absolutely packed with Mancs. It was really strange, all these people had come over to see the band. That sort of thing never happened in those days. It was like a football support thing. My mate who was driving me wanted to leave pretty fast but I persuaded him to give the Roses fifteen minutes.

'I remember John Squire coming on with his paint-spattered guitar and they started playing "Elephant Stone", and the place kicked off. The atmosphere was absolutely brilliant, people were dancing on tables. It was the best atmosphere at a gig I could ever remember. There was a lot of Leeds chants going up. Ian Brown went up to the mic, looked at the crowd, and said, "Yeah, that's right, this is Leeds," really cool and confident. Everything seemed so colourful after gigs being so dark for ages, it was a turning point really.'

Overnight Simpson was a total fan, he rang up Silvertone the next day and blagged a pre-release of the album to review for his fanzine *Avanti*. His reaction to the record was typical of the thousands who were about to be caught in the euphoria for the band. 'I loved the album. I couldn't stop listening to it. I remember going down to the chip shop and I had to go back home because I just needed to listen to the record again. It was the spring going into the summer and the weather was great. It just seemed to capture the mood of the time perfectly.'

A month later the Roses returned to Leeds to play at the much larger Polytechnic venue. In the last four weeks things had really shifted a gear as Dave Simpson remembers: 'I'd arranged to put them on the cover of my fanzine and I went along to the show to do an interview and even though it was a much larger venue it was really packed. I remember that there were loads of kids stuck outside who couldn't get in. That was definitely a rare sight in those days.

'I went back-stage to get an interview and for some reason I was told to go and ask for Cressa and this skinhead with baggy trousers comes to the door. He then goes back in to find the band – it was all a bit farcical really. We did the interview in the bar and before the tape recorder was on they were really chatty and matey. As soon as the tape went on they went schtum and difficult. Normally if you interview a band that you like everyone is really matey and chatty, but this was different. I don't know why they did that, maybe it was Gareth's idea to make them seem more enigmatic. If that was the case it certainly worked.'

It would become the Roses' interview schtick for years on end, stony silence and off-hand answers, but at first it did really work, giving the band menace and mystery. There were some classic moments as Ian Brown would stonewall eager journalists, staring back with his large glacial brown eyes at their festering attempts to nail the band down. It was always done in a polite and civil way, really unsettling for a cub reporter.

Simpson thinks though that it may have all blown up in their faces later on. 'At first it was really effective, it was a really cool thing but eventually it seemed to get a bit nasty. It was like a schoolboy being really proud that he could really piss people off in the end. It was like they had started to lose sight of who they really were.'

Simpson spoke to Brown and Mani. 'John Squire came along to the interview and sat about three feet away saying nothing at all. Ian was really bolshy, turning all the questions around, like I was asking them how massive they wanted to be, like as big as New Order who were about the biggest an indie band could get. He turned the question around and started talking about what massive really was, and decided in the end that Michael Jackson was massive and the size that they wanted.'

Simpson loved the Roses because of Reni. 'I was a drummer and that made me listen to Reni; his drumming was incredible. They were saying that he learned his drums in the cellar of his parents' pub drumming along to jazz records. He was really exciting, unbelievable, the best drummer on the scene. I thought that A Certain Ratio's drummer, Donald Johnson, was unmatchable, but this was a different league altogether.'

The Roses' gigs were becoming events; even on the toilet circuit in the UK, where dreams are broken and countless bands are burned out by the sheer cruel drudgery of the venues, the Roses were putting on a very different show.

When *The Stone Roses* eventually started its long haul in the album charts, the word soon got out that there was a new way to rock

And as soon as the word was out it went fast.

John Harris, now editor of *Select*, was at school when the Roses finally broke. 'I remember at school everyone seemed to be into *The Stone Roses*, everyone seemed to have the album on vinyl. It was the same when I went to college in the south – they seemed to be the most popular T-shirt there. Everyone went out and bought "Fool's Gold" the day it was released. I think people found them a lot easier to get into than The Happy Mondays, who didn't seem to get that massive until *Pills 'N' Thrills And Bellyaches* came out. I remember every club in Manchester used to play their album – places like Devilles seemed to play the whole album in one night. They were religious about it.'

In the weeks before its release the Roses were heading for some sort of breakthrough, and the album itself accelerated this. It proved that the band were going to deliver and it defined the whole of that crazy summer.

I WANNA BE ADORED: REACTIONS TO THE ALBUM

Maybe there is a point in your life when it all comes together. You've got the talent, the team is together, the times have changed and you're in the right place at the right time. For the Roses the release of their début album was perfection itself.

Squire's astonishing guitar talent was finally getting the space to shine, and the last twelve-month surge of songwriting adding to a stockpile of drop-dead classic songs that were left over from the Couzens-Garner line-up stood them in good stead. After all, this was a band that had been going for five years, a band that wasn't short of talent and sheer steely nerve – for The Stone Roses to have recorded a crap album would have been unthinkable.

In some ways this was their second album, the shelved Hannett album being their real début. Astute to the last, at the time they had prevented its release, instinctively realising that they weren't ready to put an album out. It was a smart move as the Hannett album would have nobbled them, whereas their eponymous début defined a generation.

The key record of its times, *The Stone Roses* set the agenda for 1990s British guitar pop. It easily stands the test of time; from the vast range of tunes, the complex song structures, the superb arrangements and the lyrics that hint at a mystery, intelligence and depth that the band weren't giving away in interviews.

It's the moment when it finally got to be in touch with roots rock'n'roll, taking on board Hendrix, Love, The Doors, psychedelia, etc. The Roses made retro a compliment and weren't ashamed to wear their influences on their sleeves. It was this moment, for some, when pop stopped going forward and swallowed its own history. For others it was when pop got back to doing what it did best, dealing in three-minute rousing anthems, sung by groups with a tough street charisma. It didn't do the Stones much harm in the 1960s, so why should it now?

Post The Jesus And Mary Chain pop musicians were getting in touch with their rock roots. The sheer spaciousness and scale of sound of *The Stone Roses* perfectly matched the hunger of the house generation. Anthemic songs that were perfect for the new large crowd vibe that was sweeping Britain after years of huddling in the underground.

It was also a great pop album, at once exhilarating and dark. Sugar-sweet melodies cloaked dark lyrics and tracks that were a stupendous rush of adrenalised playing and anthemic choruses. A slow seller, *The Stone Roses* never got into the top ten, preferring to hover around the bottom of the charts where it still intrigues the new post-Oasis pop generation.

Stunning in its scope and its playing, it was a massive jump forward for the band who had only twelve months previously been tied to rock. They sounded like an outfit greedy for change, and had a huge swaggering confidence about making those moves.

On its release in the spring of 1989 the reviews were mixed, as if there was just no space for guitar pop. It seemed unfeasible that a band could deal out six-string pop and become successful, to the point that if The Beatles had put out an album in the late 1980s they would have been dismissed. Now in the 1990s, with a whole plethora of bands dealing out the same sort of schtick, this kinda pop is day-to-day, and bands crashing in at number eighteen in the charts are considered failures, when at the time the Roses had little hope of ever getting that high. But this was the record that changed it all.

This was a new flavour, a new approach. For some pundits the Roses were a continuation of indie, but for the band this album was the end of the notion that guitar bands should be grovelling in the underground.

As Ian Brown pointed out to Mat Smith of *Melody Maker* a couple of months after the album's release, 'I don't like us being thought of as an indie band, 'cos I can't think of any good indie bands. Independent music hasn't thrown up much in the last ten years, has it? Maybe a couple of good records, "Psycho Candy" and one or two Smiths records, but the other stuff I just wouldn't entertain.'

This was Brown's line: the Roses were a proper classic rock'n'roll band. There were no apologies from his band, the first for years not to be a snivelling indie band. The Roses wanted it large and they weren't going to stop now.

In the same *Melody Maker* interview Brown broke another taboo when he claimed the band's ambition was to be on *Top Of The Pops*. 'I want to be on that show. I watched it last week and it was like *Junior Show Time*. I wanna shake them all up. We've got as far as we can by being stubborn and arrogant and unfashionable, and eventually it all comes around.'

It's that clear-cut. Things were different, the music scene was changing fast, making one of its occasional leaps forward.

'We've been bored with rock music for the last five years. Everyone I know has always liked rock music, dance music, punk and Northern Soul. I don't think it's unusual for our fans to be into dance music. Those dividing lines aren't there any more,' noted Ian Brown, in the unlikely environment of *Loving* magazine.

He also told *Rolling Stone* at the same time, 'I think pop music was saved by the advent of acid house and rap because whites have done nothing for ten years.'

Shocked, the American music paper for the touch-of-grey 1960s generation asked what the last good white record was.

'The Sex Pistols' first LP.'

In the same interview John Squire was asked why The Stone Roses were needed.

'People want to listen to *music*. They like to dance, but they are tired of that machine noise. I mean, the songs sound like they were written by a computer virus. I suppose that a lot of acid house music is guilty of the same thing, of being completely cold and devoid of any human touch, and that is what we are trying to put back,' said Squire negating a lot of the indie dance connection.

Squire also explained the band's roots. 'The Beatles were the first band everyone I knew was into, even if they were born in 1970. But The Sex Pistols were the first band we could actually go and see. They were the group that made us want to be in a group.'

Not that the Roses had actually gone to see the Sex Pistols. The Pistols' two shows in Manchester in 1976 were ill attended but witnessed by the fathers of the Manchester punk rock scene, a scene which provided the very pillars for the whole Manc musical establishment years later. The power and the negativity of the Pistols, combined with the exhilaration of their playing and the sheer bravado of their music, scored with a whole generation. At the time considered to be non-players, the Pistols have become, over the years, one of the key influential bands in British rock, along with The Beatles, whose down-to-earth approach to everything from mysticism to rock'n'roll combined with an incredible talent, saw them survive the pratfalls of fashion and become almost over-bearingly hip in the 1990s.

Of course Oasis would take the fusion of these two groups one step further and almost join them together. With The Stone Roses there were plenty of other musical factors at play.

Ian Brown was bemused by a lot of the band's comparisons. 'Everyone likes to describe us as psychedelic and say we're inspired by 1960s music, but in truth, we'd never actually heard most of those 1960s bands until we'd read the reviews making comparisons to us. People like Arthur Lee and Love, when we read that we were meant to sound like them, we went out and got an album and were surprised to find a common thread. Hendrix, though, is the biggest influence – John loves him.'

Jimi Hendrix was something else, the meeting point of everything in rock'n'roll-flash; sexy, cool as fuck and a genius guitar player, Hendrix, with a smoking-gun vocal, was also one of the great rock vocalists. He wore proper rock star clothes and had the swagger down perfectly. On his first three albums he pushed the guitar into a thousand different directions; it was a template that a lot of people have hideously abused. Squire, though, managed to pick up in his sensitivity and sensuality in his playing. 'We're all into different things. Reni is really into Sly And The Family Stone, Mani is really into reggae and acid house. We've all got different influences but we all meet at The Beatles, The Rolling Stones and Hendrix.'

It's funny that, according to some people, Reni's all-time favourite record is 'Jump' by Van Halen..

Much, over the years, has been made of the eclectism of the Manchester scene bands and it's true that many UK groups have an incredibly narrow range of influences. The city's groups, though, have tantalisingly ridiculous record collections, spanning a myriad of styles from house to Latin from punk to funk to metal to pop, to kitsch to crap and back again.

It was this strand of punk, a diversity and a hunger for new sounds and experiences, that came to an unlikely roost in Manchester, and fuelled the creativity of a wonderful and crazed bunch of home-town action.

For Brown, as he once astutely told an American magazine, 'We are striving to be part of a new movement in rock, like The Beatles were to the 1960s and The Sex Pistols to the 1970s. We've got it.' When asked just what the 'it' was, Brown replied, 'It's something indefinable, it's an X-factor. I just want you to understand that we aren't being egotistical about this. We're just trying to show our potential.'

It would be the closest he ever got to defining his own role in the Roses.

THE REVIEWS

The media were generally with the Roses now. 'Made Of Stone' was an acknowledged cool record and the Hacienda gig had done them plenty of favours. It seemed like the Roses were about to ride a wave of good press for the album.

Robin Denselow in the *Guardian* noted that 'Elizabeth My Dear' had 'dodgy' lyrics, but he also said, 'There are some good musicians at work here; they have the ability to swiftly move on when they are becoming dull. If they are this good live they should be well worth seeing.' He added 'Back in Johnny Marr's old stomping ground there is a new northern psychedelic scene (flared jeans and all) which has led to a batch of new bands. The Stone Roses seem to be the first to swop their massive cult following for international success.'

Jack Barron grabbed the album for the *NME*, and gave it seven out of ten. He liked it but he was hedging his bets: 'This is an aural Big Mac laced with a psychedelic drill. This comes from Manchester and is made by people who think that Levenshulme is a suburb of San Francisco. This is The Byrds after they've flown the coop, this is living proof that acid is good for you. Just.'

It was that kiss-off line that later made the album look even more ungainly when it was perched on top of the critics' fave albums of the 1980s. It was like no one expected anything nearly this good from the Roses. Everyone was just warming up to the fact that there was something really good here and then, bang, they went massive.

Sounds raved about the album, calling it a masterpiece, while Bob Stanley at *Melody Maker* went mad for it. Bob thought the album was God and was everything that Bobby Gillespie had been talking up for years with Primal Scream.

US mag *Billboard* took an overview on the record: 'The Stone Roses are an English quartet that crossbreeds a thick gloom rock-derived sound with more than a hint of old-time psychedelia.'

The truth is The Stone Roses became massive without anyone's permission; they became massive because this was a great album, an album that friends played to friends and raved about in a breathless whisper.

Word of mouth was king here. The Stone Roses were huge before the press really had time to have their say. This made nonsense of the claims that they were a hype. The early Manics were a far bigger hype, lots of press and no fans for a long time. The Roses were the real deal – the grapevine had been burning about this band for a few months now. But, being pioneers, they would still be riding a slow wave; it had been a long time since a pure pop band had crashed the charts.

The album never got in the top ten. For all its long and curious chart run it preferred to sell consistently. Sales currently total over 400,000 in the UK.

GET IN THE VAN . . .

That summer The Stone Roses were back on the touring circuit. This time, at last, they were packing places out everywhere and not just in Manchester. This time it was getting serious – the word was out and the wires were buzzing with the news.

Sat in the van with the Roses was Steve Cresser pumping up the sound system, blasting out a cool and eclectic mix of music, a lot of it a million miles away from the pure pop of the album. The stereo was hammering The Rolling Stones, Hendrix, Burning Spear, PIL, hip-hop and house, a cool brew to burn away those miles of tarmac.

Also in the van for a few gigs was Jack Barron, the *NME* writer who was now most definitely on their case since reviewing their album. Jack was one of the key writers of the period, switching from underground American noisenik music to acid house and the Mancs bands in an E-fuelled Paul-on-the-road-to-Damascus-style U-turn.

Ian Brown was laying down the law on one of his key influences, John Lydon. 'I sneaked into a PIL gig when I was fourteen and went back-stage and cadged a cigarette off John Lydon and I found out that he wasn't the nasty bastard that he was portrayed as. That was very influential on me.'

They were also explaining to Jack the Stones' support story. Some parts of the Roses' story are so shrouded in mythology that it's hard to know whether Gareth Evans spun a yarn or they actually happened, but one of the great tales of 1989 is how they turned down The Rolling Stones' support slots in Canada. While it seems likely that the Stones could have wanted some hip indie cred by inviting them out on to the road with them, it sometimes seems difficult to believe that the gnarled old troupers could possibly be that hip to what was happening on the streets in the UK. Of course the story was a fib!

'We were told that we had some support slots with the Stones if we wanted them in Canada but, fucking hell, we're not opening up for them. They should open up for us! It's obscene that they are even touring – they lost it years ago. It's a shame that they haven't got any friends who're willing to tell them when to quit,' spat out Brown.

Barron then asked the vocalist, who was getting a stream of comparisons to the youthful Jagger, what he would do if he met the man.

'I'd want to punch him out, really. There was a time for three or four years when the Stones were red-hot. They looked good, sounded good, and meant what they were playing. Nothing could stop them. Now they are nothing but a money-machine. Sad really.'

Spoken like a true punk. Brown shared his generation's loss of faith in the Stones, once the world's number one bad-ass band but now considered a sad parody of former greatness and a sitting-duck target for hot new singers to take pop-shots at.

Barron was worrying whether the Roses were just another rock'n'roll band, and back-stage, among the dope fumes and the brandy, there certainly seemed to be very little difference. Brown, though, realised, like many others at that time, that the fact that pop stars took drugs simply wasn't an issue any more. Everyone took drugs and lived far crazier lifestyles than any musician. Drugs were everywhere.

'I don't see us being in a rock'n'roll tradition at all. You go to a reggae gig or a punk gig or an artist's party or maybe just up to Alderley Edge to look out over Manchester, and you'll find people getting into spliffs and brandy. All kinds. That doesn't make them rock'n'roll. In fact I don't like rock'n'roll – the attitude and leather jacket. It's old hat. It's redneck.'

In the late 1980s Brown could well be perceived as a new type of rock'n'roll singer, less macho and more street. Britain was changing, and changing fast – the seismic shift caused by acid house was having repercussions. Everywhere there was a war on between the grey world of indiedom and the new psychedelic summer of love being promoted by the rave scene. The story of 1990s pop culture would be the gradual intertwining of the two cultures, with people going from one scene to the other and back again.

The Stone Roses were at the forefront of all this, either as a rock band canny enough to see where the scene was going, or as people who had always been into dance music, whether it be Northern Soul or ska.

Ian Brown related to Barron, 'I'd rather go to a club and dance, than go to a live gig because there just aren't that many exciting bands about. I hate that indie-rock-guitar mentality that people have where they won't even consider listening to dance music, which is some of the most exciting stuff around at the moment. Most of the indie rock scene is blinkered and fucked up by its own narrow-mindedness.'

They spent the months following the album release, constantly on the road. A never-ending series of gigs in Britain's small towns, slowly building up that bedrock of a following. This was no overnight success. The album had come out, hovered round the back end of the charts and remained there for years. There was no Oasis-style rise to megastardom. For the first half of 1989 the changeover was slow but it was happening. From Tunbridge Angel Centre to Birmingham's Edwards No. 8, from Shrewsbury's Fridge, to Aberystwyth University. They were grinding it out on the circuit.

Of course in Manchester it was now getting beyond serious, the 6 May headliner at the International 2 was a packed celebration, 2,000 punters surfing on the wave of Madchester, a bedrock of a following that gave them the confidence to step up later that summer to the Blackpool gig.

In London there was the 15 May ecstatically received gig in the tight space of the arty ICA and a return to Dingwalls. The word was getting out, in London the media were now totally on their side, in Manchester it was the mainstream audience and round the UK pocketfuls of fans were rallying to the cause. It was only a matter of time.

They were turning young minds all over the country. Typical of the new fans was Andy Bell, ex-Ride member and current Oasis bass player. He caught the Roses that May at Oxford Polytechnic and was blown away.

Recalls Andy, 'The first Stone Roses record I heard was "Made Of Stone". I was 18, I'd just started art school and Ride had formed just a few weeks before. I'd bought it (on 7") because I liked the sleeve. I'd never heard the band, I think I'd seen some press.

When I played the single, I liked the B-side more at the time, "Going Down", for the lyrics about Jackson Pollock and Ambre Solaire and the Byrdsy tune. Of course "Made Of Stone" is more of a heavyweight tune in the long run. To an ex-Smiths fan, John Squire made a perfect follow up for Johnny Marr as a guitar teacher. The Roses had a better image as well.'

It wasn't just the music that was captivating, it was the whole package. Adds Andy, 'There was a brilliant early picture of them taken from the ground with all the flares intertwined. Cool clothes, fantastic haircuts, proper shoes. I started cutting out all their press and saving it (never did that before or since with a band – I just liked the way it all looked).'

The Roses were to have a profound effect on a generation of musicians who were affected like Bell. 'The members of Ride had all just moved into a house together when the Roses' début album came out. You heard it and felt sad because it was so good you knew they wouldn't be "your own" secret for long. The jam at the end of "I Am The Resurrection" got me and Loz Colbert really into jamming together, guitar and drums, which had quite a big effect on the Ride sound I guess.

We were really into Young MC's track "Know How" so when John Squire namechecked it, it was good to know we were on the same wavelength. They played Oxford Poly bar, early 1989. The place held about 200 people. It was a really good time for gigs there, I remember seeing Spacemen 3, The House of Love, My Bloody Valentine all around the same period as the Roses played.'

The gig was an event. The young musicians got there early. Very early. Continues Andy, 'Me and Loz went early to watch them soundcheck. Unbelievable charisma is all I can really say. We were sitting at this table round the corner from the stage and a sullen Ian Brown came and sat with us for a bit. They looked exactly how they did on the pictures from the album sleeve. Reni's drums were all painted different, a real hotch potch. Seeing him free-forming around the kit to soundcheck the drums was fantastic.

John Squire came out after a bit and without any of those amateurish "amp-starting-up/tuning up" noises started playing dead cool Hendrix-y phrases. It was all so casually done but in another way a total performance. It must have been obvious to them that there was a little group of us checking them out.'

And then there was the gig itself. 'The gig was incredible, they were on top form. I remember it in freeze frames. Mani's face gurning as he swung round to catch Reni laughing his head off in the middle of a tune. Ian in his element, head nodding as he sings in front of a sea of bodies losing it. Seeing Loz's mad head as we flew around the moshpit singing along with "I Am The Resurrection". I went home mindblown, clutching a T-shirt.'

Andy was so inspired that he popped down to see them in Reading on 6 June.

'I saw them again a few days later at Reading Majestic. Majestic was the word. Even the crew looked like the band. Next one I saw was Alexandra Palace. When you'd meet people out and about, the first question would always be if they liked The Stone Roses, and everyone was saying that the Empress Ballroom had been the one, and this was next, so we couldn't miss it. When we arrived at the venue I remember everyone buzzing about the records being played by the DJ. There were big cheers for the tunes like Voodoo Ray and anything by the Mondays. But the place was so big that the sound when the band played was really swampy, a disappointment.'

The results of this excitement saw the formation of Ride, one of the best British guitar pop bands from that era and a band that neatly straddled the so called shoe-gazing and baggy scenes without being bogged down in the clichés of both. Ride released a series of cool records and were one of the new vanguard of bands on the Creation label.

'By this time Ride had a deal with Creation, and our first single had been recorded. We hadn't known about the Roses when Ride started (as a band we were primarily into Sonic Youth, the Valentines and The Spacemen 3) but I was totally having it as soon as I discovered them. They were a huge influence on Ride. The early themed sleeves that Ride did were a nod to the Roses and The Smiths. The sense of occasion in everything they did led us to play the Daytripper weekend with The Charlatans. The influence kind of got in everywhere.'

Multiply this influential excitement by about, ooh, 10,000 and you've got an idea of what was rippling through the UK's guitar pop rehearsal rooms that summer!

SINGLE NO. 5!: SHE BANGS THE DRUMS

On 15 July 1989 'the second summer of love' was burning bright. It was one of the hottest summers since 1976, a curious heat which always lets loose the crazed party animal just under the skin of the Brit.

With the whole of the gameplan stunningly unfolding before them The Stone Roses finally followed up 'Made Of Stone' and released a re-recorded version of 'She Bangs The Drums', flipped with 'Standing Here', 'Mersey Paradise' and 'Simone'. The single also came with another great Squire sleeve and a free postcard of one of his paintings.

'Mersey Paradise', casually tossed on to the 'B' side, along with 'Simone' is the Roses at their most confident. The song could have stood up as an 'A' side in its own right. Pure crystalline melody and effortless musicianship, with the now obligatory weird lyric. Brown is singing about something dark and nasty, there could be a murder, there is the stench of death and it's all happening in the Mersey that flowed about ten minutes' walk away from his West Didsbury flat.

Not content with this, they also put another potential 'A' side, 'Standing Here', on the flipside as well. 'Standing Here' is one of the last guitar pop anthems the Roses wrote before their tentative swing into the more groove-orientated stuff. For some this single represents the creative high water-mark of the Roses. You've just had the album and now there's these four more amazing tracks. Again the sleeve was another John Squire creation.

'That was a detail of a larger picture that was also used later on "I Wanna Be Adored". We just homed in on one section of it. We were running out of time, and I didn't have time to work on it properly.'

Riding roughshod over a pop riff which recalled the pop genius of The Monkees 'She Bangs The Drums' was a big fat slice of guitar pop. It was

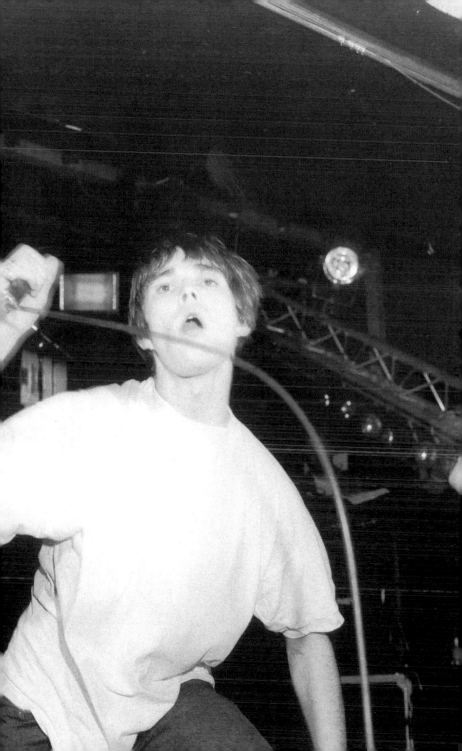

1988. Poses stolen from the Clash. The Roses had the same
strong gang identity as the influential British punk band.
Photo Ian Tilton

Granada Studios late '88. The Roses were never that good
at getting told what to do by 'the man'.
Photo Ian Tilton

A pop band just about to break, young, lean and mean,
sharp and angular. Note Cressa helping Jon with his effects.
Photo Ian Tilton

Pollocked! The Roses.
Photo Ian Tilton

1989. At the height of the 'baggy wars' – the money shirt, flares, attitude and hair. Ian Brown is 'the Skull' giving it the malevolent pretty boy look that still echoes through most British guitar bands of the late nineties.
Photo Ian Tilton

Cressa the vibemaster in action!
Photo Ian Tilton

The classic mic pose. Ian Brown as the full-on 'King Monkey', pro-active and oozing self belief with Mani at the 'One Love' video shoot, 4 May 1990.
Photo Pennie Smith

'F minor 7 dim / G flat major – sod it'. The first non-macho guitar hero in action.
Photo Ian Tilton

'No, listen, it's a number one!' The fact is, Reni can play
guitar almost as well as he plays drums.
Photo Pennie Smith

Robbie Maddix – he came, he saw, he conquered.
He had to do the impossible and fill in for Reni, the
greatest drummer of his generation. By the time of
the last stand he seemed to be running the band.
Photo Pennie Smith

They went that way!
Photo Pennie Smith

No, this way!
Photo Pennie Smith

**1990. Still riding high as the gang, the Roses were by now
full-on rock 'n' roll outlaws hiding in cornfields from the
grind of the music business machine.**
Photo Pennie Smith

Ian Brown, new soul warrior, stands proud as the band prepares to disappear for five years.
Photo Pennie Smith

The 'Rogue Rose' prepares for the acoustic section of the comeback tour. Madrid was one of the finest performances the band ever gave *according to eye witnesses.*
Photo Pennie Smith

'Come out with your hands up and bring the album with you!'
Photo Pennie Smith

pure pop. It sounded like it was from an age that oozed far more innocence. That was until Ian Brown croaked in with the classic lines, 'Kiss me where the sun don't shine, the past was yours but the future's mine.'

Brown was always up for putting the sting in the tail and these two lines were the key pop lyric of that heady summer when pop went mad. 'You're all out of time,' he sneered at contemporaries.

The single was their biggest hit so far, and their first to make the top forty, but still only managed number thirty-six. The group were unhappy as they could see from the long and winding tour that they had just been out on that they were getting bigger than this polite back-end of the chart messing around. Something was afoot – maybe Silvertone just wasn't big enough to assure them of a definite big smash, and they would have to seek a larger label to fulfil their real potential.

Ian Brown told *Melody Maker* that he would be severely disappointed if they didn't have a number one by the end of 1989.

In hindsight number thirty-six does seem like a joke. Here was a group that within weeks would be selling out the 4,000-capacity Empress ballroom in Blackpool. Maybe at that time the pop charts just weren't capable of registering a very northern phenomenon.

The Stone Roses had moved a long way from the indie scene. They were getting the Fleet Street mentions and they were getting offers from massive bands desperate to boost their credibility, and audience, by getting the band as support. As well as the aforementioned Rolling Stones, The Pixies (the American group who redesigned the rock song with the quiet verse and loud chorus that Nirvana took into the major arena) were one bizarre outfit to offer the Roses a support. But by now the Manchester band were far, far bigger than their American rivals. Next off the block were, laughably, Bros, who everyone had completely forgotten about. This would almost have been a cool gig to play as the contrast would have been terrifying – the self-contained hot new group, versus yesterday's men. New Order also offered more of a helping hand to their fellow Mancs, not that Ian Brown was impressed: 'New Order isn't massive. Michael Jackson is massive. That's what we are aiming for.'

They had their own agenda now, and a trip to Japan set them up as enormous stars there. They loved the country and the love was reciprocated. Japan was always a highlight for the Roses and a place where they were always big time.

LIFESTYLE '89

The whole myth of The Stone Roses as a dance band mushroomed throughout the late 1980s. It seems odd, now, to listen to those records and think that they were once, pompously, included in many long-winded articles about acid house, with their picture adorning the attempts to describe this new phenomenon.

True, their gigs featured a barrage of house cuts, and they even went so far as having a home-made piece of techno featuring wailing sirens as their walk-on tape to the stage, but they were, musically, firm traditionalists.

Living in Manchester, the Roses were party to a huge mushrooming of dance culture which affected everyone in the city culturally, and totally changed the way it looks today. Walking around Manchester in the new millenium you are struck by the seemingly endless explosion of poncy Continental-style chrome-and-glass bars, some of them sprouting out of run-down old Victorian red-brick warehouses, and all of them teaming with nightlife.

Years before any other city in the UK, Manchester was opening these places. It was a part of the city's culture almost from the off in the house era, booming sound systems and flash bars full of ravers, students and gangsters. It was the rough meeting the smooth that so typified the city culture.

The atmosphere around the clubs, fired by hedonism and great music, was electric. All of a sudden the city dressed looser – hair grew longer, people staggered down the street looking dazed, and everyone kept asking about this wonder-drug called E: just what was it all about? The post-punk generation were instantly suspicious of E, and it became a sink or swim thing. Those that took it discovered the ups and downs of a whole new way of life, and those who didn't went over the marker and into the section marked 'last pop generation'. For millions of people it was a life-affirming rush that totally changed their lives, while for a few it was a dismal and sad death. Ecstasy totally changed the pop and cultural landscape of the UK.

The Stone Roses could have been destroyed by Ecstasy culture; it could have left them dead, perceived as a plodding rock band, a monochrome experience now that everything had gone completely colour; but with their cultural stimuli twitching they whole-heartedly embraced the new culture.

With their newly found psychedelic edge, combined with a lightness of touch fusing their music, they caught the cultural shift and, checking on the Mondays' street urchin appeal, they moved base. They threw off the shackles of tight-ass rock'n'roll and, utilising Reni's incredible loose drum patterns, freed up the rhythm section, putting a funkier free-flowing undertow to their more traditional song structure. Fusing this with an understanding of the times they started to dress accordingly and The Stone Roses were suddenly the band in fashion.

Ian Brown, at twenty-six, was just young enough to get away with looking like 'every lad', and in the next few years he would become the totem, the leader, the icons with the looks and the attitude that matched the new pop generation.

Just in time they had shifted, and it was smart pop manoeuvring.

Already tired of the post punk regime, The Stone Roses embraced the new house-styled generation and became its figureheads.

As Ian Brown once related to the press, 'Everyone is talking about indie and dance coming together. But everyone I know has always gone into each other's scene and had dance records since they were little kids. It's not a sudden thing that has happened. It's just that it took time to be presented, packaged and made palatable for the listener. You either get a good feel off a record or you don't – and there are as many bad house records as there are good rock records.'

The Roses had grown up through an intermingling of style from punk. They travelled through soul and ska, two of the greatest forms of dance music ever made. They flirted with funk, and they always dug the Stones who are perhaps the most danced-to group of all time. Ian Brown had travelled to Northern Soul all-nighters, the natural precursors to the house scene, and the band innately understood the drugs, clothes and music combination that fires all the classic pop periods.

To split music into two camps of rock and dance was always a flat-footed conceit, and to claim always that rock had some sort of intellectual superiority over dance was totally laughable. The Stone Roses knew this and they duly profited from their lack of small-mindedness.

LIKE TROUSER, LIKE BRAIN: FLARES!

But of all the things the band achieved in their short but glorious ride to the top, it will possibly be the wearing of flared trousers that will be remembered most. For the band it was a minor detail, an interest in clothes and styles that got bizarrely exaggerated out of all proportion. To a generation reared on tight-trousered orthodoxy, it was an outrage, especially as the Roses were from that cut of cloth, so to speak.

The history of flares itself is also a curious one. Phil Saxe, the original manager of The Happy Mondays, used to have a stall in the centre of Manchester in the early 1980s where he and his brother used to sell them; they bought them up dirt-cheap, having no idea what sort of people would still be buying flares at this time. Bizarrely enough kids interested in fashion started to pick up on them and soon the early Happy Mondays were swaggering around in flares. It was the ultimate snub to the fashion drama queens, the most hated piece of denim worn with stark working-class pride, cocking a snoop at the vile taste-makers and a gesture that was more punk than the punk look that it sneered at.

Cressa, to all intents and purposes the fifth member of The Stone Roses and the street-style expert, copped the look from the Mondays, giving Ian Brown a bottle-green pair of flared cords. They suited Brown immediately and appealed to his dual sense of street style and winding people up. This was more Lydon than Lydon! And more street than the current yob look. The fact that they also totally suited his new, more dope-fuelled, shaggy persona also added to the equation. He was quoted as saying, 'I've always been into clothes. When I was twelve I used to wear twenty-one-inch hipsters. Then I stopped wearing flares for a long time and now I'm wearing them again. Flares are really comfortable and they feel right. The main reason was because no one else was wearing them. We'll have to stop wearing them soon because everyone else is. Loads of people who come to see us are wearing flares and parallels. Some of them look better than me in flares! A lot of people don't cut it though, and they shouldn't wear them just because their favourite group does. They should wear what they look good in.'

He told the press a couple of years later, 'You get a buzz when people laugh at you because you aren't wearing the same pants. It's weird how something really simple like that can make you feel special. I remember years ago at school I got a pair of straight-legged trousers and was laughed out of town because everyone else was wearing flares. With flares coming back people have to realise that you can't wear anything wider than twenty-one-inch bottoms. Anything more looks ridiculous. And they have to crumple. You just can't have half-mast trousers.'

Simon Kelly, a fan of the Roses, remembers Ian Brown crashing out in the same room as him that hectic year: 'He came in really late; his flares were all ratty and worn out at the bottom. He took them off really carefully, folded them up and put them on a chair. It seemed strange that such a worn-out pair of trousers could be looked after so much.'

For all this talk of flares, though, the picture of Brown on the inner sleeve of *The Stone Roses* captured in the Granada studios in 1988 by Ian Tilton shows him defiantly in straight-legs looking the sharp and angular supa-mod, all lean, mean and spitting attitude. It would only be in 1989 and 1990 that he would fully endorse the flared-trouser thing.

Flares were one of the main bones of contention during the Roses' reign – if there was one thing that really seemed to piss people off it was their trousers. This, of course, is a pop classic – people getting wound up by clothes.

During 1989, sales of flares rocketed. As a buyer from a UK chain of trouser shops reported, 'We tested them in four or five of our stores recently and they sold out in a few days. By April, whether you like it or not, you'll see a lot of kids wearing them.'

It was an accurate prediction. A lot of people did wear them and a lot of people did look fairly lumpen in them. Another buyer said, 'Flares offend the sensibilities of the older generation and that's why they are taking off. After a long period when father and son dressed the same and looked the same, things are going to change.'

THE ROSES AND THE MEDIA GAME

From the start of their roller-coaster ride to fame it was obvious The Stone Roses were no fools when it came to the media. They pulled their fair share of stunts (some of them were justified actions that didn't exactly harm their mythology): 'over the top' big gigs; inflammatory comments about royalty, other bands and politics; throwing paint around ex-record-company offices; made up mega gigs; pulling out of US tours – it was all great copy. One feature of the band's career has been their ability to stay on the news pages of the rock press almost permanently for years on end, including a lot of years when they did fuck all. And they did this by hardly saying anything at all.

Unlike The Manic Street Preachers, who seemed to come to every interview armed with a deadly machine-gun rattle of superb quotes, The Stone Roses would stonewall the journalist. With shy guffaws, muttered asides, dispassionate staring, foot-shuffling silences and complete mind-numbing gaps, punctuated by the odd piece of incisive home-spun philosophy from Brown, who occasionally hinted at a well-read mind. There would be a complete silence from John Squire, witty banter from Reni, and Mani spouting off if he let his guard drop.

There's a great piece of TV footage from *Music Box*, a late-night pop profile programme, when the presenter just won't stop asking questions. The band don't let their guard drop once, even when she asks Ian Brown about his rumoured Union Jack tattoo.

They seemed unprepared to enter into the breast-beating buffoonery of rock'n'roll. They gave nothing away about themselves or their past, present or future; they set up a smokescreen. They didn't lie, they just didn't say anything.

It's this enigmatic quality that helped to give them the aura that even now still cloaks them in a shroud of mystery.

Whether it was Gareth Evans who set up this smokescreen or the band themselves we'll never know. In real life they were nothing like their interviews, apart from John Squire, who spoke little to people he didn't know.

Maybe Squire didn't speak much but what he did say in short quotes really said it all. When asked about the media, he looked up: 'We hate tense people – you're only here once. It's not a rehearsal. The tense people are the twats who are only interested in making money and who ruin things for everybody else.'

When the *NME* asked Ian Brown why they didn't like getting interviewed he replied, 'I don't hate anything. It's just that sometimes the attitude of journalists and the questions they ask you can piss you off. But having said that, I don't expect anyone to get us right after meeting us for twenty minutes. Have you found us arrogant or difficult? I really don't think that we are. Too many groups feel like they have to play up to people all the time.'

The Roses never became part of the pop circus, and were hardly ever to be seen at any other gigs or clubs. Occasionally you would see Brown on his own at something like The Happy Mondays at GMex shuffling around at the back, unexpected and unrecognised, but for him and the rest of the band pop life was alien life.

For Brown his real heroes came from a very different world. 'Boxers are my heroes. I know it's a laddish thing to say, but it's true. It's the fact that they are putting themselves on the edge. They're amazing, you've got to be 100 per cent completely wised up all the way through,' he told the *NME* in 1989.

Brown, the lad's lad, perceived as the hard man, the funny man, the master blagger, the chancer who had pulled it off, was none of these things. For someone who had spent his youth in gangs, he was never comfortable with the lad tag. The Stone Roses, along with The Happy Mondays, may have kicked off the 1990s lad culture that was eventually epitomised in *Loaded*, but for the Roses' singer it couldn't be further away from where he was as a person.

STONED!

Drugs and rock'n'roll are completely inseparable; from Elvis speeding his way through his first tours to The Beatles bombed out of their brains from Hamburg onwards. Everyone is taking them, and the ones that don't have to explain their agenda to non-believers.

Every new drug completely alters people's perception of pop music and when ecstasy exploded across the UK, pop changed in a way that no one could possibly have predicted.

The Stone Roses' early years were dominated by speed. They were total speed freaks. They drank little, looking down on alcohol (interestingly enough this tallies with the early house scene, where there was an E-fuelled disdain for booze – alcohol was a slothful, dirty drug, which slowed people down and made them look like leaden fools to the E taker).

In the late 1980s the Roses started smoking pot. Ian Brown was less the crazed-amphetamine-filled frontman and their whole look became shaggier, looser. By the time E hit the scene they had the shaggy E-monster look off pat.

Drugs, clothes and music – it's the triumvirate that dominates pop.

The E rave scene totally altered the make-up of cities. Manchester changed drastically, a direct result of the house daze of the late 1980s. It became a haven for students and one of the hippest pop spots in the world, and all this came down to the rush of liberation which fell during the E explosion.

All week you could be buzzing on a Red And Black, a White Dove, some waxy pill, anything, and end up at some wild endless party. House music was the perfect soundtrack, booming across the city into the dawn hours, while rough kids, students, hooligans and music biz players were all freakin' in the crazed darkness, unopened cans of beer piled up at the side of the room as the big bass boom-boom-boom shattered the stiff upper lip, and people spilled out over the balconies.

The Stone Roses understood this, soundtracked it, paid lip service to it and indulged in it. It was that simple – they seemed to understand what was going on. In 1989 drugs were their making.

In the years that followed they were their undoing.

'Drugs and babies killed The Stone Roses,' John Squire noted later in his press interviews for The Seahorses, adding, 'Each member of the band was on a different drug. It made communication difficult.'

Inevitably it would scramble minds and help to lose the band's focus. Best to get high on life, kids!

SAY IT LOUD! SAY IT PROUD!

For a band that never said very much The Stone Roses said an awful lot, although they learned by the mistakes of previous generations, as John Squire pointed out: 'We were never into sloganeering like The Clash.'

Maybe not sloganeering but there was a real bilious hatred of the establishment. Ian Brown could always be counted on to have a potshot at the royals, 'We're all anti-royalist, anti-patriarch. When the ravens leave the tower, we want to be there shooting them,' he told *Melody Maker*.

Excellent stuff.

As noted before, Brown was well read on the political trip, and now and then in interviews he would let slip his anarchistic leaning; in the lyrics as well there would be something hinted at, something revolutionary stirring in the soul of the protagonist. Everything was left vague, a blur of hints at a far-left rhetoric, a restlessness and a dissatisfaction with an archaic system.

The Roses never dealt in specifics – that was their strength. It was up to the listener to glean information from the tantalising tidbits.

From the 1968 student riots, anti-monarchy, Tony Benn and a common touch, Brown had a restless soul and no set mandate.

Maybe that's the best way for pop – leave a trail of confusion and hint at greater possibilities, never sour the myth or the dream with the real sleaze of genuine politicians.

ON THE STREETS

They were calling it the second summer of love or the third summer of love; it just depended on where your perspectives lay. The summer of 1967 can't have been as much fun though. When Manchester came alive in 1989, it had been through the heavy cloud of depression and had decided to party like crazy. The city began to transform itself on a scale that even ten years later the echoes are still being felt. It was changing fast, the accents were becoming more marked, with everyone playing up their ruffian credentials. The Smiths seemed like an eternity ago. Everyone pretended that they knew a dealer, drugs were everywhere, people smoked dope on the bus, took acid in the pub and a few Es in the 'Hac'; and the dress style totally changed – flares, Kickers, Timberlands, long hair and goatee beards.

The Roses' gigs were peppered with chants of 'Manchester', but all this northern nationalism wasn't something that Ian Brown ever felt that comfortable with.

When Dave Haslam asked him about the 'Manchester north of England' shirts, he replied, 'Some of those T-shirts are bang out of order – "061 Cock Of The North" and "Born In The North, Die In The North" – to be so pro Manchester is verging on something really dodgy. Being territorial like that is like being pro-English in miniature. Manchester is full of great people, but there are also a lot of twats here.'

Acid house was pumping out of the bars that were starting to appear across the city centre – it was the soundtrack interspersed with the Roses and the Mondays, with a touch of the Beatles.

The clubs were packed – everyone calmed down, everyone bamboozled on E. It was about several years before the sinister violence began to creep in, and once that appeared, it showed absolutely no sign of disappearing; violence became a natural way of life for many, and once the buzz of E had gone the buzz of fighting took its place.

But in 1989 fresh-faced kids danced crazier than Bez in back corners of clubs that had no regard for fire limits. Staggering down the streets on hot summer nights there were packs of people leaving clubs, eyes on stalks, their talk peppered with the weird and their vibe very good. Daft phrases started getting picked up – 'top', 'sound', and 'nice one' chased 'nish' and 'clish' and 'in the area' around the bars; jokey words and mad handshakes, daft whistles and shouts of 'Manchester In The Area' from loonies swinging off club and bar tables.

They were crazed times but they were great times, staggering from bar to club to club, chasing the scene, wallowing in its excess and fun. Suddenly a city outdid London and was the scene of pop action and all the bands basked in this new warm glow of hipness. Some better than others, of course; The Stone Roses and The Happy Mondays were better placed than the rest of the pack. Astute observers of pop culture and also riding in on the vanguard of the new way, they were seen as champions of the new lifestyle, name-dropping the right bands, the right clubs and wearing the right clothes. Their music also captured the new flavour, subtly altering to capture the shimmer and the pulse of the times; the stoned vacancy of the stoner's face and the sharp-dressed sense of the street punk were all neatly encapsulated in the Manc bands.

Very few of the bands actually took much musically from the acid house party that was bursting out everywhere across the city. 808 State were the closest musically and even they had their own idiosyncratic take on the new pulse; The Happy Mondays, with their natural funk, remixed their tracks and eventually got Paul Oakenfield in to produce their next album. The rest, though, like James, who through brutal organisation and an ear for a great pop tune finally made it after years in the wilderness. The same went for The Inspiral Carpets, who doggedly ploughed on with their treasure chest of great garage pop tunes and were rewarded with a run of pop hits. For many bands the knock-on after-glow of living in the same city as the hippest kids in the country would be enough to assure them of superstar status.

The endless party spilt from the streets to the jails: Strangeways rioted, and on the roofs of the ancient Victorian rotting hulk were dancing figures, the surrounding streets full of relations and zonked kids shouting up at the unlikely new heroes. They seemed to signify the new Manchester feel – desperadoes dancing in the grey, huddled against the night sky shouting and wailing tunelessly into the void. It was a bizarre entertainment.

It totally encapsulated the turn of the decade in the city.

ROSES IN BLOOM! THE REST OF '89

In August the Roses triumphantly capped their new-found success with the Blackpool Empress Ballroom gig which opens this book. This was the single moment when the band, at their pinnacle, burst through. For the core fans there never would be a better moment to savour than this; it was the greatest moment in their career. There would be bigger gigs, and some good times ahead, but The Stone Roses would never again seem as fresh and as exciting as at this moment in time.

Post Blackpool, they announced an autumn show at Alexandra Palace, in London, a larger and more ambitious show for the south of England. It seemed that there would be no stopping them now. Every wild-card scheme they planned to pull off was going to work – it was just part of the exuberant optimism of the era.

A couple of months after the Blackpool show, they set out for a European tour. One of their superfans, Simon Kelly, joined them out there with his mate Stuart Deabill. 'We flew out to Hamburg and found the venue. It was a really small place with a massive barn door where you went in. We saw

John Squire just round the corner of the door and he said, "Come in, come in." They seemed pleased to see us. Loads of fans went to the Paris show but only a few of us came to the dates before. They put this tape on post-soundcheck and blasted it out over the PA. At first we weren't sure what it was – it was well over eight minutes long and it sounded awesome. When Ian started singing we realised that it was a new Roses song. They came over and asked us what we thought of the new single. It blew us away. That was the first time I heard "Fool's Gold".'

On 11 October the Roses played their first gig in Amsterdam. If there was one place that should have connected instantly with the current dope-fuelled Manc vibe, it ought to have been Amsterdam. Traditionally, the North European capital of drugs and easy living, the city has been a magnet for drug fiends for years.

Oddly enough, the Dutch audience wasn't really having it. Maybe *because* it's the dope capital of Europe, the city can sometimes seem sluggish in its reception of bands attached to that culture, or maybe everyone is just too stoned!

Simon Kelly travelled to Holland as well. 'We arrived in Amsterdam and had a two-day break. It was a nightmare, we got really stoned! Loads of coaches from London had come down for the gig. There were ten people in Europe doing the whole tour: people like Eileen Mulligan had been inter-railing round Europe, going to gigs in places like Spain and Italy. In Rome Ian Brown had met the boxer Marvin Haggler in a club. He was a massive boxing fan and recognised him straight away. He just went up to him and started chatting to him.'

The Dutch crowd were distinctly unimpressed, perhaps believing that this must have been the latest of a long line of British hypes. The Roses had no fear: they didn't care if a crowd loved them or hated them, let alone stood there impassively. Besides they'd got some serious work to do in Paris the next day.

VIVE LA FRANCE!

Twenty-one years after the student riots that almost sent De Gaulle packing, the Roses arrived at Les Inrockuptibles Festival in Paris on 12 October. Put on by the French newspaper of the same name, the festival was showcasing current raved-about British bands. It would be an opportunity to see just how the Roses stood in comparison with their nearest rivals.

Fellow travellers, and two of the greatest lost bands of the era, The La's and Felt, also played but they were already being overtaken by the Manc four-piece. The La's, who only two years before at Sefton Park in Liverpool had seemed the band most likely to break when they played with the Roses, would dither about endlessly with the production of their début album and still have a hit with it. They would then flounder and disappear, leaving bass player John Power ample time to leave the group and form the highly successful Cast. Felt main-man Lawrence would eventually find media attention as the front-man of 1970s glam pastiche merchants, Denim.

It had been a couple of months since the Blackpool show but The Stone Roses were now well and truly a pop phenomenon. Their fans were dealing with the situation more like a football team than just another rock'n'roll band. The Stone Roses were quite definitely a lifestyle. A gig in Paris was a great excuse for coachloads of fans to dress in the latest wacky British street fashions and flood the streets of a bemused European capital.

The trip to Paris was one big beano. Coachloads of crazy Englishmen in too much cloth, and with a scant regard for the Customs' position on drugs, were making the trip over the Channel for the Roses' first Euro-jaunt since those Swedish dates of a few years previously. The festival was being held in the brilliantly seedy La Cigalle, a venue that holds 1,200 people. The Roses fans made up well over half of the audience. It was home from home.

When the band hit the stage the chant of 'Manchester, Manchester' filled the air. This was regional pride as the northern boys asserted themselves in a hall that they totally dominated. It was a weird phenomenon. Could you imagine a regional band from France bringing hundreds of fans over to London dressed in some crazy pop fashion and chanting their home city's name? It was utterly bizarre.

Not that Ian Brown, a man noted for his distinct lack of interest in regionalism, was having any of it. 'Paris, Paris,' he sarcastically answered back, as he king-monkeyed around the stage. The atmosphere was truly tanked up; there was a ribald sense of celebration in the air that couldn't even be dampened by the CS canister that someone let off early in the set just before the band kicked off 'Waterfall'. Eyes were watering, people were running everywhere (should have brought some lemons!) – the band played on regardless, maybe unaware of the mayhem or getting off on the Paris '68 on the barricades' revisionary vibe.

It was wild – they had got the crowd in the palms of their hands.

Simon Kelly remembers Paris as being the show that everyone seemed to have turned up for. 'You couldn't get near the band by then – the place was full of record company people and there seemed to be thousands of fans there. It was totally different from the shows on the rest of the tour.'

Back home, the talk in the press was now that the Roses were planning to release 'What The World Is Waiting For' backed by 'Fool's Gold' as the next single. Eventually, of course, this decision would be reversed and 'Fool's Gold' would be the song that defined the Roses at their peak.

ALLY PALLY: TAKING THE NEW VIBE TO THE CAPITAL

'It's not where you're from, it's where you're at . . .'

The legendary phrase (half-inched from Muhammad Ali's trainer in the late 1960s) was muttered by Ian Brown halfway through the Ally Pally gig when the 'Manchester la-la-las' were just getting too much.

After Blackpool and Europe, the Roses were in a buoyant mood. The mould was set, and this was a band who would attempt to go beyond the norm – think big, make gigs 'events', try and avoid the usual places and take their pop machine into different spheres of influence. It went with the ambition of the time, a new hunger, a belief that they could take this all the way. Gareth was looking for a big show in London and five months after Dingwalls they felt they were ready for something big!

Casting around for the next big one, Manchester promoter Phil Jones, had hit upon the idea of Alexandra Palace, the large ornate hall that held 7,000 people in north London. Ally Pally was more suited to putting on antique fairs and exhibitions than rock'n'roll shows. But in terms of creating 'the legend', here was a spot which would suit them perfectly. Famous for its psychedelic happenings in the late 1960s, where there is footage of a rather stoned-looking John Lennon showing off his walrus moustache and catalogue Afghan coat, the Ally Pally happenings had had that curiously English psychedelic vibe, a psychedelia that had one foot in music hall and the other on super-stoned drug turf.

The 1960s happenings included the '14 Hour Technicolor Dream' in the spring before the summer of love of 1967. During the fourteen hours, Pink Floyd and Soft Machine thrilled the masses at a fundraiser for the fucked-up-by-litigation hippy newspaper, *International Times*.

On this 18 November 1989 evening, though, the atmosphere was defiantly non hippy; a laddish audience in pristine baggy were hacking at their first joints and not feeling quite as psychedelic as previous generations. This was a generation that dug football, rock'n'roll and lager. It wasn't a bunch of hippy drips. This lot were looking for a laugh but, even so, they still wanted some rock'n'roll to transcend them and take them somewhere else.

Despite the much-mooted link between the house and the rock scene, most of the crowd looked confused as the DJs filled the auditorium with house music. They stared vacantly, waiting for the band to come on, or sat cross-legged in the bar getting pissed on warm lager. Ally Pally hardly captured the burning energy of a rave, and when the band hit the stage, the crowd seemed relieved that there was a rock'n'roll band to watch.

For many people in London, this show was the one when it hit them that something really was happening.

Fan Dave Norman had never seen the Roses before. 'I didn't know that they were that popular! And all the clothes that everyone was wearing. It was totally different to any other show that I had been to – it seemed like the north had its own look. In London the indie crowd just didn't dress in flares or baggy gear – that was more of a rave look. That night the two scenes completely crossed over. It seemed like after Alexandra Palace everyone loosened up.'

This was a feature of the times: when there was a dance-orientated band on people didn't dance like they were in clubs as some promoters naively expected, but stood there and stared at the stage, just like they always had done.

After all the buzz that had gone round after Blackpool there were plenty of new faces ready to make the journey to Muswell Hill.

Ian Brown, still harking back to the rush of the Manchester warehouse shows four years previously, explained to Q magazine the reason why they chose the venue. 'Originally we wanted to play somewhere different. So we tried to get a warehouse, but with all the parties it would have been difficult, and this was the only place that we could find that wasn't a rock'n'roll gaff. The best legal alternative.'

The same line of thinking that had dominated since the warehouse parties a few of years back was still being employed, the same sort of determination to move outside the mainstream and operate on their own terms. It was a grand and brilliant arrogance and one which would unfairly saddle them with a difficult reputation.

The Ally Pally, though, was perfect for a band attempting to grab the moment. Surrounded by huge sprawling gardens, the opulent venue was in sharp contrast to the sort of dive in which most fans were expected to check out guitar music in the 1980s; it was a bold and beautiful gesture and the band went for it.

There was new power in the air. The Roses were caught up in the amazing sea change that was happening. It was a time when borders fell, people were freed and pop music became the people's music again. Brown felt that the 1990s were promising to be a hell of a decade: 'Anything is possible when people come together, like East Germany. I'm talking about people who are constantly being had over, sold short, misled, had the wool pulled over their eyes. Eventually they'll say that they are not having it any more . . .'

If only.

At the soundcheck of the big one, the hall seemed massive, almost too big. The band were on-stage jamming and playing for ages, the loosest, funkiest, sassiest shit that they ever played. Gareth Evans wandered around backstage in a knitted cardigan with a huge butterfly design on the back. He couldn't believe his luck, but was also vindicated by his eccentric vision coming together.

The place was buzzing with stage crews building up the PAs and rigging the stage. The huge Victorian hall echoed with the clank of working crews. Watching the soundcheck was Si Wolstencroft, who was hanging out. The ex-Patrol drummer now employed by The Fall looked on more proud than bitter at his lost opportunity. It had been a long and strange five years for both parties.

The soundcheck was a dream, and the sound was stunning. Reni sang a whole bunch of vocals and they jammed out the songs. The band was fluid. The vibe was well and truly up, and there was an air of excited expectancy.

As the crowds began to drift up the hill towards the venue, it was noticeable that there was a marked change in the make-up of the punters. Whereas Blackpool had seen the hip kids, by October it was a show where everyone who wanted a slice of the Roses was turning up.

Even though there was still a massive contingent of Mancs, there were also a lot of very new and very clean-looking flares and long-sleeved T-shirts and Reni hats in the crowd. There was a move away from the acid house heads who also liked the Roses and their original core Manchester following, to rock fans who hated dance but who were getting into the band.

The usual set of acid house was pumped through the PA while the audience listlessly hung out waiting for the main event. There was an electric anticipation, which the Roses played on coming on-stage as late as possible, cranking the atmosphere. As ever there was no support; this show was about The Stone Roses.

When they finally hit the stage there was a massive rush of excitement which rode over the sound which was now really shoddy compared with what it had been at the soundcheck. While the band played their set several things became obvious pretty quickly. The sound was awful in the foggy drone-filled cavernous hall. If it wasn't for the fact that they were playing the defining anthems of their time, the Roses would have got a far shorter shrift off the people. The atmosphere remained ebullient, as already the Roses meant so much to so many people. They were a special band. Muddy sound? No problem, pal, this band is too special, they soundtrack people's lives.

The fans were in a celebratory mood, as fan Geoff Hague points out: 'The sound was a bit muffled, but it was never as bad as anyone made out. I must admit that we were pretty well out of it. We spent a few hours getting stoned in the park before we got in. The total rush when the band came on seemed to last for the whole show. I'd been to loads of gigs before that and it was the first time I'd been to a gig where the atmosphere was like that. They were easily the coolest band in the world at the time.'

Here was a band that in six months had become a legend, and this gig was a celebration of the fact. They played all the usual songs, ending with a climatic version of 'I Am The Resurrection'; Ian Brown sat down playing his bongos, detached in his own world. The duff sound and dodgy venue weren't dampening this crowd.

'I was off me head that night, and I had to sleep on the station,' remembers fan Jay Nielson, 'but it was an amazing buzz, I felt like I was part of pop history.'

The reviews were, as ever, mixed. Mandi James, writing for *NME*, noted how excited she felt about going to the gig. 'It was like going to see a band for the first time,' she raved, getting into the euphoria of the night, and as astute as ever, she pointed out the shortcomings, but was still besotted enough by the power of pop to get caught up in the sheer exhilaration of the event, writing about wide-eyed fans still grooving hours later – you could just tell that Mandi spent the night dancing with the spirit of the times.

Steve Sutherland, at the time writing for *Melody Maker*, was in no mood for this new pop regime. While admitting that the Roses were a 'goodish band' he was at pains to point out that he felt that the whole thing was a hype that had got out of hand. He felt that there was a conspiracy to make the band massive and that we were all falling for it. He decided that the crap sound of the Ally Pally made it very difficult for him to tell whether the band was actually any cop or not.

The *Morning Star* was confused, detecting a magic in the air, although the band just didn't seem to be able to grasp it. 'It was often grabbed for a while but they never held it,' claimed the generally upbeat review.

As 'I Am The Resurrection' ended in a climactic thud, the crowd were up for more and they got the shock of their lives when the Roses changed the no encore rule and kicked straight into an extended work-out of 'Fool's Gold' – a song no one had heard yet.

It was several minutes of fret work from Squire, staggering a long way from the shots of pure pop that they were casually dealing out, almost into free-form Seventies Miles Davis, Can avante funk, adding to the sheer groove of 'Fool's Gold' and Reni's mighty drumming that saw him take it up a few more levels than was normally possible. It was a climactic ending.

The Roses never really played encores as it wasn't part of the aloof schtick. 'Yer pays yer money, yer gets yer show' was the deal. If you want any more you should have been checking the gig.

The Roses had no interest in giving too much away about themselves. They were working on the enigma, the enigma that was the key. There was no kow-towing to the audience.

Later on that night there was a party in a fucked-up old nightclub space in north London. The party goers all sat there waiting for the dawn and for the drugs to wear off. Publicist Philip Hall sat at the table with some of the hardcore Roses' fans. Brian Canon, who went on to design all the Oasis sleeves, was down there along with several other people, Manchester faces, scenesters and hustlers enjoying the big night out in London. In the murk and the mush of the party, one thing was agreed on: it was a great night, despite the rough sound. It was a top buzz, it was a great party. It was pop history in the making.

SINGLE NO. 6!: FOOL'S GOLD

On 1 November before Bonfire night the Roses decided to get all incendiary themselves, and released their best-ever record. With a seven-inch clocking in at 4 minutes 15 seconds and a twelve-inch at 9 minutes 53 seconds, the band were obviously about to break out of the tight formats dictated by verse/chorus guitar pop, and utilise all their strengths. After a couple of years listening to dance, checking out clubs and nailing the Es, they were also about to deliver their take on the new dance-conscious youth of the UK.

The single was going to be their first serious new track since they broke massive over the summer and would be their first shot at the top five.

'Fool's Gold' was the Roses' finest moment, an alchemy of everything that was strong about the band. John Leckie for one cranked up the Roses' awesome rhythm section and combined a neat sample with Reni's ever-inventive fluid drumming, a killer simple bass line from Mani, and John Squire's funky bad-ass wah-wah licks on top. Ian Brown intoned a husky, menacing vocal, as ever, part homely and part preacherman, with the original mystic scally dope-shot voice. It was simple, sexy and funky as fuck. It was the musical high-water mark of their career.

The original loop was either copped from 'Bra' by Cymande (they could well have grabbed the bass line from here as well) or sampled from James Brown (the guitar riff has echoes of Brown's God-like 'Say It Loud, I'm Black And I'm Proud').

Cymande were a black funk band from the mid-1970s, a golden period in music when the true psychedelic shit was being whacked out. This was righteous stuff, when black American music went weird in the 1970s with outfits like Sly And The Family Stone, Parliament and The Temptations going brilliantly crazy along with a whole generation of black musicians; they made some great strange music but didn't forget to bring the groove along. Instead of The Beatles' music-hall pastiches and the Stones' clumsy attempts at psychedelia, this was true weirdness.

This was a freaked-out intergalactic, space-cake weirdness times ten, great players who never lost the funk going out on their own cosmic journeys, but unlike the white guys in their cheesecloth and kaftans these guys never forgot the funk or the sex. Their sinuous keen music still had its pulse in the groin.

There was a whole heap of stuff to work through from Miles Davis's freaked jazz funk of *Bitches Brew* through to James Brown hustling and jamming with whoever was in his band; the aforementioned Temptations'

Psychedelic Shack; and then there was Sly And The Family Stone, with his cosmic raps, sweet voice and loose handle on reality – this was music that kicked out the funkiest dirty-assed hip jams, awesome and sexy stuff and, along with Clinton's Parliament/Funkadelic, a key influence on a whole generation of Manchester bands. You could hear these influences pumping out of Hulme bedsits, student discos and flats across the city. The mix was part of the cultural mish-mash that created the city's flavour.

In Manchester there had been an interest in rock and dance that traced its roots back to Legends in the early 1980s, when DJs like Greg Wilson were pumping out New York electro sounds years ahead of any other towns, inspiring A Certain Ratio and New Order to loose their raincoat shackles and funk up their rainy-city grooves.

The Roses were now pushing the boundaries of pop further. They now had the tuff groove of funk, and they then crossed this with the open space repetition of Krautrock kings Can. It was an audacious and bold record and, along with The Happy Mondays, they were cutting pop that defined the times perfectly.

If the second album had been put down there and then, it would have been all grooves combined with sinister vocals that were half spoken and half rapped, played by a band that were so tight that they could lock into a groove and milk it, a band that were tight as friends as well as musicians, all buzzing off each other's talents and skills. For many pundits this was the great lost moment. If only they could have gone down this road what a genius album they would have made!

At the time producer John Leckie spoke to *NME*. When asked about the Roses' indie dance connection Leckie was a tad confused: 'I'm too busy to follow dance music. If someone takes me to a club then I hear it occasionally. If I like a track I'll buy it. I'm not really known as a dance producer. It's not my forte. It's a bit like me asking your opinions on classical music.'

Well, so much for the bridge between dance and rock then. Leckie was as confused as most people by this endless connection, although he did put it into perspective. 'At the time we were listening to a lot of dance music in our recreation period in the studio, so that probably leaked into the recording by osmosis so to speak. One of the reasons that "Fool's Gold" crossed over was because it was a song. A lot of dance stuff is great but there's no song. A good track is something you can strum on an acoustic guitar or play on the piano. That's the bottom line. It seems like a natural progression for us; all this categorising of music makes no sense to me.'

The Roses, at this point, were fucking with their template, attempting to move forward, as Ian Brown explained to Dave Haslam in 1989: 'We need to be constantly changing. You've always got to change. When you realise it's not there any more, then you're chasing your tail. Then you stop. You can't degrade yourself in public and ride on the back of an old reputation. We're concentrating more on rhythm now. On the first LP it was a matter of making the melodies sound good. Now we're trying to get the rhythms to sound better. "Fool's Gold" is the most different thing that we have done for ages. It's based on a continuous bass riff. All I know is that we never intended to sound like a 1960s group.'

Incredibly, despite being acknowledged now as the classic defining moment of The Stone Roses' career, 'Fool's Gold' nearly didn't make it on to the A-side. For some reason, the more standard fare of 'What The World Is Waiting For' was the original main track.

Gareth Davies, whose company Beer Davies was doing radio promotion for The Stone Roses, was instrumental in getting the single flipped over. 'We were working a white label pre-release of the single around TV companies and we biked it over to *Rapido* and *The Late Show* people. All they would go on about was this great bass riff on the track. I didn't have a clue what they were talking about until I turned the record over and noticed that they must have been going on about "Fool's Gold". It occurred to me straight away the single was the wrong way round. The bass riff that everyone liked so much is the one that Mani plays on "Fool's Gold". I phoned Andrew Lauder at Silvertone straight away and he agreed. That's the beauty of working with a small record company – decisions can be made very quickly.'

As it turned out the band were more than happy to go with the decision. They felt that they knew even before the white labels were pressed that this was the correct way round for the record.

The decision meant that in a simple stroke The Stone Roses were looking forwards and not backwards. Here was the synthesis of dance and rock that everyone had been writing about; rhythm was king and melody was along for the ride.

On release 'Fool's Gold' provided The Stone Roses with their first top-ten hit, entering the charts at number fourteen and then going to number eight. It also provided them with their first bona fide daytime radio record. Davies looks back fondly at this crucial moment. 'I remember ringing the band up when the record was getting its first daytime plays and they were very excited.'

A top-ten hit meant *Top Of The Pops*. They were booked to appear on 23 November.

And *Top Of The Pops* meant a whole new stack of logistical problems for the normally unflappable Davies.

First, though, they were booked to play on the late-night BBC2 arts programme *The Late Show* on 21 November.

Gareth had been thinking about broadening the band's media profile. An arts programme was perfect. He sent the 'What The World Is Waiting

For'/'Fool's Gold' to *The Late Show*, one of the last bastions of art TV. It was a smart move. He figured the Hampstead arts mob would like a bit of rough on their show.

He was still surprised when the programme's researchers phoned back and said they were keen to have the band on the programme! And, hey, they loved that funky 'B' side.

That was last September. By now 'Fool's Gold' was in the charts, the Roses' biggest hit yet, and when they arrived in the studio for the run through that afternoon they were not a band that was going to get pushed around by a bunch of artsy fartsy TV people. Every time they got some sort of instruction, they stared back impassively. This was not a band that was interested in kow-towing to anybody else's idea of what a rock'n'roll band should do.

When it came to filming, the atmosphere was already fairly tense and when the band's cranked amps blew the BBC's noise limiters one minute into their live rendition of 'Made Of Stone', it was pretty well over.

Ian Brown spat into the mic, 'Amateurs, amateurs . . . we're wasting our time here lads' as the group skulked away in the background.

Late Show presenter Tracey Macleod attempted to salvage the situation, ad libbing through the tension.

The incident grabbed the band a whole bunch of press coverage and got them pretty well blanked by the BBC, apart from the odd appearance, when it came to TV coverage.

In the years that followed Gareth tried to claim that the whole incident was planned, that it was an attempt at national shit-stirring on the scale of The Sex Pistols.

On 23 November, the Roses made their début appearance on *Top Of The Pops*. Normally an appearance on Britain's premier pop show is taken with good humour or great excitement. No matter how corny or how naff it's perceived as, it's also the best pop programme ever on British TV. There's something about its chart-heavy and simple format that works beautifully. It's also the pinnacle in any promotion campaign and a crowning moment for the pluggers to get the band on to the show.

Of course things were different with this band.

'I had many proper sleepless nights over this one,' remembers Davies. 'I normally sleep like a log but the Roses on *Top Of The Pops* was a cause of major concern for me.'

It turned out that the band didn't want to be on *Top Of The Pops*; maybe like their heroes The Clash or Led Zeppelin they believed that the show would demean their work or, even cannier, they believed that the enigma that was sucking everyone in would be ruined by flouncing around on the show.

'They were certainly very smart like that. They were hardly what you would call over-exposed. It's like the only people to ever really see them perform were their true fans. It was very difficult for the casual observer to see The Stone Roses, and that became part of their allure,' admires Davies.

'They didn't want to do it. They were staying at the YMCA hotel just off Tottenham Court Road which was typical of them. You couldn't get further away from the rock'n'roll circus than that. I went over there to persuade them to do it. They didn't want to be seen miming: they wanted the amps on-stage to make it look right. I got in touch with *Top Of The Pops* producer Stan Appel, asking if they could use their amps. He said, "Why are this band so difficult? We have no problems with proper stars like Barry Manilow and Liza Minnelli." When they arrived in the taxi at the studio they told the driver to keep the cab running as they may leave at any minute. They didn't trust the programme, they didn't care, they would have just walked back out of there again. The roadies set up the gear and we waited. Gareth Evans was in a real flap. The Mondays were also on the show, and before the Roses went on he was trying to keep the two bands apart in case the Mondays spiked their drinks.'

Eventually it all went ahead smoothly. It went down as one of the legendary *Top Of The Pops*, far more legendary than Barry Manilow appearing on the show.

1990

AT LAST! THE END OF THE EIGHTIES!: FACE OFF WITH *THE FACE*

The decade had started off well, with the *Sun* newspaper predicting that The Stone Roses would be one of the bands of the Nineties if only they would stop 'slagging off the royals' and there was not much chance of that with Ian Brown's avowed hatred of Britain's most useless family.

1989 had given the band a superb impetus. Not only were they the band of the year, their début album was already being talked about in hushed whispers as a rock classic. Where, only months before, people had been talking about them as if they were pop lepers, they were now being treated as one of the bands of the Eighties.

The *NME* put together a readers' poll of the greatest moments of the crappiest pop decade on record and they scored pretty highly with no. 16 album, no. 4 hope for the Nineties and no. 15 biggest surprise of the Eighties.

That January, the first month of a brave new decade saw the Roses basking in the glow of warm press. The only dark cloud was the notorious Nick Kent feature that appeared in *The Face*.

It was a piece on The Happy Mondays and The Stone Roses and it left no one very happy with its misquotes and its condescending manner. Kent, a journalist, was a product of the mid-Seventies rock star scene.

He had cut his rock'n'roll teeth writing about Iggy Pop, Keef Richards, Sid Vicious and their ilk (couldn't really fuck that up, could you!) and was naturally suspicious of these two new bands hanging out at rock'n'roll central.

There was a whole new drugs and rock'n'roll party and he wasn't invited. Kent, a veteran of the drug wars, felt that it was his professional duty to take some ecstasy as research for the article, something that he trumpeted in his preview for the article on *The Face*'s contents page.

'It would be pretty unprofessional if I wrote about these two groups without ever trying it – trying to look in from the outside.' The biggest shock was that he must have been one of the last hipsters in the country not to have taken E.

He went down to the Mondays' and the Roses' joint *Top Of The Pops* appearance, perhaps *the* pop moment of the year and completely missed the point of what was going down. It was a cultural and generational clash.

Kent had misquoted both bands and painted them both in a not particularly flattering light. The Roses' quotes were written out in northern accents that made them sound nothing like themselves (ever met anyone who says 'fookin' he also seemed to think that the Roses' drummer was called 'Rhemmi'.

The tabloids were now on the band's case as well, Brown's anti-royal stance was the sort of sensationalist guff that they thrived upon. The *Sun* went down to Sylvan Avenue to find out what neighbours thought of the vocalists 'controversial' stance. They were gruffly rebuked.

Attention-seeking Tory MP losers like Geoffrey Dickens tried to get the group banned from *Top Of The Pops* because of the same stance. He urged viewers to switch off while the band was playing. It was completely childish but not too unexpected from the pathetic Tory party.

PAINT JOB: THE STONE ROSES GET INTO THE PAINTING AND REDECORATING BUSINESS

Bored with being the good boys in the new Manchester pop hierarchy (and it would take a brave and crazy man to outdo Shaun Ryder on the badman stakes) The Stone Roses were on the lookout for some sort of mischief.

The fact that the label Revolver FM had recently re-released their 1987 single 'Sally Cinnamon' without their consent and put together a promotional video for the single that was an ad hoc shambles of clips slapped together had wound the band up. They managed to chart the single at number 46.

The band weren't happy.

For Revolver the Roses' rise to success had been a frustrating one. Since they had released the single the band seemed to have disappeared. They had signed them when no one else would give them a look in. And now they couldn't get a whisper from the band. Nothing. Gareth just wasn't returning their calls. A big silence.

The Roses were fuming. They wanted revenge. They knew that there was no chance of striking back through the courts, things would have to be done in a street style.

On 30 January after a band meeting at the International, where the topic of revenge was brought up, the band set off to Rockfield Studios in Wales to work on their next single, 'One Love'. During the meeting they decided to visit label MD Paul Birch and his girlfriend Olivia Darling in his Wolverhampton office, which they promptly redecorated with coloured paint. Ian Brown then slipped outside and smashed the rear window of Birch's twenty-five grand Mercedes with a brick and Reni gave the car a respray, a respray that was hardly likely to add value to the vehicle.

'The video was insulting,' Brown said at the time. 'Blokes selling fruit, a few pigeons, some black woman holding a baby, a picture of me on the front of *The Face*, a few people in flares . . . So we went and painted him.'

Birch was, understandably, less than pleased and even as the band were arriving at Rockfield Studios covered in paint, making it easy for the police to spot who they were, he was starting proceedings against them for wilful damage.

The band and Steve Adge are arrested. Ian Brown, John Squire and Reni are arrested in their hotel near the studio. Mani and Steve walk into Monmouth police station to give themselves up. All are taken to Wolverhampton. Steve Adge is released without charge.

The band put an injunction on the label and prevented them from showing the video. During February with the Revolver case rumbling on, Silvertone re-released 'Elephant Stone' on 19 February (it was The Stone Roses' second Top Ten hit, crashing in at number 8) and 'Made Of Stone' a week later (surprisingly less of a hit at number 20). On the back of this 'She Bangs The Drums' re-entered the back end of the Top 40.

The Roses' past was now up for sale and there were plenty of takers.

They appeared in Wolverhampton Crown Court that March, where there was a disagreement over the amount of damage caused. Revolver claimed £22,000 and the band's representatives £8,000. The case was postponed, finally coming to fruition the following autumn.

I went down and covered the case for *Sounds*, sitting in court soaking up the near carnival atmosphere. While they were getting their wrists slapped, T-shirts with 'Ian Brown Is Innocent' emblazoned across the front were being flogged outside.

The band pleaded guilty to the charges and were fined £3,000 each plus £95 costs. The judge said that their actions were 'immature to the point of childishness'. The Roses sauntered into the court smirking.

This was a proper laugh. The band were convinced that they were totally justified in their action and they knew that the fine, although a tidy sum of money, would hardly break their piggy-banks.

After the trial they stood on the steps of the court looking cool as fuck, bad-ass rock stars in old Wolverhampton fooling with the system. They posed for pictures, laughing like guilty schoolboys, savouring every moment of the drama.

They may have been fined but they felt like they had won as they dashed to the waiting cars parked round the corner.

FELLOW MUSICIANS REACT TO THE NEW POP KINGS

The Roses' ascendancy hadn't gone unnoticed by some of the creaking rock royalty. *20/20* magazine quoted Pink Floyd man Roger Waters that spring: 'The Stone Roses reminded me of us twenty-five years ago. They've got loads of bollocks and arrogance and won't take any shit. John Leckie produced the album and he engineered bits of *The Dark Side Of The Moon* and *Wish You Were Here*. I see they've got a Jackson Pollock paint-splashed Rickenbacker bass – the first guitar I spent all my grant on – I got a friend of mine to paint mine. I like that kind of open guitar sound and it doesn't sound like there is any machinery around. They wear flares, and why not?

This kind of identity seeking in late adolescence is very crucial and will be till the end of time. Anyway people don't grow up – they just get older.'

Albeit pretty stuffy, but oddly perceptive. What a surprise that he had heard of the Roses, let alone actually listened to them.

It boggles the mind to wonder what the Lydon-influenced Ian Brown made of all this.

Post 1989, the whole scene was opening up in the UK. There were hordes of new bands fired by the Roses and some older heads were turning. Spacemen 3, who had been dabbling in psychedelics for a long time, were hooking into the whole vibe. They had played several shows in Manchester over the years and had been pretty influential on several of the up and coming local bands. The Inspiral Carpets had supported them and The Happy Mondays had checked them out, as their guitar player Sonic Boom recalls. 'After a gig a couple of smoothies came up to me and I thought that they were going to hit me,' is how he remembers his first meeting with The Happy Mondays, adding, 'What you've got with the Mondays and the Roses is really accessible music, combined with a really cool attitude.'

Ian Brown noted at the same time that there was definitely something up on the streets. 'Everyone's dressing up again – 1986 seems like a lifetime ago. A few skins have been shed since then,' he was quoted in *Sounds* that spring.

Loose drugs and looser clothes were the order of the era. Pop music, which had been under the cosh of the 1980s' dull scene was starting to find its own voice. That decade was getting rubbed out by a whole plethora of new sounds and new styles. All over the UK new bands were starting to form, fired by the possibilities that The Stone Roses presented, grooving off the confident aura of Ian Brown and the brilliant pop musicianship of the band. Chancers, dreamers and bug-eyed schemers were putting into place bands that would go on to dominate the 1990s.

The Stone Roses were currently at their catalytic best, central to the new art riot. Rumours of a massive show that summer were starting to surface. It would be the big one that would galvanise the imagination of the new pop generation.

There was talk of a strange place called 'Spike Island'.

POLICE AND THIEVES

In mid-May Ian Brown was caught up in a bizarre incident at the International 2. One that was a pointer for what the Manchester of the next few years was going to be like once the party was over.

The sinister gangster thing was starting to kick off as the drugs trade was far too profitable to be left to a few manky old hippies dealing out dope. The sharp street kids wanted in. There was a new generation of gangsters hustling for some action.

The city had become more and more tense. The so-called vibe seemed to disappear and the drug dealers looked rougher and rougher. Moss Side became synonymous with gangs, and Cheetham Hill, Moss Side and Salford fought out a drugs war in the city's clubs. Pundits reckoned that the whole drug business in Manchester was worth millions per year and there were plenty of takers.

The gunmen were starting to encroach on the music scene. Brown was watching local reggae band Ini Kamoze at the International club, when a gunman charged into the club and people went flying as bullets were shot into the roof; moments later the cops burst in and the whole place calmed down again.

It was to be like that in Manchester as the party gradually drew to a halt, as the comedown from E kicked in. The surly attitude of the pop stars was getting handed down to the streets as a licence for macho posturing. Drugs, which had sent the scene through the roof two years before were also contributing to its downfall.

Manchester was going to be in for a couple of rough and ready years.

THE ULTIMATE MEDIA STAND OFF: THE SPIKE ISLAND PRESS CONFERENCE

By the summer of 1990, for the first time since punk, a whole series of street bands were hitting the charts. The flavour of UK pop had changed and things were getting briLliantly out of hand. Not only were the Roses planning to play to 30,000 people in the middle of an industrial belt in Cheshire, but they were going to have a full-on proper press conference as well.

No one interesting had done that in pop for years.

This was a chance for the band who didn't really communicate with the media to talk to the world's pop press. A mass of journalists were all in Manchester getting ready for the Spike Island showdown. This was an opportunity for the still generally cynical media to lock horns with the UK's latest pop sensation.

The press conference was an odd and controversial occasion that was probably the brainchild of Gareth Evans, who spent the stand-off standing just to the side of the band with a grin slapped across his face.

As the midsummer day drew to a close across Manchester city centre the press, the pundits, and the blaggers started filing into the Piccadilly Hotel foyer. A curious building, Piccadilly Hotel is the revolting slab of concrete in the centre of Manchester that looks like it was donated from some fucked-up industrial town in deep Eastern Europe. The huge neon signs on the side, the shitty chip shops on the ground floor and the ugly concrete of Manchester's second-tallest building dominate the city centre, making it seem far more grim that it really is.

Most rock'n'roll bands would have used the Midland Hotel round the corner, it being one of the famous pop haunts, but for some reason the Roses went for the Piccadilly. Swigging beer and looking across the tramp-strewn wasteland of Piccadilly Gardens and on to the smog-filled mess of the bus station, the press pack were curiously less rowdy than usual. No one really knew what to expect. It wasn't going to be an easy ride.

A whole clutch of Manchester scenesters and pop fiends mingled with the high and mighty and the self-appointed guardians of the new cool.

Late, as usual, The Stone Roses mooched into the room. The atmosphere got tenser and there was a curious silence.

'Why don't you ask summat? You've flown here from all over the world,' sneered Ian Brown at the not-so-merry throng. There was plenty of foot shuffling. No one really felt like being the first to talk in such a hostile atmosphere.

'Tune in, turn off, but don't drop out,' added the singer enigmatically.

The questions that followed were the usual banal, unprepared pieces of cannon fodder that always seemed to be the feature of these events, everyone always hoping that someone else asks something smart for them to steal for their own copy.

Journalist: 'When are you coming to America?'

'When you send us the ticket,' replied Mani, the Rose who seemed most comfortable with the whole thing.

Indignant journalist: 'Answer the question.'

Stone Rose: 'We are.'

Journalist: 'Are you guys prepared for this press conference?'

Reni: 'We're not a political manifesto. We never went to a school for press conferences.'

Journalist: 'How do you think Americans will appreciate Manchester sarcasm?'

Ian Brown: 'With an American accent.'

Maybe there were shades of The Beatles at Kennedy Airport in 1964 trying to be cute fending off the more banal questions, only this time it was nastier and armed with a more 1990s brutish northern wit.

Unlike The Beatles, the press didn't like what they were hearing.

Journalist: 'Do you like The Charlatans?' referring to the Northwich-based outfit who had supported the Roses earlier in their career and who were now making inroads into the mainstream with their Roses-influenced Hammond-driven garage pop.

Roses: 'We've never heard of them.'

Journalist: 'Would you play in a bullfight arena?'

Reni: 'It's just not on, is it? We wouldn't watch it on TV, so why should we endorse it.'

The questions were starting to get dumb.

Journalist: 'What did your parents do?'

Ian Brown: 'My father was a joiner and he told me to never work on a building site, and that's what I have done.'

Someone piped up and asked about the Strangeways Prison riots that had recently dominated the news when prisoners had kept the guards at bay for several weeks from the Victorian Manchester city-centre jail.

Ian Brown perked up. 'It was great. It was like five lads keeping the whole of England at bay,' he stated, not realising that he could have been talking about the Roses themselves. 'It took a lot of strength. Anyone who has a go is a folk hero in Manchester.'

The tabloids, represented by the *Daily Star*, decided that it was time to get things on to home territory, and asked about sex, drugs and rock'n'roll.

Ian Brown, feigning intense boredom, stared glumly out at the audience.

There was finally a question about Spike Island itself.

'We asked our manager Gareth to find us somewhere near loads of people and he found us Spike Island,' Brown deadpanned, referring to the considerable complaints that had come from the local residents about the gig. He added, 'We're not getting any money out of it. It cost us 400 grand to put on and we're getting nish.'

Someone asked if the band had any rivalries with any other local outfits. This was obviously not someone from the city because the bands, although disparate in style, were always pretty tightly knit. The whole nature of the band scene was always close, most bands cheering on their so-called rivals.

'It's not a contest is it?' replied Brown, with an icy stare. 'We don't have a grudge against anyone apart from Nick Kent because he's a liar.'

Journalist: 'Hello, I am from a national paper in Spain. I want to know when your recordings on Silvertone will be available all over the world.'

Brown: 'The people to ask are standing at the back.'

The Silvertone people at the back shuffled uncomfortably. No one likes to be made to speak in a full room of people, especially a room full of press determined for a story. Luckily the drunk grabbed the mic and started talking in late 1980s Manc-speak, 'Roses in the area. Spike Island got fuck all in the area aaaaaaiieeeee!'

Journalist: 'John, are you ever going to speak?'

John: 'No.'

Journalist: 'Do you think you are the best guitarist in the world?'

John: 'Yeah!'

The madman: 'Aaaaaaiieeeeee!'

Journalist: 'Do you think that you are the new Rolling Stones?'

Brown: 'This is 1990 innit? So I say to you the Rolling Who?' (Cheers and applause.)

Journalist: 'What do you think you'll be doing in five years' time?'

Brown: 'What a stupid question, how the fuck do I know?' (Indeed it was a stupid question and one that everyone always gets asked at these sort of things. Does anyone in pop ever actually have a five-year plan?)

Journalist: 'You're being compared to some of the biggest bands in the world. How do you feel about it?'

Brown: 'Excited, bored – I'm waiting for someone to make me laugh.'

Photographer (to the gathered press): 'What I want to know is why the fuck are you all here? Why are you all so afraid to ask the band any questions?'

Brown: 'It's because we don't answer them.' (Nervous giggling and uncomfortable fidgeting.)

Journalist: 'Do you guys always bear a grudge? You've invited all these people here and you won't answer any questions.'

Brown: 'I've answered all the questions . . . except the stupid ones.' (Mumblings, atmosphere is increasingly tense and uncomfortable.)

Journalist: 'Since it's inevitable you guys are coming to America, you're obviously gonna have to do a lot of press. They'll want to ask about your private life. What are your backgrounds?'

Brown: 'I'm not telling you.' (A long gap of silence and shuffling.)

Madman: 'Wooooooagh in the area!'

Brown (belches): 'Urgh 'scuse, anyone want a cig?'

Journalist: 'Yeah, want some of this?' (Hands Brown a spliff.)

Brown: 'Who has come from the other side of the world? Hands up, you're being paid to ask the questions.' (Angry rumblings from the floor.)

Journalist: 'I paid my own fare, so fuck you, man!'

Brown: 'Ooooh.' (A row starts between two journalists and one of them turns on the Roses.)

At this point Frank Owen from *Details* magazine got to the front of the queue and, attempting to shout over a drunk mate of the band, he yelled, 'This is fucking bullshit! I'm from Manchester. I live in New York and this is bullshit. You're treating these people like fucking shit. [Another bloke starts telling him to shut up.] No, you shut up, you fucking dickhead.' (They start pushing each other.)

Brown: 'Hey, ease off, we're not treating anyone like anything.'

Owen: 'Don't give me that. I'm from here. I know when you're fucking winding people up!'

Brown: 'Sort your head out, man.'

Owen, now visibly annoyed, weighed in: 'I'm from Manchester and I know when you're winding people up. Why are you coming out with this anti-American shit?'

The Roses were momentarily startled by Owen and let him continue.

Owen: 'You're behaving like pigs to these people. Why are you dissing all these people here?'

The drunk loon made menacing steps towards him and it looked like the whole press conference may kick off with some real physical aggro. Everyone in the room tensed, expecting some hooligan action, but the drunk seemed to lack the focus necessary for the job and backed off.

Owen continued: 'It's the whole Manchester sarcasm shit. Why won't you answer the question?'

The band looked back baffled. 'What question?' they quietly replied.

Ian Brown looked up with one of his vacant stares and blanked back with one of his odd phrases that could have come from his grandmother. 'I think you've got the right stick but at the wrong end.'

This was the high tension point where all the frustration and misunderstanding between the two sides kicked in. Gareth stood to the side, his face full of glee; it was this sort of confrontation that he loved.

Journalist: 'Have you seen tapes of when the Stones came to America? Does this remind you of that?'

Brown: 'No. [To aggrieved bloke.] You still upset?'

Owen: 'Yeah. I'm fucking still upset. These people come all this way and you won't answer the questions properly.' (Everyone on the floor starts arguing and shouting at each other.)

Brown: 'What are you complaining about? You've got a free trip over to England and you're going to see a great band tomorrow. Hands up who's paid to come from the other side of the world out of their own pockets.'

A photographer went down to the front and grabbed hold of one of the Roses' mics.

'You haven't asked goddamn shit,' he snarled, 'you lot haven't asked shit for questions.' It was probably the truest comment of the night.

A member of the band's management then grabbed the mic. 'How the fuck do you think the band feel sat up there in complete silence with all you bastards staring at them, asking them fuck all! You come all this way. Drink all the free beer and you haven't asked fucking shit! You're a bunch of fucking wankers in whatever language you speak. If I was them I'd fuck off now!'

As the press conference ended the journalists and everyone else drifted out into the still Manchester air. Gareth Evans took the opportunity to show me the contents of his car boot, stacked full of T-shirts. He was rubbing his hands with joy. He was going to be minted from flogging these the next day. It was the beginning of the serious merchandise era and the smart bands were getting the T-shirts out.

After the press conference the band were shocked at the antagonism that they had kicked up, but not too displeased. A bit of controversy was always to the Roses' taste. It was their punk roots showing through.

The press conference was the culmination of the Roses' odd affair with the press. At the start the press had feted them with that Gary Johnson feature in *Sounds* from their first-ever gig, and then there had been a three-year gap until *Sounds* or anyone else picked up on them again.

From then on the press themselves covered the Roses quite faithfully, cranking a gear when it was clear that the pop zeitgeist had suddenly sided with these northerners. The Roses gave very little back, blanking interviewers.

It was a confused and bizarre situation, and one that still pervades to this day, when northerners are quoted as saying 'fookin' instead of fucking and they have their speech printed out like they were retards, whereas southern bands naturally speak in perfect grammar. The northern bands are perceived as being simple oiks and the southerners as college boys, a gross simplification of reality.

No wonder John Squire always kept his trap shut. Apart from virtually one thing: when asked by the throng who his favourite painter was, he replied, 'Ronnie Wood.'

Now that's funny.

SPIKE ISLAND

When you've burned Blackpool, set your stall at Ally Pally and you're a dreamer, you may as well go for broke. In 1989–90 anything could happen, that was the vibe. Self-belief, boosted by ecstasy and the acid house boom (which promoted community, large crowds and loadsamoney for unscrupulous promoters), were all coming together and affecting the rock scene.

During the back end of 1989 Gareth and his business partner Matthew along with promoter Phil Jones had been scouring the country looking for a suitable venue for the mega gig. All sorts of suggestions were thrown their way – disused caravan parks, old quarries, even the site from the legendary Bickershawe festival in 1972 where the Grateful Dead made their UK début. But they were looking for something wackier, something weirder.

And if the music business had thought that Blackpool was off the beaten tracks then check out what they had come up with. Some island in the Mersey near Widnes.

Fuck!

People were hungry for big spaces and big ideas. At the time festivals were just getting themselves sorted out after dipping into a 1980s malaise of leather jackets and stale lager-fuelled crap hills. No cool band would be seen dead at a festival, let alone put one on themselves.

On 21 December 1989 Evans had applied to Hatton Borough Council for a licence. The site was usually used for a local carnival and wouldn't be a problem for a concert.

All year rumours had been going round about proposed big Roses shows and the band, who were attempting to operate outside the rock'n'roll circuit, were trying to pull off the big one, flouting conventions yet again.

There is a certain circuit that a band is meant to complete, before selling out Wembley Stadium at the peak of its career. Now that every local band seemed to be playing GMex in Manchester, a 14,000-capacity hall, as if it was a small local gig, imagination was called for.

Whatever the festival was, it was going to be the band's first British date of 1990. There had been some crazy rumours going round everywhere about shows. Some of them were probably plants, some were moments of sheer lunacy and some would have been great ideas if they had been pulled off.

Like in July the wires were buzzing about a show at Buckingham Palace or in one of the royal parks nearby. 'We want to do it. We're in negotiation with Buckingham Palace at the moment,' the Roses chortled.

It would have been a great moment as the anti-monarchist Roses pulled 40,000 stoners into central London, outside the grim old Palace for a rowdy evening's mayhem.

Unfortunately it was a scam.

The idea for Spike Island was to place a gig somewhere between Liverpool and Manchester, a symbolic link between the two cities that were at each other's throats in football hooligan terms, but now, armed with their own music scenes, were rivalling London as the hippest corner of the UK.

The plan was to flood the semi-rivers around the island and build bridges, creating a natural barrier in and out of the gig. Everyone knew what a bunch of blaggers lived in the north-west; Manc guest lists were always ridiculous. Now here was a chance to blag the biggest party of the year. Anyone without a ticket or an approved blag was going to have to swim the Mersey to get in, and you can't get any more foolproof than that.

Spike Island was the big one. It was the gathering of the clans. If Blackpool had been a special moment when the Roses had proved that there was something special going on, then Spike, with the movers and shakers from all over the UK turning up, was an unprecedented show of strength for a group that had burst on to the scene only a year before.

As the warm summer evening drew to a close, and the Roses battled with the rubbish sound system, countless bands would be getting formed in the scrubby fields on the banks of the River Mersey.

Spike Island was both the peak of the Roses' career and the point where it all started to unravel. The point where the sheer speed of their sudden rise in popularity would bring nearly 30,000 people to Widnes to see them play live, but would cause all sorts of logistical and organisational nightmares.

This was the time when the cultural shift could be well and truly marked – there were hundreds of Reni hats (there were even letters to the papers about 'Reni hats' with people asking whether he had them specially made, not realising that he just bought them from junk shops, airport lounges, anywhere where he had the time and the money; he can't have realised that he was starting off a fashion craze).

Spike Island was the high-water mark of the baggy scene, as flares, baggy tops, greasy moptops and 'label' clothes totally dominated. The youth was looking to distance itself from the austere 1980s as far as possible; the baggy look would go on to dominate the 1990s, and, refined and twisted around it, came Britpop.

It was the rock kids appropriating the acid house look and lifestyle, although it was more warm larger than Ecstasy. Even now there were plenty of Es knocking about on the site and spliff was beginning to make its massive inroad into popular culture. Smoking dope, which, even up to about a year before had been more of a bohemian drug, was now curling into the mainstream. It was the start of an astonishing rise in the popularity of drugs that saw the 1990s eventually becoming the most drug-fused decade in Britain since the druids stopped chomping down the magic mushrooms in ancient times. Popular culture would never be the same again.

Warming up for Spike Island, the Roses did a short tour of Scandinavia, returning for the first time since their poverty-stricken 'Beatles In Hamburg' bonding tour of Sweden five years before. This time it was different, as with hits under their belt the Roses were stars in Scandinavia.

Sweden and the surrounding countries had always dug British groups – they were in the UK pop sphere of influence and the bands had always been well supported over there.

The main gig was in Stockholm at the Fryhuset, a large youth-club YMCA building.

The preceding two gigs had been rusty. The début in Copenhagen on 15 May wasn't one of their best, and the next show, in a small venue in Lund, had seen a crowd mainly made up of ribald punk rockers spitting at the band – just like old days.

On 17 May in Stockholm the band were buzzing about the new single 'One Love' to journalists. They were about to go back into the studio and remix it. The cut hadn't been perfect and they needed more bottom end. The choice was now between the Adrian Sherwood version or the John Leckie version. Getting the bottom right was always something the Roses, a band that listened to their reggae and dub, were keen on getting correct. Mani's bass was the heavy undertow with resonations of deep dub and Public Image Limited's great bass player Jah Wobble in its sound. It wouldn't be until Mani laid down some great bass lines for Primal Scream that his bass would get the fully bang-on sound that he had been looking for.

The band hit the stage running in Stockholm and the 1,500 punters crammed in went mad. The Roses were big time now in Sweden and the crowd went mental for the 'Adored'/'Elephant'/'Drums' opening salvo. The tour also saw the début of 'One Love', which *Melody Maker*'s Bob Stanley points out is far closer to pop radio than the dancefloor, before claiming that it's 'a dead-cert number one'; he also notes that they played 'Elizabeth My Dear', a rarely played live song, as well as débuting 'Something's Burning', the 'B' side of the upcoming single.

Post show they got on the tour bus and headed for town to see what action there was. The sound system pumped 'Jumping Jack Flash', The Misunderstood, The Beatles' 'Nowhere Man', The Byrds – all trad rock fare. They got caned in a club called Melody, arriving through the door the moment the DJ put 'Fool's Gold' on to the turntable – it was perfect timing, right then the Roses couldn't put a foot wrong.

The Spike Island site itself was like a crazed joke. Surrounded by cooling towers and hideous factories, it was, perhaps, the ugliest festival of all time. There was going to have to be a massive attempt to create some magic in the filth of the north-west landscape. The brutality of the surroundings made no apologies: this was stark, this was real. Spike Island was no Glastonbury, there was no spiritual vibe here, maaaan – this was the real raw deal.

The attempt to create some magic wasn't happening at the ground level either. Only two beer tents and a few burger stalls dealt with a crowd that would have dwarfed most premier league football clubs. Back-stage a mêlée of journalists tried to grab what little free beer there was, and got very impatient in the process. The fans, meanwhile, took it easy, despite all the handicaps. Their brand-new flares flapped in the breeze and the mood was for a party. They got stoned and they waited.

Noel Gallagher remembers one of his future band mates making the trip to Spike Island. 'Bonehead used to be a plasterer, and he had a white transit van done up with splattered paint just like the Roses' Jackson Pollock stuff, and he went to Spike Island in that – about ten of them all went at eight in the morning. They watched the gig from right at the back on the top of this transit van, and the van looked fucking amazing. I always told him he should have kept that van. It would have been a fair sight seeing these ten plasterers sat on top of this van at Spike Island.'

John Harris, ex-editor of *Select*, remembers arriving at the site. 'I had a great time at Spike Island – despite Gareth's droogs taking my lager off me and my mates when we arrived at the gate. This meant that we had to go and buy more beer at the tiny stalls. All the journalists hated it just because the back-stage bar shut down early. At the time we could sense that people had it in for the Roses. For us it was a great day out.'

In the background the huge cooling towers that shrouded the never-ending ICI factories on the banks of the Mersey formed the backdrop and the air was stale with industrial filth being pumped into the air. In some ways it was the perfect setting, a challenge. Could great rock'n'roll be created in such disgusting surroundings?

Spike Island was organised on a shoestring. It also nearly didn't go ahead. Danny MacIntosh, one of Manchester's best sound engineers and manager of the excellent Snow Patrol, was earning a wedge that week before the show helping to set up the stage. He remembers the nail-biting tension as the company he worked for waited for Gareth and Matthew to pay up the money that they were owed. 'Three days before the show they were still owed thirty grand and they weren't happy. They said that they wouldn't put up the stage if they didn't get paid. They still hadn't been paid even the night before, so I was sent up in an XR2 from Bedford, where the company was, to Widnes to pick up the money. They had left several ansaphone messages about me picking the money up. So I was already pretty nervous about the meeting. It was like something out of a gangster film. I had to meet Matthew [Cummings, Gareth Evans's partner] at a bus stop in Widnes, and I had never met the guy before in my life. He just gave me the bag of cash, thirty grand in a plastic bag! And I drove all the way back to Bedford at about 140 miles an hour. I was totally shitting myself. I thought that I was going to get done over!'

The last-minute nature of the festival affected its efficiency, but on the day, as it creaked and groaned into place, there was a definite air of excitement, as the new generation of pop fans waited for deliverance.

Of course putting a major rock festival on in Widnes was not going to be without its difficulties and it's to Jones's credit that he made the whole thing happen. The problems seemed insurmountable. The local council were strictly monitoring sound levels and the road crew setting up the stage complained of weird blisters caused by the chemical ooze being pumped out by the factories across the river.

On the day it felt like there was more than the 30,500 punters who had tickets on the island. The guest list itself was five thousand strong. Outside the stench of burgers and cheap merchandise, cheap blow and warm booze, the atmosphere was excellent. The baggy boom had now gone mainstream way beyond the cool kids. It was now for everyone.

Back-stage there was a weird tension as the London set descended upon this grubby corner of the north-west. The usual crew of Manc ruffians hung out with middling indie bands and soap opera stars. The free beer, of course, ran out quickly, until someone climbed in behind the tent and switched on the beer pumps, freaking out the beer company.

The oddball support bill included the excellent African musician Thomas Mapfumo and his drum orchestra, followed by the heavy duty bass rattle of Jah Wobble (the very same Wobble that was a loose influence on Mani's bass sound). Cranked through the ON U sound system Wobble was going way over everyone's heads. Shame, as he was dealing some great music that afternoon.

Minutes before show time, the Roses mounted the huge stage, clambering up the stairs and the ramps at the back of the stage. They looked like four tiny matchstick figures as they walked out to the enormous roar of the bored-shitless fans who had only just moved their rock allegiance this far. These pop fans were definitely not ready for the DJs sets or the supporting ON U sound system whose avante dub funk just went way over their heads.

Most of them were at their first-ever rock festival, let alone 'rave', and went berserk. For thousands of people it was their first chance to see a band that had played to barely fifty people in their local town just a year before.

As the set kicked off with 'I Wanna Be Adored' the atmosphere was cranked despite the sound seeming delayed. Enigmatic as ever, Brown did the pimp roll, walking on-stage in the same white top that he had worn for the press conference the day before. He was dealing the lolloping chimp moves that only he could stamp any sort of cool over. Keeping schtum for the whole show, all he could say was, 'The time . . . the time is now. Do it now, do it now.'

More Brown philosophy, more simple-speak that made perfect sense – grabbing the positive rush of the times and riding it hard. The night before, Brown had claimed that the crowd was the star and that anyone could have it. These were words that would echo through the UK's rehearsal rooms as legions of pop kids traded in their flares for guitars and started to rebuild the UK pop scene in the wake of the Roses' magnificent putsch, a putsch powered by their musical talent and Brown's charisma.

Whether he was carrying the large plastic globe around like he did at Spike or playing the bongos, Brown was doing the rock star cool thing with a consummate ease. A Jim Morrison from the DHSS, every move was legendary.

For the fans it was a great day out. Carl, who was twenty-one at the time, still remembers it clearly: 'It was like a giant party, man. We felt free, at ease in the field. Me and some mates from Preston just went down there and we got totally stoned. We were out of it. The Roses were amazing that day. I don't care what anyone says, but that was such a great day out.'

Jenny, who was eighteen at the time, says, 'It was a real hassle getting a drink, but Spike Island really meant something. It felt like our generation had its own thing. We just sat in the sun and got really out of it and when the Roses came on we just danced like mad. Their songs were amazing. It just felt like you had known those tunes all your life.'

For some it was a disappointment. Gez looks back less fondly: 'The sound was crap – you couldn't hear a thing, it was really muffled and there was all the poseurs who turned up – people who you had never seen before, in their Reni hats and flares. Blackpool was miles better. That was the one for us. That was the one that really counted.'

Remarkably there were only four arrests at Spike Island. There were two warnings about the volume (apparently a third one would have meant that the show would have been shut down by Widnes Council, though what they would have done with 30,000 pretty irate punters if it had been shut down halfway through is difficult to imagine).

The night ended with a fireworks display which cost over five grand. Some of the more stoned members of the audience stared into the sky, not sure if it was their heads exploding or the heavens.

Then for us it was a fast car back to Manchester for the very low-key post-show shindig at the International 1, where, for a couple of hours, aptly enough, attempts were made to get the sound system up and running to play some records. A bunch of people waiting for the comedown stood around, got bored and then fucked off home.

Spike Island may have not worked as a rock'n'roll show, but for a field full of new-generation pop fans it was the alpha moment when Britpop/baggy or whatever banal hookline there was went fully national. Try as they might, the Roses, with all their special events etc., would be as powerless as anyone to break down the tradition of gigs.

And maybe it's a bloody good job as well. Rock gigs are the bottom line; despite shitty venues, grunt bouncers, appalling rip-off promoters and lousy sound systems, they are great fun! A superb band can transcend the most difficult conditions to provide the people with some magic in their lives.

That night that was what The Stone Roses were dealing in.

COMING DOWN: GLASGOW GREEN

On 9 June the Roses got their tent out and played Glasgow Green, a show that was, for many, perhaps their finest ever live performance. Two days before the tent had been in Belfast where they had gone down a storm. The gigs were meant to be the first of many big top gigs. Attempting to break out of the touring circuit and away from the traditional venues, the Roses and Gareth had gone for the idea of a touring circus tent. As it turned out, Glasgow was their last show for five years and the last time that Reni ever played drums on stage, which is pretty fucking tragic.

The big top idea was perfection. The Roses wouldn't come to town and play the normal crabby venue. They would bring the venue with them! Each show would be an event. They would bring their own bands, their own DJs – even their own crowd, dammit.

At the time of Glasgow Green, there were plans to bring the tent to London and there was talk of the Roses headlining on the Isle of Wight – mad rumours, insane ideas, some true and some made up by Gareth!

The tickets for the show were for sale in Scotland only and sold out like a shot. It was the Roses' first Scottish date since the 1989 club tour. Since then Glasgow had really gone for the 'Manchester' thing in a big way. You really noticed it when you arrived there that weekend – the city was awash with kids decked out in Manc baggy clobber. It was flares a go-go. The kids were dressed up like Mancs all over the city and even years later the clubs still do 'Manchester' nights.

In return many Mancs felt an affinity with Glasgow – a tough working-class city with a tradition of arty bohemianism and socialist politics. Both cities were hammered by the powers-that-be in London but refused to buckle down to the Tory scum. The same went for Belfast. The show there on the 7th at the Maysfield Leisure Centre had been great. When we arrived at the Glasgow Big Top just before the soundcheck the road crew were buzzing about the Irish gig. The band were hot. Spike Island has been painted as the point where it all started to unravel for the Roses but these two shows saw the band hitting a top gear, really exploring all the possibilities of that quintessential line-up.

If Belfast had been the band hitting a laid-back chillin' groove, Glasgow was fierce, full on rock'n'roll.

Mani has said in interviews since that this was their favourite ever gig. 'When we were on stage that day, we all looked at each other, and then just went up another level.'

The show itself was a killer. The sound problems of Spike Island were ironed out – it was blistering and it was loud. Squire's guitar, cranked, massive and hard, was fuzzing at the edges, almost like The Sex Pistols. It nearly sounded like Oasis years early. The gig was the missing link, soundwise, between the two bands except the Roses were making some transcendental rock'n'roll (although Oasis have cut some classic pop, the Roses at their peak had a special magic).

Ian's voice is great, in total command, uplifting, perfect. 'Adored' sends the tent up several notches of excitement. The crowd sings along throughout the set, even on 'Elizabeth My Dear', and by the time 'Resurrection' is going through its chops you know that you are at one of the best rock'n'roll gigs you will ever go to.

The tent was sweltering hot, sweat dripped off the roof back on to the kids who were rammed in there. The atmosphere was electric, buzzing. Wandering round the venue you'd see some of the same faces that travelled all over the country to see the band, as well as a whole new never-ending stream of spotty kids who were getting transported by the first proper band they would see in their lives.

And what an introduction!

As 'Resurrection' clatters to a halt and Reni leaves the stage for the last time. If the Roses had not blown out the American tour two weeks after this show, if the Roses had just kept gigs like this coming, the pop landscape would have been so different. The second raters who grabbed their own crown would have had to wait in line. There was so much great rock'n'roll left in this line-up. But barely one year after they hit the UK big time they were about to grind to a frustrating halt.

After the gig, at a curiously empty back-stage, the band sat drained and quietly polite in a small caravan. The atmosphere was hardly celebratory but the awesome rush of playing to so many people must have taken its toll. The Roses really meant something to this audience and they had given everything that they had to fire them and it had worked.

Later on there was a party at the Sub Club, the hippest house club in Glasgow where everyone got totally blasted till the wee small hours. It was a night of mega strong E and endless drinking, beautiful girls, spazzy dancing and a large contingent of Mancs getting down with the Glaswegians. Somewhere in the blur, Mani was bouncing around – the affable party man – while the rest of the Roses crew held court in a corner of the club. It was a night of so much sweat that I had to throw my sweat-soaked socks and shirt out through Ian Tilton's car window, the next day, on the drive back to Manchester, in the glorious sunshine.

At this point it seemed like The Stone Roses were invincible, an unstoppable force, a band that touched people's hearts and souls. They had the tunes and the attitude. They seemed to understand the pop culture codes and they had that indefinable X factor that struck home with countless people from all walks of life. They had that street thing nailed down tight. Versed in pop culture they had a rough understanding of what was happening and just rode with it.

If they had managed to keep the inertia running from this point in then they could have had it all. Large.

In reality Glasgow Green was the last gig the band played in Britain for five years.

ONE LOVE

On 25 June the Roses' new single, 'One Love' finally got its release. It eventually came out in early July, caused by a bizarre and unintentional glitch in the artwork.

The layout of the latest John Squire sleeve had looked like a swastika when viewed from certain angles. Squire himself noticed it first when he was checking the proofs of the sleeve. Shocked he recalled the artwork and cut it all up and rearranged it as a collage.

'We don't want some kid to get attacked in a bar in somewhere like Barcelona because he's got that design on a T-shirt,' reasoned Ian Brown. Indeed one of the band's own roadies was stopped from going into the Hacienda with the design on a T-shirt.

The sleeve design brings up the whole Nazi thing yet again. There have always been rumours about the Roses' right-wing past.

Admittedly there were some very confused ideas knocking about in the early Eighties. NF skinheads dancing to the Jamaican folk music of ska, a post-punk right-wing confusion that had more to do with violence than politics. If you grew up in that era like I did, you would have seen people having their heads turned by the hate politics of the right. The Roses would have seen this as well, but how far would someone like Ian Brown with his Bruce Lee and Mohammed Ali fixation and socialist parents get into that kind of mess? Seems unlikely to me.

Maybe the 'One Love' sleeve was unintentional, maybe it was a misguided attempt to grab back the original meaning of the swastika (it's a peace and good luck symbol in India where you see it carved on to every gatepost). Squire himself is quite adamant that the swastika was completely unintentional.

All this contrasts sharply with the sentiments behind the 'One Love' single and it's music which oozes the prime time swing of the blackest of musics, funk

'One Love' was the sound of a band moving on. Attempting to ride a fusion between Can and pure pop, it was under-rated at the time. Taking the formula of 'Fool's Gold' and stretching it out over several minutes, 'One Love' was funky loose chops and a neat spiralling wah-wah guitar. Brown went for the sinister whispered vocal, giving the song a menacing air. 'One Love' was mean, sinuous and funky, flipping over into a chorus that was anthemic as well as massive.

'One Love' was yet another example of the much mooted 'new direction' of the post 'Fool's Gold' groove, the sound of a band playing inside out itself, Brown again doing the drop-an-octave-mystic-scally bit, intoning some kinda street wisdom over the band's workout. The main let down was the chorus – it sounded hasty and glued on. Says Ian, 'We were trying too hard to write an anthem.'

If you want the real business then flip the record over for 'Something's Burning'. This is where the Roses of 1990 were really cooking, visiting The Can's vibe and fleshed out with a jazzy xylophone. It was a sultry, smoking record and both tracks boded well for the second album. They seemed to be moving away from the crystalline pop and towards a more groove-orientated sound, utilising the shit hot drums of Reni and really combining the rock and the dance. They were getting fluid, losing their British skin, getting funky, getting black, getting to the roots of what this whole rock'n'roll thing was really about.

Where the 'A' side is merely competent, this is the band stalking Seventies Miles Davis territory (if you like this kinda feel then go out and buy Miles's *Bitches Brew* right now!), effortless and awesome and with added xylophone. Brown intones some biblical morality piece over the top, ancient wisdom copped from the good book, digging deeper into the bible for inspiration.

When it was finally released the single crashed into the charts at Number 4, not Number 1 as expected – the meteoric rise had stalled. Before 'One Love', before Spike Island, everything had seemed possible. Afterwards the band slowly came back down to earth, became a normal band.

All the delaying tactics before the release had many wondering if they were building up the advance orders – looking for a Number 1. Even at their peak, they just didn't have enough fans to knock Elton John off the top or Fatty Pavorotti or the *Neighbours* 'star' Craig McLachlin out of the way, leaving them stuck at Number 4.

That week's chart also included the Soup Dragons' 'I'm Free', the latest in a long line of baggy bands. The Soup Dragons were a Glasgow indie band who had gone 'indie/dance' and were now coining it worldwide with their own hit, a cover of The Rolling Stones' oldie. It was a perfectly executed pop trick and was selling a stack load in the Roses' wake. They were typical of a whole new generation of bands who were starting to crash in on the new pop scene, from Blur's Roses pastiche, 'There's No Other Way', to The Charlatans' sudden mass popularity on the back of a great pop album. There were a myriad of different versions of the Roses wherever you looked.

The pop times were also changing. All round it was World Cup fever – New Order's 'World In Motion' was a big hit and everyone was getting into football after years of pretending to be bored with sport. The new 'lad' was starting to rear his beery head in the wake of 'E' culture. The Roses had unwittingly heralded a new era of blokedom, something that they never felt really comfortable with. It was into this new landscape that their single was unleashed.

TV CRIMES: THE WOGAN NON-APPEARANCE

As 'One Love' crashed into the charts, it opened up more TV opportunities for the band. Plugger Beer Davies was working the record hard. The band were now mainstream and were, in their plugger's eyes, ready for some teatime TV. At this level, *Top Of The Pops* is a foregone conclusion, but what about mums' and dads' TV? What about *Wogan*?

If *The Late Show* was Beer Davies working overtime grabbing cool TV opportunities, getting the group on to the *Wogan* show was hustling beyond the call of duty. At the back end of the Eighties the insufferable Terry Wogan had a nightly chat show. For years he'd been the housewives' choice on Radio Two, tucked away from the rest of the populace, but now you could hardly avoid him.

Persuading the researchers that having The Stone Roses on their show would be a really cool idea because it would get the younger generation into watching the show was the easy part. Getting the band to play by the rule books was going to be rather trickier. Gareth from Beer Davies remembers the latest set of TV problems.

'They insisted that they would have to be interviewed as well. Wogan's people were not too keen on this idea – they grumbled that there could be some sort of trouble planned. It was some time later that I found out that they actually planned to pull Wogan's wig off on live TV. They understood the value of publicity, it would have ended their TV career, but they would have become really famous if they had pulled it off.'

It would have been a great TV moment, the humiliation of the pillar of the establishment by the band that didn't give a fuck. Of course this story was half true, yet another mixture of myth, wishful thinking and half truths that dominate the Roses' story at this stage.

Wogan's people were right in their assumption and promptly blocked the group's appearance. There would be little TV left for the band; the enigma was still in place.

1991

ENTERING THE WILDERNESS YEARS

Most bands who are at the top of the tree and powering a generation into hyperdrive take the bit between their teeth and go somewhere, but not The Stone Roses. Maybe the sheer shock of being appointed generation leaders was too much for them, maybe they had lost the muse, or maybe they were trapped by that overwork that kills the creative impulse of a lot of bands: the tour/interview non-stop schedule that gives bands little time to be creative, preventing songwriting, and adding to burnout.

The Roses' development was already very different from that of any other band. They had spent five years putting together the first album and if they felt like spending five years putting together the second, then that was their prerogative. The Stone Roses, being a gang, were self-sufficient – they thought they didn't need to play the game. They got this far in the 'dirtiest business', and now it was time for that business to play by their rules.

It was January 1991 and they were just getting round to putting together rehearsal sessions to work on the new album. Nearly two years since the release of *The Stone Roses*, which had at once defined them and their generation, they were back together in an effort to start work on the follow-up.

On 13 January they decamped to Bluestone rehearsal studio in the beautiful wilds of Pembrokeshire. Bored in the country, the Roses soon started dossing around, doing anything to avoid getting down to the real business at hand. According to an *NME* report, they played baseball with pool cues, smashed windows, and threw aerosol cans into a bonfire, an ace laugh as pieces of burning red can explode everywhere.

John Squire took an expensive set of Harrods carving knives and, as a special present for Doreen, the owner of the studio, built a giant cock-and-ball statue – a piece of artwork went over the locals' heads – and they dubbed Doreen the 'old cock and ball', a nickname that stuck like dirt.

NME also claimed that all the band ate were chips, and when the studio served them baked potatoes they just threw them into the bonfire, pissing off the rehearsal space's cook, Pippa, whose culinary skills must have been put to a severe test in cooking the potatoes.

That's life in these country rehearsal spaces. There's nothing much to do but rehearse, and bands quickly find all sorts of school prankery to get up to instead. The vibe is that of a school trip and the most banal of practical jokes quickly becomes hilarious.

Eventually in February a van came to pick them up, and all they had to show for their month's stay was a ragbag of stupid stories and a burning desire to escape. The snow drifts were so deep that a tractor was required to haul the van out of the mire.

It's almost a metaphor for the band themselves.

Maybe it served them right for trying to get their heads together in the country. There's something about urban rock'n'roll that just doesn't work when it's transported to the countryside. The fast-burning urban sex and pollution that is ingrained in all great rock'n'roll is so much part of all the coolest bands' early stories that the slacking off in the fields and wilderness that inevitably follows when they stretch out and enjoy their new wealth often means some truly crap music gets made.

Not that the Roses were going to make any crap music – it was just going to take them longer to rekindle the fire. In hindsight they should have hit the road, got the band feeling back again, and kept in touch with the street. The glory of the Roses was their anthems, their arrogance, their city music.

According to *NME*, when they signed the visitors' book on leaving the studios, John Squire, ever polite, promised that all damages would be paid for. The signatures themselves are probably the closest the band ever got to telling the truth about themselves. Brown signed his name 'the laziest man in showbizness', Reni with 'What Time Is It', his calling card when he spent the last month in a bored daze, and Mani, the court jester, wrote, 'Nothing off for good behaviour, vive la proletariat'. John Squire simply signed his name in introverted small letters.

Even in September 1989 there had been rumbles of the band leaving Silvertone. The deal that Silvertone had was adequate for a struggling outfit desperate for a deal, but with all their new-found success the band wanted to make changes. That's how Gareth had set up the deal. Sign now and negotiate later. That's what had been agreed back in 1988. By the end of 1990 the rumblings were getting louder. After Spike Island Gareth firmly expected Silvertone to renegotiate, treat the band as the potential U2-size stadium outfit that they were on the fast track of becoming. Spike had been the pinnacle. It was obvious that this was a different sort of situation than in 1988.

In the Roses camp there was also dissatisfaction with their chart placings for 'One Love' which had stalled at Number 4 when they felt it should have been a Number 1. All this was eating into the band's relationship with Silvertone. They figured that with a bigger company they could get the mass audience that they felt was theirs.

Lob into this equation the eccentric management method of Gareth, the obstinate nature of the band and the fact that Roddy McKenna, the one link between the label and the band, was working in the US and you've got a very chaotic situation. Every band goes through this. The A&R that signs them moves on and they are left high and dry. Only in the Roses' case they held all the cards. The band was now massive, perhaps the biggest band in the UK and were ripe for a bigger label to come in and snap them up.

A band in the Roses' position was worth big money. Their meteoric rise had not gone unnoticed, there were hints of spectacular money on the horizon. Could Zomba match this? Were they willing to take the chance?

There were new offers but Gareth was already looking elsewhere. How could Zomba at one moment offer a deal that was the best they could do then suddenly up it under pressure. Things had moved on massively since 1988. Then the band believed they would be world beaters now? Now they were potentially world beaters.

Ironically it was this attempt to break out of the small deal that probably stymied the Roses' rise for good – the litigation, the arguments, the fallouts . . . The next few years the only headline The Stone Roses got were boring ones, full of lawyers' names and details of record deals. Good business maybe but fuck all to do with rock'n'roll.

Gareth had been wheeling and dealing, attempting to free the band from the deal and finally announced that on 4 March they would go to court to free themselves from the contract.

On 4 March Silvertone attempted to have the 1988 contract with the band declared enforceable, and seek an injunction to stop the group recording for any other company. The interim injunction would stay in place pending the outcome of the case. A case that was now in action.

The *NME* quoted the Roses' lawyer John Kennedy talking about the injunction that prevented them from recording: 'It was agreed at the time that the group could go back to court and apply to have the injunction lifted if it was interfering with their career. Obviously the right to record and release an album is central to their career. Now the band want to record an LP so we will be making an appeal against the injunction in February.'

During 18–22 March the band appeared in the Law Courts in The Strand, London, to hear the testimony of Geoffrey Howard, their solicitor at the time of signing the Silvertone deal. Later in the week, the band's lawyer, John Kennedy, reported that they had been offered a deal with Geffen Records. Rumours of a Roses summer concert started.

On 23 March, the *Melody Maker* reported Ian Brown saying that if the case went against them the band would give up music and go on the dole. In the *Melody Maker* The Stone Roses were quoted as saying 'Silvertone have got us for thirty-five years – we'd have only got ten for armed robbery.'

Silvertone were baffled by this unhappiness. They claimed that no one signed deals for thirty-five years and that the deal was based on the number of records released. There was a bit of posturing from both sides, squaring up for action. Silvertone, though, had no intention of losing the band and slapped an injunction on the Roses to prevent them from releasing any other records with anybody else until it was all settled in court.

Silvertone told the *Melody Maker*, 'We're fans as much as anyone else, we want them to make another record.'

On 25–26 March the band appeared in court in connection with the Silvertone contract – although Reni was ill and couldn't attend. The reasons behind the band's non-appearance on Wogan in July 1989 were discussed. It was revealed in court that Roses manager Gareth Evans's real name was Ian Bromley. He changed it while working at Vidal Sassoon's in the 1960s.

The press had been swiftly on the case of the band's label disruption. The first *NME* of the year had printed a huge story about the band taking Silvertone to court. The story claimed that the band would have to wait until November to get the case into court and the chance of getting material out seemed very slim.

The Roses' lawyer John Kennedy, who is considered to be the doyen of music biz lawyers (and went on to represent Sony as an expert witness against George Michael in one of the other celebrated music biz cases of the Nineties), prepared a 40-page document detailing why the contract that they had originally signed was not legally binding.

Gareth Evans seemed to love being in court; the drama and the tension was all fuel to him. Like all rock'n'roll managers, he loved being on stage. They all dream of fronting a band or at least of fucking the lead singer. Gareth was definitely not interested in the latter and he had no chance of the former, so the court was his stage. You can imagine him being almost relieved that to get out of Silvertone would require a long protracted court case that would have the music business sitting up and checking its procedures.

Silvertone were represented by Peter Prescott, QC, who kicked off by saying that The Stone Roses 'Can't now be heard to say "boo hoo I now want to get out of the contract".'

He also added, 'When The Stone Roses' career began to take off their success had been pretty modest. It is particularly galling for my clients that the group said that the contract is invalid and they are free to go off with another company.'

Silvertone were being aggressive but even they must have realised that they were on a hiding to nothing when the rumours started to appear that Gary Gersh, the leading A&R man at Geffen Records (and the man that signed Nirvana to Geffen) was on the Roses' case and was promising to pay all the legal fees (up to £300,000) and whatever it took to get them out of their contract. The big guns were lining up – the necessary finance was being made available and Silvertone were soon under the cosh.

Geffen were rightly hungry for the Roses. At this point in time if the band had kick started their career again, they could have been one of the biggest bands in the world – they had the UK, they had Japan, Europe was getting interested and some hard touring would have sorted out the States.

Evans himself was lapping it up, staying in the posh Russell Hotel in London, walking around like a man possessed, giving journalists the run around and grinning the shit-eating grin of managers who realise that their time has come.

When Geoffrey Howard, the brief who represented them when they signed to Silvertone in the first place, turned up in court to give evidence, the band turned up as well, looking suitably out of place at the proceedings.

They were there to hear Evans be described by the Roses' own QC Barbara Dohman as 'inexperienced in the music business'. These trial revelations would eventually prove to be the undoing of Gareth's grip on them as a manager. By December 1991 rumours were rife of his going to accept a new job on the West Coast of the USA as an A&R man.

It emerged in court that one of the first major cracks that had appeared between the band and the record label was the group's lack of enthusiasm about appearing on the *Wogan* show to promote the 'One Love' single. They believed that the show was a touch naff. Ian Mill, counsel for the band and Gareth Evans, pointed this out to Silvertone in court.

'Terry Wogan is the housewife's choice and the people that appear on his show reflect that fact, do they not?'

Mr Jenkins, managing director of Zomba, replied: 'No, he has various musical guests – he has to have topical guests from all areas of music.'

Mr Mills replied: 'You do not think that there would be a perception among any part of the fan base of The Stone Roses that the group would be selling out by appearing on the Wogan show?'

Jenkins conceded that the band could have seen it that way before adding: 'I do not think so. It's one of those shows which is well established.'

It was these ridiculous snippets that kept the press well entertained throughout the spring of 1991 and showed just how banal the workings of pop really were.

On 27 March Evans backed up Ian Brown's story that the band had been paid poorly by Silvertone. They each earned £70 per week before tax eventually rising to £200 per week as the hits started to come in, not bad if you can get it but laughable for a band in their position. Evans talked about why he had signed the deal in the first place.

'I knew Zomba were a hard company. I didn't want to rock the boat. I wanted to get on with the whole thing and relied on the prospect of a new contract as a reward. We built Silvertone up into what it is now.'

Asked why he had signed the band to a ten-year management deal, Evans replied, 'I wanted to be with this band for a long time. We'd been at it for five years and a lot of bands are following what we did.'

The case was helping to spell the end of Evans's tenure with the Roses. It also burst the bubble they had created as a band. Court always reduces everything to the black and white, exposing the workings and machinations of a group. It wrecked their aura. It ruined Silvertone's credibility. No one wins in these situations. Except the lawyers.

'Contracts and lawyers, they are bullshit,' as someone once pointed out.

Meanwhile, outside the court room, the rumour mill was chewing over a story that the Roses were planning a huge comeback concert in the south-east of England. Like most of these rumours there was probably little more than wishful thinking involved in the story. It was the type of tale that would plague the news pages of the music papers for the next five years as the press looked for any tidbits of information on a band that at one moment had been everywhere and the next had completely disappeared. People were baffled by the way the band had seemingly turned its back on the big time, and the enigma fascinated everybody.

With April's usual blast of spring in the air, and not much to do, Ian Brown and Mani turned up at the typically protracted court proceedings and sat with thrilled fans. It was a Rolling Stones moment.

One of the classic images for many pop freaks is that of the Stones' court busts in the original summer of love, when the sharp-dressed dandies swaggered in and out of court and, apart from Brian Jones, got one over the stuffy establishment. There always seemed to be something romantic and swashbuckling and something very rock'n'roll about rolling in and out of court. Getting that rush of adrenalin, stalking across the Victorian portals of the ancient hallways and into the stuffy confines of the court itself. Heads turned, mouths were agape. It was like going on stage.

Brown paused from his big day in court, to speak to the *Melody Maker*, relating how bored he was with the whole affair.

'It's more fun when there are witnesses because at least there's something to stare at. I'm getting a little bored with all these people pulling coloured flags from their mouths, but at least I'm beginning to understand their double speak.'

Meanwhile, back on the front line, Evans was under the hammer. Silvertone, in an attempt to loosen his control over his charges, revealed that he took a third of their money and had them signed to a ten-year deal – a shockingly long-term contract that is far far more than a manager normally takes. They also pointed out that he didn't give the band any accounts of his company 'Starscreen Management'.

In his favour, Evans claimed he had signed the ten-year deal because he was putting a lot of money into the band. He had a long-term vision for the Roses, a vision that was crucial to their success. His crazed ideas and his lack of knowledge about the way the music business actually worked were brilliant for the band.

Here was a man who dared to dream.

The case itself rumbled on. It was revealed that the contract had odd clauses like the fact that the label wasn't obliged to release Roses' products anywhere in the world and that the band would only get half the royalty rate from a greatest hits package. The tide was turning in the Roses' favour at last.

On 29 May Judge Humphries found in favour of The Stone Roses camp and the contract was annulled. The band was free. Instantly the press was full of talk over who was going to get the Roses' signature. There had been plenty of takers. Gareth himself had been over in LA, flown out there by interested parties. He had been in talks with several labels.

It was on that trip in LA that David Geffen, head of the maverick major Geffen Records, got in touch with Evans. Alerted to the Roses by his head of A&R Gary Gersh, Geffen was fired up. In the past twenty years Geffen had built a fearsome reputation for himself, first as a manager before setting up Asylum, signing the likes of The Eagles. He then set up Geffen Records and had made big bucks out of Guns 'N' Roses and a whole host of big time Eighties outfits.

He had also masterminded, ironically, the John Lennon comeback of 1980 after a five-year hiatus.

It was reported that the money the Roses would have got if they delivered all their albums from the deal was awesome. This truly was the payday.

For their new album they received a million pound advance and would receive a further million when the record was released. Then each album onwards the advances would correlate to the success of failure of the previous records. It was a great record deal, the total opposite of the Silvertone one and one that reflected the band's current standing in the world of pop.

For the second album (the one after *Second Coming*) they would receive a minimum of $1.5 million, a maximum of $3 million; for the third 2–4 million; for the fourth $2.25 4.5 million; for the fifth $2.5–5 million, and on top of this a royalty rate of 29 per cent in all major world territories like the UK, the UK and Japan and 27 per cent elsewhere – the normal rates are between 12 and 18 per cent. It was a staggering deal; they were in the stratosphere; only major league superstars get to breathe this sort of moneyfied air.

By 1991 Geffen was hot. This was a big money operation and was easily challenging the big boys. Breaking an outfit like The Stone Roses into the States would be great kudos as well as big money.

In Geffen's eyes the Roses were pretty well their band.

SIGN ON THE DOTTED LINE . . .

When the rumour broke that the band was going to get out of their contract the major label vultures were in like a shot and a bidding war kicked off. This, after all, was the biggest buzz band in Britain and they were dealing a pretty trad guitar pop sound that wasn't stained with any of that weird punk rock stuff that mainstream America still hadn't really got its head round. Make no mistake, at this point The Stone Roses were worth a lot of money.

The album had sold 250,000 in America alone. A good start.

The bidding war was coming to a head. That summer the Roses and Gareth convened to the Halcyon Hotel in Holland Park in London. Ostensibly to sign the Geffen deal, there was a meeting with David Geffen that morning then a break for lunch. Even this close to the wire there were four other major labels in the hotel hoping to persuade the Roses to sign to them. The band were confused and Gareth was edgy.

The final decision was to go with Geffen and for a wheeze they made the wacky snap decision to sign the contract on a bus! So dragging all the lawyers, the Geffen people out of the hotel they jumped on to a passing bus and ran upstairs sniggering. Briefcases were snapped open and the bizarre spectacle of a band signing a multi-million pound contract on a bus unfurled itself.

Looking for a witness to the contract, they were going to get an old man who innocently sat near them to sign his name, but just before he had put his name to paper, the Roses lawyer John Kennedy made Gareth put his name down as the witness. A momentous decision. For if the band would ever think of getting rid of Gareth, trying to claim that he had drifted away from the band prior to the signing of the Geffen deal then what was his name doing at the bottom of the contract?

Not that the band were going to get shot of their manager – or were they?

The Geffen deal was potentially a big payer. Millions could be earned by the band as each album came out during the Nineties. Now all they had to do was stop fucking about in court and get down to some serious songwriting. Get back to band business.

THE INERTIA KICKS IN: ROSES IN 1991

The band themselves spent part of May in a house in north Manchester rehearsing new material, but the sessions crumbled when John Squire flew with his girlfriend Helen to Tenerife for a holiday. The rest of the band flew to Rotterdam to see Manchester United beat Barcelona 2–1 in the Cup Winners Cup Final, celebrating when Mark Hughes scored the winner.

At the time it was also reported in the *NME* that Reni was spending his time flying to most of United's games around the country. After years of struggle and poverty the band were enjoying lounging around like rock star millionaires. Fun but fatal – the real work was still to be done.

Smarting from their court defeat and out of pocket from the result, Silvertone announced that they were to appeal against the verdict. Just when it seemed like the Roses might start functioning as a normal band again they were back against the wall. The appeal itself wouldn't happen for another nine months, stymiing the band's creative flow.

This was when the real rot set in. The Roses ceased to exist as a really full-on creative unit at this point and retreated into the wilderness years, spending most of their time playing and watching football.

On Tuesday nights down at the plastic turf at Man City's training ground in Platt Fields near Moss Side there was a football game – Reni started playing all the time. The game was tough and fast and a certain level of fitness is required to keep up. The standard was pretty high – some members of Yargo and A Certain Ratio also put in appearances and Ian Brown occasionally turned up as well.

Now and then when they felt like being a band again they phoned up publicist Philip Hall and filled him in on what was going on. The fact that they talked more about football was a giveaway to their current inertia.

It was deep into the summer and they still hadn't got down to the second album. Even if they recorded it this week they couldn't release it for another year. They were well and truly knackered by the music biz, a business that has little concern for people's dreams unless they can make plenty of big money cash out of them.

Reckoning that they were down £1 million from the Roses court cases etc., Silvertone decided that it was time to get some dosh back into the coffers. In August they released 'I Wanna Be Adored' as a single and reformatted the album in a gatefold package.

Bored, Reni started to get into trouble. His first case saw him in court on four charges. They included disorderly behaviour and illegal parking. The court case revealed that he owned three houses in Manchester, including one of those funky little flats behind the Peveril Of The Peak pub near the GMex Centre in the city centre.

Reni was renting out his flats. It was also reported in the NME that Reni's girlfriend, a paediatric doctor at St Mary's Hospital, had given birth to a son called Cody.

In September Reni's case finally came through – he was found guilty at Manchester Magistrates Court on charges of disorderly behaviour as well as two offences of parking in a no-waiting zone and causing an obstruction because he refused to move his car from the side of Burton Road, the bedsit bohemian high street of south Manchester in West Didsbury.

He also admitted two offences of parking in a no-waiting zone and causing an obstruction and was fined £50. Furious, Reni complained about the police. 'I have already lodged a complaint about the way I was physically abused by the police,' he stated in court.

He was not a happy bunny.

In September Ian Brown and Adge, noting the sudden rise in Roses bootleg tapes floating around Manchester, go down to Strawberry Studios to buy up the old master tapes of the Martin Hannett-produced album that was shelved years back. This was the album that Andy Couzens would stir up a shit storm in in the mid Nineties by releasing.

That October, Silvertone continued in their no-holds-barred getting-the money-back campaign when they released The Stone Roses: Blackpool Live video through Windsong.

Clocking in at just under an hour, the video was a pretty poorly filmed document of the now two-year-old legendary Blackpool show. The ropey sound quality did the band few favours and it's difficult to grasp the sheer exhilaration and magic of what was already a piece of pop history. The previous month Silvertone had re-released the début album as two 45 rpm discs inside a gatefold sleeve while CDs and cassettes had 'Elephant Stone' added on as extra incentive for any collectors out there that needed mopping up. The sets were all numbered with a limited edition getting pressed up for the vinyl version with a bunch of John Squire Pollock artwork and black-and-white pictures of the band thrown in for good measure.

On a more positive note that September, John Squire and his girlfriend announced that they had just given birth to twins, a boy and a girl.

As 1991 ground to a close all the Roses had to show was a frustrating year of nothing. It was all court cases and attempts at writing material for the new album. An album that was already getting itself a high expectations rating from a hungry media and audience.

The music press were by now wondering just where this album was. A December Melody Maker asked current indie celebs what they thought of the band's continued hiatus.

People were pretty sceptical.

Mike Edwards, the singer with the then successful Jesus Jones, was obviously not much of a fan: 'I didn't think they were off to much of a start in the first place, though obviously a lot of people disagree with me. No, I don't think they've blown it. From a musician's point of view, I'm glad they got out of that contract, which, I gather, was one of the most oppressive I've heard about. I don't really care to be honest. I enjoyed bits of the first album, but they're a band who've been incredibly influential and they really shouldn't have been. I mean, we're down to fifth-generation Roses copyists now, which is really depressing.'

Miles Hunt, the vociferous vocalist with The Wonder Stuff, could always be relied on for good copy. 'Can they do it again? I don't think they did it the first time, to be honest. It's a pretty good album, but again the British music press got out of hand. I think they'll probably make a really good record, but there is no way they'll live up to what this country expects of them. They can't win really.'

It was like The Clash and their second album, *Give 'Em Enough Rope*. Their début had changed lives and their follow-up was buried under the weight of expectations. It could never be anywhere near as good. Sometimes bands are put under enormous creative pressure, but bands like these meant so much more to people than normal groups, expectations were always going to be inevitably high.

Maybe a year had been frittered away but expectations were still really high that soon the Roses would deliver something.

The band themselves, despite spending the last month wasting time in rehearsal rooms in Wales, were rumoured by mates through Chinese whispers to have nearly two albums of material lying around. In all probability they just had 'Ten Storey Love Song' finished – a drop-dead gorgeous song.

But try as they might they couldn't quite ignite that old spark, that inspiration. It didn't seem to be the same any more. Spike Island had been where they had shot their wad, now it was the morning after, the long hangover, everything they had worked furiously for had been achieved. They had proved their point.

They didn't even live in the same town any more. Ian Brown had moved to Wales by the coast and John Squire had got himself a place near Morecambe Bay. No longer hungry young men, they were in their late twenties, positively ancient in rock'n'roll terms and were putting their feet up after ten tough years building this thing up. Their rhythm section remained in town, but the geographical distances were starting to affect the band. No longer was it possible to sit them all down in the International to rehearse every day.

Money in the bank, objectives achieved, the Roses seemed to be slowly falling apart.

1992

MY GOD, IT'S 1992 ALREADY!: THE WILDERNESS YEARS CONTINUED

With a whole year wasted in court and their fast lane lives slowly returning to normal, the Roses realised that even at best they were not going to get any new material out till the autumn. The running jokes and gossip about where the fuck the band were had started to circulate.

Not only this but the band's creative edge was becoming decidedly blunted. Scurrilous rumours reported that John Squire had shown the band a bunch of new songs that he had written and they had turned them down. As a story it doesn't fit. What was starting to emerge was John's complete dominance of the music. The Brown/Squire songwriting partnership was effectively over. John was in creative hyperdrive, he was moving deeper into Led Zeppelin territory, moving away from the groove-based direction, and pure pop that they had cut their reputation on.

As the band sat there wallowing in Zep, Ian Brown was disgusted. 'What are you listening to them for, they haven't got what you've got,' he pleaded.

Brown knew in his guts that going the rock route was the wrong way. Of course it was playsafe and would possibly be the direct road to the mega-success that Geffen craved for the band, but this was the Roses! Where was the arrogance that made them stand out! Surely they weren't going to end up as just another band?

The rest of the band were gradually being frozen out. Brown was not called upon for lyrics, there were more and more drum loops and Mani's bass was disappearing behind the guitars. This is no crime, of course, as Squire was a fantastic guitar player. It's just that the Roses' strength was accommodating each other's talents.

The band themselves had planned to get into the studio and record as soon as possible but they decided to get on with getting more tunes sorted out before they went in there. 'They realised they couldn't rely on hype,' the insiders explained to the *NME*.

Early in 1992, a slightly concerned Geffen called a summit meeting with the Roses, and Gareth, in one of his last managerial roles, straightened out a battle plan. Geffen had signed a band that was on the edge of the big breakthrough and now they had ground to a halt. They had realised that the band were no young bucks looking for never-ending world tours but they were seeing them as a band that could slot next to REM in the US market, a band for the maturing and vast indie guitar audience to grow up with.

Many musicians at this stage of the game are barely out of their teens. Life is a ball, they have nowhere to live so they live off the fruits of the road. Their idealism is not yet tainted and the sex, drugs and rock'n'roll is still a golden ambition. For the slightly older Roses, they were dealing with pregnancies, kids and mortgages – all real life stuff. They were also dealing with court cases and an indecisiveness about management.

Keeping the band together as a creative unit was becoming more and more difficult – not living in each other's pockets any more was not helping. Small differences can seem a lot bigger when bands start to live apart. Everyone grows up, the gang is no longer a gang but a collection of individuals.

Since the court case they had started wondering about Gareth. The revelations had surprised them and they began to think that maybe it was time for a change. That maybe he was not working in their favour.

GARETH

Gareth had been the closest anyone had ever got to being in the gang. But he always realised the band would eventually need to move on. And now in early '92 the decision had been made.

The court case had taken its toll on their relationship. To lose Gareth was a traumatic decision but a vital one.

OK in theory, but getting shot of a wily character like Gareth was not going to be that easy.

It was going to cost them dearly in terms of time and money as Evans was a man who had already shown he loved a court battle and was not going to go without a fight.

Sometimes the bullshit piled up so high in The Stone Roses camp that you needed wings to fly above it all.

Evans himself figured that the band should have kept him on for another six months. He was baffled when they turned down a series of big American shows, claiming that these gigs, with the full force of Geffen behind them, would have set up the Roses in the US. Personally he would have made damn sure those gigs had got played.

But now he was out of the picture and the band blew the gigs, pissing off the more sensitive American music business, a mistake that could well be costly in the long term.

Evans, though, was hardly a peripheral figure in the Roses story. It's always a grey area, management and whose idea it was to do what but a music press story in the mid Nineties credited him with Spike Island, Alexandra Palace, the idea of not talking in interviews, Ian Brown's large blown-up globe onstage at Spike, even the paint-throwing incident at Revolver FM, all down to the maverick manager – each one vital moments in The Stone Roses' career. When asked in the same article what he thought The Stone Roses' future as, the former manager replied, 'They will pull through, but they won't be massive. They aren't quite clever enough without me.'

And watching all this were several big American management teams, including Michael Jackson's heavyweight team. It seemed like every management team with an eye for the main chance was out there waiting.

So what did the Roses do? They went to ground. To North Wales to be exact – to Ian Brown's new place – to start work again on the new album.

Feeling more positive about their situation after taking the bold stroke of sacking Evans, the band finally decided to move into the studio and record the second album.

Now starts one of the weirdest periods in the history of any British rock'n'roll band – an immensely talented band caught in a bizarre creative and business limbo. In March they moved their operation up to Brown's place in North Wales – probably drawn by the beautiful countryside, and the quiet-away-from-all-the-hassle vibes of the area. Geffen got excited and wanted to release the album in the late summer.

Scouring North Wales for suitable studios the Roses found out what most of the local Welsh bands already knew – the local studios were crap. But, hey, they were loaded, 'If Mohammed was not going to the mountain, let the mountain come to Mohammed' and they hired in the Rolling Stones mobile studio, called John Leckie and parked it at The Old Brewery in Ewloe, a rehearsal studio with 12 bedrooms.

Again the lack of discipline began to bite immediately. The sessions would start very late afternoon and drag through the night.

Leckie noted that the band had six songs which they brought to the sessions and they began work on these amongst the usual tomfoolery of throwing eggs at each other and goofing about.

Brown kept himself fit and chased away the studio fug by skipping and boxing, Squire himself drank only a few glasses of wine and the Roses rock'n'roll reputation was left to Mani who was now calling himself the 'Rogue Rose' although this went no further than beer and a passion for the ladies.

Four years since they had started to record their début and things were very very different round the Roses camp. They had jettisoned their management, their record label, had become legends and were working in the shadow of that début album.

They were in the mobile for six weeks and shaped up some demos. However the pressure of the first album, an album that when it was released only got mixed reviews but was now slowly starting to get legendary status; was getting to them.

The Stone Roses was starting to become the blueprint to a whole host of new bands. It was getting mentioned all over the place, a massive sea-change had happened in the British music scene and the Roses were not present to reap the reward. People were already saying that if the first album was so good the second album must be awesome. It was a hideous pressure for a band to be under and the longer they took to put the album together the worse the pressure was going to get.

In March it also became clear that the Roses were not going to be playing the massive outdoor Oxfam gig that had been rumoured months before. Unfortunately for the punters The Cure were chosen instead and the gig quickly lost any legendary status.

As the spring drifted into summer, it passed the three-year mark since the début album was released.

The Roses returned to the Old Brewery to work on some new material with John Leckie. They were in there for a month. They now had ten songs down. Some of these songs formed the eventual backbone of the *Second Coming*, songs like 'Love Spreads', 'Tightrope', 'Breaking Into Heaven' and 'Driving South'.

Already there was a marked difference in the band's sound. Squire has upped the guitar ante – delving deeper into the blues and digging up whole heaps of filthy Zeppelin riffs. 'Love Spreads', in particular, zigzags on the dirtiest riff of them all.

The Roses were different now: they sounded like men compared to the boys on the first album. They had tired of the crystalline pop that dominated the début. The new songs were about broken love, sadness, personal pain. The lyrics were coming from John Squire, giving the record a very different flavour. The optimistic rush of the first album was replaced by the pain of growing up and an almost world-weary vibe descended upon the record.

Squire, feeling the pressure in the studio, the creative burden he was placing on his own shoulders, was resorting to cocaine to bolster his flimsy confidence. It was the first big wedge between him and Brown who still preferred his marijuana. The different drugs at different times scenario was beginning to kick in.

And while John sweated on his porta-studio working on those overdubs and tunes, the rhythm section began a series of never-ending jams – Mani and Reni grooving to the loose funk that had dominated their creative peak. Fuck what would you pay to hear some of those tunes!

John Leckie was becoming increasingly frustrated with the band and their new songs. Some of the tunes were half finished and some of the others just didn't cut it.

A great producer, he did what producers must do in these situations and told the band that they simply didn't have the material to record an album. Take some time out he pleaded, and ironically he told them to rest up and then write some new material.

Of course they ignored him and booked themselves into Square One in

Bury for the New Year to continue work on the handful of songs. Astonishingly so far no-one from Geffen had turned up to check on their massive investment in the studio. They thought that this is how the Roses must work and they left the band to their own devices.

A band with no manager, an increasingly frustrated producer, bogged down in court cases and under increasing pressure . . . this would have been a good time for Geffen to come in and pull the band out of the mire.

Meanwhile, as The Stone Roses were wrestling with their difficult second album, the naffly titled baggy scene – of which they were meant to be the figurehead – had disappeared. Pop had moved on, bands that appeared in their slipstream like The Charlatans and The Inspiral Carpets were forging their own careers.

In the bowels of the Manchester Boardwalk rehearsal rooms, Noel Gallagher was working with his brother Liam's group and they were about to make pop history with a band that was modelled on the Roses. The vibe that the Roses and the Mondays had helped to create had disappeared and the gangsters had moved in. The clubs were racked with violence – the party was over.

The Happy Mondays were fading fast, after an interview in the NME with Stephen Wells where they went on about 'faggots' combined with a disappointing fourth album, had seen their last tour oozing with a sour atmosphere. The shows were dominated by support band Stereo MCs who were rising fast with a whiteboy, Brit hip-hop sound that somehow combined the swagger of the Roses and the street suss of the Mondays in a blistering street-pop package. It was ironic that they too would disappear into the nowhere land of attempting to record a follow-up.

In the pubs of Camden a new twist on the guitar scene that the Roses had kicked off was slowly moving into the music papers ready for a complete takeover . . . Britpop (a shitty term for a music scene which I made up as a joke in 1988 when reviewing the La's in Sounds).

As 1992 slid to a close there was very little activity in the Roses' camp – it was obvious that the album was not going to be ready till the following spring or the autumn. Geffen were still not panicking and the rock press busied itself with reports of the Roses getting spotted all over Manchester.

It seemed like they were doing absolutely fuck all, sitting around the Beech and the Horse and Jockey in Chorlton, chewing the fat or following the revived Manchester United all over the place. At one point they were spotted in Mantos on Canal Street celebrating United's Derby match victory over their less fortunate neighbours City.

It had been a long and frustrating year of false starts and dashed hopes, another year watching their crown slip.

1993

STILL NOTHING GOING ON: THE WILDERNESS YEARS, PART 3

So roll on 1993 and with still no sign of any music at all, in fact no sign of anything – even the mooted sessions at Square One – the still managerless Stone Roses were starting to cause concern at Geffen Records. The multinational label had tried its hardest to be hip and modern and all Nineties about the situation and left the band to their own concerns, but with this amount of money invested in the band, maybe it was time for them to sort something out.

They perceived the band was intensely talented but difficult to deal with. Gary Walsh from Geffen came over and sat down with the band. He needed some answers. Like, just what the fuck was going on and have they managed to find a manager yet? It had been nearly a year since Gareth had been sacked and the band were virtually looking after themselves with Steve Adge.

There was talk of a summer single, just enough talk to get Geffen sent packing happy. It would have been a great time to put a single out, it may have been a long gap but the Roses were still massively popular and Oasis were yet to break and steal their thunder. This would have been the perfect time for the comeback.

The rest of the band arsed around at the football or popped over to Lanzarote for holidays. There was a distinct lack of inertia in the Roses' camp. It was more fun doing everything else apart from being in the studio. After all, after a decade of gloomy rehearsal rooms who wouldn't want to party?

Still, at some point the holiday had to end, the party has to be brought to a short, sharp stop and as the fourth anniversary of the release of the début album loomed in March, Gary Gersh made one of his six monthly visits to the band and their ersatz manager Steve Adge and insisted they recall John Leckie. Get something done. Get that summer single out!

They put in a surprise call to John Leckie and told him that they were ready to go into the studio and start recording.

Leckie who hadn't worked with the band for almost six months was puzzled by this unprecedented outbreak of activity and hi-tailed it north.

There were nearly a dozen songs ready, with new tunes like the English folk melody drenched 'Your Star Will Shine', the driving 'Begging You' (written by Squire as he attempted to master computer programming and emulate the dense hypnotic backing tracks of Public Enemy with whom he had become obsessed – not quite the Zep freak of legend!) and the nearly completed 'Ten Storey Love Song' – a total classic that had John Leckie gasping. It screamed a hit. If only they could have got it together, got the record out for the summer of '93, it would have been a dead cert Top Five, a possible Number 1! In their absence the Roses legend was growing. An awesome tune like that would have been one fuck of a comeback.

With the band back in the studio Geffen sensed that there may just be some action on the horizon. What they need to do was give the group a push, get their act together and start planning the campaign, the relaunch. What the Roses really needed was a manager, someone that they could deal with, so they went shopping for bosses.

They looked at Elliot Rashman, the very successful manager of Simply Red, and a figure widely respected in the music business for his ability to check huge egos.

Affable and straight-talking and a man who lived in Manchester, he seemed perfect for the job. Rashman, though, begged to differ. He was too tied up with Mick Hucknall and didn't feel that he was quite right. He suggested Nathan McGough, the fast-talking wheeler dealer ex-manager of The Happy Mondays, who was currently working in A&R at WEA. McGough, though, was worn out after dealing with The Happy Mondays and turned them down.

Noticing that it was four years since that album got released, the *NME* travelled up to Bury to try and doorstep an interview with The Stone Roses. The band, seeing the journalist Gina Morris waiting to interview them, were as polite as ever but refused to be interviewed. They said 'Come back in a few months and we'll do a proper interview.'

A month or so into the session, producer John Leckie was beginning to feel weirded out by the strange vibe that surrounded that band, especially the way that nothing seemed to get done and their whole bizarre way of operating. Meanwhile Chris Griffiths and Phil Smith and the rest of the band's crew were starting to get itchy feet. Despite still being on the payroll they had nothing better to do than sit around in Phil's back garden playing chess. This was not what they had planned when they went on the road with The Stone Roses. It wouldn't be long before they upped sticks and went to work with the emergent Oasis, yet another lifeline between the two bands.

After twenty-six years of trying, Manchester United finally won the 1992/93 League championship and there were wild scenes in the city as thousands of fans hit the streets to party. Mani was spotted getting pissed in Leggets bar in Failsworth. Naturally things got out of hand and the police were called. Recalls Mani, 'That was a top buzz. It was rocking around the Pole in Failsworth. I remember we nipped off to the Broadway in Moston for a while and when we got back the riot police had Oldham Road completely blocked off. United won the League for the first time in twenty-six years and it's "kicking off" like revolution. The Old Bill were completely over the top that night, they must have all been gutted City fans.'

The Roses lost a link with Geffen, when the A&R man that signed them, Gary Gersh, moved over to Capitol Records.

By now Geffen sensed the game was up. The Roses were fucking about. They would still be treated as a big act, but not a priority act. Time to cut losses and concentrate on other acts.

Finally in June the Roses checked into the Rockfield Studios for the first time since 1989 ostensibly to get the damned album recorded.

Rockfield itself is more than a studio, it's a legend. It had been set up by Kingsley Ward, whose kid brother owns Monnow Valley Studios just down the road. The two studios had built up some sort of rivalry over the years, to the point where they wouldn't lend each other microphones. The two brothers just did not get on.

Years before the pair of them had been in a band produced by the legendary Joe Meek. Lying around Rockfield were some of the compressors and Valve EQ equipment built by Meek himself who was born just up the road in Newent.

KingsleyWard, an eccentric figure (he had recently been managing T' Pau) would pace the grounds with his yapping spaniels in tow and pretend to be bemused by what these musicians got up to. He had tales of Iggy and Bowie and every damned rock star you could name coming through the studios and their never-ending pranks.

Rockfield was actually two studios – one was in a coach house and one was in the stables. When you get there it doesn't even look that spectacular, not like, say, Abbey Road. Rockfield is cluttered with boxes and looks like the back room of a farm. It actually is a great sounding room with all the warmth for a classic rock recording aided by a funky old Nieve desk – the perfect piece of equipment to harness what the Roses were looking for.

On 26 July John Leckie arrived at the studio to talk about the album. The Stone Roses were again locked into a bizarre studio timetable. It was as if no one wanted to grasp the nettle – maybe the pressure of the remarkable début was too much. Maybe nobody in the band wanted to take the lead and push the band on, maybe the power balance in the group had been disturbed again. The Squire/Brown axis had already been wobbled and now Squire was taking the lead.

Squire was now in creative overdrive – he may have not wanted to bulldoze the rest of the band but, on the other hand, because they were doshed up, smoking dope and sat in the rolling Welsh countryside, they were inevitably taking it easy.

Brown railed against John's cocaine habit, but really it was just a thin veneer over the deeper problems in the band's relationships. Reni, too, was getting ostracised, getting out of the, ahem, loop.

There was talk of breakbeats replacing the drummer. Outrageous! But then bumping into Reni one afternoon in Manchester he seemed quite chirpy and even talked about how he was replacing himself with breakbeats, how 'you've got to move on.' Of course this never happened in the end but wherever you looked the intense bond that had cemented the Roses was no more. They were great players in a great band but they were no longer special.

John Leckie wasn't sure about the direction the band were going in and worn out by the band's slow work rate quickly quit the sessions. He went on to work with The Verve and Radiohead and then on to Kula Shaker, becoming one of the main producers of the 1990s – another spin-off success from the energy released by the Roses' success.

The Roses had been happy with the sounds Leckie had got up in Wales. As they started at Rockfield, they told John Leckie that this was the kind of sound they were after for the rest of the album. As Ian told *Guitar* magazine, 'When it came time for the proper recording Leckie said he didn't think we had the songs. We'd given him three of the best tracks on the album! I thought "Daybreak" was fantastic as it was.'

After just one night at Rockfield, after being persuaded back into the studio by Geffen, Leckie decided that he had had enough of a project that he felt was suffering from under-rehearsal, lack of spirit and focus. Ian: 'When we first met John we were on the dole, and we'd go in and make a record in a day. Now it's different.'

There were still snatches of Leckie's production work that made the final cut, the atmospheric intro to 'Breaking Into Heaven', parts of 'How Do You Sleep' and some parts of 'Begging You'.

John was confused by the producer's departure. 'He was taking us aside one by one and waving bits of paper under our noses. He also started worrying more about the money, it seemed to me. It was good in a way 'cause it made us angry and you can really use anger.'

Squire, though, was looking for a warmer guitar sound, a more rock'n'roll feel for his guitar than the 'monochrome' sound of their début. Leckie's trademark 'fizzy' sound, the cold, trebly manner in which he recorded guitars had always been a moot point. Says John, 'I'm not sure I like that saccharine and chrome-plated Leckie sound anyway,' says Squire. 'It sounded too neutered for the kind of record we wanted.'

John Leckie looks back on the album sessions wearily, as he told *Guitar Magazine*, 'My role as producer is simply to capture that magic take. I'd tried, I really had, and contrary to what Ian says, I had no problems with the songs – they were great. John would come down from his bedroom, deliver them to the band and they'd be great, but I invested two years of my life in that record, on and off, and it seemed to be going nowhere. There was no discipline, no urgency and they just didn't have that magic in them at that point. It was a different band from the one that made "I Am The Resurrection".

'We'd had two sessions with the Stones' mobile and in the first four weeks we did three tracks and in the second six week session we did just one, "Ten Storey Love Song". They just didn't have any life in them. I told them there's no point in hiring an expensive studio and coming out with demos so I said, "Go away, sort yourselves out and we'll try again." They were spending a grand a day and producing nothing! I was under contract to keep the album within budget, although I was never told what that budget was. If it had gone over budget I was liable personally for the costs. In the end it just got too much. There comes a point where you have to devote some time to your own life, other albums and projects.'

'We talked about me leaving the album for a while, in fact we had two or three big meetings about just that. I didn't want to go to Rockfield and I told them, but they managed to convince me it would work. I lasted one night.'

Leckie's parting shot was to suggest that the band get John Paul Jones, the Zeppelin bass player to produce the album. The idea was never considered and they played on regardless. It was a definite pointer to the direction the music was going in.

The band decided to carry on at Rockfield and promote engineer Paul Schroeder to the production role in August. Engineers in most studio sessions do most of the dog work and have a perfectly good idea of what the producer was up to, so a promotion like this was never totally out of order. Local boy and tape-op Simon Dawson was moved up one rung to become the engineer.

Schroeder was no stranger to the band's working methods. He had also worked on 'Fool's Gold' and 'Don't Stop'.

Listening through to what they had already recorded, the band decided to ditch everything, using it as demos and start recording everything from scratch. In a studio that cost nearly a grand a day they were spending money like madmen . . . or rich men.

Starting to feel sluggish from the stuffy late-night environment of the studio, they began to take up mountain bike riding. John Squire got heavily into it and would eventually spend hours cycling back home over the Yorkshire moors. It was a passion that he would eventually share with his younger brother Matt. Squire also trashed nearly every rock'n'roll convention by taking up kite flying.

They also travelled beyond Monmouth and twenty miles down the road to TJs – the great Welsh club looked on by many as the home of hardcore, a club where the likes of the Butthole Surfers, Hole etc. had cut their teeth in the UK and where Kurt Cobain had proposed to Courtney Love. TJs was a real dosshole in the best possible way and usually packed with wild, drinking, punk rock Welshmen up for a good time.

It's here that they become tight with a great local band called Novocaine who played a hard-assed but melodic pop punk.

Brown's friendship with singer Steve eventually saw him writing a lyric for Novocaine's song 'Brain'.

Back in the studio they were locked into the nocturnal rock'n'roll shift. Sessions often end just before breakfast time. It's bizarre how anyone can work these long shifts, past about two in the morning ears start getting wasted – you lose track of the treble end and start cranking the cutting-edge sounds, making things tinnier and thinner.

For recording, a late-night session is a nightmare but the Roses weren't even recording yet. They were jamming endless all-night songs – hammering the tunes out, flexing the riffs, getting their fluidity back – working the chops, attempting to re-awaken the great band that had lain dormant for a good stretch of time.

They often left the tapes running, piling up hours of material, searching for the moment. A great way to capture greatness but a nightmare to edit back together again afterwards.

As easy atmosphere hung over the studio, they drew a crap cartoon with felt tips on the back of the studio door (it's still there) local musicians popped out to hang with the Roses, especially the affable Reni and Ian Brown. They sat around getting stoned and laughing at the crap local TV. Ian Brown talked about anything that was going down, particularly John Lennon and Greek mythology. They joined their new-found buddies in drinking in downtown Monmouth, in the Nag's Head and the Bull.

Monmouth is a curious place, a small sleepy Welsh market town that thinks it's English. The town's youth were by now getting used to the influx of rock stars on to their patch. It was nothing to see a Stone Rose or eventually a member of Oasis in the Nag's Head. It caused a small stir, someone more funky to hang out with – some distant warrior from the rock'n'roll front line to doss around with. The town seemed to be able to accommodate these rock stars in its sleepy wake.

As the Roses gradually immersed themselves in the local culture, Mani began to get deeper and deeper into the local scene. Coming from north Manchester he'd seen friends fuck up badly on smack. He'd tired of city living and the bullshit that goes with it. He got his chance and he wanted to take it. Eventually he married a local girl and lived in Monmouth. The rest of the band abandoned him to his new country squire lifestyle – which included visiting a falconry centre in Cliffords Mesne.

John Squire seemed less interested in getting down with the locals and spent a lot of his time painting and playing his guitar, working out tunes on his porta-studio, locked in his room. Communication, as Led Zeppelin would say, was in breakdown. Band members would turn up at different times in the studio, but the gang had gone.

As the summer stretched into the autumn, the sessions went on and on, but again they seemed to lose interest. Taking time out for holidays, flying off to the football, spending their large advance and generally avoiding getting that second album together. With money coming out of their ears and no manager or record label to crack the whip, the Roses were again coming apart at the seams.

The former tight partnership between John and Ian was over. You can hear the tension on studio out-takes with John losing patience with Ian's attempts to sing 'Your Star Will Shine'.

Sessions were abandoned for a few weeks and ironically the band that slowly but surely seemed to be replacing them in the public's affections, The Charlatans, moved into the available studio space and started recording.

Finally in November the Roses got themselves back into the studio to get on with some more work. The year was nearly over and, apart from a heap of jamming sessions down on tape, there was nothing concrete to speak of.

Also in the studio were Lush, the affable, easy-going indie band fronted by Miki and Emma – two girls who know how to party. They became the latest band to get included in the Roses' chugging, never-ending party zone. Mani and Paul Schroeder in particular hung out with Lush.

The oldest Rose, Mani, celebrated his 29th birthday at the Bull in Monmouth. A wild night kicked off with champagne and tequila slammers with the band, the Monmouth drinking crew, Lush and their producer Mike Hedges getting out of it with the Roses' wildcard bass player. Also in attendance was Ronnie Rogers, the former guitar player with T'Pau. It all started getting bleary in the countryside.

The night ended with Mani and Lush's Emma Anderson getting a cab back to the studio where Emma was promptly sick all over the place.

Rock'n'roll – it's a crazy life, isn't it?

Meanwhile the media were again becoming worried about the Roses. Like just where were they? Where were the figureheads of the new pop revolution. They hadn't been spotted for years now, disappeared over the edge into nowhere land. There was no precedent for this sort of behaviour, bands don't just make it and then seemingly give up.

Maybe Brown's oft-quoted maxim that he hoped the band would make it and then just fade away was coming true.

In the news pages and the gossip columns the stories continued. Some of them crazy, some of them true, and all of them entertaining. The band were getting more press coverage by doing nothing than by playing the game.

It was a long time down the trail from being skinhead scooter punk mods and hanging out in south Manchester. They had been in a band for nearly ten years and released one album and had become perceived as the most important new band in the country. They were trapped in that eternal and strange bubble of youth that bands get into.

There was some vague talk from Mani about a comeback and how he thought Spike Island and Alexandra Palace were complete farces. He mentioned that the band far preferred Glasgow Green and that they might take the big tent out again for a big tour. It was an idea that Dodgy would use to great success a few years later with their summer Big Top tours.

In December, their publicist Philip Hall, curious about what was exactly going on, travelled up to Rockfield to listen to rough mixes of the album. Hall, along with his brother Martin, was slowly beginning to build up a rock'n'roll empire (managing the likes of The Manic Street Preachers) with a combination of cool taste, a massive rock'n'roll enthusiasm, a level-headed common sense and an affability that made him very popular within the business.

He had been doing the press for years for the Roses after Evans had been given the publicist's number by a music biz insider on a train to London and had phoned him up.

Hall Or Nothing, his company, was regarded as the best in the business and Hall, an ex-*Record Mirror* journalist, had built his reputation masterminding the PR campaign for the likes of The Pogues.

While in Wales, after being blown away by the finally recorded new material, Hall sat down with the band and, during a four-hour meeting, was asked to be their manager. He would have been a perfect choice with stacks of enthusiasm, a calm sense of what was going on and a big heart in a mean and vicious scene. He had put £45,000 of his own money, re-mortgaging his house, into The Manic Street Preachers; he had even let them live in his cramped West London flat where they had done all his washing and cleaning for him without being asked! This was a committed man.

Hall accepted the Roses' offer. It was a decision that would have put the band back on course.

Unfortunately within weeks Philip had died of cancer. A complete and utter tragedy, as one of the nicest people of the scene was taken away by the meanest of mean diseases.

The band made a rare trip to London to attend his funeral. It was a wretched affair. They returned to Rockfield and again grappled with the album.

Another bizarre report in the *NME* was that the band were racing their flash advance payrolled cars around the country roads and back lanes of Monmouth, and that engineer Simon Dawson crashed his into a ditch but luckily crawled out unscathed. The band later denied these stories but it was a sad portent of what was to come when four years later The Charlatans' keyboard player, Rob Collins, crashed his car on the same roads – when returning from the pub to Rockfield for a session for The Charlatans.

Listening to Neil Young, the blues, Led Zeppelin (John) and hardcore underground rap and dub and Bob Marley (Ian and Mani), they were attempting to work these influences into staggering long sessions and fiddle around with their songs. It was like trying to get two entirely different qualities into a piece of music – a nigh on impossible task which could only contribute to the nightmare of the sessions.

On the other hand there were still songs going down, some great stuff was getting recorded. It was just the time it was taking, the money it was costing, the slothful slowdown of the band, but despite all this there were tunes in the can.

Ian, maybe in an attempt to get back to his lean and mean sharp and angular roots, shaved his head; so did Reni.

The sessions were finally coming to an end and, towards Christmas, with some of the tracks shaping up, Geffen finally put their foot down and set a delivery date for the record. John Squire had finished the artwork and there was talk of a first release on Valentine's Day, 1994, of 'Love Spreads', the bluesy old testament fused rocker that was to be the first single.

Geffen also talked of a March release for the album. They still obviously didn't really realise what they had on their hands here. A week before Christmas Ian made a trip down to TJs in Newport and was hassled by a reporter from the *Western Mail* for an interview, an interview which he declined; 'Speak to me as I am, not with a tape recorder' was his riposte.

The last of the wilderness years drew to a close, with a bulk of the material in the can. The band were finally putting the finishing touches to what they hoped would be *the* second coming.

1994

MY GOD, THERE'S SOMETHING STIRRING

Early in 1994, with a new album looming, the Roses decided that they needed to sort out some sort of management. They knew that they had a big job afoot and they needed the right person at the helm to guide the project home. By now, though, their reputation preceded them. Because they didn't act like humble buffoons and serfs like most musicians, they had gathered a reputation for being difficult, for being a band that you just couldn't manage.

Some managers just want to hang around with the gang. They are the band's Number 1 super fans, caught up in the male braggadocio and bravado of the 'group as gang' thing. Some managers are wheelers and dealers – they haven't got a clue about the music business but they can cut a deal with anyone. The Stone Roses had already had one of those, they wanted someone more 'music business' this time, someone who could kick start their career in America for them.

In January 1994 they flew to New York City to meet up with Peter Leake, who was manager of The Waterboys and The Cowboy Junkies but, again, their plans fell through.

With February looming, 'Love Spreads' slipped off the release sheets again and the schedule was put back. It was coming up to five years since *The Stone Roses* and the band had become shrouded in legend. Now this new band Oasis were happening. It was the calm before the storm – Britpop was starting to kick off big style and the heritage of the Roses is finally going to hit pay dirt. As the bands that were influenced by them and the space that they created finally got their act together and swamped the mainstream. The only band missing, was, ironically, the Roses themselves.

Paul Schroeder, the engineer, who had been promoted up to producer for the album, had left Rockfield Studios for London. Due to a prior commitment of producing his sister's band, however, he reluctantly had to leave. 'He'd have been an arsehole not to go,' says Brown. 'Family commitments are important.'

Schroeder had produced 'Breaking Into Heaven', 'Driving South' and 'Good Times', the old school rock'n'roll tunes.

Now they promoted Simon Dawson, the son of the Rockfield owners, up to producer; their third producer. He had been in on the sessions right from the start so it was a logical move and kept the ship stable, recording and producing the final version of 'Love Spreads', one of the last songs to be completed early in 1994.

Geffen, obviously living on a different planet to everyone else, put the album, now officially titled *Second Coming*, into the schedules for April. It was yet another date that would be trashed.

One afternoon at the tail end of the sessions two generations of Manchester rock'n'roll collided. While in Monmouth, Ian Brown was walking out of the newsagents WH Smiths on the High Street and bumped right into Noel and Liam Gallagher. The night before he had listened to Steve Lamacq on Radio One and had heard the two brothers in full flow playing new Oasis tracks. He was impressed, recognising a great new rock'n'roll band on the block and probably pleased that the quiet boy that used to roadie (well hang around with) The Inspiral Carpets, Noel Gallagher, was getting a big head of steam on him.

Maybe recognising that the baton was finally being handed on from the Roses to the next generation, Brown was magnanimous as ever. Most musicians would have been bitter that they were being usurped by the new breed, but not Brown.

Spotting the Gallaghers, Brown shadow boxed towards the two bemused brothers. He'd got the Muhammad Ali moves down. He was looking lean and looking good. The Gallaghers, who were at the beautiful Monnow Valley studio down the road recording *Definitely Maybe* and had probably spent most of the session discussing what the fuck the Roses were up to at Rockfield just under a mile away, were secretly thrilled.

'You're the guys out of Oasis, aren't you? "Cigarettes And Alcohol", fucking hell. Great song,' he rasped, staring with his large brown eyes.

Noel Gallagher told the *NME*, 'We were recording our album in Monnow Valley studios and The Stone Roses were two miles up the road in Rockfield. There's this little village called Monmouth right, and although me and Liam know Mani – we've never met Ian Brown, he's never seen us, even.

'Anyway me and Liam went to the shops one day and Ian Brown bounces out of WH Smiths, shadow boxing like Muhammad Ali. He knew that we were Oasis and he knew that it was about time.'

Noel was asked about the Roses album and, in true Manchester style, was supportive. 'With any luck it will get them back to the way that it was. Where all them fuckers and pure chancers like 2 Unlimited and all that junk food music will be gone and there'll be loads of real bands like The Kinks, the Stones, The Beatles, The Small Faces and the Roses and everyone will go, isn't it great to be alive.'

It was a dream that was coming true fast for Noel.

Brown shadow boxing in front of the Gallaghers on Monmouth High Street. It was a classic rock'n'roll moment, the past meets the future and it comes out fighting. It was the moment when Oasis assumed the mantle and Roses took the back seat, the master and his pupils. This was the point where Oasis got on board and the Roses stood back helpless – bogged down in the courts and in the studio while the hard-working Gallaghers roared away.

Relations, however, between the two bands remained strong. Midnight tractor rides in the fields around Monmouth were reported in the *NME*. Constant name-drops in the press mean that the lineage between the two groups remained strong.

Things seem to be chugging slowly towards a release date, but there was another spanner in the works. Ex-manager Gareth Evans was back on the scene and he was just about to hit the band with a writ for an unspecified multi-million pound sum.

The Roses reconvened again at Rockfield for another two-week spell. There were a few loose ends to finish off. The album was nearing completion and they must have been getting pretty excited about the shape of it. It was a noticeable jump forward – it was, as some pundits promptly pointed out on eventual release, like listening to the third album and missing out the second one.

That May the *NME*, fed up with waiting for the album, sent out another crack team of reporters to look for the Roses. It was the fifth anniversary of the début and they just wanted to know what the fuck was happening.

The piece, by Stuart Baillie, was great. It added to the mystery of the band – various music biz figures who had heard the album attempted to describe it. All were frothing at the mouth. Matthew Priest, the Dodgy drummer had had a sneak preview.

'They had a huge bag of grass that they were skinning up over an Aerosmith LP, so that gives you an idea of where they were at. The stuff that we heard doesn't have any vocals. It's like Led Zep but with a trancey vibe.'

That phrase kept coming up in all descriptions – Led Zep. It seemed that the band and John Squire in particular had been listening to a whole heap of Jimmy Page's Brit blues band of the early Seventies and it was affecting their sound.

Led Zeppelin were certainly an awesome outfit. Their funky rip off of old blues riffs and knack for neat songwriting, combined with Bonzo's heavy drums had made them a classic band, especially in the States, where they were one of the biggest bands of all time. The fact that the media hated them and they were always music-business mavericks who could stand on their own two feet must have appealed to the Roses who at this stage must have felt so far away from the music business that they were positive outsiders to the whole circus.

After a fortnight they were off again. John left for the south of France to go mountain biking, probably the best cure for the studio fog that must be filling his head now. It had been a long, hard and weary battle but the record was finally nearly made.

It was reported in *NME* that Reni was recovering from a debilitating illness, though the nature of the disease was not disclosed.

Geffen, feeling bolshy, started talking up the album – dropping Led Zeppelin references. Fans were now starting to wonder just what sort of record was getting put together out there in Wales. They were expecting another pop stained opus and they were getting promised Zep – there was a distinct unease among the fan base.

John Kennedy, the band's lawyer, was promising everybody that it really would be a second coming. The record was already so talked up that there was an air of excitement as the mythical figures prepared for a return to the real world.

As the summer of '94 approached, the Roses were well and truly overtaken by Oasis. For many the waiting was over and the Manc megamouth band has returned, only this time it was fronted by the Gallaghers and not by Ian Brown.

With Noel's brilliant songwriting, no bullshit interviews and Liam's simplifying of the Ian Brown stagecraft, Oasis knocked all the strange edges off the Roses' model and created the biggest British pop phenomenon since The Beatles.

Oasis had well and truly stolen the Roses' thunder. The dithering about had meant that although expectations were still really high most people knew that the crown had been stolen by another outfit. Forget the second coming, the new gods were the Burnage boys, and the Roses were, at best, Moses or John The Baptist, the old prophets coming down from mountains with dark tales of pop wars past.

During the summer, Mani was back-stage at the Glastonbury Festival taking handshakes and looking very confident, basking in the brilliant hot sun of one of those golden summer days that makes old Blighty one of the best places to be in the world. He didn't look like a man panicking as Oasis rocked the *NME* stage – their first truly big stage appearance that they took with ease. He claimed that the album was nearly finished and sang its praises.

Geffen, getting tired of moving the release back and getting a tad worried about their investment, sent Tom Zutaut over to Wales more and more to check the 'progress' of the record, while the band kept on talking to Peter Leake, desperately attempting to get him to take them on.

Tom Zutaut finally got to hear the unmixed album and he was blown away. The Roses were starting to feel more confident about what they had got on their hands. They invited their radio pluggers Beer Davies over.

Gareth Davies and James Chappell-Gill made the trip.

It was a strange feeling for the radio pluggers. They would be the first people outside a tightly knit circle not only to hear the record but actually see the Roses since they mooched off the stage at Glasgow Green four years ago!

While the pluggers were making their journey over to the studio, 'a desperate, bizarre incident took place' when two fans had decided to head down to Rockfield Studios to see what was going on. They arrived in Monmouth then headed up to the studios, which were just outside the town. They wandered up the drive and asked a mysterious-looking man hanging around at the end of the road in the night darkness if this was the Rockfield Studios that those Roses were recording at. 'Yeah' replied the gaunt figure, before telling them that the album was great as well.

Justin Hammond was one of the fans.

'We were shocked to see Ian Brown just wandering about. We thought that he would be really moody and pissed off that we had just turned up but he was really made up. He was wandering around with an acoustic guitar and a Bob Marley songbook. He had been sat around learning to play the guitar. He knew a couple of chords. He said he was going into the studio to put down "Redemption Song" (you can hear his plaintive version complete with a great vocal on one of the Roses bootlegs that does the rounds . . . recommended). He then asked if we wanted to hear the album.'

Brown seemed out of it, other worldly.

'He was speaking really slowly. He was slagging the NME off for turning up and doing those pictures of them. We went into the studio and the engineer was sat there. He was just paid to sit there all day in case one of them turned up and wanted something. We asked Ian where John Squire was and he shrugged his shoulders and said, "Probably cycling somewhere." Mani was in the main house part of the place watching the World Cup and every time someone scored he would phone up the studio. Ian got the engineer to put the album on and we sat there listening to it. It sounded great. He asked us what we thought of the record and he seemed to be really made up that we liked the tracks. He was dancing around the room clicking his fingers. It was really weird, you wouldn't think that he cared what we thought of the record. He kept saying that the record was going to prove that the Roses were one of the best two bands in the world and my mate said like The Smiths and New Order. Ian Brown just stared at him and said, "No The Beatles and The Stone Roses." totally seriously.'

Justin remembers the weird vibe around the studio. The band were in the Couch House, a Seventies-styled snug studio complex on the farm. The Roses had been there a long time, long enough to etch a drawing of the devil on the door of the studio.

'It was like he [Brown] didn't want to be there really. He seemed like he was missing his kid. It didn't seem like anyone wanted to be there. He was really cool to us, though, and he seemed really quiet and intense.'

Later on the Beer Davies pluggers arrived and Ian and Reni played the album back to them. James was completely blown away. The two Mancs sat there nodding their heads.

Not to be overtaken in the makeshift promo stakes, Mani played Steve from Novocaine a tape of the album as he drove back from Monmouth in his car.

Steve was blown away. For the Roses it was the record that they had been working on for years and like all bands they now had difficulty in hearing how good or bad the record was. It seemed that the snippets that they played out to people sounded awesome. As a record that stood on its own it was indeed a great album but with all the attendant cultural baggage it was going to have to carry with it when it finally did come out, it had a big fight on its hands.

The Roses had dug in deep with the local band scene. Always affable, they easily got on with other bands. When they first came into Rockfield they hooked up with local outfit the Blood Brothers who then split into Dub War and 60 ft Dolls, two of the most successful bands who came out of the nascent Newport Scene. Newport itself, being a hotbed for hardcore and left-field noise bands, always boasted a great music scene and Rockfield being only twenty miles up the road was a perfect magnet.

Ian and Mani were telling all in earshot that the record had taken so long to finish because they wanted to make something perfect and that they were bursting to get out and play live as soon as possible. The Roses were getting ready to get back to business – quite possibly not realising that the pop scene had moved a million miles away from where they were last standing when the début came out. The times were meaner, the groups were more and more brutal and the summer of love had well and truly pissed off.

In October, with yet another year running out the Roses moved the whole operation to Metropolis Studios in Chiswick to get the album's final mix fine-tuned with Bill Price. The legendary fixer had salvaged The Clash's *Combat Rock* as well as producing the same band, The Sex Pistols, Mott the Hoople and Guns 'N' Roses. Perhaps one of the greatest rock'n'roll producers in the world, Price was legendary in his ability to get life out of battered tapes.

The Roses' sessions were a mess, they just needed some level of continuity. They had been recorded in so many different locations, from a 16-track Fostex machine to a full-blown 48-track setup. Some tracks were recorded in the full-on studio environment while others were tarted up rough and ready demos ('Tightrope', recorded in the Rockfield TV lounge using just a stereo Neumann, being the obvious example). Price tidied up the record, cleaning up the army of guitars that Squire had laid down repairing the record, getting it ready for delivery. And by the spring of 1994 the record was just about ready.

The big question now was: was the world ready for The Stone Roses again?

The tapes were now finally finished and compiled and the Roses finally had their second album ready. It must have been a strange and empty day when the final tape was put into its box.

At last they had something to play to Geffen and the band flew to LA to play the company the tapes where they got an enthusiastic thumbs up. The album's rockier feel and more Led Zeppelin touches put it perfectly into the stream for some action in the United States, more so than the first album. The Stone Roses had got something that could really kick off in the USA.

The next appointment was with Hall Or Nothing, their British press people, to work out the promo campaign for the comeback. Typically they failed to show for the projected meeting, the lackadaisical air still hanging over the band.

There was, of course, a lot of interest in the record – the amount of time they had been away had built expectations up to fever pitch. The old warriors were back from the wars but the land that they once inhabited had changed drastically – they were going to have to jostle for position with the rest of the pack.

This, of course, is something that they were not prepared to do. So a careful battle plan was going to have to be thought up.

The band insisted on a late November release date for the single with the album to follow in the difficult Christmas market. This was complete madness. Christmas was the time when the music business goes crazy and the Mr Blobby season starts. Foul old entertainers like Cliff Richard get the Christian spirit and go for raking in as much cash as possible with schmaltzy vile songs. It's a dull and frustrating time of year for the rock freak and there is no space for a serious act like the Roses. They would be out competing with the old dossers that always clog up the Top Ten at that time of the year.

But this was *Second Coming*! Aptly titled for Christmas release and feeling bolshy as ever the Roses decided to go for it. It was a bold and crazy gesture and one that could have cemented them into the mainstream if they had totally pulled it off.

Geffen UK took Beer Davies off the radio and TV plugging account, a fatal mistake since the company had built the band's profile up from the start and decided to plug the record in-house, losing the crucial personal touch of the affable pluggers.

Their first plan was to exaggerate the secrecy of its release, build up the crescendo of the buzz that already resounded off the record. The track that everyone in the music business was dying to hear and yet no one could.

They sent the 'Love Spreads' single down to Radio One in a security van, played it to them once and left. The exclusive play was on Steve Lamacq's show on Monday, 7 November. It was a corny trick but then rock'n'roll always thrived on mythology.

I heard it for the first time later that day in a van hurtling across the Moors at four in the morning played on the Claire Sturgess Show. Its dirty blues undercarriage and spooked ambience were perfect for the mist-swilled night high in the hills above Manchester – the sign-off line 'The Messiah is my sister, ain't no King, ain't no Queen' repeated till the fade, was a classic Roses Old Testament anthem. It had Ian Brown, the spiritual soothsayer, stamped all over it, but it turned out later that John Squire wrote the words!

It sounded awesome.

Four years after 'One Love' there was finally some Stone Roses vinyl out. And it was a markedly different sounding band that was leaving the wilderness years behind.

LOVE SPREADS

Described by Primal Scream's Bobby Gillespie as 'The greatest comeback song ever', 'Love Spreads', released December 1994, was a swaggering avalanche of dark-hearted blues, a proud and bold slice of great rock'n'roll that blew away any conceptions about the band being a spent force.

It was also a brave move releasing that close to Christmas and holding back 'Ten Storey Love Song', the dead-cert Number 1 for the second single. 'Love Spreads' still hit the charts at Number two. There was also a lot of curiosity out there but 'Ten Storey' would have easily nailed the Number 1 with its classic Roses pop ooze.

Still that takes nothing away from this song and the Roses were pushing their audience's expectations of what this band was about.

Dig deep though and there are still some of the hallmarks of the classic Roses. The biblical imagery lyrics. Ian's hoarse stoner prophet vocal as débuted on 'Fool's Gold' all those years back and a powerhouse groove that only the Roses among their contemporaries could deal out. Oh and Mani deals a killer bassline in among that mountain of zig-zagging guitars.

When the song came out, everyone thought it had been penned by Brown, the lyrics were so much in his style (the lyrics by Squire ponder Jesus being a black woman, and in John Squire's words are about 'the hijacking of a religion'). The 'B' side of 'Love Spreads' featured 'Your Star Will Shine', 'Breakout' and on some versions an extra track, 'Groove Harder'.

The Squire artwork is a clean break from the past as well. The Pollock cut-ups are gone, replaced by a snap of an cherub's head from the bridge in Newport town centre.

'I took that. I drove past it in Newport, went and bought a Polaroid camera and drove back to the bridge. The fag in its mouth [on *Second Coming* cover] is what appealed to me.'

The cherub sat over a coat of arms would be the Roses' comeback logo. Fans were travelling from all over the world, having their picture taken beneath it. Some of the more light-fingered kept stealing the cherubs – the band paying for replacements. Just another chapter in the cherub's history!

The gold shield with the upright red chevron dated back to the sixteenth century. Originally it was the shield of the Duke of Buckingham who was the Lord of the Castle and the Borough of Newport. It was incorporated into the seal of the town.

When on 17 May 1521, almost 468 years before the release of the Roses début, the Duke of Buckingham was beheaded, his lands were handed over to the crown, the colours being symbolically reversed.

Some claim that the shield was inverted under orders from Queen Victoria after the Chartist uprising of 1839 when workers attacked the Queen's soldiers at the Westage hotel back in the days when the Welsh took no shit from the English.

The elders of Newport dispute this, explaining that the shield was reversed just to make it stand out from Buckingham's shield. The coat of arms though was not officially approved by the town until 1939.

The cherub that sits on top of the shield had no explanation apart from artistic licence; its origins were a full-blown mystery but for most people now the whole piece of artwork was the cover of the Roses début comeback single.

In 1957 they decided on something more significant to the town's history and stopped using the cherub and coat of arms for the insignia, not realising that nearly forty years later some damned pop group would make the whole thing history again.

So off the bridge went the cherub's head and into the pockets of eager fans seeking a small token of Roses-inspired artwork. This really pissed the locals off and surprisingly it didn't make the band too happy either.

Ian Brown, a man not always noted for his respect for local architecture, was quoted as saying. 'People should have more respect for architecture.' His tongue was probably rammed into his cheek with that one.

The Borough Council were a bit more forthcoming. 'They were stolen once before in the past. Then they were found dumped on the riverbank and put back in place. This time it would probably be a case of using the original moulds to replace them.'

The cherub itself had already been used on artwork when Frug Records, a Newport-based independent label had put out a compilation using the supercilious motif. They weren't happy but there was very little a tiny label could do about it.

Never has a piece of artwork caused so many ridiculous problems. Squire must have sat back and wished that he had used the usual paint splashes.

'Love Spreads' is a classic slice of kick-ass dirty rock'n'roll and quite different from anything The Stone Roses had done before. It is low-down dirty and nasty, Ian Brown's voice sounds shot and weary – and it is perfect for the song. It's a great vocal, conveying a sinister world-weariness. The vocals' very understated nature is the perfect complement to the heaps of nasty guitars piled in there by John Squire.

It seemed that the Roses were well and truly back. They had got their own vibe, a new sound, a new attitude.

The single came accompanied by a video designed to add to the enigma. Lo-fi cine-8 footage of them fooling around in the studio. It was like the Roses themselves had disappeared and gone all fuzzy at the edges and they were slowly returning from the murk.

The pop nation craned their necks like mad just to see what the band looked like – had Ian Brown turned into Demis Roussos? Had Mani gone completely mad? The smudged images showed that they have hardly changed at all. Scarily time had stood still in the Roses camp. They still looked lean and hungry – it's a Dorian Gray situation – the world has moved on and they had remained in a time-zone where, physically, it is 1989 for ever.

But their music shows that a dark angel was casting its shadow over the band – there have been some black goings on in their lives – there had been relationship turmoils, drugs and death to deal with – each personal incident scouring the band's soul.

This was a band with a heavier and darker heart oozing through a commitment to the blues that still packed a powerful melodic brew. The single crashed in at Number two. The aura was still there to power them to the top end of the charts.

ARE YOU READY FOR THE SECOND COMING?

In late '94 with the album weeks away from release, Steve Adge went down to Rockfield to collect the last of the tapes that had piled up since the jamming sessions started. His answer-phone message was a small child shouting 'You'll Never Take Me Alive Copper.' The phone is inundated with requests. The mystery was over and the world wanted to grab a slice of the returning band.

Geffen were going to extraordinary lengths to keep the album secret, but it was leaking out in the most unlikely of places.

A Japanese magazine printed a track list and the artwork of the album. Typically the media was rife with rumours about what the album was like. The single had cranked expectations. It was a lot better than many people had feared. Everyone now knew that the album was called *Second Coming*. Some believed the Roses could just about pull this off.

On a grey afternoon in late autumn, they stumble out of the hotel across the road from the Cornerhouse in central Manchester, on the way to a photo shoot with Pennie Smith. It was the first time that the whole band had been spotted in public for years. I ran smack bang into them in the street and do an impromptu semi-interview with the band that the *Melody Maker* run on the news page the following week. Heads turn as we chat as even after five years the Roses are still legends in Manchester. The band are affable, confident and despite many people noting that they no longer hang like a gang in the photo sessions the way they did years ago, they seem to be in jovial mood. Reni is particularly talkative and Ian Brown is as friendly and forthcoming as ever.

The wraps were off. *Second Coming* was ready.

FINALLY IT'S HERE: THE *SECOND COMING* THAT CAME AND WENT

With 'Love Spreads' at Number two, The Stone Roses' biggest ever hit, Geffen's campaign seemed to be working. Now, in mid-December, it was time for the album. They were putting so much front on the release that nothing less than a Number one would do. The press campaign played up the enigma. It was decided to just do an interview in the *Big Issue* (the street magazine sold by people who had fallen into the poverty trap) and skip the normal media route. The pop press were appalled as Gary Crossing at the *Big Issue* got the big exclusive and the band's relationship with the press soured. Philip Hall had come up with the idea, one of the last ideas he had before his death. It was a brilliant move.

It kept the band out of reach and it made the *Big Issue* a fortune.

The music press, though, were very pissed off. The claws were out. The Roses were going to get a kicking.

And when the reviewers finally heard the album they were confused. This was definitely not the album that anyone was expecting. There was a very mixed bag of reviews.

So where do we all stand on *Second Coming* now? The long wait and the band's status as living legends for the nu-pop generation meant that this was a record that was never going to get a normal reception.

Some people expected manna of the gods, some people expected a great pop album like the début, some people were ready for the return of the Roses, some had their knives out, some couldn't care less.

Times had moved on. The band may have been at the centre of British pop in the late Eighties but the whole new scene of bands that they had unwittingly kicked off had gone and got massive. Now the Roses seemed mortal, no longer the gods; they seemed like just another band.

The talk was of Britpop and it was no longer unusual to see UK guitar bands chew up the charts with their latest single or album. In fact things had moved on much more than that – Oasis were locked into a sales spiral that would leave them with the second best-selling album of all time. In their wake came a whole slew of bands making big money.

The Roses' return was a mixture of massively heightened expectations and muted disinterest. Into this vacuum would arrive an album that wasn't playing easy to get, with a marked move away from the pretty pop and dark-heart melodies of the début. This time there was a collection of songs that were not instantly accessible melodically and were far heavier than those on the Stone Roses.

Even the sleeve was different. It was darker, meaner, harder to make out, murkier and hinting at something more menacing than the pop strokes of the first album. Says John, 'It wasn't supposed to be that dark, that was a mistake. I got a little carried away with the paint, I got distracted – I put it on, went for a piss and it had dried. I was hoping to wipe it off a lot more than I managed to. It was a nightmare, it took ages to make. I made the material by sewing rectangles together. I was going to make a shirt, but I got bored and dumped it. Recycled it by dipping it in wood glue and draping it over a board.

Nothing seemed to be easy!

Christ, even the band's photos snapped in Manchester's Chinatown by legendary lens woman Pennie Smith (whose collection of shots of The Clash ranks as the finest collection of shots of a rock'n'roll band ever) showed a group looking more pensive and less surly than the late Eighties shots, not looking that comfortable in each other's company. It was almost like they had forgotten how to pose as a gang.

Had they forgotten how to make records?

SECOND COMING

Give the album another listen, kid! Sure there are weak spots but there is some great rock'n'roll on this record.

Second Coming kicks off with a swathe of vicious feedback before segueing into a tape of the River Monnow, the cold Welsh river water sluicing down the mountain on its way to the Bristol Channel captured by Ian Brown on a portable DAT player. Shades of *Apocalypse Now* soundtrack, especially as in the background there are swathes of dark feedback. Also slashes of the FX laden guitar noise that used to punctuate the Roses' songs way back.

The track fuses gently into Reni's drum pattern, a tribal workout that sounds almost like Fleetwood Mac's *Tusk*. Squire kicks in and we're finally off into the album's début track, 'Breaking Into Heaven', and we are into classic rock country. There are shades of Jimmy Page and the whole album has the much mooted Led Zep stamp on it. There are several layers of guitar – most of them forwards and some of them sliding in backwards, joining the occasional backwards snares that slurp in and out of the sound collage.

Clocking in at eleven minutes it was to be the Roses' longest-ever song.

The track was one of several jammed versions of the song. 'Breakout', the flipside of 'Love Spreads', was yet another version of the tune. The jam sessions were one of the keys to the album, as producer Simon Dawson told the *Melody Maker*. At least it gave a chance for the rest of the band to feel involved!

'We spent a lot of time getting the backing tracks feeling good. They'd go in and just jam it for maybe a few days. They'd sort of play it all afternoon and maybe get bored with it and play something else and come back to the first song later with a slightly different feel. They just like playing together as a band, so that's what they wanted to try and capture. If you want to make an album that sounds live, it's as simple as that. They did spend a lot of time jamming in the studio, and a lot of different feels came out of that.'

Brown sings with a strong nasally northern accent. It's a million miles away from the American blues tradition and puts a northern stamp all over the track. His voice is husky and rough. It sounds like a man dragged out of bed; it suits the deadly poison of the song. Reni's backing vocals on the chorus are great.

It would be more than the drums that he was finally missed for.

About eight minutes into the song there is a great chord change and the song shifts a gear. *'How many times do I have to tell you that you don't have to wait to die.'* Brown intones as the song builds towards a climax.

It's a fucking great song, a long way from the three-minute pop most people were waiting for but exactly where the Roses should be ten years down the line.

There is no play safe here. Most bands put on a punchy radio tune to get things going. From the off, though, you can tell that this is Squire's record. There are heaps of guitars on here, great licks, Zep guitar squalls, adept, artsy, clever rock'n'roll.

It's guitar heaven! There are piles of them dominating the band's sound, layers and layers of guitar sounds much like the way Jimmy Page piled up the six strings in his days with the Zep. His 59 Les Paul cranked through a hotwired Fender Twin. It's unfair to say that the guitars ruined the record, on tracks like this Squire's work is awesome.

Mani's Rickenbacker bass is deeper than ever before – an almost bowel shaking tone – if only it was higher in the mix you could then fully appreciate its Jah Wobble that dominated Public Image's finest moments.

The album is that combination of hard rock and English folksiness that Zeppelin mastered; it's music that slots into US Rock. Except that the Roses had maintained some sort of edge, a smattering of Manchester city tuffness that stopped their music tipping over into rawk boredom.

Maybe this was down to Ian Brown's voice. When he finally kicks in five minutes into 'Breaking Into Heaven' he still sounds like classic Brown. Of course he 'sure can't sing', but somehow he makes his voice work with the music, it's all attitude, flat vowels, northern accent bending the US-styled rock'n'roll back to the UK and that's just the verse!

When they kick into the chorus it still has that effortless rush of all the classic Roses' choruses, especially with Reni's backing vocals.

Brown's vocals are one of the key points of the album. Sometimes sounding listless and bored and sometimes displaying a curiously emotional cracked intensity, he sounds like a man at the end of his tether and remarkably squeezes some sort of emotion in a menacing and laid-back manner out of John Squire's words.

Squire wrote nearly everything on *Second Coming*, whereas on the Roses' début the lyric writing had been a shared thing. Ian: 'We shared writing the lyrics. "Adored" is all me, "She Bangs The Drums" is half and half, I did the verses, he did the chorus, "Waterfall" – John did most lyrics on "Waterfall", "Don't Stop" is about fifty–fifty, "Badman" about fifty–fifty, "Elizabeth My Dear" I wrote, "Made Of Stone" I wrote 90 per cent, "Shoot You Down" we both wrote, "This Is The One" I wrote, "Resurrection" I wrote. So John wrote some of the lyrics, yeah. But we both wrote melodies, and the melodies and the music were made at the same time.'

It's never easy singing someone else's lyrics. Brown, when pressed on this, said that 'He was constantly writing really good stuff so there was no point in me doing anything.'

The lyrics sometimes, though, are the album's main weak point – there are too many 'crossroads' and rawk lyrics drowning out the cutting personal insights. They don't come near the class of the début when homespun philosophy, dark jokes and revolutionary anger are mixed into what are perceived as love songs.

Brown all at once sounds disinterested, dispassionate, mean and lovelorn; all this with a voice that barely rises above a hoarse whisper.

'Driving South' is twelve-bar Zep boogie driving on a mean riff. It contains the hilarious line 'Well you ain't too young or pretty/And you sure as hell can't sing,' a John Squire lyric that Ian Brown must have sung with a smirk! A bad day in the studio!

Again the guitars totally dominate. It's as close to Zeppelin as they get, like 'Immigrant Song' crossed with 'Whole Lotta Love', a twelve-bar boogie and the bass end is reduced to a massive mush in the battle for attention. A lot of Roses fans skip this track, the band having wandered a long way from what they love about them, but the song does have a certain kick ass charm about it and Reni's rolling drum beat is classic Roses.

Already the difference between the two albums is becoming apparent – on the début maybe the Roses played as a team, as a sum of their parts but now they are all plying their separate paths, all chasing those heaps of Squire guitars.

Not that Reni is panicking. His drums are effortlessly brilliant throughout, deceptively simple skip beats and great timings. This guy is a constant, totally amazing. He never even changed the skins on his kit and was still using the same drum kit from the first album. Reni was not adverse to messing around with his rhythms. As Simon Dawson remembers.

'Reni is well into taking bits of something, sticking it into a sampler and re-triggering it and see what comes out, getting a groove from that. We'd go down that line for weeks sometimes.'

And just when it seems the Roses had fucked off in a totally different direction, one of the best songs they ever wrote kicks in. After 60 seconds of guitar noodle, 'Ten Storey Love Song' sounds like it is tagged on to the end of studio jam – all drums and guitars attempting to find the song before the song itself slopes in.

And when it comes in it sends the heart soaring. Heaps of melody pile up, each change in the song is yet another great tune heaped up all the way to the stunning chorus. This is 'Made Of Stone' taken up another level, it's the effortless pop Roses of old, the spiritual affirming rush that they were almost unwittingly adept at. 'Ten Storey Love Song' is the album's link to the old days, melodically and lyrically.

Brown's vocal on this is great. One of the key points of the track, all cracked and broken. It sounds one part like the fallen choirboy of old and a worn out old soul on the other. Squire's guitar is a simple chime and nails the melody down. Suddenly it feels like the first two tracks make sense as teasers building towards this, one of the great crystalline moments of the Roses' career and one of the best songs that they ever wrote.

'Ten Storey Love Song' segues straight into 'Daybreak' which again moves along great fractured drums. At first the song sounds disjointed, unfinished . . . but, fuck, it gets under your skin, it sounds like hot players really jamming good. Reni's drums are loose-limbed, you can hear the fuckers as well! His snare work is brilliant, chasing the beat all over the room, locking with that insistent bass, the guitar either hooks the funky riff or slashes all over the tune and when the Hammond crashes in at the end it sounds low down and dirty. The song also features some of the best lyrics on the album (Ian Brown back on lyric duties sees a shift from the rock mythology back to the political), being a homage to Rosa Lee Parks who refused to give up her seat on a bus in Montgomery, Alabama, to a white passenger, in the days of racial segregation – a brave move. This in turn inspired Martin Luther King to initiate the bus boycott, making Rosa Parks the 'daybreak' of the Civil Rights Movement.

Brown, in one of his best vocal performances on a Roses track, intones 'Sister Rosalee Parks/Love forever her name in your hearts'.

'Your Star Will Shine', already released on the 'B' side of 'Love Spreads', is a short acoustic tune that Squire wrote about missing his daughter growing up. 'Your Star Will Shine' is an acoustic workout with the added spice of the line about the bullet being aimed 'right between your daddy's eyes'.

For many fans the album's low point is Brown's one and only track, 'Straight To The Man'. But listen again. Its eccentricity, its mooching groove and its oddness give it a charm of its own. Armed with an easy shuffling groove, neat slide guitar and odd bounce, it has a sleazy swagger all of its own. A swagger that Shaun Ryder would capture with Black Grape's début months later. The Jew's harp in the track gives it an almost redneck biblical preacher man feel.

The lyrics deal out a sharp rebuke against British colonialism – or they seem to, you can never tell with Brown whose words are sometimes left deliberately open-ended and vague.

'Begging You' sees the Roses finally cut a track that could be perceived as indie/dance. Its disturbed helter-skelter pile-driving nature is perfect for remixing and when it finally came out as a single months later it was reworked several times. The Roses worked with a lot of loops and samples, sometimes running the loops through monitors and jamming along to them building up whole new tracks.

The mood is completely switched with 'Begging You', the Roses' out and out distorted breakbeat monster that rides in on a massive groove and is complete with distorted vocals. One of the last songs that Ian and John actually wrote together, 'Begging You' is another suggested new direction for the band and was an attempt by John Squire to capture the dense dark feel that Public Image so brilliantly captured on their stunning albums.

'Tightrope's gentle almost English folk acoustic guitar workout and plaintive heartfelt lyrical imagery makes it one of the fans' favourite tracks on the album. You can hear the band hunched around the one mic in the TV room in Rockfield, a camp fire sing-along!

After this the Roses switch deep into Led Zep territory, there had been hints, even close skirmishes, with the misty mountain hop of prime-time Zep throughout the album and now they really cut loose and enter the mystical world of Zeppelin. Like most of the punk generation they initially had a fear of the Zep but by now most of the band were deep into the mythology and music that Jimmy Page was giving out in the mid-Seventies (apart from Brown who you can almost see shaking his head sadly at this madness!).

'Good Times' and 'Tears' are side two's excursions into the classic Brit-rock fused with Peter Green Brit Blues. 'Tears' is mid-Seventies long hair. You can hear the acoustic arpeggios of 'Stairway To Heaven' dripping through the tune. The song is bolstered by Ian really pushing his voice, really singing out, a long way from the scowling prophet he naturally favours. The two songs sum up the cul-de-sac that the Roses were jamming themselves into. Of course the musicianship is awesome – it just doesn't suit them.

The two songs are so sprawling, so untypical that you almost completely miss the classic pop shakes of 'How Do You Sleep', a neat and concise return to their début album brisk pop. The great forgotten song of the album, 'Sleep' would sit easily on the Lemon album, with its brisk near jazzy chords, sugar melodies and dark sinister lyrics from John. It's classic Roses, sweet tunes and dark haunting lyrics clashing . . . great chord change into the chorus as well – oh and a beautiful solo on the song's outro.

The album ends with the mystical magic of the first single culled from it. 'Love Spreads' is the zig-zag wanderer, a dirty assed blues howl and another of the Roses' total classics and is as good as anything they ever wrote. It storms in, cutting through the acoustic mid-Seventies mush much in the same way that punk did in the Roses' far off youth.

Brown was buzzing when John Squire gave him the lyrics to 'Love Spreads'. A critical song dealing in religious imagery, as 'I Am The Resurrection' had on the first album, 'Love Spreads' contemplated the idea that Jesus should have been a black woman. A powerful idea, a twist on the patriarchal imagery of the church.

And that was it, unless you left the CD running for about ten minutes till it hit track 64, 'The Fox', when you were treated to the Roses dossing around with violins and a plinky plonk piano for a very drunken sounding exit.

And that's it – *Second Coming* all boxed up and ready to go.

Five years of work and now it was time for release . . .

DECEMBER 1994: *SECOND COMING* – WHAT THE WORLD IS WAITING FOR?

When Steve Lamacq played 'Love Spreads' for the first time that November on Radio One, the UK pop scene was singing to a very different tune than the last time the Roses had wandered the earth. The ball that they had started rolling in 1989 had really rolled. Big time! Now the charts were full of guitar bands, there was the tail end of baggy, there was Britpop, and there was Oasis – the Gallagher brothers had picked up that baton and really run with it. They were now the biggest British group since The Beatles. It was as if all Ian Brown's big talk had come to life!

The Roses were still a big deal, their legend had grown in their absence but they were no longer the leaders. They were the prodigal sons making a return. But where would they now fit in?

The single was delivered to Radio One in a security van in a ridiculous display of top secrecy. An ostentatious display of hype that just didn't suit them.

And there was the interview in *Big Issue*.

This was different. The Roses hadn't been interviewed since 1990. There had been attempts to track them down but they had managed to avoid the press for years. They had spent the Nineties hogging the news pages of the rock press and now with the album ready to go it was firmly expected that they would do the usual round of press. Talk to the *NME* or *The Face* and then to *Melody Maker* before moving on to other papers – it's a well-worn road, a system to build up the hype on a band.

Nope.

The Stone Roses being stubborn old sods decided to do a *Big Issue* interview first. Uh?

No one did interviews with the *Big Issue* unless they were a couple of months into their 'promotional campaign'. The *Big Issue* was a paper set up by The Body Shop's Anita Roddick and was sold on the streets by the homeless to make a few quid for themselves and try and set themselves up in life.

People were so fascinated to find out where the band was at that they bought thousands of the magazines, it was the *Big Issue*'s best-selling copy ever, making plenty of money for the needy.

They did the interview on 21 November with journalist Gary Crossing. The Roses, of course, were giving nothing away. So some things hadn't changed. The *Big Issue* had its biggest ever selling issue, money for the poor! Punk rock! The Clash would have been proud!

But this interview combined with the record's endless delays and the atmosphere of secrecy around the album only served to set the band up for a rough ride in the papers. In the weeks before Christmas *Second Coming* came in for some pretty damning reviews. The band were shellshocked.

Says Ian Brown, 'We were really surprised with the reaction to the album, we thought it a great record,' he sniffed.

It had come out to some very mixed reviews – the *NME* scratched their heads, Everett True typically went against the grain and gave the album a great review in *Melody Maker* (he also managed to capture just what made the album work). No one was very sure about it.

Under the headline 'Wonky', Danny Kelly gave it two stars in *Q*, adding 'the *Second Coming* is just OK, which is a disappointment', reminding readers of just how great the first album was and of how far the band had wandered into a mid-Seventies mushy pop rock.

The *Big Issue* interview had done them a lot of damage. The mainstream rock press was severely pissed off that it had lost the exclusive piece on what they considered to be their band.

In media terms *Second Coming* was a brag too far and the Roses were getting a kicking – they were too far gone, too Led Zep (what is this paranoia about Zep?, a fantastic band) and more importantly . . . too late!

Out on the streets, of course, things were very different.

The single had crashed into the charts at Number two and no one was complaining about the quality of that record. The fan base were hungry for The Stone Roses and excitement was building for the album.

And at last, after all the wait, all the hype and all the bullshit . . . *Second Coming* was to be released on 5 December, the worst time of the year for a rock band. From the off it would be battling with all the Christmas crackers. No time for a serious record.

On the night before the album release the city centre of Manchester was buzzing. Sunday night, at midnight, the stores opened as a neat promo stunt. I went down with Ian Tilton and we interviewed freezing kids patiently queued up in the streets. At midnight the store opened and the fans filed in to buy the album. In the background the record played on a continuous tape loop and the kids craned to hear what was going on there. If they were waiting for a series of straight pop anthems when they got home they were going to be sorely disappointed. The great *Second Coming* debate was about to kick off around the city's bedsits!

Virgin and HMV had queues of kids going round the block, seeking some pop magic. As an exercise it was highly successful, the record was soon to be Number one in the midweek chart. The buzz was selling the Roses. By the weekend, though, the Christmas malaise combined with confusion over the music that was actually on the record was pushing it back down the charts. Charts, which, that weekend had the album listed at Number 4. Not bad for a normal band but not exactly the second coming!

In the weeks that followed, the truth kicked in. Despite being a big-selling record, its chart positions of 4, 14, 21, 14, 14, 13 and 19 were telling their own story – that even though it was charting higher than the début – the public was confused by the Roses comeback.

It was a second coming that didn't really come.

1995

COUNTDOWN TO TOUR: JANUARY

1995 and now what?

The road, that's what!

Time to tour!

But how? How do you go back on the road when the last full-on tour you did was in 1989? And you've built your reputation on doing off-the-wall shows, unusual shows? In January there was talk of a series of low-key gigs that were announced only on the day of the gig on local radio. Keep it secret. Get a buzz. A touch of the warehouse gigs. Perhaps Steve Adge had come up with the plan. Still in the frame Steve had pretty well become the Roses manager. The Adge was holding the fort, he was quite capable of managing the band but to hook into the American market they were going to have to get some big shot in.

So just how do you go back on the road when you were the band that didn't do normal tours? The Roses had spent 1989 breaking the big audience with a run of imaginative secret gigs, or a Glastonbury headliner. Michael Eavis had asked the band if they wanted to headline the Saturday night. They seemed keen. It would be a triumphant return to the big stage. A perfect way to reinstate that damn myth!

In mid-January they went down to London to mix the 'B' sides to the next single to be pulled off the album. The talk was of it being 'Ten Storey Love Song', an obvious choice. From there they flew straight out to the States to do the pre-promotion on the *Second Coming* which was due for release over there on 16 January – the album had done 300,000 in the UK and there were high expectations that the rocked-up Roses may just be ready for America.

In an interview towards the end of the month Reni admitted, 'Personally I'm sick of underachieving.' It was an ominous remark that meant little at the time but a few months later would be put into a far firmer context. The managerial problem was seemingly closer to getting resolved with the latest unlikely addition to The Stone Roses canon.

Doug Goldstein had cut his teeth managing Guns 'N' Roses since 1988, the US metal band whose singer Axl Rose was legendary for his tantrums and keen adherence to the rock'n'roll lifestyle. Very much a US industry man, Goldstein seemed a bizarre choice as manager for the maverick band, but with the band getting very keen on breaking into the US, a scene that had been notoriously difficult for UK bands to break into for several years, heavyweight help was required.

The Roses were not exactly going out of their way to creep to managers. Their whole attitude to the affair was almost jocular. They had faxed Ed

Bicknall, the manager of Dire Straits, with the simple and blunt message: 'The Stone Roses are auditioning managers.' He wasn't impressed!

Goldstein flew into Manchester and booked into the Charterhouse Hotel and rang up Steve Adge. It was an audacious move but it got the band interested. They went down to the hotel and hit it off with the US big shot.

A spokesman for the Roses concluded: 'The Roses didn't just want a manager, they wanted someone who could make them laugh – and Doug Goldstein does that.'

Goldstein was duly appointed but it was going to be a short and rocky ride.

FEBRUARY

The Roses went on a radio tour of the US to flog the album that was starting to open a few doors for the band Stateside (in its first week it was number forty-seven, selling 21,953).

At the time, before Oasis really went in there and mopped up (seven tours in two years, the Gallaghers were serious about doing good business in the States) the Roses were considered to be the spearhead of a new British band insurgence into the States. They were the first of that generation of guitar bands to break into the US top fifty.

The Americans, since the New Romantic wave of the early Eighties, had been gradually getting more and more bored with British bands. The US market, dominated by hard-touring MTV-friendly outfits, found very little space for UK acts and their whingey ideas of cool. It made no sense translated across the Atlantic. In America it was all big gestures and back-slapping. The Stone Roses, obviously, would have no part in this charade but with the might of Geffen behind them they were beginning to make tiny inroads into the vast US pop scene.

America is the big one. It's the pot of gold, the biggest record market in the world – it is also the most influential. A big success there has a huge knock on effect across the whole globe. Post grunge though it had been looking more and more inwards, promoting its own bands. Maybe it was a sign of the times, a part of the slow US withdrawal from the world stage or it was part of the xenophobia that was going on all over the world. A xenophobia that was witnessed back home with the rise of such stupid notions as 'Britpop' . . . the new nationalism, it was getting scary.

The fact that there hadn't been any big British bands since The Cure, Flock Of Seagulls and Depeche Mode may, on one level, be self-explanatory, but it was getting to be a worrying vacuum.

On the January promo tour of the US Ian Brown stirred up a piece of Lydonesque controversy. On a Los Angeles radio station he urged the American army to stop killing babies, hundreds of listeners jammed the phone lines complaining about Brown's comments. It was the sort of talk that could get a man into deep trouble among the more gung-ho sections of the US community.

America was there for the taking. The fact that the Roses would piss it all away is a mere footnote in history. They could have had it. They could have toured like fuck, put out the third album and watched it do top ten business but they seemed to lose total interest.

Eventually it would be Oasis, Bush and then The Chemical Brothers and The Prodigy that would mop up, the latter two being a brilliant example of what British pop was really about in the late Nineties.

The Roses also claimed in another US radio interview that British bands were 'cry babies' because they couldn't break the States, adding 'a lot of bands expect to be heroes there – they play ten dates and go home and expect to be heroes. The only reason a British band hasn't cracked it is because there hasn't been any great ones recently.'

While 'Love Spreads' was chosen as the theme tune for a German quiz show, Albanian state TV were also using the track as opening music for a sports programme! It was announced that the second single from the album, 'Ten Storey Love Song' was due for release on 27 February.

In mid-February the band filmed the video for the single in London. At the same time Gareth Evans was re-emerging with his name being linked to The Ya Ya's – an Oldham guitar band who had been on the local circuit for a long time without making much of an impact (they would re-surface in 2000 as the excellent Morning Star).

Gareth was reported as saying of the Ya Yas in the *Manchester Evening News*, 'I've had loads of tapes and offers but until I heard The Ya Yas I just haven't been interested. But I've got the buzz again. These guys can happen. They are more wholesome than the Roses. They actually like people. They smile.' But then that was the whole appeal of the Roses in the first place.

Evans, now forty-five, had been annoyed by his departure from the band. After being a major player in the rise of the band, his bolshy attitude, ability to talk things up and that belief in them had done them no harm in their swift rise to the top. It was Evans who had given away stacks of tickets at those early International gigs that had started to build up their following; his vision with the special big shows had been coupled with the band's talent and self-belief – and that heady mixture that had built them up fast in the late Eighties.

The management deal that he struck with the band, though, was the bone of contention.

According to an *Observer* article written by Jay Rayner it was a complex situation, 'Evans claimed that the Roses and John Squire in particular insisted that all earnings must be divided equally. When the money did start coming in, Evans says the deal reverted by mutual agreement to the standard management cut of 20 per cent, a claim which will be argued over in court in March.'

Evans was talking about his contribution to the whole caboodle in the same piece. 'What I gave them was their mystique. I told them look at other bands, when they came off stage, they mix with their fans. You shouldn't do that.'

He also claimed in the same piece that his vision was long term, that the whole process was slowly building up towards something. 'Everything that we had done up to that point, the free T-shirts, the free tickets, the big gigs, all of that was aimed at the US. We put in over 100 grand from the money that we made at the International club and took nothing back in manager's commission.'

It was more stuff to be argued about in court.

In the US the Roses video for 'Love Spreads' was rejected by MTV because it was claimed that it was of 'poor quality'. They promptly reshot the video with Steve Hanft, whom Beck had used for his 'Loser' video.

Speaking to the *Los Angeles Times* John Squire came clean about his cocaine problem. 'I made this mistake of using cocaine for a while, thinking that it would make me more productive, but it made me unsure, more paranoid. For one thing it gives you endurance. A lot of what I do comes from spending time on guitar . . . just getting locked into a private world and turning things around, and something will grow from that.'

In the same article Squire claimed that the band eventually pulled back from the drugs that stopped them working, although in post-Roses interviews he claimed that drugs were one of the main reasons for splitting up.

So much crap is talked about drugs but nowhere near as much crap as is talked while actually on cocaine.

Cocaine hinders creativity and produces banal work which is bolstered by the feeble self-confidence and big-mouthed arrogance that the band produces.

Insiders to the Roses camp claim that one of the problems with the five-year hiatus is that 'all four members of the band were on different drugs all at once.'

No wonder communication was difficult. You would have thought that a band as fantastically talented as this would have got the rush from just jamming – getting that amazing feeling of power that playing together at the height of your powers produces.

Squire, though, was under a lot of pressure to produce something special with *Second Coming*. Expectations were ridiculously high. When asked about the stress in the *LA Times* he replied, 'I certainly felt it. But we weren't sitting in the studio asking ourselves what the critics are thinking, or even what the fans are thinking. I wasn't caught up in thinking of us as the saviours of UK rock'n'roll or worried about too much time going by.

'The pressure was more of a result of wondering if you could live up to your own standards. I think every time you sit down and write, you worry that the last song you wrote was the last one.'

This is the constant fear of the artist. That they have captured the moment, that they have burned out, dried up, that there is nothing left to give. Some people try and fill this void or try to grab the moment again with drugs. It's a very easy trap to fall into and Squire was ensnared for a while.

The mooted small club tour was announced and then a few days later cancelled because John Squire had pneumonia. Yet more frustration!

They did another round of press to promote the upcoming 'Ten Storey Love Song' single but this time there are only three of them doing the interviews. No Reni.

'TEN STOREY LOVE SONG'

At the end of February they finally got round to doing what most people figured they should have done in the first place and released 'Ten Storey Love Song' as a single. It was the obvious classic on the album and the track that melted most fans' hearts. Flipped with the Zep fused instrumental 'Moses' and the plum-stir crazy 'Ride On', it would just miss the top ten. Two months previously it would have been a number one. Most people now had bought the album, scuppering the single's chances of the big one.

'Moses' was smoking slowed down trip hop groove written by the band. Recorded that January it was to be the last thing all four of them recorded together in the studio. Some fans claim that they can hear a slowed down 'Breaking Into Heaven' in the song but I haven't picked this out yet.

'Ride On' was also put down at the same sessions and again is another trip-hop mooch, perhaps a vague attempt at a new direction from the band in the form of an experimental 'B' side. This time it came complete with a vocal from Brown who was deep into some sort of preacher man mysticism and weird Dylanesque imagery. With the songwriting credit going to Brown/Squire, it was the last time the classic team would work together.

Squire's riff out of the song has been around: it started off in the sessions for 'Daybreak' and ended up on Brown's solo album, having been copped by Aziz Ibrahim for the Squire slating 'Can't See Me'!

Bagged in the least Roses – like artwork from Squire so far ('It was 24 Michelango's Davids that I saw in an Oxfam shop in Stretford. I shot them up with an air pistol') the single peaked at number eleven that spring. It would have been number one if it had come out before Christmas.

COUNTDOWN TO TOUR: MARCH

On 10 March 1995, with the Gareth Evans case against the Roses about to kick off at the High Court in The Strand in London, Gareth received a fax from the band. They wanted to settle out of court and for a large sum of money. Gareth did just that, although the settlement was nowhere near the ten million pound mark that had been floating around the press.

Late March and there was talk of another set of small club dates in the UK. At last the band were back on the road!

They announced a gig at Liverpool State Ballroom on 6 April. It was to be their first UK date in five years. They were also to play five gigs in mid-April, before going to Europe and Japan. The small date comeback tour of the likes of Blackwood (Manics country!), Liverpool and Ipswich was postponed and eventually blown out yet again. The leaked dates had caused too much advance publicity in the press. The secret gigs were no longer secret! The band who had been in extensive rehearsals in Manchester were frustrated yet again.

None was more frustrated than their drummer.

RENI HAS LEFT THE BUILDING!

Looking back now you can see the cracks. The Roses drummer wasn't happy. As had always been suspected Reni was more than 'just the drummer'. Here was someone who was a great singer, a really good guitar player and had even been writing his own tunes. That February on the American radio interview tour he had hinted at his dissatisfaction and his own personal creativity.

'I've written my own stuff, my problem is finishing it. The last few years I've been learning the guitar; I'm a very basic strummer but I just can't help writing songs. In fact my drumming suffered 'cause I was always working on songs on my 4-track at home. I've got a keyboard and a guitar and you can play those at home whereas you can't play drums – at least not where I live 'cause it would annoy the neighbours. I've been working on some Gang Starr loops that I've put stuff over that sound great. I could develop those ideas. If it takes us this long to record another album I'll have my solo LP out first.'

At the time no one thought much of this. Reni was hardly going to quit the Roses! This was the gang! The tightest ship in rock'n'roll. But that was from the outside. On the inside of the camp the unity had gone. The gang had fizzled out. Everyone had outgrown everyone else partly due to the use of different drugs at different times. Lob into this equation kids, mortgages, houses in different towns and what you have is the real world creeping in.

And then add on to that the fact that the Roses were turning into the John Squire Experience! Reni felt edged out. It had been bad enough years ago when the Brown/Squire songwriting credit was slapped on the songs. After all he was no average drummer – fuck, he was the first reason anyone really loved this band. 'Go and see the Roses, their drummer is amazing' is what people used to say. And now in the eternal twilight of the *Second Coming* sessions he would sit there jamming with Mani. John had his own agenda, he was talented and he was running the show, but that didn't make Reni's life any easier.

And then there was the stop/start shambles of the last few months. It seemed like an eternal state of limbo as the Roses attempted to resurrect their legend and everything seemed to conspire against it.

It was time to go.

On 5 April it was announced on the Jo Whiley Show that he had quit. It came as a massive shock. The dream was over. How could they even think about carrying on without Reni, the hat boy with the fantastic drum barrage! But he was gone and the Roses were planning to continue. Since those 'B' sides they recorded in January and that American promo tour Reni had in effect quit – they had done photo sessions and interviews without him; fuck, even the video for 'Ten Storey Love Song' had a roadie with a mask on pretending to be Reni. He simply wasn't turning up any more. They probably hoped he would return like he had done years ago but, nope, this time it was for keeps and after the announcement there was no turning back.

For that week Reni appeared all over town, uncharacteristically bouncing round bars, celebrating, the burden off his back. The negativity and cynicism of the Roses was gone. There was some life to be lived.

On 14 April Reni broke his silence about the split. 'That's it now. I've quit. I'm not drumming any more. There's other things going on, but I'm not drumming. I want to spend more time with my family – I haven't seen them for a month.' The rock'n'roll world held no more magic for the drummer, the pull of family life was stronger.

There was talk of a golden handshake. A few weeks later John spoke about the split and Reni, even hinting that some of the album delays may have been down to Reni losing interest in the whole project. 'He had very strong opinions about everything. He was very funny as well, but he was showing all the signs that he wanted to leave. I'm not trying to blame him for the delay, but it was apparent he wasn't really interested. He wasn't there a lot of the time.'

John is closest on record to admitting that the loss of Reni was pretty well the end of the Roses. 'The thing is, I don't think it'll ever be the same as it

was, because part of the spirit died when he left. I think the four members
of the band, at that time, meant it was greater than the sum of its parts; the
fact that we'd all started from nothing, and worked our way up there made
it somehow *special*. There was that inner core, and we could all look at each
other and know what we were thinking. It's bound to be different when
someone new comes in, who applied for the job. You feel different about
yourself too, once you're choosing people to play with. It can never be the
same, because anyone new isn't going to spend time on the dole with us,
waiting for buses, holding guitars . . .'

The drummer's loss of interest had been noted by other members of the
band. Says Ian, 'We knew he was going to leave, 'cos he said so. All the
time.'

Already Reni had retreated back to his house in Whalley Range with his
eight-track, and began the patient-long-slow-work on his tunes and this
time it wouldn't matter how long it would take. It was his own stuff after
all!

IF THAT WASN'T BAD ENOUGH THERE IS A TOUR TO DO!

A Scandinavian tour at the end of April, the beginnings of a world tour, all
those British gigs that had been booked and unbooked. Had the Roses
bottled out of playing in Britain? Was the pressure on them just too
ridiculous? Would the Roses ever hit the road? All that sort of talk. But they
did have gigs. There was a return to Scandinavia at the end of the month.
Fuck. How difficult was this all getting!

Obviously they needed a drummer. Auditions were set up almost eleven
years to the day when Reni had burst into Decibel Studios and changed the
band. They were checking out drummers. Two unnamed guys passed
through the sessions but they weren't right. Not quite what they wanted.
Not quite able to fill the drum stool. This was more than an average job after
all!

Wasn't it Joe Strummer who once opined 'you're only as good as your
drummer' when he was pressed on what The Clash were like after the
monumental Topper quit. They had soldiered on but it had never been the
same again.

But they only had two weeks to prepare for the upcoming gigs.

Despite the trauma of Reni leaving, there was no choice but to still go out
on the road. The dates were booked, and to blow out now would have put
unbearable pressure on the group. It was time to get out there and play.
Maybe a tad too soon with their new drummer, Robbie Maddix, the Roses
flew out to Norway that April for the Scandinavian leg of the world tour.

So often the Viking countries seemed to be the place where they warmed
up or put the band together. Never in their history can there ever have been

a time when the pressure was like this, though. It seemed like the media was willing them to implode. Shock had followed Reni's decision to quit, followed by disbelief that they were actually going to continue without him. The knives were out at the début show on 19 April at the Oslo Rockefeller Music Hall.

Finally back on stage after years and years – they hadn't played live since Glasgow Green in the summer of 1990 – it must have been a weird experience to limber up the old bones into rock'n'roll mode after a long time out in the wilderness. Typically they managed to hit the stage months after the album was released. There was intense media speculation about the Oslo show, and it grabbed a mixed bag of reviews.

It was obvious to anyone who was at those initial dates that the Roses were just not together. All those years off the road had definitely left a few rusty edges. Eye witnesses and fans will all attest to the drums not quite being on it, Ian's vocals being off key and even John Squire sounding sloppy on some songs. There were some moments of magic of course, some moments when the power of the Roses cut through, but there were plenty of teething problems as the band attempted to remember just who the fuck they were!

As they toured Scandinavia that late April and then Amsterdam and Brussels in early May, the band were at sixes and sevens. Their show on 9 May in Lyon, France, is considered one of the worst gigs that they have ever played with Ian not even bothering to sing on some of the songs. It was a bizarre spectacle, a band of this size and importance displaying such a fragile and human edge. But then just when it looked like they had completely caved in, their Paris show on 11 May saw them recapturing what made the band so important in the first place.

Egged on by a rapturous crowd the Roses clicked back into gear and gave the best display of their European tour.

No wonder they had avoided England! They would have been torn to shreds! But going on the road so soon after losing Reni was a mixture of plain crazy and plain brave. No matter how good a drummer Maddix was he was given one hell of a job catching up with all that distinctive drum action in ten days. Ten days when the band obviously had spent more time teaching their drummer the old songs than learning them themselves. And let's not forget that after five years of not playing, bands can totally forget what a band is meant to do.

The local press slammed them, pointing out their 'lack of stage presence' and there were mentions of 'out of key vocals'. *Melody Maker*'s Dave Simpson was sent out to the show to interview the band and to see if they could cut it after such a long gap in the schedule. 'When I got there, their reactions at the hotel seemed really mixed. They remembered me from years ago when I met them back in 1989 in Leeds. John Squire looked at me like I was shit, but that might just have been me being paranoid because he was friendly enough afterwards. At the soundcheck Mani was stood on his own on-stage, playing Love songs on his guitar. We picked him up and went around Oslo doing photographs. It was weird seeing Ian do his goldfish mouth thing again after all this time! When they finally came on-stage after all that time I missed the big entrance! What a nightmare – after all that waiting I was down the road eating when they played the first two songs, I was so pissed off!'

For Simpson, the man who had loved Reni's work years before, the sight of Robbie Maddix was really strange. 'It was odd them having a new drummer; Reni was so much part of what they did. On certain songs it didn't quite work, but he was a good drummer. It was just trying to fit in where someone had really made an impression before – that must have been really hard. After a few gigs, though, he did gel with the band.'

There was some talk of this gig being substandard. 'Well, that was really weird because it was a great gig and the crowd was really going for it. Certain sections of the media really had it in for the band. They were determined to get them. They rang up someone who worked in the bar at the club who obviously didn't like the Roses anyway, and asked them what they thought of the show. It was a weird situation,' says Simpson.

After the show he went back-stage and saw the band in a situation that it hadn't experienced for a long time. 'Back-stage they were literally pinned into the dressing-room by hundreds of manic Norwegian fans. They didn't seem to know what to do. It must have been really odd after all that time to have these really intense fans trying to talk to you. It seemed like they didn't know quite what to do.'

Simpson interviewed them for *Melody Maker* on the tour bus, an interview that took, unusually for the Roses, four hours. 'I asked them exactly a hundred questions. I never usually write any questions down at all but this was such an important interview for me I remember getting up to question sixty-seven, and John Squire asked me what number we were up to and groaned!'

Rebecca Goodwin was in Madrid with her boyfriend, Tom Piper, and the show blew her mind. 'That was such a great concert. There was like, 2,000 people crammed into a medium-sized hall going crazy for the Roses. It was the pure Stone Roses experience, none of the pomp or media hype of Spike Island. I went down there at the soundcheck and the band seemed to be really chuffed that there was someone from Manchester at the show. They really looked after us. Mani said that there had hardly been any Mancs out in Europe for those dates. He also said that it was the best show that they had played so far on that tour. It was one of the best nights of my life and the best that I had ever seen the Roses, and you've got to remember that I went to Blackpool as well.'

Rebecca noted that the band didn't play 'Fool's Gold' – it was the big hole in the new set and a pointer to how much that song was built up around Reni's idiosyncratic drumming. It was always going to be a nightmare to replicate.

They finished off the short, bumpy European jaunt with a date in Paris on 11 May. Three days later they would be playing their first show in the US, a début show eleven whole years into their existence.

NOT SO BORED WITH THE USA!

On 14 May the American tour started in Atlanta at the unlikely Mid-Town Music Festival where they played with bands as diverse as Del Amitri and Adam Ant. Elsewhere they broke the box-office records in Toronto, selling out a 3,500-capacity venue in five minutes while their Los Angeles gig was moved from a 1,200-capacity venue to a 3,500-capacity arena due to demand for tickets. America was starting to wake up to the band. Another couple of years, another couple of tours and it would be theirs!

Finally the Roses made it to the US. The pot of gold. The country where you have to make it to prove your rock'n'roll credentials. With the new 'American friendly' rock vibe of *Second Coming*, Geffen was fairly confident that the record would set the Roses up in the traditional British rock'n'roll pantheon of heroes like the Stones, The Who, Led Zeppelin – the world-beating British bands of the Seventies who are still, decades later, the standard bearers of great rock action.

By the Nineties, though, things had changed. Really changed. Maybe after The Beatles, British bands could stomp around the world cleaning up everywhere. I mean, for fuck's sake, Herman's Hermits were the world's biggest-selling band in 1965 (bigger than The Beatles!). There was a love for all things British and pop-based. This infatuation continued into the Seventies with rock giants delivering and outfits as unlikely as ELO regularly scoring number one Stateside. It was seen almost as birthright to have a number one in the States.

Punk temporarily upset the apple cart with only The Clash having any major crossover success but the New Romantics had conquered MTV and the American heartland in the early Eighties. Since then, though, there had been an appreciable tailing off. Bands like New Order and The Smiths had made a dent but they were not mainstream, and this new baggy thing, this 'Madchester sound', y'know, groups like the Charlatans UK and the Soup Dragons, were like cool man, but were never going to get past 200,000 sales and now there are these Stone Roses, what are they about?

The Roses' delay in getting to the States had made them, in some people's eyes, a band jumping on their own bandwagon, but as 'Love Spreads' hit number one on the college radio charts and the album scraped into the bottom end of the top fifty there was enough residual interest in the band to see them easily sell out 3,000 capacity venues across the US. In fact in some cities the tickets were positively flying out.

Five years ago they had blown out that big stadium mini-tour, a cancellation that Gareth Evans had always seen as a major blight on their career span, but now here they were, still capable of putting punters into medium-sized halls. For a first tour of the USA it was all very promising.

The band was still rough live, although they were coming together gradually. There were still mistakes, songs fell apart and band members played out of time. Despite this, there were some ecstatic responses from the US audiences, proving that the band were on the verge of something quite special Stateside. If they had managed to hold it together and return the following year after they had finally managed to get their act together, who knows?

On the road however, relations between band members were getting more and more strained. The final cracks between the two key members of the band were becoming more and more apparent.

Towards the end of the tour they started delivering shows that again promised the magic inherent in the band. The gig in San Francisco saw the band suddenly clicking together, connecting with the powerful music that was tantalisingly close to them if they could just reach out and grab it.

It's also worth noting that no matter how loose the band played, the shows all kicked off, the people loved this band, an indefinable love and respect but a powerful one between the band and its audience.

On the horizon they were being offered the chance to really kick in and set their stall again! There was the offer to headline the Saturday at Glastonbury in June. This would be the righteous return to the main stage – the moment when the Roses would headline the world's most major music festival and the gig that would put them back on top of the pile. The band was really gelling, kicking ass, ready to go.

I mean what could possible go wrong now?

THE BADDEST BREAK IN THE WORLD!

So there was John Squire on his mountain bike on 2 June, relaxing a few days after the stressful but successful eleven-date tour of the US. They were taking time out before travelling to Japan and Australia. Squire was keeping fit high in the hills above San Francisco, getting a rush from cruising the rough terrain. The sheer adrenalin of tackling the mountains, man and machine; it's an exhilarating rush. Suddenly he hit a lump and was on the floor, fucking knackered, but that's the way of the bike – you get a few knocks and a few bruises.

But as time went on it started to look a lot more serious. With only three weeks to go until Glastonbury, Squire had broken his collarbone and shoulder blade, and it began to dawn on the band and their management that they would have to cancel their Glastonbury show – a disaster, as Glastonbury was to be the big UK comeback. It should have been a key moment in their second coming. But there was no way they could play with a one-armed guitarist; those were damned difficult guitar parts for a two-armed player, and a one-armed man had no chance.

The announcements of the withdrawal were made and were met with astonishment. The press thought that the band were faking, and the audience likewise. It seemed like everyone believed that the Roses had lost their bottle.

All this was going on while Squire was back in England, sitting with John McGregor, the ex-Manchester United physio, desperately trying to get his arm fixed up. A steel plate and six pins were inserted across the bone but it was to no avail.

It must have been a hell of a frustrating position to be in. There was no way the band would bottle this show intentionally, and everyone was on tenterhooks.

The Roses also had to cancel a ten-date tour of Japan – a country where they were still rock'n'roll gods! Disaster was stalking the band at every move; it was the payback.

JUNE

Losing the chance of playing Glastonbury, and blowing the place apart and re-stating their case as the premier Britpop outfit, must have been one that really rankled. Many fans had already bought tickets for the show and there were some dark mumblings at the grass roots.

Uncharitably for many, this was the moment when The Stone Roses blew it. It would need a remarkably good UK tour that autumn to win them back many favours.

Incidentally the Roses' blow-out gave Pulp the big break. The Sheffield band, who had been bottom-of-the-bill outsiders for many years, but who were starting to break through with a run of quirky pop singles, were asked to step in at the last moment. This gave them the air of saviours and they played a great set and were perhaps the best-received band at the whole of Glastonbury that year. They had the so-called 'common people' in their pocket and Jarvis Cocker, after years on the outside looking in, was finally knighted as one of pop's key spokesmen.

By late July Squire's arm had healed up again, and the battle-scarred band were ready to resume their world tour. Where else do you go to break yourself in? They returned to Scandinavia for four dates in Sweden and Finland before flying in to Ireland on 6 August for the Feile festival in Cork, a show that half counted as a sort of homecoming show for the long-suffering fans. It might have been a foreign country but, fuck, it was near enough to count and many made the trip to Cork.

This gig was also the début of the Roses' new keyboard player, Nigel Ipinson, who was formally with Orchestral Manoeuvres In The Dark and lived in Southport. There were reports of them rehearsing out at his place by the seaside.

Fan Peter Jenkins, who was at the gig, remembers seeing Ian Brown walk out into the crowd. 'There was one band headlining or playing – I think it was Tricky or someone – and Ian Brown walked out of the back-stage and out into the audience. The crowd totally freaked out and everyone ran over to where he was. There were loads of people just hanging around him. It left the front of the stage totally empty.'

Caitlin Moran, reviewing the gig for *The Times*, pointed out, 'I have seen Take That, and the hysterics of their audience was nothing like the Roses fever at Feile. As the band took the stage the crowd started piling over the crash barriers before they had even played a note.' Ian Brown would go on to say that this was one of the Roses' greatest ever gigs, an opinion shared by those who were there.

Again after despondency and disaster it seemed like the band were back at last on the right track – at any point they could be massive if only things could get into gear and stay there.

When asked about the plethora of British guitar acts that had followed the Roses' call to arms, Brown was quoted as saying, 'Nah, I never feel we've been overtaken by everyone else. All the bands that were around in 1989 – it was a great time for music, but things have gone back, not forward. There's been a lull. We're here to bring things forward, we do what we want. All these bands who want to sound like Ray Davies or Paul McCartney . . . that's just retro shit.'

Even now you will bump into punters who go all misty-eyed about the festival. Coach loads had travelled over to Britain to see the Roses. This was the closest the Roses had been to Britain for five years, and even if the gig was still displaying a few of those rough edges that everyone had heard about in Europe, it was like, fucking hell! The Roses! The band that had provided the touchstone album of a baggy generation. People were here to pay their respects to the band.

So what if Ian was singing a bit flat now and then. This was the band that had changed lives, made something magical out of guitars, bass and drums, made music that transcended everything. Even without Reni's fluid dexterity they could still grab the magic out of thin air. The band was playing really well now, this was the gig when the Roses really started to remember just who the fuck they were and started to play like it as well. And the crowd was going mental . . . before the band had even come on stage! This was still the

Roses and living fuckin' legends . . . And there were not too many of them stalking the Britpop landscape. There might have been some alright bands knocking about, but not bands that really meant something.

People loved the Roses.

There was talk of a British tour that autumn. And despite all the negativity of the past year, even weary cynics were buzzing with excitement. If only the band got on the road, finally return to the British circuit that had made them.

After two weeks off they play a 'secret gig', their first British gig since that 1990 show at Glasgow Green, five bleedin' years ago. On 1 September finally it was touchdown in Britain.

As an apology to Michael Eavis and the Glastonbury people, The Stone Roses played on Pilton village green. The show was an annual event with the money going to the village nearest the Glastonbury festival that gets disrupted every year by it. Support came from Dodgy, a fruit-and-veg contest and a competition for local pets.

A crowd of about 1,500 made their way down for the show. Dodgy were totally thrilled; the Roses were their heroes and they were getting the support at the legendary homecoming of the first British dates since Glasgow Green, a whole pop generation ago.

The Roses turned in a killer set. The touring was paying off, and they were a band getting well into gear now.

As he left the stage Ian Brown realised it was time for one of his weird one liners. 'You're the trip, see you in November,' he muttered.

The pop aristocracy was there to check them out, Noel and Liam as well as Bobby Gillespie from Primal Scream – all the different generations of Roses-style pop checking the show.

The Bristol listings mag *Venue* was there and thought the show was great, calling it the gig of the year. 'All through those five dark years of law suits, rumours, cancellations and disappointments, you knew that The Stone Roses had one perfect gig lurking deep inside them. This was the show. Stone me, what a night.'

The scene was now set for a great tour. Perhaps now after all those false starts and disappointments, the second coming could finally take place.

A couple of days after the Pilton show they travel just up the road and back to Rockfield Studios to re-record 'Love Spreads' for the *Warchild* charity album for the war orphans of the fucked-up situation in the Balkans. The record already has a sleeve artwork donated by John Squire. The band, as if to disprove their slothful image, did the track in one day.

To promote the *Warchild* record Ian and Robbie had to do a round of interviews. Brown's hair is noted for returning to the classic baggy mop of yore, replacing the intermittent skinhead and one inch crop he had been sporting most of the year. 'It's always the same. I grow my hair quite long, and then I get it cut off really short. I just happened to have a crop when the album was released – I didn't grow it out because I thought it was a mistake. I'll do the same – get it cut when it gets longer.'

And then, on 7 September, it was finally off to play the Japanese leg of their world tour, the date which had been postponed after John broke his collarbone. The Roses were ecstatically received by their big Japanese audience, the band still bonding tight.

Before they left they announced the British tour dates, and the tickets flew out, selling in a couple of hours, with queues around the block. The band was coming home and the fans were hungry.

Ian Brown was feeling under the weather after being spat on by a drunken Australian tourist in a Tokyo bar a few days previously. It was a bizarre incident that saw the removal of two of Ian's teeth in an unprovoked attack, meaning he needed a trip to the dentist to get some more gnashers put in.

Speaking about the incident at Sydney's JJJ studios a week later, at the commencement of the Australian leg of the tour, Brown said, 'I wanted to bottle him but I didn't,' as he sat there with a swollen mouth and a black eye. 'He threw his drink on me, so I threw one back. Then he punched me so I've been in pain since I got here, been on painkillers and shit. Every day I get toothache. It's wearing me out. I just come here to do the shows. Every show we've done in Australia there's been a sea of smiling faces with their arms up in the air,' he explained to *Melody Maker*.

In the same interview Mani was in a belligerent mood, talking up the British tour: 'We put tickets on sale and they all went in two hours. *NME* will tell you that we're finished; the people on the street will tell you that we're definitely fucking not, mate. England's waiting for us still, we ain't gonna let 'em down.'

They played four shows in Australia that were rapturously received.

'We're at the start of our career,' Mani told local radio prior to the Melbourne show on 5 October. 'After all, we've only done two albums,' he cheekily said. *Mojo* magazine was there and described a packed 2,000 crowd digging the Roses. The talk was that they could have done four or five nights as the tickets sold out so fast.

The Roses played the usual show but were plagued with sound problems. Brown was subdued, probably due to having a swollen gob.

That night they stormed through 'Breaking Into Heaven', 'I Wanna Be Adored', 'She Bangs The Drums', 'Waterfall', 'Ten Storey Love Song', 'Daybreak', 'Tightrope', 'Your Star Will Shine', 'Tears', 'Good Times', 'Made Of Stone', 'Driving South' and 'I Am The Resurrection'.

The band left Melbourne on 10 October feeling confident. A reviewer reckoned that they could play in Australia for years. In fact they would never return.

They ended the tour with dates in Perth and Adelaide on 8 October. Now it was to be Britain's turn. The tour was turning into one of the highlights of the autumn season, if not *the* tour.

The time was right, the stage was set, at last it was the grand return.

'BEGGING YOU'

Previewing their upcoming tour, the Roses released on 30 October the track, 'Begging You', off the album. The single was multi-formatted and was a value-for-money thirty minutes with five mixes, including one from Robbie Jay Maddix, as well as by the Stone Corporation who tripped into handbag territory, the Chic mix and the Young American Primitive remix, which was distinctive with its helicopters, plus also a mix by Carl Cox. 'Begging You' was the closest the Roses ever got to a so-called indie/dance record.

'Begging You' was also maybe the Roses' best track for remixing. The band have never really sounded that convincing when they get remixed, perhaps because Reni's drums were too damn good to get messed with. The pointless money raking cash-ins have all testified to this fact, that some band's material is better left alone.

'Begging You' was to be the band's last proper single release and charted at number fifteen. It came bagged up in another John Squire sleeve. A sleeve that tells a part of the story of the creation of the tune. Says John, 'I got hooked on Public Enemy's "Fear of a Black Planet", and I wanted to make music like that, deconstruct it and reassemble it – so a guy called Si Crompton was showing me how to use the sequencers and samplers. But it wasn't for me. Too much like a science lesson. So I ripped up the floppy disks I had used and set them in plaster. I pinched all the colours from a Degas painting.'

It was released the same week as Oasis released 'Wonderwall', the cut that would take them away from all of this and into the stratosphere. 'Begging You' was a great twisting slice of techno-fused rock weirdness, but you couldn't sing it on the terraces and there would be no catching up with Oasis now; no one, not even The Beatles, would get in their way.

Early in November *The Complete Stone Roses* video compilation was released. Directed by Douglas Hart, who had been making pop promos for years, since his days as the bass player in The Jesus and Mary Chain, one of the few bands that the Roses really admired back when they started in this whole rock'n'roll malarkey.

The video's début screening was at the Yo Yo club in Ricos, Greenock. The promoter there was Andrew McDermid, a Roses fanatic who would eventually promote John Squire's second comeback show, and who, as manager of Roses' fans White Out, had given Oasis their first support tour of the UK.

SOD THE WORLD, IT'S TOURING HOME THAT COUNTS

At last, at bleedin' last, the band had rediscovered their chops, they had been all around the world trying to recapture the genie and shove it back into the bottle, they had coasted on the love of the fans, they still had the charisma to retain the legend and they still had the songs to rock the crowds but sometimes each one of them (apart from Mani!) had let the side down.

But now back in the UK they were hitting that groove and, fucking hell, the shows were the Roses playing like they did in 1990. Leicester de Montford Hall on 9 December is numbered as one of the greatest Roses shows *ever*! Check the bootleg – it oozes class, it's worth listening to just to hear how beautiful Ian's voice can be when he gives out. The belligerent stoned Ian giving way to the fallen angel voice that was, at the end of the day, *the* key component of the Roses sound. When Ian sings like this the Roses are untouchable. The best band of their ilk. And when the band take off like they do on this set they really do break into heaven. They could easily coast on the charisma, the legend, the awesome records, every damn thing, but when they bring the music along to the party as well, then it's a shame that it all fell apart.

Finally, yeah finally, the Roses were back prowling the UK stages. On 28 November they played the tour's first show at Bridlington Spa, and the local papers were full of stories of fans queuing for the last few tickets released just before the show. This was their first big UK show since Glasgow Green.

Despite the excitement there was a definite scepticism in the air too. They had blown too many chances, and stretched their credibility point just a little bit too far. People weren't believing in them in the same way any more. Even people like Damon Albarn from Blur, a band whose first break had come with 'There's No Other Way', a hit single that made no bones about cashing in on the Roses' success half a decade or so back. With its wah guitar, light tune and video with the band suitably baggied up, Blur were arch manipulators of pop. Albarn was putting the boot in: 'It ain't over until the flat laddie sings,' he quipped.

Not that the Roses cared about any of this piffle. 'Did you miss us?' said Brown, as the band took the stage in front of the sell-out audience. The five years seemed to have had very little effect on the size of the Roses as a live draw. A whole new audience was suckered into their pure pop. They were by now widely looked on as the saviours, the band that kick-started the whole Britpop thing, and everyone was in to pay their dues. The unlikely Humberside town of Bridlington was the focal point of the pop media that week and fans were scurrying up to this little visited corner of the UK to see if the Roses could still cut it.

Taylor Parkes from *Melody Maker* was a man who never exactly minced his words. 'I like them but I've never believed in them. Belief is such a fucked-up condition. This idea that you get a certain number of men and, yes, it's always men, ensure they are sufficiently straightforward, play very old fashioned music and the end result is a band you can believe in,' he astutely pointed out, before going to stand aghast at the opening three songs. 'They play the opening three songs off the début album in order after all this time!'

Parkes was shocked by Ian Brown's voice (comparing it, hilariously, to Arthur Mullard), talking about his 'doped doleful drone', and found the whole show, although entertaining, hardly transcendental.

With the Roses now the fans were expecting something ridiculously unattainable. Such was the power of the myth, that when they were merely mortal they were in deep trouble.

The new set was a neat blend of the first album and *Second Coming*, the songs fitting together far better live than the differing styles of the two albums would suggest.

With maybe a nod to some sort of maturity, the Roses even slotted in a mid-set acoustic spot with the house lights on.

The show was also the début of Ian Brown's knitted ski-hat.

The following night they were at the Civic Hall in Wolverhampton, and the local press's write-ups were ecstatic – 'There is something strangely magical and unique about The Stone Roses' hit it on the nail, even if Oasis were by far out-selling them and were waltzing their way through much bigger gigs on a road that would lead to Knebworth, one of the biggest gigs of all time.

The Roses still possessed something that none of their rivals had; they had a strange and powerful magic which transcended everything.

This last British tour was a run of odd gigs with strange atmospheres. They weren't like normal gigs. They were events beyond rock'n'roll . . . emotional, exciting celebrations, played by a band that looked like it was coming apart at the seams on the stage. Careful observers remarked that group members seemed distant from each other and that there was hardly any rapport between the musicians.

On-stage there was a weird tension about the group. Ian Brown mainly stood there aloof, out of it, like he wasn't really there. John Squire detached himself from the rest of the band, and Mani, his hair scraped back into a pigtail, looked thrilled to be back on-stage. And Maddix was just about holding on. A good drummer in his own right, he was filling the biggest shoes of the times; Reni was no easy act to follow, and if there was one obvious hole in the band's sound it was the missing Reni. There was no one who could follow him, not even Maddix.

Most of the audience seemed shocked that they could actually see the band, having got used to the idea that the legendary outfit had disappeared for ever. It was an added bonus to actually have them back. Although the expectations for the gigs were high and for the most part they delivered, for many fans the tour itself pissed all over the album. It was where the band really delivered those new songs.

One thing the tour proved was that, despite the obvious tensions, The Stone Roses were still a great live band.

On 1 December they checked into the Corn Exchange in Cambridge, before returning to Brighton for the first time since a handful of bored people stood watching them at the Richmond. This time they were at the huge Brighton Centre.

Coasting into Brighton, the town with a deep history of pop culture from mods and rockers onwards, the Roses were now on a roll. The town was buzzing, as fans from London and the south-east made the trip. The words was out; the Roses were on top form. This wasn't a limp nostalgic show but a band that was kicking ass. The show itself nearly didn't take place, though, because Ian Brown's child had fallen over at home and was rushed to hospital with a suspected head wound – no X-rays could be taken because he was under two years old. Brown was naturally worried as fuck and wanted to pull the show and go home, but with assurances that things weren't as serious as first thought the gig went ahead. He hurried home the next day.

If anything typified the band's comeback trail it was these teething problems. With families to look after and new responsibilities, the Roses were no longer a few yobs in a van trailing up and down the country. Things could and would go wrong. They were an extended family now and the gods weren't always smiling upon them.

Back-stage, the band were noted to be standing in opposite corners of the room – the old gang spirit still hadn't returned. The only party animal now was Mani, as ever the rogue Roses, who tried to get into the Zap club, and was thwarted at one forty-five in the morning.

A few days later on 4 December the tour resumed at the Newport Centre in South Wales. The gig was as close to a riot as the Roses' gigs ever got.

Ian Brown, never a big man for football, almost started off a ruck by putting on a Cardiff City shirt at the Newport gig. A football fan would have known that there was a massive tension between Cardiff and Swansea fans, Cardiff having a reputation for having some of the worst hooligans in Britain, with the core thugs calling themselves the Soul Crew, leaving calling cards with, 'If you like a lot of fighting at your football, join our crew.'

Brown's shirt was a red rag to a bull. Cardiff fans started chanting 'Bluebirds', their nickname, and sporadic fighting kicked off.

The band had spent a lot of the year on the road and were reaching the peak of their powers. The all-nighter at Brixton Academy is looked upon as the best show of the whole tour. They played one of their classic shows, of which Karen Black was a witness: 'I don't even like them that much and I went down that night because someone blagged me a free ticket. The atmosphere was amazing and when the Roses played they were completely brilliant. They really blew me away – it was one of those classic gigs.'

It was a memory that tallied with many others at every show on the tour.

On 13 December they played Leeds Town and Country Club, and the show was recorded live for BBC Radio One and broadcast the following March.

Journalist Dave Simpson was there and noticed that something was amiss. 'John seemed to be stood there in his own little world. I'd interviewed him three weeks before and he sounded really unhappy. There seemed to be something going wrong. He mentioned Reni leaving and how it wasn't the same any more. He said that the band weren't really speaking to each other, that it was like a marriage – just passing each other in the corridor – but no one thinks of doing anything about it. I thought nothing of what he was saying really. At the time it just seemed like a temporary thing.'

They played Liverpool's Royal Court on 15 December. Ian swopped the knitted hat for a Santa Claus hat; reviewers called the show 'the greatest gig of the decade'.

MANCHESTER, ENGLAND!

The Apollo is burning up. It's a special Manchester evening. The atmosphere is righteous, wild. The Roses haven't been in town on-stage for years. This is a special occasion and everyone is out for it. It's the hottest ticket in town. A rock'n'roll Christmas present for the faithful. People can't quite believe it. The band that kick-started the party is back in town. There is, of course, no support. The whole tour is typified by the Roses playing alone and plenty of DJing action building up to their big entrance.

The rain lashes down outside and Reni isn't going to be here (although there are rumours that he will get on-stage for the encore – rumours that turn out to be untrue).

The stage has a great set, with long strips of gold hanging from the ceiling and strip lights combining. It's sombre, almost requiem like.

The Roses hit the stage late. The atmosphere is highly cranked and when the bassline to 'I Wanna Be Adored' lopes from the stage the place goes wild. It's a great night; they have really got a set together that works. Even the acoustic section is cool. Standouts are 'Made Of Stone', which still sends shivers down the spine, and 'Love Spreads', a huge zigzagging crazy beast.

John Squire is now the complete virtuoso, standing slightly aloof stage-left – playing an amazing slew of riffs. Mani is yelling at the crowd. New man Nigel Ipinson was pushing his keyboards up, adding a funky chop house piano break to 'Love Spreads', and putting new Hammond parts in where he could, as well as filling in the backing vocals. Robbie Maddix holds down the beat tight and hard, but lacks that bounce, that indefinable extra that Reni provided. It would take a hell of a drummer to replace the man and Maddix is working hard against the tide of history.

Ian Brown is ice cool, wearing a Puffa jacket with the hood pulled over his head; he doesn't seem to sweat a drop. He moves little on-stage, stares impassively at the crowd and lays out his vocals, which are cranked through a freezing reverb.

The neatest moment of the show was during 'Daybreak' was when a banner that read 'Reni Lives' was getting waved at the band. It caught Ian Brown's attention, and there was a moment of tension when he pointed at it asking for it to be put on to the stage. The crowd sensed that there could be trouble but Brown completely swerved expectations and held the banner aloft for the whole of the next song in a weird tribute to the missing soul of the band.

At the after-show party Brown sauntered around still ensconced in the swollen jacket and still not sweating a drop.

Noel Gallagher was buzzing about just what the Roses were capable of, in fact everyone was. Those two shows are perhaps two of the best Roses gigs I have been to, and although you really missed Reni, the band had started to gel, had started to turn into something else, a Roses Mark 2 maybe? John Squire's guitar playing was awesome. It's hard to believe one person could make those many notes! 'Soloing like a bastard,' as Noel typically and succinctly put it.

The crowd was ecstatic, so buzzed up on the Roses that even Liam Gallagher was pretty well left alone to watch the show in peace. There's always something quite powerful about the bond between The Stone Roses and Manchester and it seemed quite fitting that these two, virtually the last two proper gigs they ever played, would be here, in the town that sent them on their way.

On 28 December they played the massive Sheffield Arena. The gig wasn't as good as the Manc shows. It couldn't be, but it really underlined their pulling power and set them up for the Wembley Arena gig the next day.

Now it was time for London, and in 1990s pop terms this was an historical gig. It was the Roses' last stand with John Squire, as well as the

Manics' first big show without Richey Edwards (their guitarist) who had disappeared months before after apparently committing suicide. It was the moment when the Roses fizzled out and the Manics started to really move into the mainstream.

This was the big one; Wembley Arena is a cold, hungry aircraft hangar where things like atmosphere are banished by the draughty hall.

It's functional, chilly and unfriendly – hardly the communal celebration that rock bands seek. First on were the Manics with their comeback gig, an initial arduous task on a road that would see them, the most unlikely band of their generation, end up being vindicated as one of the great British rock bands of the 1990s.

The Roses' final stand saw them still grabbing critical plaudits to the last – in *Melody Maker* Everett True went berserk and astutely pointed out that John Squire had reinvented the guitar hero as someone without leather trousers or 'a Mars bar stuck down their pants'.

The show – their longest ever at 85 minutes! – was a vindication and further proof that, despite the odds, the Roses, even without the magnificent Reni, were on burning spectral form. They had played a spellbinding British tour.

1996

EXIT JOHN SQUIRE

That Xmas as they left the stage at Wembley there were no set plans for the band. They went their separate ways for the new year.

The UK tour had been a result! The fans were ecstatic, even most of the reviews were pretty good. But the tour only clouded over the actual picture. The band were still managerless. Says John at the time, 'It's hard to get a unanimous decision out of this band.'

Perhaps jumpy after their experiences with Gareth and Goldstein, the Roses were not making any decisions at all. They were a rudderless ship. If they had managed to get a manager years back this whole fragmentation could have been avoided. But as 1996 continued the band were in limbo. Drifting.

In early '96, as the whole band apart from John reconvened to write some tunes, occasionally the band would bump into John down at Old Trafford, where Mani and John would watch United. The pair of them were even talking football with the *Red Issue* fanzine, an interview which is the last-ever interview that John did as a Stone Rose.

In that interview John claims that there were eight or nine new Roses songs and some half-finished bits and pieces for the band to jam on (one of which, 'Standing On Your Head', he would use later on). It's not clear if he's including the six songs the rest of the band claim to have written – six songs that include 'Ice Cold Cube' and 'High Times'.

In March 1996 John received a letter from a lawyer representing the other three members of the band. It started 'Positive noises are being made about the group going into the studio . . .'

John, who had been considering quitting for months, stalling the inevitable, wondering what to do, was stunned by the letter. Was this where the band stood now? Letters from lawyers? How far apart was the much touted gang now?

On 21 March he phoned the other three members of the band. He was leaving. On the last tour he'd felt like a phony and couldn't do it any more. When Ian asked what 'it' was he replied shakily, 'play guitar'.

And with that brief flurry of phone calls, John Squire had quit the band that he had helped to form twelve years previously.

No longer would we see Squire's sunburst '59 Gibson Les Paul Standard on-stage with the Roses. Almost exactly a year after Reni left the band, The Stone Roses were dealt the mortal blow – John Squire had left.

The split had been a long time coming. Maybe carrying the baggage of the Roses legend had proved too much or maybe the band had grown too far apart. Anyone who watched this last tour could see that this was no longer a tight gang unit.

Squire told *Q* magazine that his decision to leave the group had come when he realised just how far they had all drifted apart.

'I got a letter from the group's lawyer saying that positive noises were being made about going into the studio, which is indicative of the dysfunction of the group. The fact that it had come to that. I just thought that it was . . . fair. I wouldn't have scuppered a tour or an album, but as we were in a rest period, that was the time to do it. And I feel a lot better for it.'

Time had taken its toll on the band.

'I just wasn't in the band that I had joined. I don't think any of us were. All that kept us together during the break was the name. We saw very little of each other. We just . . . drifted apart. Crumbled.'

The split was announced nationally on 25 March on the Jo Whiley Show on Radio One. Even while the announcement was being made there was a flurry of activity as the band vainly attempted to patch up the situation.

The remains of the band were shell-shocked. For the first time for a long time there were phone calls between band members and at an eventual meeting at their lawyer John Kennedy's office, the other four tried to persuade Squire to remain and work on the third album. It must have been a tense meeting, the first time they had actually all been together since the Wembley show the previous December. Squire, though, had made up his mind – he was off. He was adamant that that was that – the band had drifted too far apart, it just wasn't the same without Reni. He missed his drumming and his camaraderie. The lack of communication between band members became apparent in the terse statements that followed the split.

Says John, 'When I told Ian I was leaving it was, like, the first time I'd spoken to him for a good few years. I don't really know who he is now.' He added, 'People change, relationships change, hair styles change, that's life isn't it?'

Q cheekily asked Squire if he had left because of Brown's singing.

'No, I knew that he was doing his best. It wasn't sabotage. We all started out from the same amateur level. None of us were any good apart from Reni. He was the only natural, I'll deny any attempt to say that I left because of Ian's voice. This thing is all very difficult to talk about. I do feel this obligation: to the gang. It does feel dishonourable to discuss the band without them being present.'

The remaining three Roses elected to carry on in the face of a barrage of hostile criticism from the media. It was assumed that post Squire this really was a dead band. They swiftly announced that they would be playing Reading Festival, but in what form? How could they replace John? Names like Bernard Butler were put forward as well as, bizarrely, the former guitar player from Girlschool. It seemed like this was a band clutching at straws.

The remaining Roses released a tense press release; they had decided to come out fighting. 'We feel as cheated as everyone else who has heard the news. We were in the middle of recording the next LP. We're disgusted, yet feeling stronger and more optimistic than ever.'

John Squire's press release was, inevitably, more balanced. 'After lengthy deliberation, it is with great regret that I feel compelled to announce my decision to leave. I believe that all concerned will benefit from a parting of the ways at this point and I see this as the inevitable conclusion to the gradual social and musical separation we have undergone in the past few years. I wish them every success and hope they go on to greater things. My intentions are to continue writing while looking for partners in a new band and to begin working again as soon as possible. Thanks for everything, John Squire.'

THE LAST STAND: READING FESTIVAL

Reading Festival 1996. The winds were howling and the rain poured down. The hardy pitched their tents in the wild summer squalls. It was a freezing first night and a miserable one for the late arrivals in the field around the rock'n'roll electric amphitheatre.

Reading 1996 was a watershed for the Manchester prime movers of the late 1980s: on the Saturday Black Grape played a shambolic show that was still a triumph – no matter how sloppy Shaun and Kermit and their crew got, their congenial party vibe was perfect for a crowd that was willing to match them for chemical excess.

All through the weekend, though, the talk was of the Roses. Could Ian Brown really pull it off again? Now the chips really were down would the enormous pressure that the band was under make them collapse? Would the expectations finally crush them?

A couple of weeks before, they had played the Benicassum festival near Madrid, and varying reports filtered back – some went on about a 'dancing girl' and some mentioned the début of new guitar player Aziz Ibrahim, another Manc from Burnage with the unlikely background of Simply Red and prog rockers Asia. Aziz, a brilliant guitar player, had seemingly learned all the John Squire parts in a fortnight. It was going to be one of the hardest jobs in rock. If he wasn't nervous before going on-stage at Reading he must have had nerves of steel and a hide of leather.

HAVE GUITAR WILL TRAVEL: AZIZ IBRAHIM

Of Pakistani roots, the dapper, urbane, seemingly egoless Aziz Ibrahim was born, bred and lived his whole life in Longsight, Manchester. The classic 'have guitar will travel' sideman, Ibrahim had spent the last decade in a confusing sprawl of bands learning his craft.

At first the idea of the Roses having a session guitar player in their line-up and one who had played in Asia and Simply Red seemed bizarre, not something that the Roses was about. But Aziz had roots in the city's music scene and the knowledge of far better musics than his CV was owning up to.

Aziz came from a strict religious background where even 'wearing jeans was considered rebellious!' He got into guitar at an early age and quickly became the kid at school who was always carrying a guitar (bizarrely enough he was in the same class at school as Pete Garner . . . 'he was an arty guy, a cool guy, very funny . . .' Aziz remembers, chuckling). His range of influences was breathtakingly eclectic.

'I sneakily listened to everything, rockabilly, punk, blues, rock . . . I was into all kinds of music, Bollywood stuff. And my roots are Pakistani traditional music . . . I'm second generation. When I was a kid I was not allowed to listen to western music.'

When you listen to Aziz playing you can hear the eastern flavours. He may have learned John Squire's music note for note, he may have slotted into the background of Simply Red, but his real sound is a mixture of his roots, the western rock roots mixed with traditional ancient guitar scales, an interesting fusion of guitar action.

In his youth he played in a bewildering series of local bands meeting Robbie Maddix who was playing in Gina Gina, a black rock group. With his easy-going nature and awesome technical skill and ability to play in several different styles it was inevitable that he would become a session player.

Says Aziz, 'I became a session player by accident. I never intended music as a career, let alone session. I was playing reggae in 4th Generation, that's where I cut my teeth, Simply Red came from that. Word got out that Hucknall was looking for someone who understood his reggae and jazz vibes. I'd done some work for a band whose manager worked at their office and that's how that came about in the early Eighties . . .'

Simply Red was an experience he doesn't have the fondest memories of. 'I was a sideman, just playing what I was told to play. It was a weird experience. After Simply Red ended most people thought I wanted too much money and that I'd broken away from the local scene. I was looking to form a band with the guys from Gina Gina but nothing came of it, so I did more session work with Rebel MC, Dennis Brown, Barrington Levi, Freddy MacGregor, Ruby Turner and Errol Brown's Hot Chocolate and PM Dawn. I joined Asia for some time and left because it had run its course, I didn't fancy wearing sky blue jewellery any longer!'

A few months, in early 1996, later the call came from the Roses who although ostensibly were still in existence needed a guitar player to help them on some demos they were putting together.

'I didn't know the Roses personally then. The first I'd heard of them was years ago when Gareth Evans was asking me what I reckoned to this band that he was starting to manage. I said, "What do I know"!'

His connection was, of course, Robbie Maddix, whom he knew from the sprawl of local bands they had been connected with. He went down to meet the band. Aziz quickly hit it off with Ian Brown.

'The first time I met Ian we were chatting for ages. I was teaching guitar at the time and I taught Ian a couple of tunes! He was heavily into the Hendrix chord . . . E7 sharp! . . . Ian is a really spiritual guy. He's read a fair amount of the Koran, he was intrigued with me being involved in rock'n'roll and also being a Muslim . . . And I am without a doubt. I don't believe this world exists without help from above. I was helping out on demos they were putting together, then news broke that John didn't want to do it no more. A few weeks later I got the call from Robbie. They'd been to see John Squire and it wasn't happening. I was jumping up and down with excitement. There is nothing like being in a band, a proper band.'

The new line-up starting rehearsing over at Ipinson's place in Southport. 'We started rehearsing in Southport. But word got out and everyone was queuing outside the doors. We then moved to this other rehearsal room in Salford behind Renaissance gym. Robbie knew the owner.'

Before they hit Reading there were a few festivals in Europe to play. The new line-up were going to début in the rawest environment; the no soundcheck, big crowd outdoor scenario. The handful of shows were typified by the Benicassim Festival in Spain, where some of the tightness problems that had dogged the band in 1995 were still apparent. Aziz held down the guitar parts well, although it was impossible for him to get the feel that John Squire had brought to the band. The audience was confused but attempted to stay with the band and the appearance of the partially clothed dancing girl gyrating through the set was ridiculously out of place.

It was a hotch-potch Roses that was staggering across Europe. Fans who were reporting back were scratching their heads. It wasn't like the band was awful – they were playing OK and Ian's singing was fine. It just wasn't really the Roses up there. It was obvious to everyone that they had lost one too many members.

The last Euro date was in Portugal and the band headed back to play the Sunday night headline slot at Reading Festival, ironically their first-ever British festival appearance (that they actually managed to play).

They still rehearsed on the edge of Salford, and one of the other bands rehearsing in there remembers, 'This band moved in the room upstairs. We thought that they were a Roses covers band. They sounded really untogether. One day we went out in the corridor and there was loads of gear out there, far too much for a covers band, and we thought, fucking hell, it *is* The Stone Roses!'

During the weekend Brown popped up back-stage at Reading, hanging out with old cronies like Steve Cresser or just standing around on his own – an out-of-sorts figure, looking too famous to be mingling back-stage at the village-fete-like atmosphere of the festival.

Brown also wandered out into the crowd, a detached figure in rock star fatigues – all velvets, loose trousers and shirts . . . stoned, immaculate, the lost prophet of Britpop, limbering up for what couldn't help but be the last stand.

Mani was in a far more down-to-earth mood, with finger snapping handshakes and buoyant confidence. 'We're having it large,' he steamed back-stage.

'They'll pull it off,' the rump guard of the Roses' believers shouted in the heated back-stage arguments. The Sunday night would be the last chance for the much-damaged outfit, now patched up with an oddball collection of session players – ex-OMD members and guitar players like Aziz, who, despite awesome technical ability, just didn't feel right. The beauty of the Roses had been that gang, the crew, the bunch of lads who had bust out and made good. All the great British rock'n'roll bands had been like that for years.

The moment when it seemed like things were getting desperate was at the press conference. Unlike the pre-Spike-Island press conference, when the band's cold indifference to the bemused press pack had actually worked, their rabbit-caught-in-the-headlights of the hostile press at Reading was a disaster.

Mani shot his mouth off about John Squire, making comments that he would later regret, while Ian Brown was cutting and cruel. Squire had been dignified on his departure, but this bickering was out of character for the band who had always held a united front even at times of crisis.

But then like the marriages and close affairs that bands seem to cruelly resemble, the hatred was a natural reaction to the deep hurt caused by the departure of one of their best friends.

The Roses were on death row and even they were sensing it now.

As the day drew on and Sonic Youth played one of their mind-blowing sets, the Roses were looking like they were on a hiding to nothing. On the NME stage the newly triumphant Underworld were limbering up for what would be a victorious exit from Reading Festival; it had been a great year for them, topped by 'Born Slippy', their surprise smash hit from the Trainspotting soundtrack. The fact that they were playing directly against the hot new dance act could only add to their problems.

Still, this was the fucking Roses! Ian Brown had never let anyone down before and for a lot of the audience they were a legend – the band that started the whole damn 1990s Britpop thing, and here they were at last live on-stage at a huge festival.

And there was Mani, boisterous as ever and having it large, the familiar rumble of the bass, so often the signifier to the great pop moment, and 'I Wanna Be Adored' burst out. There was an appreciable sigh of relief from the crowd – could the Roses be about to pull the whole damn thing off? The guitar was swirling around a bit oddly but then the familiar figure kicked in, followed by the 4/4 thump of the bass drum; the crowd chugged along, ready for the revival. There was a genuine feeling that the band could pull it off at this stage.

Ian Brown sauntered on-stage, and some young fans were heard to gasp, 'It's Liam Gallagher' – the toll of the five years out of the limelight was beginning to tell. Oasis had recently packed out Maine Road football ground for two nights; they were now massive legends well on the way to being bigger than the fucking Beatles, and yet here was the band that set the blueprint and built the foundations.

Brown looked good, limbering up, doing some boxing moves; and then he started singing, skidding around the tune, 'I don't have to sell my soul.' It was OK, but a bit cracked, a bit nervous.

As the set went on Brown's vocal sounded not just flat, which was never a major concern, but bored, disconsolate, detached – it wasn't like the Brown of old, the exuberant positive pop messiah, late 1980s generation. This was a shell of that man.

They played two new songs. One, 'Ice Cold Cube', a mundane twelve-bar with a title that was reputed to be a band nickname for John Squire, was rattled out with a perfunctory chunder. This was a band that lacked the majesty of the old days; the sheer inspirational euphoria that had been their calling card had gone. Ian Brown stood there just going through the motions. It wasn't John Squire's absence that nobbled The Stone Roses that day: it was Ian Brown's.

Aziz was holding the guitar down well – he had learned Squire's licks fast, a major achievement considering just how good Squire was. But there was no soul, apart from Mani, who was virtually carrying the gig, trying to hold a massive legend upon his shoulders; he wouldn't cave in, even to the bitter end. The man on the streets, Mani knew what the legend looked like from the outside. At least it couldn't get any worse.

It couldn't get any worse? Suddenly a dancing girl was on the podium gyrating to the Roses' music. It was all wrong – the Roses were always aloof and they never had things like dancing girls. The last straw was someone shouting, 'C'mon, put your hands together.' The spell was broken. It was all wrong; the diehards walked away, people were laughing or groaning and leaving in droves, faces from the old days shook their heads in shame. To be fair, very young fans who had never seen the band before were still caught up in the remnants of the legend and the songs which were still classics.

'I'd never been to a festival before and The Stone Roses were the best band on all weekend,' remembers Jane Scott, who was seventeen at the time. 'I couldn't understand why everyone slagged them off afterwards.'

Back-stage Cressa was fuming. 'It's a nightmare, it's awful,' he snarled, staring at the floor. 'Get back-stage and tell him, just tell him how crap it was, tell him to finish it, it's a travesty.'

'You tell him, he's your mate,' everyone replied.

Cressa turned on his heels and disappeared into the throng back-stage.

This was the band that had inspired the formation of nearly every guitar pop band in Britain in a brilliant eighteen-month period when they were untouchable. When you've been that good, meant that much, you simply can't let people down. You are just far too important.

The band were, to all intents and purposes, now finished. Most pundits thought that this was definitely the last stand, the final moment. As the closing chords reverberated out of their amps the legend of The Stone Roses would ebb away with the sound.

No one bothered to tell the Roses that, though.

Ian was later to comment, 'I didn't go to bed the night before, like a dick. We'd done five shows in Europe, and we'd been getting better each one. I saw Cressa the night before and I went on the piss with him. Smoking weed all night. I was so excited. Normally I don't drink. No powder, no. I haven't touched powder since 1990. But I must have fucked me voice. At the time, I didn't realise it was all going wrong. From the stage, I couldn't see anyone crying or leaving. But later, when I heard the tape, I knew I sounded terrible. It was a cabaret version.'

THE LEGACY

The band spent all their money from the Reading Festival on buying up Square One studios in Bury and renaming it 'The Rose Garden'. They had planned to put the third album together in their own studio, on their own terms. Geffen had already shown very little interest in putting the record out, so it looked like they were on a hiding to nothing.

If this was a normal band then that would be that. But the Roses touched far more people in bigger ways than all this would suggest. They changed the whole soundscape of British pop, inspired bands, fired up people. Mistakenly Suede get the credit for inventing Britpop, but you can't rewrite history for ever – the key band *was* The Stone Roses. The musicians know, the people understand, the Roses' name is still talked about in hushed adoring whispers, and their albums still float around the bottom end of the charts years later.

The Roses made indie guitar, white-boy pop music sexy again, and they smashed down the doors of the charts; before then the closest anyone got was with The Jesus And Mary Chain and they always seemed to get stalled at number forty-one.

Now, when a teen-band's hearts break when they don't get on *Top Of The Pops* with the first single, the Roses' achievements seem smaller. But The Stone Roses changed the notion of what a pop band was allowed to do. Before, in the righteous schedule of post punk, bands tried to smash rock'n'roll to pieces; this was great in some cases, as some truly startling genius music was made, but it also doomed a lot of bands to failure.

The Roses and the Mondays were the most inspirational bands since punk rock. How many bands were inspired by 1980s rock gods like U2 or Simple Minds? Erm, about none at all.

Some bands like The Bluetones took the Roses' blueprint all the way and seemed to model themselves on the band, while others like The Manic Street Preachers used them as something to measure themselves against while admitting a secret respect for the band.

Others such as Ride saw the Roses live in 1989 and formed a band instantly; some like Liam Gallagher saw the Roses play and just knew what to do with their lives; some people saw the Roses and became journalists or superfans who eventually worked within the music industry.

They were a clean broom, a new way of doing the same old thing. Ian Brown, unlike most of the twerps in bands in the 1980s, was a folk hero, something that people like Bono would die for but never achieve. John Squire made musicianship hip again, and their songs soundtracked a generation growing up with ecstasy and acid house, and the new hope and optimism of the late 1980s.

Primal Scream managed to resurrect their career in the space provided by the Roses, and a whole host of lesser imitators carved out short careers in their fallout. A slew of Manchester bands had their five minutes of fame and then got burned.

The Charlatans, a band hugely inspired by the Roses – even supporting them at many early gigs – gradually got taken more and more seriously, and bypassed desperate tragedy to become one of the great British rock bands of the 1990s. Even now, though, there are echoes of Ian Brown in Tim Burgess's stagecraft and his singing voice – that husky whisper and studied cool reflect the Roses' frontman at his peak. The stoned nonchalance and stone-dead stare that turned on a generation are still there in every gangling sub-Liam-Gallagher frontman mooching about in the UK's rehearsal rooms.

The Inspiral Carpets arrived stage left and exited stage right with a heap of under-rated singles, the Stranglers of the 1990s, they were never hip but were consistent enough to be respected by a huge fan base. The Roses' fans drifted into dance or back to where they had come from. They had been a part of a time when pop went mad and elected fresh heroes, new fucked-up leaders and flawed bands.

Never career animals, the Roses were at one time the tightest and tuffest gang on the block.

They ripped themselves apart, but their legacy lives on, and now British pop has been well and truly resurrected.

Just a few days after the Reading appearance Ian Brown bounded into press agents Hall Or Nothing's London based office as if it was business as usual.

It was as if the gig was not a disaster or a temporary blip or even a fuck up. Brown was buzzing, upbeat.

Reading had been a pricking of the myth. A deflating of the legend and that was perhaps all that was great about the show. Mani who had stayed loyal to the end finally took the Primal Scream job that he had been offered months earlier. John was rumoured to be putting a band together and Reni was still working up tunes on his 8-track.

Ian Brown knew the game was up and offered the following press statement on 29 October and then fucked off to Morocco to get his head and his life back together.

'Having spent the last ten years in the filthiest business in the universe it's a pleasure to announce the end of The Stone Roses. May God bless all who gave us their love and supported us throughout this time. Special thanks to the people of Manchester who sent us on our way. Peace be upon you.'

And that was it. The Roses was finally over.

Ian Brown got on a plane and went on holiday to Morocco. It looked like it was the last time the world was going to see the King Monkey in action. All that was left for Roses fans was this new band that John Squire was putting together.

The Solo Years

APOCALYPSE NOW! SQUIRE LEAVES THE ROSES AND GETS REBORN AS A SEAHORSE!

That final phone call hadn't been easy to make. But John Squire, like Reni the year before, was owning up to the truth. The Stone Roses only really existed in name. The band as that mythic gang had gone years ago, they had grown up. Changed. They were all in a different place now. They had married, divorced, had kids, got mortgages, got lost in drugs, got into very different music, that's the way. You change. The soundtrack changes. Who hangs around with childhood friends when they hit their mid-thirties?

Making *Second Coming* had been a strain. Putting it out and touring had been worse. Everything possible had gone wrong. They were not really getting on. And when that letter arrived c/o the lawyers, well that said everything, didn't it?

John phoned Ian Brown from York where he was hanging out with his guitar tech Martin. He said it was all over. He felt like a phony. He just couldn't do it any more. Of course it was a difficult call. But when he had done it he felt strangely relieved. He no longer had to carry the burden, the burden of ridiculous expectation that The Stone Roses had become.

To celebrate he went out on the town with Martin and got plastered. They stumbled round the tight-knit pubs in York's carefully maintained medieval tourist trap centre. In one pub there was a band blasting through a James Brown cover in the back room. Naturally they sat down and checked them out. It's irresistible when you're a player, you have to keep listening. The band were busily getting pissed blasting out tunes, having a whale of a time. They ended their set with a Chuck Berry cover. The band was The Blueflies, a classic bar band, good time beer and fags music, a few quid for a few covers.

John was struck by the young bass player in the band, just how good he was, how he'd be great to play with. Maybe, ridiculously, he could grab the bass player and start a new band now. Just get going again. Already.

It was a lucky break for the 20-year-old Stuart Fletcher who was approached by the legendary guitar player after the gig. He was only standing in that night because the band's normal bass player had RSI and couldn't make the gig. He'd been playing bass since he was eleven and had even passed through one of the earlier line ups of local heroes Shed 7.

As he stood there getting pissed at the bar with these two older guys talking about his bass playing and this band that they were putting together he had no idea that it was John Squire from The Stone Roses. He was, of course, bemused . . . But what the fuck, it was a gig!

As he left the pub, according to *Guitar Magazine*, John Squire banged his head on a fibre glass sea horse that was hanging on the door.

Now he knew his new band would be called: the Headbangers!

John had been too drunk to take Stuart's phone number. Luckily Martin was together enough to grab the goatied bass player's phone number. A quick phone call was made the next day and he went over and met the pair again.

Of course, in the cold sober light of day, Fletcher realised exactly what was going on. This was John Squire and he'd left the fucking Roses and he wanted him to be in his new band. And he hadn't even realised the Roses had split. But then it hadn't even been announced yet!

John played him some of his porta studio demos of the new songs that he had – 'Happiness Is Egg Shaped' and 'Standing On Your Head – songs that could have been the backbone of the third Roses album. The only condition for joining the band he was told was to be 'independent and flexible'.

It seemed an easy enough ticket and he was in. 'Meeting Stuart just hours after I'd left The Stone Roses can't be just coincidence,' Squire offers quietly. 'It was fate.'

Squire had the kernel of a group. Now all he had to do was get a frontman!

A mate of John's was walking down York High Street when he spotted a busker. The shaggy-haired young man singing his heart out might be interesting. He put a call through to Squire who was equally taken aback. Good job he went to York! The place seemed to be teeming with band members.

That's lucky!

The 25-year-old Chris Helme had just returned from a busking tour of France in his own outfit, Chutzpah. Returning from the tour he had lived in a squat in Brighton with his girlfriend, robbing food from the local supermarket, an existence so meagre that he went back to York at the first opportunity.

Landing back on his feet he was back on the streets busking. Picking his spot outside Woolworths on Sunday afternoons it was a particularly exuberant version of the Stones' 'No Expectations' that caught the ear of the drunken mate of Squire's staggering past. He told Helme that Squire was looking for people and told him to send a demo tape and passport to this address.

John was, apparently, not that knocked out with the tape but still intrigued enough to go and check Helme out singing in Fibbers, the main circuit venue in York. Of course with so much riding on the 'audition' everything went badly wrong, the strings flew off his guitar, snapped by heavy-handed nervous strumming, he was well drunk and by the time he crashed into 'No Expectations' his eyes were screwed shut with the nerves, a mannerism that annoyed Squire no end.

Squire looked at the singer on the stage. Did he look right? After all, he was going to be the public face of The Seahorses, this was going to be the person who was going to personify the songs that John was writing. Helme looked like a busker, shaggy-haired, folky even – not hip, but then maybe that was what John was after, something away from the street hip that had been the Roses' ticket. Something more traditional.

Chris was given another chance to audition. A straight gig in Manchester at the Roadhouse, away from his mates, gave him another chance. Obviously there was something that intrigued Squire.

The Roadhouse audition went well and The Seahorses were now three. They retreated to Conniston in the Lake District to a cottage up in the hills and during that long hot summer of '96 started piecing together the début album.

While the rump of the Roses were self-destructing at Reading Festival, The Seahorses were putting the finishing touches to the tunes that would form the backbone of the album. John refutes claims that The Seahorses was somehow pre-planned during the final days of the Roses.

'There's only one song on *Do It Yourself, Standing On Your Head*, that was completed before I left The Stone Roses – but I didn't write it with the intention of it being the start of a secret store of songs that I could use for any solo project. It was just something I held back from *Second Coming* because I felt we had enough to work on at that time. Things were going so slowly I just didn't want to add another song to the pot. But looking back on it, it does seem strange that The Seahorses came together so quickly.'

The endless summer in the idyll countryside was broken by just one appearance. The now legendary Oasis show at Knebworth – the biggest ever rock gig by one band in the UK. The Roses' understudies had, by the summer of 1996, gone so ridiculously massive even they couldn't believe it. And here was John Squire as special guest during the spiralling psychedelic freak out encores of 'Champagne Supernova' and 'I Am The Walrus'.

'Here's John Squire . . . with Oasis,' an unbelieving Liam Gallagher grinned, still at heart the kid at International 2, as Squire leaned back and broke out into a massive explosion of guitar notes. The crowd went wild. What a perfect moment – two generations of Manchester colliding at this, the high water mark of the city's musical popularity.

Noel was equally impressed, 'He's playing all this mad Jimmy Page stuff and I'm thinking this is a moment in my life.'

DOING IT HIMSELF: SQUIRE COMPLETES THE SEAHORSES

The Seahorses also now had a drummer. Andy Watts was again pulled in from the fog of the York pub scene, a bespectacled, much travelled

Londoner who could sing as well as play drums. He was quickly assimilated into the line-up which was soon ready to play its first gigs.

They had announced their name to the press, attracting the attention of a band from Liverpool who had been going for years with the same name. There was a row and some sort of legal squaring up. Somehow the Geffen-backed Seahorses won the rights to the name. That's showbiz.

And finally. They were ready to go public.

How do you start again? From scratch? Well, you start from the bottom and work up.

Interest in The Seahorses was of course, high. But going out on a fully blown tour was not Squire style. Break it in from the grass roots. Work up.

Their first show was in North Wales at the Buckley Tivoli, the ornate hall that had been a circuit gig for many indie bands on the verge of the breakthrough. The gig showcased a band that was quite definitely trad rock, 'Dadrock' even. All the mid-Seventies hallmarks were there, the sort of music that punk had blown away rediscovered by the former fans of the movement. For John it was his natural terrain anyway, the melodic guitar hero based music of his pre-youth.

The next gig was in Greenock at Ricos, the gig booked by the talkative Roses fan Andrew McDermid who was also managing White Out at the time. Greenock, like nearby Glasgow, was staunch Roses country, and the gig, of course, was a hot sweaty affair. Andrew was quickly on the phone buzzing about the show, about Squire's guitar playing, about how good The Seahorses were. The young crowd at Ricos reared on the Roses' legend had no uneasiness about the guitar player's new safe direction, this generation was into their trad Rock . . . where else could the bands go after Britpop?

Late that autumn 1996 the band relocated to Los Angeles to record 'Do It Yourself' with Tony Visconti, the man who had produced T Rex and Bowie and a whole plethora of classic-sounding Seventies glam records. It seemed like an odd choice at first but not as odd as the other choice that Squire had.

'Tony was one of Geffen's suggestions,' Squire explains. 'I actually wanted to get Steve Albini but I was told they couldn't track him down.'

Albini had made his name on the US underground recording loud, raw powerful records. Recently he had burst into the mainstream with Nirvana's *In Utero*, a raw dark and uncompromisingly powerful record with a massive thumping drum sound that recalled the great Bonham's primal explosive drums. Despite what people say, Albini's recording really caught the band perfectly.

With Albini you got what you played, you felt you were standing right in the room with the band. His recording techniques, utilising suitcases of vintage mics he brought to the sessions and an ear for uncompromising sound; would have been perfect for The Seahorses – an unlikely marriage that would have pulled them away from being 'too safe.' But it wasn't to happen.

Squire enjoyed working with Visconti, as he told *Guitar Magazine*. Tony flew over to Manchester Airport and when we met him he was just a really nice bloke, none of the attitude problems you'd think you might get from a guy who's worked with Bowie and what have you. Because he was so down to earth I thought he'd be really good for the rest of the band, as they'd obviously not worked at that sort of level before.

'Tony was great in the studio. He's a musician himself and plays all sorts of instruments; the producers I've worked with in the past all came through engineering and didn't have a musical background, whereas Tony could converse in that language. There were no situations where, when a song comes off the rails, the producer just says: "It's not 'right'; can you do it again?" And again, and again . . . there were no abstract terms like that. Tony also had great organisational sense; he got us all in on time, basically. A lot of the mood aspect of the recording can be attributed to Tony.'

The resulting album, *Do It Yourself*, was a move away from the Roses' legacy as Squire pointed out to *Guitar Magazine*, 'I was very conscious of that time away. There was a philosophy with *Do It Yourself* of taking it back to basics. I didn't want this record to sound like a continuation of the Roses, a sequel to *Second Coming*; I wanted it to sound like a début album, so we contrived to capture the live sound and not spend too much time slicking it up and layering. *Second Coming* was just overworked . . . on the basis of the fact that we weren't a cohesive unit and we were spending just too long in the studio. The luxury of endless hours and endless overdubs meant the freshness was lost. Some songs on *Second Coming* were the third or even fourth recorded versions; things were lying around on master tapes from the first week of recording there was no drive there, no immediacy.'

The resulting album was an unadventurous set of catchy rock songs that saw it fly to the top of the album charts. Critics point out its safe trad nature, but what was anyone expecting? Squire was in his mid-thirties and the Roses had never been that experimental anyway, their whole schtick had been to make the familiar sound new, the traditional sound contemporary . . . from the *Second Coming* onwards it was obvious the direction the guitar player was heading. But there were some good songs on there like the anthemic 'Love Is The Law'.

In many ways the album is an escape from the dark heart of *Second Coming*, daft lyrics about weetabix and giant squid replace the negative twists that had underlined so many of John's words on the Roses' two albums; the tone was lighter, more poppy, more song-based. The album was a well-worked set of melodic guitar action. The post Britpop kids adored it. Here was the man that kicked off their scene and he was back and he was making music that slotted neatly into the retro nature of the mid-Nineties.

Eighteen-year-olds digging the same records as their polytechnic reared parents. Harking back to a time when rock ruled the earth and the guitar hero was the main conduit of rock'n'roll.

Squire had escaped from the Roses' legacy and was poised to release his first post-Roses record.

'Love Is The Law' was The Seahorses' début single, released on 28 April 1997. Flipped with Christ Helme's Beatle-tinged 'Dreamer' and Squire's own 'Sale Of The Century'. The single entered the UK charts at number three – it was Squire's highest chart position other than 'Love Spreads'. The Seahorses were top five and John Squire was back in business.

The band was going well. They toured the UK, the big halls, like Manchester Academy. I caught up with them there and the venue was rammed full and the atmosphere was pretty magic, as magic as it would be for the Ian Brown shows. The Roses' aura would cloak any of the ex members and was not just the exclusive preserve of Ian Brown.

The gig was typified by John unleashing huge guitar breaks moving on stage slightly, delicately, just like his idol Jimmy Page had done in Zep all those years ago. Chris Helme walked on to the stage to screams! He was considered a bit of a bohemian pin-up at the time!

The *Do It Yourself* album followed on 27 May. The reviews were a mixed bag, but then for every Squire record from *The Stone Roses* onwards that has been the case! The record entered the album charts at number two, with only the long-forgotten boy band buffoon Gary Barlow out-selling it.

The full track listing for *Do It Yourself* was 'I Want You To Know', 'Blinded By The Sun', 'Suicide Drive', 'The Boy In The Picture', 'Love Is The Law', 'Happiness Is Eggshaped', 'Love Me And Leave Me', 'Round The Universe', '1999', 'Standing On Your Head' and 'Hello', songs that continued in the Hendrix/Zep flavour that had so dominated John's late Roses work.

'Love Me And Leave Me' was co-written by Liam Gallagher of Oasis, the Burnage bother boys' frontman's first-ever songwriting credit ten full years after being the gobsmacked kid at the Roses' International 2 gig.

The second single from *Do It Yourself* was 'Blinded By The Sun'. Released in the UK on 14 July and hitting the charts at number seven it was the first ever 'A' side of any band that involved John but was not actually written by him. 'Blinded By The Sun' was written by Chris Helme and backed with Squire's 'Kill Pussycat Kill', and Chris's 'Movin' On'.

The next single, the 'Liam Gallagher one', pulled off the album caught the attention of the over-zealous self-righteous censors at MTV America, meaning a trip back to the studio to change a line. Originally 'Don't believe in Jesus', it is now wittily re-recorded as 'Don't Believe in Censors'. But that poleaxed the original meaning of the song as explained by Liam Gallagher in the middle of a particularly funny rant in GQ magazine (the one where he went on about fighting Sixties popstars in the middle of Primrose Hill).

'John Squire come round me house one night for some aspirin and we ended up having a rant – a bit of this, a bit of that – and the paracetamol was a bit too strong for him, so we wrote that song. I've had this thing in me head for ages – I don't believe in Jesus, I don't believe in Jah – I don't believe in religion basically. I was brought up going to church and after circumstances in my life changed, I thought – f*** Jesus, f*** 'em all. It was because of me Mam and her divorce, how she couldn't take the Body of Christ anymore. They're telling her it's a big sin, she can't go to heaven and all that bollocks. She's put her whole faith in the church, but where's their faith in her?'

Not as big a hit as the first two singles, the record peaked at number fifteen in the charts; the album meanwhile was selling strongly. Squire was now well established outside the Roses.

Four big singles and one big album in one year. The Seahorses were well on their way to becoming one of the mid-Nineties' major bands – not loved like the Roses, but capable of 'doing good business'.

But then it all started to fall apart.

The lopsided nature of the band with the superstar guitar player and the three York boys was always going to make it difficult to function. Watts was the first to go. He left for the over-subscribed 'musical differences' while, in Manchester, pundits were wondering just what it was with John and drummers! Watts had just had his first child and The Seahorses non-stop touring schedule may have been too much for him to cope with.

After a long search, they found 27-year-old Mark Heaney from Peterborough. Heaney had previously been in the army and played in rock and jazz bands, as well as doing some tuition.

Again The Seahorses went out and played a series of secret gigs to break in the new line-up and during which some new material was played. No new titles were given away except for one song, 'City In The Sky'. That summer they started work on the new album as well as popping out for the odd mid-bill slot at that summer's festivals. Performances that were described as 'pretty bluesy' were given at their T in the Park performance. More new song titles were revealed as 'Tomb Raid', 'City In The Sky', 'One In A Million' and 'Moth'.

However the second album never happened. In early 1999 The Seahorses split. Maybe Chris Helme was feeling edged out, it was a difficult situation to be in – the singer in someone else's band. He got a few songs in there, but he was trying to get the songs past John Squire, someone with their own mega track record of success. Chris quit and the band folded.

As Helme himself explained at the time, 'I was having to sing lyrics I did not want to sing. I didn't like his melodies, either, so the whole thing was unsatisfying. I started on the second album and didn't like any of it. I could see from a mile off it wasn't going to work. He's a good bloke, but we didn't see eye to eye musically.'

Chris Helme had tried to keep going after he had left the relative safety of The Seahorses, there was a low-key gig in London, a set of demos but outside the Planet Squire he was back down to earth with a bump. There were a few bitter exchanges in the music press between Helme and his former band mates. Noticeably, John Squire was absent from this debate. Helme explained to NME.com,

'I've been listening to Jackson Browne and early Van Morrison a lot, so there's no muso wanking like on Seahorses. I've got enough for two albums at the minute. It's confessional stuff.' Helme was hawking his demos around but there was still no record deal. He pointed out that it was because he was still tied in to his old management deal. 'It's tough when your career's in someone else's hands. But that's sorted now. I'm not desperately seeking a new deal, but I've been talking to a few people who seem to like what they've heard.'

He also clarified, to some extent, the split. 'There was a personality clash during rehearsals. When John came up with new stuff I didn't like his lyrics or tunes. I could have gone with it and made quite a lot of money, but I wasn't interested.'

The Seahorses' e-mailing list added an interesting adjoiner to this story with John Fletcher, father of Stuart Fletcher (bassist in The Seahorses) responding, 'I think it's a shame for Chris to slag off John Squire in the music press. Chris owes JS a lot – regardless of the fact that he wasn't keen on John's lyrics or tunes. However, it was these very things that turned Chris into a household (?) name, and to broadcast their differences just smacks of sour grapes. My personal opinion, is that Chris should have recorded the second album, having come so far with it, and then cited musical differences and left the band. I don't care what he says – the Horses were a great band, and to give the impression that he hated every minute does him no credit at all.'

It was only a few months after the split so the wounds were still pretty raw. The bad feeling spilling out into the press underlined one thing. The Seahorses was quite definitely over.

And John Squire's musical career had ground to a halt. And this time the singer had left him!

BACK TO THE DRAWING BOARD (SQUIRE STARTS AGAIN!)

Groundhog Day! Squire was starting from scratch with yet another band. Just like The Patrol, The Waterfront, the Roses, The Seahorses: time to find another singer to join Andy Couzens, Kaiser, Ian Brown and Chris Helme as the vessel for his songs, the mouthpiece for his lyrics.

John the instigator was left to pull the strands back together. And midsummer 1999, the ever-industrious guitar player acted swiftly.

He still had his deal with Geffen, no wonder with those record sales! The next couple of years Squire went to ground, prompting plenty of rumours, plenty of false trails.

At first there were rumours of the band being called Reluctance. In October ex-Verve bass player Simon Jones was working with John writing new material in a Manchester rehearsal room. The rhythm section was completed by ex-Seahorses drummer Mark Heaney. The name Reluctance seems to have been replaced by Skunk Works, named after a Californian weapons system plant where the U2 spy plane was developed for the American government, although this was just loose talk as it also seems that they never really decided on a name.

Oh well, there is still the Angry Young Teddy Bears!

An insider told the *NME*: 'It's all going really well apparently. Simon [Jones] is excited about it and it takes something special for him to get excited.'

There was talk that the new band were still working on some of the leftover Seahorses songs but that didn't seem that likely with the guitarist's avowed mission to keep moving forward.

Late August John Squire and Mani were spotted chatting back-stage at an Oasis party. John was still sporting the Jimmy Page-style beard that had sprouted in May. There was also a grass-roots rumour from a band in the same rehearsal rooms as Squire that they had overheard the new outfit rehearsing a version of Arthur Brown's 'Fire' and other songs which sounded like *Second Coming* era Stone Roses. Rumours, rumours, rumours . . . just like the *Second Coming* days!

For John, that summer was one step forwards and two steps backwards – first he finally found a new singer in ex-model Duncan Baxter, but then in August Jones and Heaney quit the project. Simon Jones's heart 'wasn't into it any more' and he quit.

The pair of them continued to work on the project. Speaking to sources very close to the 'band', I was told that the music was returning to the pure pop of the earlier Roses and was veering away from the heavyweight guitar workouts that had dominated Squire's works for the past decade. Good job, as in December there was talk that Geffen had dropped Squire from its rosta, although, typically this was unconfirmed.

As 1999 rolled into 2000 John Squire disappeared further and further from view. There were occasional snippets of information round town about what John Squire was up to.

In February 2000, in an interview with the *Guardian* newspaper, Ian Brown revealed that John Squire sent him some Maltesers with a note saying, 'I still love you' while he was in prison. Apparently when they were kids they used to give each other a box of Maltesers for Christmas.

2001 and John Squire is back out there in the mythic hills, growing beards and putting together bands. Can the legendary guitarist pull it off again?

MANI: HAVING IT LARGER THAN LARGE – THE ROGUE ROSE JOINING PRIMAL SCREAM, KNOW WHAT I MEAN!

Perhaps the greatest free transfer in the history of rock'n'roll, Mani's move to Primal Scream was so perfect, so right, that it couldn't have been planned any better.

I mean, what other band in the UK had punk rock roots, working-class righteousness, a psychedelic pop edge, a huge vested interest in the house scene and a completely ramshackle anarchic mode of operation! No sir, the Primals were perfect for the mighty bassman and after a series of phone calls put in place even before the infamous last stand at Reading, he was planning his move.

Not that Mani would ever let his old muckers down. To the end he was still firing on full Roses cylinders at Reading, giving it his usual 100 per cent, thrusting his bass at the crowd.

In the weeks after the show he made his mind up fast. It was obvious that the Roses game was up so he jumped ship and moved to the only other band that would accommodate his punk-funk bass and wildass lifestyle. He announced, 'After much speculation I've decided, along with Ian Brown, that it's time to end the Roses saga. I will be joining Primal Scream, who are one of only three other bands I would ever consider joining. I'm absolutely delighted and am relishing the opportunity of playing with Bobby and friends.'

It seemed like the most natural thing in the world. Mani had arrived, and with him a new leash of life for Primal Scream.

Mani had been noting the Scream's progress throughout the years. 'I'd always been aware of the Scream. Just from the fact we're all music lovers. We were always listening and conscious of what was going on around us. There were a lot of parallels between The Stone Roses and Primal Scream, quite similar backgrounds musically and culturally. It's kismet that I ended up with them.'

The first meeting between the two godheads of British acid rock'n'roll punk rock was in Brighton way back in 1988.

'I probably first met them in an ecstasy haze, probably in the Hacienda. I can remember when we went down to play at the Zap in Brighton in '88, '89, and someone had forgotten my bass amp and all my equipment, and there were about thirty people at the gig – a large contingent of which were the Scream mob. I think we did something like four songs and just went "Fuck it, we can't be arsed" and steamed off. Bob remembers that gig as a blinder, full of attitude.'

And when the call came from the Scream camp for Mani, at the tail end of the Roses, his exuberant spirit was just what the group needed.

Gillespie, Innes, Young and Duffy had just put together an eight-track studio getting near Creation's office in north London and were together ideas for a new album. Or at least Innes their guitarist was.

It was difficult, slow-going. Alex Nightingale, manager at the time, pointed out. 'A lot of people had written them off and eventually they started saying "Fuck it, we'll come out fighting." Then there was Mani – a godsend. The best signing since Cantona.'

'When Mani joined us, it seemed like a band again,' agrees Bobby Gillespie. 'I think if Mani hadn't joined I would never have played live again. He was like a nuclear fucking explosion. He saved our lives.'

Certainly Primal Scream needed the energy of Mani

And what better band could he join.

Their career had run in parallel with the Roses with ups and downs, punk roots, creative highs and lows, acid house, post acid house, rejuvenate guitar music, a political edge; uncompromising hard ass bands with soft melodic songs, intelligent scowling presences on *Top Of The Pops*.

Fuck, where else could Mani go?

After their ground-breaking *Screamadelica* set of 1991 when they seemed to be setting the agenda with the Roses and the Mondays, the Primals had seemed to hit the same sort of slowdown. There had been *Give Out But Don't Give Up*, a far rockier affair, a record pasted by most reviewers who labelled the band 'dance traitors,' but one that stands up really well listening to it years later. 'Rocks' is still one great shit-kicking slice of rock'n'roll and the term 'dance traitors' has to be considered a bit of a joke when you hear this track live in a club electrifying the dance floor. It does open the debate of what dance music was anyway. Dance is not just acid house. Let's not forget The Rolling Stones are probably the world's biggest dance band! Add on to this 'Jailbird' and a few other choice cuts and you ignore a record that is far better than most people seem to remember.

The only problem is that as good as the Primals rock music is, the expectations are for something more, something darker and more dangerous.

After all this is a band that has singer Bobby Gillespie wacking dustbins in a liftshaft in a vague approximation of German noise avant-gardists Einsterzende Neubaten. And the fevered mind of reticent guitar player Andrew Innes, who even then was learning how to fuck with the controls in the studio.

Throw into this mix a bass player free of the constraints of his beloved band and hungry to create some new space for himself and you've got a hot mix.

All through Mani's Roses stint there had been hints of something a bit darker and more twisted, a bit more underground than the Roses pop template allowed. Hints of Can would occasionally bubble up to the surface in 'Fool's Gold' or 'Something's Burnin'.

Unleashed in Primal Scream and allowed to run amok in their seemingly impossible agenda of criss-crossing the greats from *Bitches Brew* Davis to Can, to PIL, to the MC5 and Mani was very much in his element.

Now that the Primals had decided to throw off the yoke of 'classic songwriting' and go back to their post-punk roots of fucking with the form they suddenly opened wasps' nests of sound.

The first single from this new line-up was the stunning 'Kowalski' single, a piece of sound driven by one killa Mani bass line. Gillespie's whispered vocal hints of paranoia, the hook 'soul on ice' a quote from Eldridge Cleaver's biography of Marcus Garvey.

The fact that the single was a Top Ten hit proved the strength of Primal Scream's following and the hunger for some brave music out there. When the *Vanishing Point* album followed, it blew open the Primal Scream debate.

No longer considered a burned out bunch of lost indie rockers, Primal Scream were now entering new territory. For some it was their hangover album, the comedown from the acid house high to the smack and filth infested mid-Nineties hellhole, it was the necessary kickback after all those highs. A bleak, freaked record it was electric soundscapes and dark, dank paranoias, like PIL's incredible *Metal Box* from 1979. This was the record that came out after the party but was somehow still made with enough resolute strength to capture the strange dark hue of the period.

For such a non-conformist, dark-hearted howl of a record to go to number eight was fantastic.

Of course, being in Primal Scream, life was never easy. There were bizarre, untogether gigs with a drum machine, a dark descent into a chemical hell and messed up lives. Post *Vanishing Point* was a bumpy ride but they eventually got their live show together. Harnessed those demons.

How the fuck they managed to regroup and record the amazing *XTRMNTR* is a testament to their inner strength. The album is perhaps the key British release of the past ten years, the only major league rock'n'roll band that seems to be in touch with the modern world – no fucking Beatles, or fucking Gerry And The Pacemakers, a tuff-as-nails V-sign to the establishment – political and musical.

Their 2001 tour saw some awesome gigs – Bobby hunched up waif-like on the mic like John Lydon when he was cool; the added figure of My Bloody Valentine's Kevin Shields adding his warped guitar noise over the top like he had done on the recent album, just added to the insanity. Soundchecks with punk covers, gigs that reached at all points of the rebel music universe, how fucking good could a band get. And Mani, the garrulous king of the bass virtually fronting the show!

So what if they had lost all their money due to some problems with their book-keeping, that they had to sack their manager, that their long-term record label Creation didn't exist any more. Primal Scream seem to thrive in a crisis.

And through it all is the bass player, swinging the bass around, driving the songs, virtually fronting the band, shouting good times at the crowd, living the rock'n'roll life to the full hilt and playing some great bass at the same time.

Offstage he is still Mani popping up all over town. Good times. Good tunes. Now and then he will issue a rallying call to the rest of the Roses to get together for some festival, go out on a high note, bury the hatchet, show 'em who's the best . . . Unfinished business he likes to call it. Anyone else prepared to pick up that baton?

RENI: 'JOHN THE BAPTIST' – THE BEARD YEARS

In 1993 wandering through town I bumped into Reni. The cheeky scamp was mooching down Oxford Road unrecognised by the passing pop kids. Kicking his heels in a pair of baggy jeans and deck shoes. It had been a few years since I'd seen him, in fact it seemed like another pop lifetime since anyone had seen the Roses.

They had disappeared deep into Wales and then, er, nothing.

As we walked down Oxford Road and towards the Salutation in Hulme where the penniless drummer scabbed a drink off me and sat out in the sun, Reni talked about the album and how he was not even going to drum on it. 'I'm into programming now,' he explained. 'I don't need to have my drums on the record,' he added as I wondered why it was taking so long to make the record. Reni revealed that he was taking his drums off the already recorded songs and replacing them, and that the band was going to go 'in a Fool's Gold' direction.

Two years later the album finally came out and after a brief promotional tour Reni quit the band.

In the years after he left the Roses Reni has disappeared into a mythic rock'n'roll half-life. Rumours preceded the drummer who was actually living quietly in Whalley Range bringing up his kids and getting his own music together. Everyone wondered why he quit – was it drugs? was it heroin? was it money? was it a personality clash?

There has never been any kind of explanation. Just a fistful of myths.

Drugs and the ongoing smack theory can be put to rest. Reni never dabbled in the brown . . .

Perhaps the money issue could have been a problem, with most of the credits taken by Brown and Squire and by Squire himself on the second album. It didn't leave much change for the rhythm section. And we're not talking about your average rhythm section here. Mani was a killer bass player and Reni was as already noted, one of the greatest rock'n'roll drummers that ever came out of Blighty. Lob on to that his crucial backing vocals and you have to wonder about the band's royalty arrangements!

More likely than anything it just seems that Reni was frozen out of the band by the increasingly dogmatic nature of John Squire's songwriting . . .

The endless jams in Rockfield between Reni and Mani had been pretty well ignored and *Second Coming* eventually ended up being a near John Squire solo record.

And so to Whalley Range where he's spent the past few years in his upstairs studio working on tunes. A whole mountain of songs have been piled up, with Reni singing and playing guitar in the outfit.

'You've got to remember that Reni was always a brilliant guitar player,' points out Pete Garner who was actually playing bass with Reni for a year in 1997.

They hooked up a rehearsal room and started putting a band together properly. Rumour to be trading under the name of Hunkpapa for a few months, it looked like Reni was ready to emerge from the shadows again.

'But Reni is so meticulous,' points out a friend. 'He wants to get everything completely note perfect before he lets it out. The stuff I heard sounded spot on but he still wasn't happy with it.'

The band continued to rehearse into 1998 but then Pete left . . . and rejoined . . . and left again! It seemed like a weekly occurrence. Pete and Reni just couldn't get on, stuck in the same room, stuck in the same band. Eventually Pete left for good, happier just to be mates with Reni than play in the same band as him.

Since then Reni has carried on working with the new drummer and retreated back to his bedroom 8-track polishing those songs up. There was even a demo tape floating around . . .

During the late Nineties Reni would pop up now and then. Bizarrely he and Pete appeared on a local Granada TV programme for a short interview. Reni was long-haired and big-bearded, looking like a wild man from the mountains and certainly filling the part of the long lost musician, half returning from some sort of self-imposed exile. But then Pete left again, although there was no real fallout, and they are still mates. Reni recruited local sound engineer Tom Evans to play bass with him but has yet to get a full line-up

Ian Brown noted Reni's drastic change of appearance. 'He's got big hair and a beard and I call him John The Baptist.' Ian also pointed out. 'There's every possibility that we'll play together. I was jamming with Reni last week. He's now singing, playing guitar.' There was low level talk that Reni may be joining Brown in some sort of capacity either live or in the studio. In the end Ian used the Rockfield jam with Mani as 'Can't See Me' on his *Unfinished Monkey Business*.

There is a bootleg of his band floating around, tight melodic songs, touches of The Police, the powerful melodies of Love, clever songs, a blues rock, like Led Zeppelin in their non-metal moments. The tape has gone round the majors, there is talk of deals. There are songs called things like 'Kaleida', 'Soul Full' and 'Savvy'. There was talk of a single called 'Selective Indignation'. But just how hungry is Reni? The man had children, rock'n'roll can seem a bit pointless when the real world takes over.

Six years in the making, finally, Reni was ready. His band, the Rub were out on the circuit. A bunch of dates in the spring of 1991 met with a mixed response. But there were glimmers of something here. Finally the last Rose had emerged from the mod shadows.

In a Foo Fighter to Nirvana style stepping out from behind his kit, Reni was fronting his new outfit proving those rumours of guitar skills and vocal ability were more than mere chit chat.

In Manchester at the Hop and Grape the tight packed room had gone crazy, there was a rush of electricity, some mealy mouthed scally yob had got the microphone and was shouting 'give it up for Reni' and generally larging it about on stage like he does this sort of thing for a living . . . 'Fuckin' hell it's Mani!!' correctly observes the geezer next to me and indeed it was the other half of that legendary Roses rhythm section doing the compere bit, bigging up his former sticksman.

The Rub shuffled on stage and started picking out some sort of groove and there he was, Reni, looking good for his thirty-five odd years – fag in gob, the trademark smirk, cockiness intact picking out the incessant groove of The Rub's very rhythmic muse.

The crowd, of course, were with him, hoping for the third coming. This was Manchester and Manchester had always loved the Roses (whether they are written out of the Hacienda film or not). The Roses inspired a special bond with their fans and a decade later they are still there willing them on.

No one knows the tunes and to be fair its hard to pick them out at first. There's a couple of shimmering pop moments that could be early Roses, like pop thrills, most of the rest of the stuff sounds like jammed out workouts, a band feeling its way round riffs. In these hands it works a lot better than that sounds, there's a tightness about the music and a hypnotic adherence to the first rule of groove – a groove that was less funk than rhythm guitar, chopping onto the snare tuff backbeat of prime-time power pop.

Reni, of course, has a good voice, anyone listening to the Roses knows that, and you can hear that sweet croon that underpinned the Roses classiest moments picking out what tunes there are.

For some reason Reni stands on the side of the stage, not in the mddle, whilst in the background lurks Pete Garner, the Roses first bass player, shaking maracas. It's the first time he and Reni have shared stage space since the Manchester International way back in 1987, but then Pete was a mate and he nearly played bass in The Rub.

Keep it in the family, Roses style.

Reni was back, but where this one was going to go was anyone's guess.

But no matter how great this project could get, there was the nagging feeling that you want to see Wren behind his drums, the man with a god-given gift . . .

And therein, ha! ha! lies the rub!

The rest of the tour brought many different reactions . . . fans looking for the meat melodic touches and the effortless grooves of the prime-time Roses were left feeling baffled, whilst some were prepared to embrace whatever direction Reni was choosing to take and all were waiting for the first recorded stuff (unreleased at the time of writing) to make their final decision.

Reni, the perfectionist, is there every day, working on his music and one day, when he is ready he will release it. But you can't help feeling that no matter how good his new band is and no matter what a great singer he is, you just want to see him sat behind a drum kit again. There just aren't enough drummers who are that good, are there?

STONE ALONE! IAN BROWN

The Seahorses were in full flow, Mani was rocking out with the Primals but where was Ian Brown?

The icon of baggy, the touchstone of that generation seemed to have disappeared. The whole messy demise of the Roses seemed to have crushed his will to make music.

Of all four Roses Brown had the easiest and yet perversly most difficult set of choices in front of him. As the frontman he could easily gather up a band and get back out there again and yet as the only non-musician in the Roses he would find it difficult to make music.

If he wanted to make music at all.

He had last been spotted heading to Morocco, where his head was turned. His spiritual side strengthened in the Muslim country and his disdain for the decadent rock'n'roll lifestyle further bolstered by the way Morocco had been treated by hipsters in the last few years.

He witnessed the muezzin call to prayer – a powerful sound that cuts through daily life, people singing without any commercial purpose, purely spiritual, an expression of Islam. Stuff like that can affect you.

'It lifted me off my feet, like a Saturday afternoon when I was fourteen – it was so rough and raw, echoing off the walls. The most uplifting thing I've heard for a long time.'

A million miles away from the empty world of rock'n'roll. The new Brown was now fracturing into a myriad of contradictory parts; there was the spiritual Brown, the Koran-reading righteous anti-drugs and booze rock'n'roll street preacher who still had one foot inside the world of rock'n'roll; there was still the political animal now with an added Old Testament edge; and there was a commitment to speaking his mind, speaking the truth no matter who it might offend; a personal truth, his truth whatever it may be.

Less accepting of the bohemian types who have used North Africa to indulge their sensual whims, Ian comments, 'There used to be a thousand brothels in Tangiers. Westerners used to go to get smashed out of their faces, to pick up women and kids. '60s intellectuals and pop stars – they all went over there to abuse the people. William Burroughs, he was another bum. He abused his life and he wrote a book about it. There's nothing more boring than hearing someone else's drug stories. But he's held up as some kind of literary great. For me, he was just a bum.'

Then there were reports of Ian returning to England. Going to ground. There were rumours of beards and biblical style forty days and forty nights soul searching, reading the Bible. Says Ian, 'I know about the lies and the abuse that goes on in organised religions. But yes, I've read the Koran. Me sister bought me it in 1991. It's a beautiful book.'

Ian spent months reading religious wisdom and smoking Sensi (the strongest draw) with a Rastaman righteousness and the deep spiritual vibe that burns from classic Jamaican music – from Dub, to Ska, to Reggae, to Dancehall, to Ragga. Y'know that biblical righteousness combined with the anger of Babylon, the cry for freedom tempered with occasional sexism and homophobia. A weird and wild mass of contradictions, like the Bible itself. How far Ian Brown was into this trip was open to speculation. He had certainly picked up on the anti-decadence schtick, the anti-rock'n'roll lifestyle arrogance. There was even talk of him becoming a gardener! Of giving rock'n'roll up completely.

'I'd seriously considered gardening. Fuck it, everything I'd believed in was finished. John had left me. Me best mates were robbing money off me. I had summonses up to here. I didn't want to know any of it. Fuck it, I'll do gardening for old people. But then I'm going out and kids are coming up saying "When are you going to do something?" In the end, I thought I probably should.'

Manchester has produced its fair share of musical mavericks over the years. Unconventional musicians who bludgeon their own way through the rule book and end up with their own style of music. Post Roses Ian Brown wasn't about to change this.

Brown was caught between two stools. It was pretty inevitable, being the virtual spokesman of a baggy generation and a turn of the decade icon, he was pretty well placed to get some sort of solo career off the ground. On the other hand the near mythic status that he had accrued since The Stone Roses was going to be a huge burden on him.

Expectations had been high for the second Roses album, expectations that had only resulted in disappointment.

Burned out, Ian Brown retreated to Lymm and grew a beard.

The unpleasant end of The Stone Roses had left a foul taste in his mouth. He was thirty-four, an unemployed icon, no record deal and a fistful of boring business problems.

It was a good time for some sunshine. Time to bail out. As Ian told *Record Collector*: 'After the split I went to Morocco. I felt great while I was there. I was away from the west . . . I could sit back and look at what the Roses did; I was always looking forward, I never looked back during the Roses, and I could now look back on Spike Island or when we played in New York or whatever. That cleansed me. And then I came back. I said to myself, okay, I've done my bit, John doesn't want to continue, I finish it – No, sorry, that came after Reading. Cressa, who used to dance with us, he said to me, people say it's not the Roses anymore, you have to finish it. So I went to Morocco, came back and it was winter '96.'

And the music just started to seep out . . .

'And I felt like, I'm gonna stick in me room, put carpet upon the walls, I won't go out until I've got at least ten or twelve songs together. And that's what I did. So by this time last year it all came to an end, I booked into a studio and started to record it.'

Back home Ian started messing about on his roughly constructed porta studio. Buying bits of equipment. Messing about with gear and bits of tunes. He set up his own small studio, read the manuals and started to make some music. Never the musician in the Roses, Brown was obviously in the most difficult position to kick start a solo career from scratch.

He had spent some time during *Second Coming* learning the guitar. Some rudimentary chords plucked from the Bob Marley Song Book, chords to get by, something to build songs on to.

He was working at his own pace, letting the creativity come naturally. He'd been dropped by Geffen but that was cool – no more schedules, no more stupid concessions to industry standards. Just making your own music at your own pace.

A few months after Reading, Aziz dropped by. 'After Reading there was a nothingness. Everybody vanished. Nobody could be contacted. All there was was this bad press. That was all I ever heard. Mani was first to jump ship . . . He was always planning this anyway. He was also in a meeting with Alex Nightingale before Reading. I couldn't get in touch with anyone after that. I called round at his [Ian's] house. The first time I'd seen him for ages and he said that he wasn't doing it no more, he'd had enough. After that I called round as a mate. I'd have a guitar with me like always and showed him some tunes, some chords. Pretty soon we were writing tunes, jamming. I had a couple of things like the "My Star" riff and the bits of things that became "Corpses" and he had got the lyrics for "Corpses" and "My Star".'

They quickly got working upstairs in Brown's mini studio. Says Aziz, 'He's got a little set up in his bedroom. Got all the gear together, working out how to use it. I'd help out with programming. Got him going. He'd switch on the 8-track. Couple days later he'd come up with the finished lyrics for the songs. They were great lyrics, really made the songs. I went back to my house on my porta studio and finished the music to "My Star". I took it back to Ian's and we worked a bit more on it there. Later on in the proper studio we added over dubs. NASA loops and military drums. We'd go to the house to do his stuff, four-tracks of vocals and harmonica.'

It was the first time that Ian Brown had written with anyone else apart from John Squire. Now he was out on his own writing by himself or collaborating with Aziz or whoever was on hand, learning as he went along. Stumbling along, creating a record from scratch. These were all factors that helped to give the songs that were coming together their idiosyncratic flavour.

Almost as a reaction to the years of polish and hanging about that had gone into *Second Coming*, this record was coming together fast. A record that was reflecting exactly where he was at.

Against this burst of creativity John Squire was achieving take-off with The Seahorses – selling out tours and records, playing onstage with Oasis at their record-breaking 1996 Knebworth gig, carrying their guitar flag that he had unfurled for *Second Coming*, leading the post Roses breakout.

And while John was out there succeeding Ian's songs were nearing completion and studio time was booked. The Roses actually owned their own studio, the Rose Garden in Bury.

Fleeting from studio to studio, they worked on the tunes. The record gradually gained its own momentum.

It was clear that Brown was operating on his own agenda. This was not a band thing. An ad hoc series of musicians passed through the sessions. Some of the tracks were worked out by Brown utilising his rudimentary guitar skills, scrubbing basic chords out of his acoustic guitars, some were brought to the party by Aziz, the master session player with a heap of unused licks from his frustrating sideman years; some were brought in by Robbie Maddix and Nigel Ipinson; some parts even came from a Roses jam between Reni and Mani from the *Second Coming* sessions. Scraps of music, bits of sound, anything that caught Brown's attention and needed turning into a song . . .

Now the deal was done with Polydor. They knew how to handle this situation – just leave the man alone. Brown delivered the album. Most labels would have scoffed at the raw music handed over, but Polydor knew that they were on to something good. After all, the Roses' mystique had grown stronger in the years since the final collapse. Although many in the music business considered Brown burned out, a relic from the past, John Squire was getting looked on as the true torch bearer of the Spirit of '89.

But the kids, the generation that had grown up with the Roses were waiting for the singer to get back in touch.

The rumours of the record deal and the upcoming releases sent a buzz of excitement round.

Ian Brown was going to be back in business but what, exactly, was he going to sound like?

It was easy to work out what John Squire would be doing but no one knew what sort of songs Ian Brown wrote. This record could go anywhere.

And when they started playing 'My Star' on the radio you could feel the relief. It sounded like the Roses, all guitars and husky vocals and a great melody to boot.

'MY STAR'

The release of 'My Star' in January 1998, three years after *Second Coming* broke a long silence for Brown. As the pre-release tapes floated round eyebrows were raised. For a start it was a fantastic slice of pop music. Built around Aziz's descending guitar shape copped from The Beatles' often-raided 'Dear Prudence'. As a slice of guitar pop it was easily the equal of anything that the Roses themselves had recorded and fitted easily into their canon of sombre majestic guitar pop.

The dark-hearted tune was underlined by Brown's convincing vocal, it was swiftly noted that this was a deeper darker voice, a new voice, much less the angelic rush of yore, the fallen choirboy that had soundtracked the kings of the baggy blitz. Brown sounded more mature, he also sounded smokier, lived-in.

On 'My Star' Brown was picking up the political baton put down at some point during the long months in between the two Roses albums. 'I see it more as social comment than politics. I've always been principled. I was brought up that way. The song's just pointing out that we have these wonderful space programmes, but they're mainly used for military purposes. It's vitriolic, but positive as well. I'm interested in the fact that two-thirds of people on the earth don't have enough to eat, but that billions are spent on rockets and bombs.'

In the two years since the Roses had imploded at Reading Festival, the musical landscape had shifted somewhat. The Britpop/baggy whatever-you-want-to-call-it scene was fast coming off the rails. Boy bands were beginning their never-ending dominance of the charts, the Oasis hangover was still in full effect and The Verve, fronted by former Roses fan Richard Ashcroft (who had been a regular face on the '89 breakthrough tour) were the biggest outfit in the so-called 'indie' genre. Their hit 'Bitter Sweet Symphony' became the anthem of the year.

From the release of the single to the album, Ian Brown set out on a non-stop round of interviews. This was a very different plan of attack than the Roses days. Instead of the guarded interviews, Brown seemed like a man who wanted to get a few things off his chest.

Sizzla is the charismatic new king of reggae, yet another stunning twist in the never ending musical production line from the Caribbean island. Jamaica, with its endless source of great music from Soca, to Mento, to Ska, to Dancehall, to Reggae, to Dub, to Ragga – is a small place with so much musical talent.

Sizzla was giving Brown plenty of inspiration. He was talking in a deeper, more clipped, hoarse voice, talking about the Bible, coming over on the spiritual tip. Gone was the clean-cut pop star of the Roses days, Ian Brown in the late Nineties was Old Testament spiritual mystical, like a dub prophet. 'My Star' gave little clue to this kind of talk. As it turned out, it was the closest musically to the Roses on the upcoming album, a classic slice of shimmering guitar with that strange dark undertow that always lurked in the background of the Roses' prettiest tunes.

His musical taste was a long way away from Brit white boy indie and in interviews it showed! Brown was slating every other band on the scene. The bands that had been inspired by the Roses were getting the sharp edge of his tongue. He was openly bemused at Tim Burgess, scornful of Oasis and damning of indie music in general. He was shouting up hip-hop and ragga.

The interviews also showed a very human side to Brown. Obviously still feeling the hurt from the exit of his former best mate John Squire from The Stone Roses, he was laying into his former partner in pop.

It's always difficult for any fan of any band to watch their former heroes tear each other apart in the press. For many long time Roses followers, the vicious digs at Squire seemed to be very out of character – after all the band had presented a united front, they were the ultimate pop gang, close-knit, us-versus-them, 'the-band-against-the-world' type of outfit. For the press it's great copy and for the disinterested it makes great visceral reading.

The Roses' long, slow, split had left its scars and Brown was displaying them in public. Obviously very pissed off by the manner of John's departure Ian Brown was giving no mercy. Other features of the new Brown was an anti-drug stance. He still may have smoked draw but it was the man-made drugs he railed against and cocaine especially. Cocaine was by 1998 enjoying a fast rise in hipness, London was caught in a snow storm, people who never used to take drugs were hogging the toilets at parties, cocaine was greasing the wheels of the music industry.

His anti-drug stance goes right back to the late Seventies, when the Pistols drew a line between themselves and the previous hippie generation with their anti-drug attitude. It left a spark in the minds of a new generation.

At first the Roses didn't even drink, but were, in classic punk style, speed freaks. This was reflected in their wired, intense performances and Brown's wild stage antics. When they switched to marijuana their whole schtick slowed down, the music was tinged with psychedelic edges and the band were motionless on stage.

Brown has remained there.

TOO MUCH MONKEY BUSINESS, PART 2!

Released in March 1998, *Unfinished Monkey Business* came as a surprise. Wrong-footed by the tumbling arpeggio near Roses pop of 'My Star', some people seemed to be expecting a *third* coming, a guitar-laden series of obvious songs. Some people were going to be very surprised.

Brown may have been the Roses frontman but no one was sure if he was a songwriter as such. He may have lugged that steam organ over to John Squire's house to work on vocal melodies in the old days, but did he actually write songs or just vocal melodies?

Monkey Business, with its raw production, half-finished songs and open heart vitriol and anger, came on like John Lennon's first couple of post-Beatles albums. Truth and plain honesty were the order of the day. The music was halfway between the grandiose Roses guitar assaults and the electronic post acid house daze that Brown was hooked into.

There were songs about former bandmates. Three accusatory songs that left little to the imagination. Brown wasn't beating about the bush.

'Ice Cold Cube' was a reworking of the song that featured at those last Roses shows in '96, the song title a nickname that Reni had for John and the lyrics a personal dig at the attitudes of coke-snorting associates; but no one is saying if it's specific or general.

'What Happened To Ya' co-written by Nigel Ipinson and Robb Maddix, makes the listener wonder if the song is written about John Squire. But the lyrics were not even written by Brown but by the two guys who wrote the song. Says Ian, 'I've got a feeling that at the time that they wrote it, certain situations had been mentioned, yeah.'

And finally 'Deep Pile Dreams' sneers at the dumb rock-star lifestyle, the temptations of luxury and powders and there's even a personnel remonstration here. Says Ian, 'I think my mind had fallen into that category, definitely. We'd been given too much love; too many people believed in us.

But Brown was a smoker, surely that was as mind altering as cocaine? 'No. I smoke weed. You can't ban a plant. It's a natural thing – it comes from the earth. Whoever heard of banning a plant? I've got a friend who was taken to court for growing it, and he refused to plead unless they changed the charge from growing marijuana on common land to growing marijuana on God's earth.'

The album came as a shock. The looseness, the toughness, the growing-up-in-public sound, made it very much a début album. Compared to the over-produced *Second Coming* it was a turn in a very different direction. Brown seemed almost determined to make this record his and if that meant ditching those tedious long hours of sitting around doing fuck all in the middle of the Welsh countryside, then all the better for it. Ian told *Hot Press* in an excellent 1998 interview, 'I didn't know if I could make anything musical. I didn't want it to sound like punk. But I wanted to destroy the mystery of sound production and the pretentiousness of musicians. That's what I was after. Where's this singer who can't sing? Now he's playing all the instruments.'

Gathering up an ad-hoc collection of players from his current inner circle and learning as he went along Brown was wearing a lot of hats on this record. Songwriter, musician, producer . . . it would have been easy for Brown to have grabbed a bunch of cold session faces and put together a slick bunch of tunes.

He could have also bluffed his way through on his own and done it all himself. But with Aziz knocking on the door and other willing players a phone call away, a mixture of faces could only benefit these ideas.

Ian explained his ad-hoc set-up to *Record Collector*, 'I couldn't have done it all myself. I'm not a virtuoso. But I play bass, acoustic guitar, keyboards, drums, harmonica, and a trumpet! Then there's Reni, Mani, Simon Moore, a brilliant drummer, Aziz, Nigel Ipinson, keyboardist with the 1995–96 Roses. I've got the buzz now, I am writing all the time.'

Brown himself also continued to learn how to play guitar and a whole pile of other instruments. Although he is still a pretty rudimentary guitar player, having Aziz on board opened up a lot of possibilities. Brown himself was buzzing on working with Aziz. 'Aziz plays on six tracks, he's ɔ-written four. He's perfect for me because he doesn't drink and he doesn't ɔake drugs. And he'll chat.'

Post Roses his musical crash course continued. As he went along he started writing songs. Picking up scraps of melody from this rudimentary guitar playing, finding his way through songs, creating his own pile of tunes.

But this was a very personal effort with a loose ragbag of musicians and mates and with a lot of the programming and playing done by himself (including a return to the bass guitar on a couple of tracks, the instrument he had first picked up a couple of decades earlier in The Patrol). The album had a home-made feel to it, kinda like McCartney's or Lennon's débuts.

The record was very much Ian Brown. There were teasing touches of pop brilliance on 'Corpses In Their Mouths' and 'My Star', the incessant hook of 'Nah Nah', wandering drum machine driven workouts like 'Lions' and a set of lyrics that seem to strike out in many different directions.

Many thought 'Corpses' was another Brown put-down of John Squire. A vitriolic attack on cocaine was considered by some a continuation of his interviews when he discussed his alleged accusations of John Squire's drug intake but again he denied this. Says Ian, 'I didn't write that one . . . that's about girls who hang round people in bands for cocaine.'

Mani and Reni provided the link with the Roses with their jammed groove from Rockfield sessions for *Second Coming* getting a reprise. 'Can't See Me' is many people's favourite track on the album, a missing link (ha!) between the Roses' funk of 'Fool's Gold', with more than a nod to the melody of 'Breaking Into Heaven' from the second album The drooling funk of the track is a neat hint of what could have been, the mythical 1991 Roses-second-album-that-never-was could have been a delicious groove workout.

'It's a DAT that I had from '95 of Mani and Reni. I play bass over the top of it. I phoned them up and said "Can I use it?" – and they were cool. There's every possibility that we'll play together. I was jamming with Reni last week. He's now singing, playing guitar. In '95, me and him were in New York and we saw this kid playing drums on Times Square. Reni was looking at this kid and he knew the kid was better than him. It gutted him. He didn't pick up his sticks for a year. But now he's playing drums better than ever. He's got big hair and a beard and I call him John The Baptist. "Can't See Me" is my favourite, yeah. Very fresh. We never followed up "Fools Gold" because John never rated it! He felt embarrassed to play the funk.'

The track itself, 'Can't See Me', sees Ian Brown the righteous soul surrounded by corruption and careerism. Brown drawls in his husky Manc take on patois. 'All Babylon all around. And those that are close, you can't

see who you are, and what you're doing. There's more to life than your o
selfish ambition.'

Brown himself played on several tracks. 'I spent last winter holed up
with a bass, an acoustic guitar and a drum machine, learning audio
techniques to add to the things I'd picked up over the years. The first
song I came up with was "Lions" on the acoustic. I thought – "I can do
this".'

'Lions', built around an incessant chanted hook and featuring Denise
Johnson's typically great counterpoint vocal, was the longest track on the
album. Its meandering structure makes it appealingly non-musical, a V-
sign to the tight structures and trad middle eight 'classic' songwriting of the
Beatle loving Britpop bores. There was method to the madness and built
into the story a typically Brown lyrical idea.

'I got the idea from the England–Germany game. I thought it was
pathetic, grown men crying. Years ago there was a religious programme on
BBC2, and they had a dread answering questions about his faith. And, as
the credits went up, this dread's beating his staff going "There are no Lions
in England." Why do they have lions in Trafalgar Square and on the
England shirt? There's never been any lions here."'

The sessions had started soon after the Roses' final, bitter fallout.
Muddling around on his home four-track, then getting help from Aziz and
from four-track to four-track, bedroom to bedroom, they worked up the
tunes.

The project was then moved to Forge Studios in Oswestry, a studio
chosen because Aziz knew someone who worked there and from there the
final recording and mixdown were put together in the valve studios of
Chiswick Reach.

Meticulously assembled with valve equipment, Chiswick Reach was
perfect for capturing the 'warm' end of the classic guitar bass and drums
line up. It was picked because most of the Trojan singles were recorded
there. It could even be used to warm up the dry hard sound of technology
and sample based tracks. It may have seemed like an odd choice of studio
for a key comeback album, being more used to wilful eccentrics and lovers
of the pure sound that its equipment gave to recordings. The sort of
musicians who went there to make records had little or no interest in any
kind of chart action. Cult underground maniacs who were more concerned
with the sound of their records than the tedious pop parade of the Top 30.

Says Aziz, 'Ian's philosophy was to use valve gear and record on to tape
not DAT . . . We transferred what we had on to two inch and added things.'

The album recorded, the offers were piling up. Some labels were ruled
out when they asked Brown to remix the album.

Brown was holding all the cards with the album. He was evading the
music biz rat-race.

I wanted to avoid it. In the end I paid for the record myself, finished it and said to the company [Polydor], "Here it is." I sold it to them rather than et them pay for the recording and have them telling me what to do. I said 'Look, I've got no band, I'm not planning any live shows. This is it.'"

Take it or leave it. How Manc!

The album was bagged in with a great picture of Brown pulling a mental face in a fuzzy snapshot. The title itself alluded to the fallout of the Roses and to Brown's media nickname . . . As Brown explained to *Record Collector*, 'When the Roses had disappeared, recording *Second Coming*, the press were desperate for any stories of what we were up to. The drummer from Dodgy told this *Guardian* journalist that I was making everyone call me "King Monkey". I thought it was really funny.'

Crashing in at number two, the album sold 300,000 copies. The King Monkey had now regained his throne!

. . .AND DOWN AGAIN!

And then in one single *Melody Maker* review Ian Brown well and truly blew his whole 'good relationship' with the press.

The off-the-cuff comment about homosexuality touched a raw pop nerve and had a whole legion of commentators out for Brown's blood. Just when it seemed that the whole pop scene had slumped to an apolitical disinterested party mode, Brown had kicked off one of the last great pop political debates . . .

The *Melody Maker* would invite some pop star of the day in to talk about that week's singles. Something to alleviate the boredom of doing the singles. Brown dutifully made Audioweb the single of the week and hated Prolapse the most and put it in the dumper. But that's not what that week's singles will be remembered for.

In the pile of singles was Divine Comedy, the earnestly ironic Irish outfit who were having a few mini hit singles at the time with their foppish Noël Coward lite pop. It set Brown off on a rant, the gist of which, as remembered by Brown in *Select*, is as follows (oddly enough Polydor, Brown's label will send you the whole press kit with the *Melody Maker* singles review page photocopied in it minus the controversial review!),

'Julius Caesar was known as every man's wife. Romans were homosexuals. The top Nazis were homosexuals. Greece was homosexual. Most of the things that we had to suffer, the teachings of the Greeks, the philosophers – they're homosexual men. Now when they opened the gymnasiums and stripped the young boys, these were homosexual practices. I'm sayin' that that's what the West has been built on. It seems like the biggest heroes in Britain are homosexuals. Elton John, Danny la

Rue, Noël Coward, whether you're from working-class people or v
you're the Queen Mother, you're looking up to these guys who're dr
up as women . . .'

Brown then added, 'You know what I'm saying, I'm not saying it's a
thing. I'm just saying that's the way it is . . .'

And then the shit hit the fan.

The letters page was deluged with complaints. Brown had stirred up a
hornet's nest of controversy. And the gist of what he seemed to be saying
was that the Romans' and the Greeks' powerbase was homosexual – it's
whether you take that to mean that there is some kind of link between
homosexuality, power and culture.

Brown claims that he was trying to make a point and that two
paragraphs on the singles page were not the right place to make that point.

And while that's certainly true, the gist of what he said had left him
branded as being homophobic and this was the same Ian Brown who went
on the Clause 28 march in Manchester years ago, not as a publicity stunt,
just one of many marchers who believed in fighting against the
oppression.

The shock was for most Roses fans who believed the band stood for
something more open-minded than this. Had Ian changed over the years?

To be fair the singles review was trying to say something about the
nature of European culture – the way it's built upon ancient empires, the
homosexuality angle was just an irrelevant added observation, not
something that's needed in this line of argument.

Whatever was trying to get said, it ended up being boiled down to 'Ian
Brown is homophobic' and it did his reputation no good at all.

The rest of 1998 seemed to see the tide of goodwill turn against Ian
Brown. Reviews seemed to get sour, his image was suffering even if his
record sales were still good. His 'truth attacks' in the press had stung; the
Britpop bands, the Manc bands, the baggy bands he had ostracised were
sniping back. People didn't like what they were hearing.

The people, though, were still enthralled and he was playing to packed
houses of devoted fans, many of whom would have been too young to have
been into the Roses in the first place.

TOO MUCH MONKEY BUSINESS: FROM RAGE TO 'B' WING

The summer had been spent touring. Brown had a cool band together, a
touring band that featured Aziz on guitar alongside Inder Mathura
(percussion), Simon Moore (drums) and Sylvan Richardson (bass). Ian
played a five-day sweaty club tour, followed by impressive appearances at
the 1998 Glastonbury Festival and V98.

there were shadows. Another problem collected earlier in the year going to rear its ugly head that autumn.

Ian Brown had thought the reaction to the Select article had been strong n what happened on flight BA 1611 from Charles de Gaulle Airport on 13 ebruary was going to really blow up! The case had hung around for months, orgotten by the take-off of the album, at the back of minds during the press controversy and then starting to loom again that autumn.

And when the details emerged in court it was obvious that things were not going to go well for Brown.

There they were, Brown and band, flying rock star class, all up front. There was an innocent bit of gesticulating, a stand-off and an arrest. Of course both sides have their own story to tell. In court the prosecution claims that the air hostess Christine Cooper, approached Ian Brown and his band thinking that he'd gestured for her attention. When she got there she realised they hadn't called for her attention and motioned with her hand apologetically. Ian was alledgedly abusive.

Pilot Martin Drake was called to the incident. According to the prosecution, Ian was also abusive to him.

The final incident and the one that was to cause Brown the most problems was, according to the prosecution, when the plane landed. He is said to have hammered on the cockpit door which prompted Drake to call the police.

Ian Brown, naturally, sees the whole thing very differently. He told *Select*, 'They said I was beating on the cockpit door as the plane was landing, yet they never charged me with endangering lives which, if I had have done it, they would have done.'

Aziz backs up Ian's story. But it was to no avail. No matter what you think of overcrowded planes, the way the big companies will resell your seat if you turn up 'late' – less 'air rage' more 'corporate air rage' – it's the loud-mouthed passenger that will always lose.

Getting off the plane Brown was arrested. 1998 was going to end on one motherfucker of a sour note.

Coming after a few months of various so-called 'air rage' incidents he didn't stand a chance in court. It was time to make an example of someone and Brown copped the rap.

Magistrates heard how Brown approached the door of the flight deck when the seatbelt signs were on and the plane was coming in to land, and knocked repeatedly for twenty or thirty seconds. Captain Drake radioed for police help after becoming concerned that someone was 'potentially attempting to break into the flight deck'.

Brown, who had denied the charges, asked magistrates to suspend the sentence for the sake of his two children, but was immediately taken into custody.

Sentencing magistrate Alan Frost said, 'Mr Brown, having regard to recent case law, we find that the offence is so serious that only a custodial sentence is appropriate. The words that you used were threatening, abusive and insulting, resulting in the stewardess's extreme distress. Had the pilot not locked the cabin door, other passengers' safety might have been in jeopardy. A relatively small incident may have had catastrophic consequences.'

He went down for four months.

I FOUGHT THE LAW AND THE LAW WON: BROWN GOES DOWN

'A hundred and ninety-eight . . . 199 . . . 200.'

Prisoner number B9311 was doing his sit-ups. His feet jammed under the metal rim of the bed, keeping in shape with the same relentless discipline that had pushed him through to his black belt in his youth.

It was November 1998 and Ian Brown was in Strangeways, the renovated and world-famous prison that glowers just to the north of Manchester City centre.

Strangeways, the prison that had hit the headlines back in the baggy days with the thirty-day sit-in on the roof, bang smack in the middle of the Manchester E party. The party spirit of Manchester even in that fuckin' jail! The whole city was going mad.

And who was that swaggering along the corridor, it was none other than Ian Brown, one of the prime motivators of that long gone era.

Now instead of writing anthems for the flared generation, he was getting knocked up at 7.30 AM, going down for his breakfast, and then spending the rest of the day in his cell doing sit-ups and press-ups followed by half an hour wandering round the yard, 'exercise time' and then half an hour 'association time' where the choice was a shower, watching TV or playing pool.

It's all a part of the dehumanisation, prison life. A tough regime.

And then it's back in the cell for hours a day. Long hours. Long empty hours which Brown fills in lyric writing, reading books like Eldrige Cleaver's *Soul On Ice*, the biography of black activist Marcus Garvey. Grabbing information, keeping his mind alert, avoiding his mind turning to mush.

Lights out at 8.00 PM. It's a disappointing scenario.

Is this how 1998 is to end? He'd gone from outsider to critically acclaimed hero. Then it was the bitter enemy of the rock'n'roll business, the man who hated all he had spawned and had fallen out bitterly with ex-band mates, the positives were fast turning into negatives. He was the now maligned 'homophobic', the bitter outsider, the press enemy, and finally prisoner B9311.

What a bizarre see-saw of a year.

And there was plenty of time to reflect on this in prison.

He'd been banged up since the end of the trial on 23 October, and then in the van en route to Risley he had heard the story of his own incarceration being read out on the news. A surreal situation. After a weekend in the notorious Risley he was moved to the more laid-back environment of Kirkham Prison. The last time he'd gone up the M55 was for Blackpool in '89. Now he was near Blackpool for some very different business.

Being the pop star in prison had its own problems. Sitting down for his first meal, a scouser had made a sneering threat, only to be shouted down by a Manchester ecstasy dealer that Ian knew back from '88, and guaranteeing Brown a certain passage of safety.

Brown was still hopeful. The appeal was in a week and he was bound to get out, the charge was ridiculous. Whoever heard of anyone getting four months for a bit of a stand-off on a plane?

But the appeal was thrown out and Brown was on his way to the grim Victoriana of Strangeways. Shunted from wing to wing, he even had a job putting screws into electrical components for cookers.

The governor of Strangeways confessed that his son was a fan and gave him a pen and told him to write some songs. So Brown came up with the words for 'Free My Way', 'So Many Soldiers' and 'Set My Baby Free', the eventual backbone for the album that he was planning for '99. The songs gave the album its flavour.

In the end he was put on B-wing and allowed out of his cell for twelve hours a day, wandering about, semi-free, signing autographs for fellow inmates, trying to avoid the guards who would try and wind him up, knowing that any retaliation would cost him twenty-one more days in the prison.

But the last two weeks had been mostly a laugh. Says Ian, 'It was like school dinnertime.'

And then halfway through the four-month sentence, he was up for parole, released and free to go home for Christmas. The prison was buzzing. Ian is still clearly moved by the experience. 'Kids were running up to me, giving me hugs, risking twenty-one more days in there. The love I got on that last night was equal to Spike Island.'

On the morning of Christmas Eve of the most chaotic year of his life, Ian Brown walked out of Strangeways, out of the prison gates then down past the run-down shops, past Victoria Station and then down Deansgate, Manchester's posh shopping street, unnoticed in the last-minute Christmas rush. He walked the length of Deansgate till his feet were sore, soft from eight weeks of sitting around in prison. He walked past Atlas Bar and then into Deansgate Station and got the train back to his parents' house, back to the south of the city.

Four days later he was with his Mexican girlfriend Fabiola, lying on a beach smoking a spliff, grinning his Cheshire cat grin.

A free man.

GOLDEN GREATS FOR A NEW MILLENNIUM

Washing those prison blues right out of his hair, Brown was swiftly in the studio putting together the second album.

The plan was to move on from the début, get some production on board, move further away from guitars, pull in some of those acid house flavours, make a record for the 21st century.

The result, *Golden Greats*, released 1999, was a resounding success and a massive move from *Unfinished Monkey Business*. A new direction.

Never one to rest on his laurels, Brown had started work virtually on his release from Strangeways.

Early in 1999, he was booked into Metropolis studios for sixty days, a very different recording environment than the first album, a different environment that is reflected in the record. The second Brown album was a big departure from his début. Indeed it was almost a reaction to the near lo-fi flavour of the début.

Richly produced by Brown himself and engineered by Tim Willis, the record left any kind of indie roots far far behind.

Not that this was an attempt to make a smooth record for the mainstream. *Golden Greats* resonates with darkness and reeks of claustrophobia, of prison and paranoia, haunted by bars and an increasingly vitriolic music press who were now viewing Brown very differently than during his comeback.

The closest kind of atmosphere to the record would be Joy Division's later work when they took on a more electronic flavour which captured their stormy atmospherics.

Golden Greats took Ian Brown into a very different direction. The first noticeable change was the album's electronic nature. The record saw Brown moving away from the indie guitar stained début and deeper into the electronica pulse of the music that he had been constantly talking up in interviews.

His obvious disdain for most of the post Roses bands and indie music in general was obvious. The sort of music he was talking about was ragga, and electronic and although the record was never a straight acid record, it was a push in a very different direction. Moody, dank, dark, soundscapes suiting his voice.

Not that the record was purely electronic soundscapes. The guitar was not dead yet. Says Aziz, 'The most guitars on the record are on the opening track "Getting High". It's a Free/Bad Company riff! A classic rock riff!

,ain like the first album we did it on the portastudio at home.'

Aziz also points out that both albums have parts of the same song meshed into them, I have this track, "Morassi", a Chinese instrumental sort of thing and Ian really liked it. He took sections out of it for both the albums. It's that little snippet before "Getting High" and on the first album it's also in "Underneath The Paving Stones". It's part of that sound-collage with kids talking . . . on both albums . . . I'm really proud of that song. It's a beautiful little journey this tune . . . I want everybody to have it . . .'

But this was no dance record. Instead of the fractured ragga beats or the dancehall vibes of contemporary Jamaican musics that Ian was giving props to in interviews, it was actually closer to the dark side, the left-field, underground of post-punk Manchester. The sort of near avant-garde music that Brown himself has never proffered much taste for publicly.

Ostensibly still a pop record, the songs' sparse electronic backdrops and off the wall structures were more the result of the singer's lack of experience in writing songs in the so-called 'classic' songwriting mode. Put this against a post-Oasis backdrop of the so-called 'Dadrock' scene when every band in Britain seemed to be in thrall to The Beatles and the Stones, and the whole damn encyclopaedia of rock and it makes the record seem a far braver and more individual effort than it's often given credit for.

Aziz's oriental flavoured instrumental at the top of the album gives a false impression.

Within a minute the mood has switched.

The first salvos of a big rawk riff kick in. Built around a hypnotic loop 'Gettin' High' is the closest to straight rock that Brown has ever got.

'Aziz played me this riff,' says Ian. 'It was the classic rock'n'roll riff like Free's "All Right Now". It's the first track, I wanted it to sound definitive.'

With lyrics about a friend too stoned to see the talent of those around him, it seems that Ian is still aggrieved at the John Squire fallout, although he has never alluded to this time.

Oozing in is the single, 'Love Like A Fountain', the shuffling rhythm and the hypnotic melody riding over the bubbling old skool house bubbling synths. It's one of the best songs Brown has ever been involved with and is the first indication of the stylistic switch in the album. Guitars are down, rhythms are up, the space suits Brown's voice – there's plenty of room for it. The record sounds like the sort of post acid house non-trad guitar record that Brown had been talking up for years.

Of course it's not hip-hop, but it has the same kind of structure, the same kind of space. If hip-hop is a very American form, maybe it's more honest for the British with their different roots, different lives, to bring a different flavour to the most influential music form of the Nineties.

Now things get really moody with 'Free My Way', one of the three sets of lyrics that Brown had written in jail. With its jangling key intro (a no the Stones' 'We Love You'?) dark vibes, prison lyrics and scowling sy. strings thesong switches from sonorous undertones to James Brown's 'I. A Man's World', plucked sections. The vocal is at once belligerent an doleful as it intones the dark mood of jail life.

Brown's favourite track on the album, 'Set My Baby Free' was built around a distorted funky chop keyboard loop he was given by Anif Akinola, who had worked with the classic Guy Called Gerald 'Voodoo Ray' track, one of the best tracks to come out of the acid house thing, a song that is so evocative of that era that it is pretty well a signature song of the Madchester period. 'Voodoo Ray' is a song that still sounds as strong today as when it was originally released in the late Eighties. The song is stark, simple and powerful and melodic in its sombre vibe.

Another jail lyric, the title came from a letter that Brown had been sent in prison by Fabiola.

'So Many Soldiers' continues the spooked darkness that haunts the record as Brown, in a strong northern accent, switches the subject from his personal jail experiences to an anti-war tirade over a sparse trip hop workout.

Coming in with castanets and a Spanish neo-flamenco acoustic that hints at 'Love' circa *Forever Changes*, 'Golden Gaze' at first alludes to Brown's avowed attempts to learn Spanish before switching to a crunching riff as the singer states the simple transcendental pleasure of life. The semi-stoned ooze of 'Golden Gaze' caught a perfect moment a million miles away from the claustrophobic grimness of prison.

'It came from a visit to Jamaica, sitting in a straw hut on the beach, with the sun rays pouring through the roof. All I could see was gold.'

The coolest thing about this tune is the way it is completely unmusical. The maverick spirit reading the manual and playing one fingered keyboard, still lurks in this album, only this time there is some added polish and some expertise from engineer Tim Willis and programmer Dave McCracken (keyboards, percussion); Sylvan Richardson Jr. (bass); and back on drums! . . . Simon Wolstencroft – some team!

The number of songs written about monkeys returning to the ocean to evolve into dolphins can probably get counted on one finger let alone one flipper. 'Dolphins Were Monkeys', bouncing around on phat funky keyboard chop and more of those bubbling old skool acid squelches, picks the pace up. The song comes complete with a great vocal.

'Neptune' brings the pace back down again – an ambient wash, a relaxing stoned chill out, while 'First World' is Brown digging at the cultural imperialism and Empirical arrogance of the world's major powers, still crushing the so-called 'Third World'.

The album ends with 'Babasonics', a lilting chiming guitar thing provided by an Argentinian group of the same name. Ian liked the track so

...h that he took it and made his own song from it, running the track in ...e studio, adding a shuffling drum loop behind it and a resigned sounding ...ocal ('lady got no soul') over the top. It sounds like a lazy ending to the ...ecord but its sheer oddness works.

Golden Greats is Brown finally breaking free from the shackles of the Roses. There are hardly any songs referring to the band or John Squire. The music is a million miles away from the Roses. The stark samples and dark moods dripping from the album make it a great listen. The scope of sounds and the broad vision marked it out as one of the best records of 1999, the year that baggy/Britpop or British guitar pop came to the end of its run and Nu Metal and left-field dance were the only two musics moving in any interesting directions.

It was bagged in a striking painting of Brown. 'The cover happened after this guy sent me a picture he'd done of Mike Tyson in orange and green and yellow. He said he wanted to paint me, so I sent him a photo. He's called Ian Wright. He's a really talented artist. In an interview with some magazine, Jarvis Cocker said, "Ian Brown, he's no oil painting." He is now!'

Golden Greats in one fell swoop re-established the singer as a creative force and was greeted with some rave reviews.

Brown was back in business.

A STONE ALONE: BROWN GREETS THE NU MILLENNIUM

1999 ended with the triumphant return to Manchester Apollo. As usual the atmosphere was intense and Ian made the most of the night, delivering a faultless show. The stripped down band, the simplicity of the songs, made a powerful base for his vocals which were bang on.

All that was missing was Aziz's guitar for tunes like 'My Star' and 'Corpses', a fact that the genial Aziz would only grin about when I asked him at the gig as we hung around at the back of the Apollo. Perhaps the best gig of his solo career so far, Ian Brown was leaving 1999 on a high note, no jail, no major bust-ups, a great cutting-edge record, a good slab of UK sales and some critical acclaim. Fuck, he was making this pop star thing seem almost too easy.

The year ended at the millennium show at the Castlefield basin in Manchester where 10,000 plus partygoers checked out Brown, the main attraction to the end of the millennium in a classic Manchester drizzle, the best thing in a huge non-event of a night.

2000 was a fairly quiet year. There was a spate of festivals and a bunch of shows with Aziz back on guitar. The last time I caught up with Ian Brown was at Reading Festival where he blew the roof off the tent with the best show yet. The constantly evolving band of the past two years was pretty well honed to perfection, Si Wolstencroft looking ageless and razor sharp as ever laying down the back beat twenty fucking years after playing with Ian in The Patrol! And Aziz back on guitar, filling the gaps in the early period solo stuff and being a good foil to the stark, cold, electronics. The atmosphere in the tent was of course outrageous but now, instead of coasting along on the past, Ian Brown was looking to the future, still looking for the cutting edge, still changing his music. Affable back-stage and easy-going on stage, it seems that Ian Brown has finally found an even keel, a groove.

Talk is his third album is the best yet . . .

WITHER THE ROSES?

In the new mellennium everything is so so different. The Hacienda is a pile of rubble. Another block of over-priced yuppie flats is planned in its place. Manchester city centre is full of designer wine bars. The clubs are stuck in a limbo. The music scene has revived, moved away from the so called 'baggy' boom, now its singer-songwriters are Badly Drawn Boy, bands like Elbow and the Doves, a different mood, a different music . . .

The ex-Roses still make headlines, its business as usual. The rumour mill is pumping up Ian Brown's third solo album, Reni has just taken The Rub round the circuit for the fist time, Mani has just got back from the States playing some gigs with the MC5's Wayne Kramer and is about to start work on the new Primals album and John Squire seems to have dissappeared for the time being . . .

Every now and then someone tries to reform the band. Mani still wants it and is on record as being fired up for the great comeback, the third coming, and truth be told there is unfinished business there. A third album, a realisation of all that potential, a tying up of those loose ends.

Millions of quid are talked about. The carrot gets bigger. The craving stronger . . . then you hear Reni won't do it, Ian's got a new album, someone wants more money than everyone else, John is too busy.

The truth is The Roses have grown apart. Musically they have drifted far away from each other . . .

And business-wise there are still all sorts of raw nerves. *Garage Flowers* came out and there was plenty of tension between old band members. Then you hear that someone has fallen out with someone else and then everyone's mates again . . . and after all that splitting up trauma you can imagine how difficult it would be to get John and Ian back together.

But what would you give for one last throw of the dice, one last chance to see that amazing rhythm section just go off on one, John Squire's guitar get all crystalline and pure pop before soaring off into some solo that actually made you feel something, and that pimp roll executed properly by the King Monkey himself? What would you give for one last resurrection of this great British rock'n'roll band . . . THE third coming?